Rx Help Handbook

Rx HELP HANDBOOK

YOUR A-TO-Z GUIDE TO FREE AND MONEY SAVING PRESCRIPTION DRUG PROGRAMS

Brett LaCroix

gatekeeper press

Columbus, Ohio

Rx Help Handbook: Your A-to-Z Guide to Free and Money Saving Prescription Drug Programs

Published by Gatekeeper Press

2167 Stringtown Rd, Suite 109

Columbus, OH 43123-2989

www.GatekeeperPress.com

ISBN (paperback): 9781642374964

Library of Congress Control Number: 2018968521

Printed in the United States of America

Contents

Introduction

As a paramedic with over 27 years of experience, I have responded to countless number of 911 calls.

Throughout my career, I have seen the incredible impact that prescription medications have on the lives of patients.

People are living longer and better, thanks in part to the abundance of pharmaceuticals available to treat or control nearly every type of health problem.

However, medications are only effective if they are taken as your doctor prescribed, and you can only take them if you can afford to purchase them in the first place.

If you are uninsured or have insurance with sky high deductibles, finding the money each month to pay for your medications can be a challenge.

Too many people are skipping doses or leaving some of their expensive prescriptions unfilled. This type of "medication rationing" can lead to unnecessary/preventable emergency room visits, hospitalizations, and worsening of chronic medical conditions.

Seeing the ongoing struggle that patients endure, prompted me to do research regarding prescription drug savings programs... and I was totally blown away by what I discovered.

The more I looked, the more programs I found designed to help those who are uninsured, as well as those who have insurance with very large deductibles and co-payments.

Drug company savings offers, co-pay cards and patient assistance programs (covering people of nearly every income range) seemed to be everywhere.

I have to admit, like most people who watch and read the news these days, I was led to believe that the pharmaceutical companies were big, impersonal, profit driven entities that really didn't care about patients.

My research, as demonstrated by this Rx Help Handbook, tells a much different story.

Warnings & Disclaimers

This handbook is the result of 1000+ hours of research.

Although all info was triple checked for accuracy, errors and/or omissions may be present in this book.

No warranties are expressed or implied as to the information presented here.

All information was gathered from publically available sources, collected and organized, then included in this handbook under the umbrella of "fair use".

All brand name medications (and some of the program names) are registered trademarks of their respective owners/companies, and are indicated with the use of symbols ™ and ® in this handbook.

Inclusion of information regarding a pharmaceutical company's medications, savings programs, patient assistance programs, website addresses, phone numbers, and/or other company specific info, does not indicate or imply endorsement of this Rx Help Handbook by that entity.

Income limits for programs have been rounded down to the nearest thousand, for simplicity.

Information contained herein was accurate when compiled, however all programs are subject to change, modification, and/or cancellation by their respective companies.

For each program/offer listed, there may be additional requirements not listed in this handbook. For the most up-to-date information about a given program/offer, please call the pharmaceutical companies or program administrators directly.

No information contained in this handbook is meant to be medical or health advice. The programs presented here are for individuals who have already been prescribed medications by their doctor.

Any questions regarding your current medications, future medications, or a switch from generic version to brand name version of a medication, should be discussed with your doctor, pharmacist, or other appropriate health care professional.

For questions regarding how the use of patient assistance programs or copay cards may affect your prescription drug coverage, deductible, copays, or coinsurance, contact your health insurance company.

Why the Generic Drug Option is <u>Not</u> Always your Best Choice

This Rx Help Handbook lists brand name prescription drug assistance programs currently offered by the major pharmaceutical companies.

Sometimes, choosing a brand name medication (instead of a generic), can save you money.

Case Study #1

Sarah has no medical insurance and started experiencing intermitten chest discomfort.

She visited her doctor, underwent several tests and was eventually prescribed an expensive heart medication to manage her symptoms.

At the pharmacy, Sarah was informed that her new prescription would cost $328 per month.

There was absolutely no way she could afford this, so the pharmacist offered to substitute a cheaper, generic medication that would only be $140 per month.

This would still be a very big strain on her budget, but Sarah felt she had no other choice.

Sarah now struggles to come up with the $140 needed each month to refill her Rx. She often has to skip meals or delay paying some bills just to make ends meet and pay for her prescription.

Was this a good deal for Sarah?

No… not at all.

You see, Sarah's income is $34,000 per year. The pharmaceutical company that manufactures the original, brand name medication her doctor initially prescribed, had a patient assistance program Sarah would have easily qualified for.

Instead of struggling, each month, to pay for the $140 generic prescription… Sarah could very well have qualified to receive the brand name heart medication, absolutely free.

> **TIP:** Don't pay for a generic prescription drug, if you qualify to receive the brand name version of that medication (via a patient assistance program) for free.

Case Study #2

Scott has commercial health insurance thru his work and takes a daily medication to manage his diabetes.

The insurance company has different copay prices for generic and brand name prescriptions.

During his last trip to the pharmacy, Scott was told that the insurance copay for his diabetes medication was $55 per month for the brand name medication, or $35 for the generic drug.

Without hesitating, Scott chose the generic option and now pays $35 out-of-pocket each and every month.

Was this a good deal for Scott?

Actually... No.

Had Scott done a little research, he would have discovered that a "$0 copay card" was available from the manufacturer of the brand name medication.

Instead of paying $35 each month for a generic version of his medication, Scott could have simply downloaded a copay card from the pharmaceutical company's website and paid $0 out-of-pocket each month for the brand name diabetes medication.

> **TIP:** Don't assume that a generic drug is the best option. Often, you can get the brand name medication for a lower (or often $0) copay thru a pharmaceutical company's savings program.

Case Study #3

Janet has a high deductible health care plan.

She manages her chronic conditions well (avoiding hospital stays), but takes several expensive medications.

Because of her high deductible, she chooses generic medications whenever possible, since she is basically paying for her meds "out of pocket" for the first few months of each year.

Does this save Janet money?

Maybe not.

Many brand name medication copay cards help cover of the cost of the Rx, even if you haven't met your yearly deductible... and some insurance companies even apply this towards paying down your deductible.

> **TIP:** Compare your actual costs for generic drugs, with your total out-of-pocket expenses using brand name medication copay cards. You may pay less choosing the brand name Rx.

Patient Assistance Programs and You

When you see the term "Patient Assistance Program" in this handbook, it is usually referring to a program offered by a pharmaceutical company (or a non-profit/foundation established by that company) to help uninsured patients gain access to needed medications.

Qualifying for one of these programs is almost always based on your household income and your financial need (i.e. you cannot afford to pay for your prescribed medications).

Income levels vary widely from company to company, and in many cases, from medication to medication.

You don't always have to be "dirt poor" to qualify. There are programs that cover people with household incomes of $80k... $100k... and even as high as $150,000/year.

Another important fact to remember is that most of these programs look at your income, household size, and expenses when determining if you qualify for assistance.

If you are taking multiple medications and/or have other ongoing medical treatment costs, you should consider applying for all the patient assistance programs that cover the medications you take.

Some programs allow you to apply for assistance even if you are covered by insurance. With today's high deductibles and coinsurance payments, simply "having insurance" is no guarantee you can afford your portion of the out-of-pocket costs for your medications.

> **TIP:** When in doubt... call the patient assistance program phone number and fully explain your current situation. You may qualify for assistance based on other factors and guidelines.

This Rx Help Handbook covers programs for brand name medications, but also includes generic names in the A-to-Z listings. This allows you to lookup any current generic medications you may be taking, to see if switching to a brand name version might allow you to qualify for that pharmaceutical company's patient assistance program or co-pay assistance program.

The goal of this handbook is for you to find programs you may qualify for, to reduce (or even eliminate) your out-of-pocket medication costs.

> **TIP:** Don't pay out-of-pocket for a generic Rx drug, if you can qualify to receive the brand name version of that medication (via a patient assistance program) for free.

The Magic of CoPay Cards

A large number of listings in this guide are programs designed to lower (or eliminate) your out-of-pocket costs for brand name medications.

These programs have many different names... copay cards, discount cards, savings cards, copay assistance programs, etc... but they all work in a very similar manner:

1. Download or print a coupon/card from the pharmaceutical company's website
2. Call a toll-free number to "activate" your card
3. Show your card to the pharmacist when filling your Rx
4. The drug manufacturer pays a large portion (or all) of your out-of-pocket costs for that medication

Many of these programs require you to have commercial/private insurance, but quite a few also provide a large discount for uninsured/cash paying patients.

> **NOTE:** Copay cards are designed to help patients afford their prescriptions when insurance companies require high co-insurance and/or deductibles for brand name medications.

Most copay cards do not apply if you are covered by government insurance (Medicare, Medicaid, VA, etc...).

Copay card programs handle deductibles (the amount you have to pay out-of-pocket before your insurance starts to cover the costs) in two different ways:

Some cards only apply after you have met your insurance company's deductible for the year.

Other programs, however, provide a fixed amount of assistance (per calendar year) that will pay more towards your Rx costs during the time when your insurance is not helping you pay for your meds.

For example, you may see a $5 copay card with a maximum benefit of $7500 per year.

If you use that card before you have met your insurance deductible, the card might cover the full price of that medication, minus your $5 copay portion.

Later on in the year, after you have reached your deductible, the card would simply cover what your insurance company doesn't cover, minus your $5 copay.

> **TIP:** When you use a copay card, the pharmaceutical company is basically paying a portion of your medication costs for you. Some insurance companies apply these payments towards your deductible, so using the copay card saves you money and can help pay down your deductible!

A few savings programs offer the <u>same</u> low copay amount for both 30 day <u>and</u> 90 day prescriptions.

In these cases, switching to a 90 day Rx means you pay the same out-of-pocket for more medication.

Another possible benefit of a 90 day prescription is faster pay down of your deductible. If your insurance company applies the pharmaceutical company's portion (covered by the copay card) towards your deductible, filling 90-day Rx's in the beginning of the year can help pay down your deductible faster.

And think about it... if the copay card you use in the beginning of the year is helping pay down your deductible... that means it is also helping you pay less for all your medical costs, by having your insurance coverage "kick in" sooner.

(Not all insurance companies apply copay card assistance payments to your deductible, but some do.)

> **TIP:** Be sure to check the terms of the copay card, you could save even more $$ by asking your doctor for a 90 day prescription, instead of a 30 day Rx.

IMPORTANT INFO for <u>California Residents</u>:

If you live in California, your use of copay cards is limited by law.

Unfortunately, if there is a generic (or therapeutically equivalent) version of a medication you are prescribed, you are not allowed to choose the brand name drug <u>and</u> use a copay card lower your out-of-pocket expenses.

For example...

If you wanted to fill a prescription for SYNTHROID® (a brand name medication from AbbVie), you would not be able to use a manufacturer's copay card because a generic version (levothyroxine) is available.

You could fill the prescription for the brand name version if you are willing to pay full price, or pay the higher copay amount your insurance may require for choosing the brand name version.

But you would not be able to use a copay card to reduce your out-of-pocket costs for SYNTHROID®.

On the other hand...

If you filled a prescription for SYMBICORT® (a brand name medication by AstraZeneca), you would be allowed to use a copay card, because there is currently no generic alternative for that medication.

Bottom line is this... if you live in California, you may have to ask your pharmacist if the medications you take are covered by your state's copay card restriction.

How to Use this Handbook

This Rx Help Handbook was designed as a simple to use, quick reference guide for assistance programs offered by brand name drug manufacturers.

Medication names (both generic and brand name) are listed from A-to-Z.

If you look up a drug by its generic name, you will see an arrow pointing to the corresponding brand name.

Example:

adalimumab → HUMIRA®

> **TIP:** Generic drugs are not always your least expensive option. You could pay less for a brand name Rx by using a copay card. You may even qualify for FREE meds based on your income.

When you look up a medication by its brand name, the complete program info is shown, like this:

HUMIRA® (adalimumab)   AbbVie, INC.

HUMIRA® Complete Savings Card   1-800-448-6472   *www.humira.com*

Income Limits **NONE** Rx cost → $5 Per Month $ No Medical Insurance ✗ Commercial Insurance ✓ Medicare Part D ✗

Eligible patients with commercial insurance pay as little as $5/month for their HUMIRA® Rx.

AbbVie Patient Assistance Foundation   1-800-222-6885   *www.abbviepaf.org*

Income Limits **$60k Single $82k Couple** Rx cost → FREE $ No Medical Insurance ✓ Commercial Insurance ✓ Medicare Part D ✓

Rx assistance available to patients who are uninsured and meet program eligibility requirements. Patients with Commercial Insurance or Medicare Part D, who are struggling to pay for their medications, are encouraged to apply.

For each brand name medication, there will be one or more programs listed... all following the same format.

The Brand Name (usually shown in ALL CAPS and **BOLD**) is followed by the generic name, with the pharmaceutical company name listed to the far right side of the page:

HUMIRA® (adalimumab)   AbbVie, INC.

Next you will see the name of the program, a phone number, and a website URL:

HUMIRA® Complete Savings Card   1-800-448-6472   *www.humira.com*

Due to space limitations, only the main website address (for a given medication/program) is listed. When you visit the URL, you may have to click on additional links to reach the specific program details.

Look for links on the pharmaceutical websites with descriptions such as "Patient Assistance", "Savings Program", "CoPay Card", "Save on your medication costs", "Affording your medications", etc...

> 💡 **TIP:** CoPay offers seem to be more "do-it-yourself" (visit the website to signup or print card), whereas Patient Assistance Programs often require a phone call to start the application process.

Next in the listings, you will see income limits for each program. This is the maximum yearly income you can have and still qualify for a given program.

If the income limits are not published, or unknown, you will see:

$ Income Limits | Call to Verify ?   To find out the income limits for these listings, simply call the program phone number to determine current income qualifications.

Programs with no income limits, or one limit for the entire household, will be indicated by:

$ Income Limits | NONE   **$ Income Limits | $100K Household**   **$ Income Limits | $125K Household**   **$ Income Limits | $150K Household**

All other programs will show income limits, for singles and couples, based on a percentage of the federal poverty guidelines.

For example, 250% of poverty level is $30,350 for a single person and $41,150 for a couple.

Due to space constraints, we have rounded the limits down to the nearest thousand:

$ Income Limits | $30k Single / $41k Couple   **$ Income Limits | $36k Single / $49k Couple**   **$ Income Limits | $48k Single / $65k Couple**   **$ Income Limits | $60k Single / $82k Couple**

These, however, have higher limits for larger families, which are not shown on individual listings:

$ Income Limits	$30k Single / $41k Couple	$ Income Limits	$36k Single / $49k Couple	$ Income Limits	$48k Single / $65k Couple	$ Income Limits	$60k Single / $82k Couple
Household Size	Three $51k / Four $62k / Five $73k	Household Size	Three $62k / Four $75k / Five $88k	Household Size	Three $83k / Four $100k / Five $117k	Household Size	Three $103k / Four $125k / Five $147k

If your household has more than 2 people in it, be sure to call program phone number to determine the current income limits for your situation.

> 💡 **TIP:** If you live in Alaska or Hawaii, your cost of living is higher, so your income limits to qualify for these programs are higher. Be sure to call to find out full details.

Next we list your estimated out-of-pocket cost for the medication covered by the program.

If the amount is not published, or unknown, you will see:

 To find out the medication cost, call the program phone number for details.

Some copay programs have different medication costs based on size of Rx (number of pills), dosage, etc...

In those cases, you will see:  Simply Look at copay card or call program for info.

If the listing is a *Patient Assistance Program* and you can receive medications at no cost, we use the word "FREE". If the listing is a *CoPay Card*, and there is no out-of-pocket cost to you, we use "$0 CoPay".

Otherwise, the amount of copay (or in some cases... discount amount), is shown like this:

Next, we indicate whether or not a person without health insurance coverage qualifies for the program...

Whether or not a person with commercial/private insurance coverage qualifies for the program...

And whether or not a person with Medicare coverage qualifies for the program...

A "**?**" (question mark) indicates that either the information is not published on the pharmaceutical company's website or there are certain qualifying restrictions. Additional info may be listed in each program listing description. If not, call the program's phone number for complete information.

TIP: When in doubt... call the program and explain your situation. You may qualify for assistance.

"A-to-Z" Medication Program Listings

abacavir → ZIAGEN® Oral Solution

abacavir, dolutegravir, and lamivudine → TRIUMEQ®

abacavir and lamivudine → EPZICOM®

abacavir, lamivudine, and zidovudine → TRIZIVIR®

abaloparatide injection → TYMLOS®

abatacept → ORENCIA®

abemaciclib → VERZENIO®

ABILIFY® (aripiprazole)

OTSUKA AMERICA PHARMACEUTICAL, INC.

Abilify Savings Card   1-888-922-4543   *www.abilify.com*

| $ Income Limits | Call to Verify ? | Rx cost → | $5 Per Month $ | No Medical Insurance ✗ | Commercial Insurance ✓ | Medicare Part D ✗ |

Pay as little as $5 per month, you must have commercial insurance coverage to qualify for savings card.

Patient Assistance Program   1-855-727-6274   *www.otsukapatientassistance.com*

| $ Income Limits | $30k Single $41k Couple | Rx cost → | FREE $ | No Medical Insurance ✓ | Commercial Insurance ✓ | Medicare Part D ✓ |

Provides medications to eligible uninsured individuals who cannot afford treatment. If you have Rx drug coverage and meet income limits, your annual Rx costs must exceed 5% of your adjusted gross income to qualify for assistance.

abiraterone acetate → ZYTIGA®

abobotulinumtoxinA → DYSPORT®

ABRAXANE® (albumin-bound paclitaxel)

CELGENE CORPORATION

Co-Pay Assistance Program   1-800-931-8691   *www.celgenepatientsupport.com*

| $ Income Limits | $100K Household | Rx cost → | $0 CoPay $ | No Medical Insurance ✗ | Commercial Insurance ✓ | Medicare Part D ✗ |

Program can provide up to $10,000/year in Deductible/Co-Pay Assistance, making your Rx cost as low as $0/month.

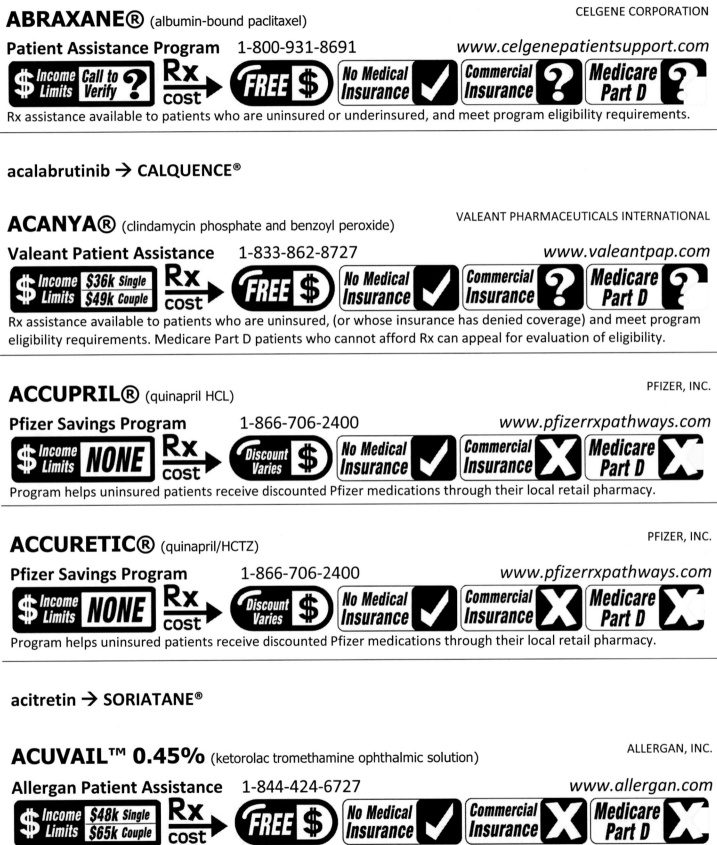

ABRAXANE® (albumin-bound paclitaxel) CELGENE CORPORATION

Patient Assistance Program 1-800-931-8691 *www.celgenepatientsupport.com*

$ Income Limits | Call to Verify ? | **Rx** cost → | FREE $ | No Medical Insurance ✓ | Commercial Insurance ? | Medicare Part D ?

Rx assistance available to patients who are uninsured or underinsured, and meet program eligibility requirements.

acalabrutinib → **CALQUENCE®**

ACANYA® (clindamycin phosphate and benzoyl peroxide) VALEANT PHARMACEUTICALS INTERNATIONAL

Valeant Patient Assistance 1-833-862-8727 *www.valeantpap.com*

$ Income Limits | $36k Single $49k Couple | **Rx** cost → | FREE $ | No Medical Insurance ✓ | Commercial Insurance ? | Medicare Part D ?

Rx assistance available to patients who are uninsured, (or whose insurance has denied coverage) and meet program eligibility requirements. Medicare Part D patients who cannot afford Rx can appeal for evaluation of eligibility.

ACCUPRIL® (quinapril HCL) PFIZER, INC.

Pfizer Savings Program 1-866-706-2400 *www.pfizerrxpathways.com*

$ Income Limits | NONE | **Rx** cost → | Discount Varies $ | No Medical Insurance ✓ | Commercial Insurance ✗ | Medicare Part D ✗

Program helps uninsured patients receive discounted Pfizer medications through their local retail pharmacy.

ACCURETIC® (quinapril/HCTZ) PFIZER, INC.

Pfizer Savings Program 1-866-706-2400 *www.pfizerrxpathways.com*

$ Income Limits | NONE | **Rx** cost → | Discount Varies $ | No Medical Insurance ✓ | Commercial Insurance ✗ | Medicare Part D ✗

Program helps uninsured patients receive discounted Pfizer medications through their local retail pharmacy.

acitretin → **SORIATANE®**

ACUVAIL™ 0.45% (ketorolac tromethamine ophthalmic solution) ALLERGAN, INC.

Allergan Patient Assistance 1-844-424-6727 *www.allergan.com*

$ Income Limits | $48k Single $65k Couple | **Rx** cost → | FREE $ | No Medical Insurance ✓ | Commercial Insurance ✗ | Medicare Part D ✗

Eye and Dermatology program provides medications to patients who are uninsured and meet program guidelines.

ACTIVASE® (alteplase)

GENENTECH, INC.

Genentech Rheumatology Access Solutions   1-866-681-3261   www.activase.com

Program provides Activase to patients who are uninsured or have been denied treatment by their insurance company. Those patients eligible for Medicare Part D (but not enrolled) may also qualify for this program. Assistance may also be available for Medicare patients in coverage gap (aka "the donut hole"). Call for details.

---

aclidinium bromide inhalation powder → TUDORZA® Pressair®

ACTEMRA® (tocilizumab)

GENENTECH, INC.

ACTEMRA® Co-Pay Card Program   1-855-722-6729   www.racopay.com

Program provides up to $15,000/year in co-pay assistance. Eligible patients pay as little $5/month for ACTEMRA®.

Rheumatology Access Solutions   1-866-681-3261   www.genentech-access.com

Program provides Actemra to patients who are uninsured or have been denied treatment by their insurance company. Those patients eligible for Medicare Part D (but not enrolled) may also qualify for this program. Assistance may also be available for Medicare patients in coverage gap (aka "the donut hole"). Call for details.

ACTIMMUNE® (interferon gamma-1b)

HORIZON PHARMA USA, INC.

Co-Pay Assistance Program   1-877-305-7704   www.compassforpatients.com

Program covers co-pay/co-insurance amount for those with private insurance. No "out of pocket" costs for patients.

Patient Assistance Program (PAP)   1-877-305-7704   www.compassforpatients.com

Program provides meds to patients who are uninsured or have been denied treatment by their insurance company.

---

acyclovir cream 5%→ ZOVIRAX®

acyclovir and hydrocortisone → XERESE®

ACZONE® Gel 5%/7.5% (dapsone)

ALLERGAN, INC.

Aczone Savings Card — 1-855-821-4234 — *www.aczone.com*

| $ Income Limits | **NONE** | Rx cost → | **$35 $** | No Medical Insurance **X** | Commercial Insurance **✔** | Medicare Part D **X** |

Commercially insured patients pay as little as $35 per Rx if they have met their deductible, or $75 if they have not.

Allergan Patient Assistance Program — 1-844-424-6727 — *www.allergan.com*

| $ Income Limits | **$48k Single** **$65k Couple** | Rx cost → | **FREE $** | No Medical Insurance **✔** | Commercial Insurance **X** | Medicare Part D **X** |

Eye and Dermatology program provides medications to patients who are uninsured and meet program guidelines.

---

adalimumab → HUMIRA®

adapalene and benzoyl peroxide → EPIDUO® FORTE

ADCIRCA® (tadalafil)

UNITED THERAPEUTICS CORPORATION

Adcirca Co-Pay Assistance Card — 1-877-864-8437 — *www.utcopay.com*

| $ Income Limits | **NONE** | Rx cost → | **$10 Per Month $** | No Medical Insurance **X** | Commercial Insurance **✔** | Medicare Part D **X** |

Commercially Insured patients pay as little as $10 per month, maximum savings $800 per Rx.

ASSIST Patient Assistance Program — 1-877-864-8437 — *www.adcirca.com*

| $ Income Limits | **Call to Verify ?** | Rx cost → | **FREE $** | No Medical Insurance **✔** | Commercial Insurance **X** | Medicare Part D **X** |

Provides medication free of charge to qualified individuals who are uninsured and cannot afford their Rx.

ADEMPAS® (riociguat)

BAYER HEALTHCARE PHARMACEUTICALS

Co-Pay Assistance Program — 1-855-423-3672 — *www.adempas-us.com*

| $ Income Limits | **NONE** | Rx cost → | **$0 CoPay $** | No Medical Insurance **X** | Commercial Insurance **✔** | Medicare Part D **X** |

Program covers up to 100% of co-pay/co-insurance amount for those with private insurance. Pay as low as $0 for Rx.

Patient Assistance Program (PAP) — 1-855-423-3672 — *www.adempas-us.com*

| $ Income Limits | **Call to Verify ?** | Rx cost → | **FREE $** | No Medical Insurance **✔** | Commercial Insurance **?** | Medicare Part D **✔** |

Helps those who are uninsured (no insurance coverage at all) or underinsured (no prescription coverage, a benefits cap, denial of coverage, etc), and cannot afford medications. Medicare Part D patients can apply and may qualify.

ADLYXIN™ (lixisenatide) injection
SANOFI-AVENTIS U.S. LLC.

Adlyxin Savings Card
1-866-390-5622   www.adlyxin.com

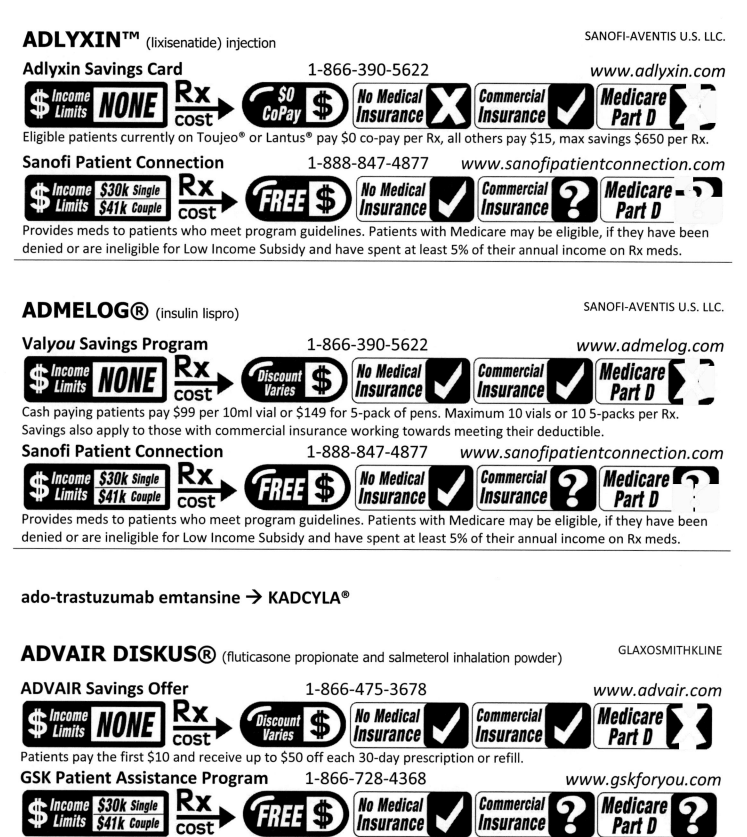

$ Income Limits **NONE** | Rx cost → | $0 CoPay $ | No Medical Insurance ✗ | Commercial Insurance ✔ | Medicare Part D ✗

Eligible patients currently on Toujeo® or Lantus® pay $0 co-pay per Rx, all others pay $15, max savings $650 per Rx.

Sanofi Patient Connection
1-888-847-4877   www.sanofipatientconnection.com

$ Income Limits **$30k Single / $41k Couple** | Rx cost → | FREE $ | No Medical Insurance ✔ | Commercial Insurance ? | Medicare Part D ?

Provides meds to patients who meet program guidelines. Patients with Medicare may be eligible, if they have been denied or are ineligible for Low Income Subsidy and have spent at least 5% of their annual income on Rx meds.

ADMELOG® (insulin lispro)
SANOFI-AVENTIS U.S. LLC.

Valyou Savings Program
1-866-390-5622   www.admelog.com

$ Income Limits **NONE** | Rx cost → | Discount Varies $ | No Medical Insurance ✔ | Commercial Insurance ✔ | Medicare Part D ✗

Cash paying patients pay $99 per 10ml vial or $149 for 5-pack of pens. Maximum 10 vials or 10 5-packs per Rx. Savings also apply to those with commercial insurance working towards meeting their deductible.

Sanofi Patient Connection
1-888-847-4877   www.sanofipatientconnection.com

$ Income Limits **$30k Single / $41k Couple** | Rx cost → | FREE $ | No Medical Insurance ✔ | Commercial Insurance ? | Medicare Part D ?

Provides meds to patients who meet program guidelines. Patients with Medicare may be eligible, if they have been denied or are ineligible for Low Income Subsidy and have spent at least 5% of their annual income on Rx meds.

ado-trastuzumab emtansine → KADCYLA®

ADVAIR DISKUS® (fluticasone propionate and salmeterol inhalation powder)
GLAXOSMITHKLINE

ADVAIR Savings Offer
1-866-475-3678   www.advair.com

$ Income Limits **NONE** | Rx cost → | Discount Varies $ | No Medical Insurance ✔ | Commercial Insurance ✔ | Medicare Part D ✗

Patients pay the first $10 and receive up to $50 off each 30-day prescription or refill.

GSK Patient Assistance Program
1-866-728-4368   www.gskforyou.com

$ Income Limits **$30k Single / $41k Couple** | Rx cost → | FREE $ | No Medical Insurance ✔ | Commercial Insurance ? | Medicare Part D ?

Uninsured patients who meet certain financial criteria may be able to get meds for free. Medicare Part D patients who have spent $600 or more on Rx drugs may also apply for assistance.

ADVAIR HFA® (fluticasone propionate and salmeterol)

ADVAIR Savings Offer   1-866-475-3678   *www.advair.com*

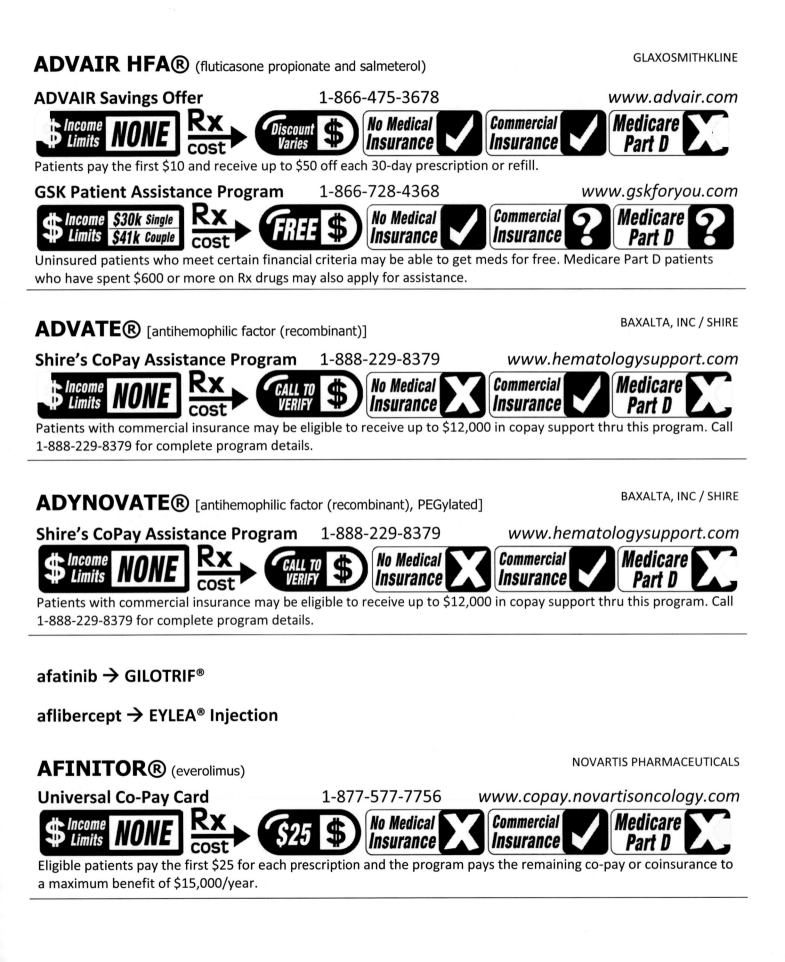

Patients pay the first $10 and receive up to $50 off each 30-day prescription or refill.

GSK Patient Assistance Program   1-866-728-4368   *www.gskforyou.com*

Uninsured patients who meet certain financial criteria may be able to get meds for free. Medicare Part D patients who have spent $600 or more on Rx drugs may also apply for assistance.

ADVATE® [antihemophilic factor (recombinant)]

BAXALTA, INC / SHIRE

Shire's CoPay Assistance Program   1-888-229-8379   *www.hematologysupport.com*

Patients with commercial insurance may be eligible to receive up to $12,000 in copay support thru this program. Call 1-888-229-8379 for complete program details.

ADYNOVATE® [antihemophilic factor (recombinant), PEGylated]

BAXALTA, INC / SHIRE

Shire's CoPay Assistance Program   1-888-229-8379   *www.hematologysupport.com*

Patients with commercial insurance may be eligible to receive up to $12,000 in copay support thru this program. Call 1-888-229-8379 for complete program details.

afatinib → GILOTRIF®

aflibercept → EYLEA® Injection

AFINITOR® (everolimus)

NOVARTIS PHARMACEUTICALS

Universal Co-Pay Card   1-877-577-7756   *www.copay.novartisoncology.com*

Eligible patients pay the first $25 for each prescription and the program pays the remaining co-pay or coinsurance to a maximum benefit of $15,000/year.

AFINITOR® (everolimus)
NOVARTIS PHARMACEUTICALS

Novartis Patient Assistance Foundation   1-800-277-2254   *www.pap.novartis.com*

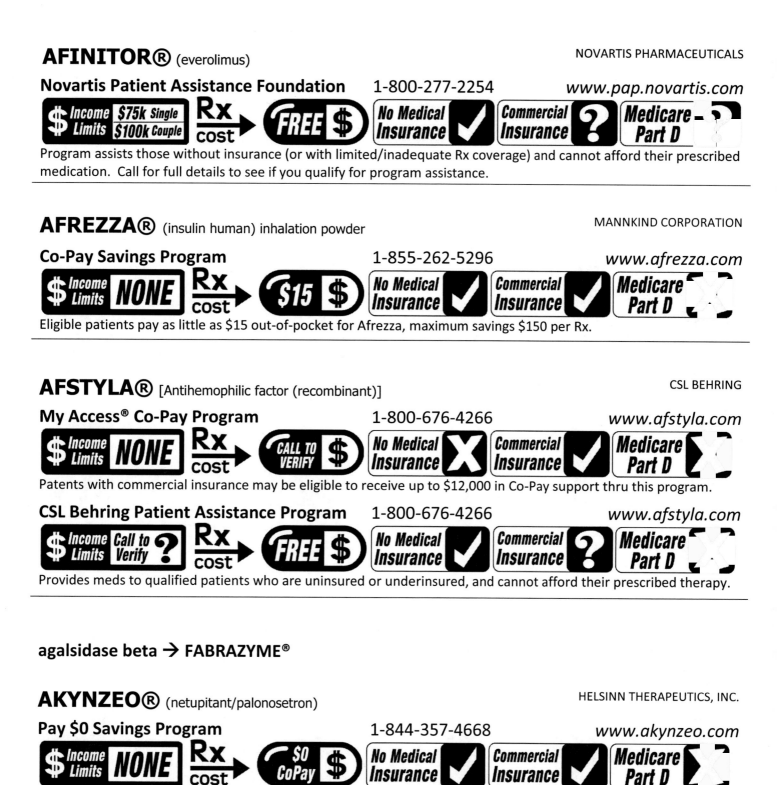

Program assists those without insurance (or with limited/inadequate Rx coverage) and cannot afford their prescribed medication. Call for full details to see if you qualify for program assistance.

AFREZZA® (insulin human) inhalation powder
MANNKIND CORPORATION

Co-Pay Savings Program   1-855-262-5296   *www.afrezza.com*

Eligible patients pay as little as $15 out-of-pocket for Afrezza, maximum savings $150 per Rx.

AFSTYLA® [Antihemophilic factor (recombinant)]
CSL BEHRING

My Access® Co-Pay Program   1-800-676-4266   *www.afstyla.com*

Patents with commercial insurance may be eligible to receive up to $12,000 in Co-Pay support thru this program.

CSL Behring Patient Assistance Program   1-800-676-4266   *www.afstyla.com*

Provides meds to qualified patients who are uninsured or underinsured, and cannot afford their prescribed therapy.

agalsidase beta → FABRAZYME®

AKYNZEO® (netupitant/palonosetron)
HELSINN THERAPEUTICS, INC.

Pay $0 Savings Program   1-844-357-4668   *www.akynzeo.com*

Eligible insured patients pay as low as $0/month with a maximum savings of $1800 off the patient's out-of-pocket costs per year. Patients paying cash receive $150 off each Rx, maximum savings $1800/year.

Patient Assistance Program   1-844-357-4668   *www.acynzeo.com*

Eligible uninsured/underinsured patients, including those with Medicare Part D, can receive AKYNZEO free of charge.

albuterol sulfate → ProAir® HFA

albuterol sulfate → VENTOLIN® HFA

albuterol sulfate Inhalation aerosol → PROVENTIL® HFA

albuterol sulfate inhalation powder → ProAir RespiClick®

alcaftadine ophthalmic solution 0.25% → LASTACAFT®

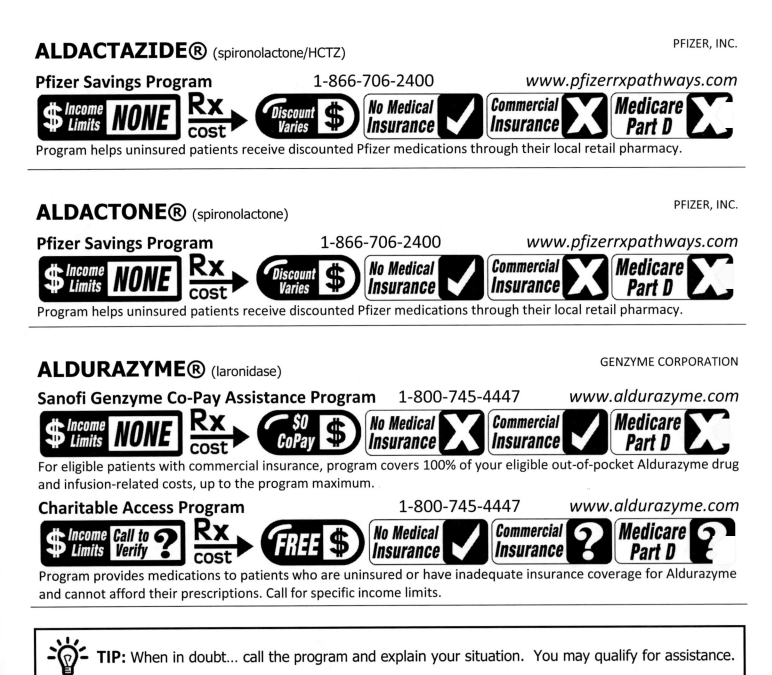

ALDACTAZIDE® (spironolactone/HCTZ)   PFIZER, INC.

Pfizer Savings Program   1-866-706-2400   *www.pfizerrxpathways.com*

Income Limits **NONE** | Rx cost → | Discount Varies $ | **No Medical Insurance** ✔ | **Commercial Insurance** ✗ | **Medicare Part D** ✗

Program helps uninsured patients receive discounted Pfizer medications through their local retail pharmacy.

ALDACTONE® (spironolactone)   PFIZER, INC.

Pfizer Savings Program   1-866-706-2400   *www.pfizerrxpathways.com*

Income Limits **NONE** | Rx cost → | Discount Varies $ | **No Medical Insurance** ✔ | **Commercial Insurance** ✗ | **Medicare Part D** ✗

Program helps uninsured patients receive discounted Pfizer medications through their local retail pharmacy.

ALDURAZYME® (laronidase)   GENZYME CORPORATION

Sanofi Genzyme Co-Pay Assistance Program   1-800-745-4447   *www.aldurazyme.com*

Income Limits **NONE** | Rx cost → | $0 CoPay $ | **No Medical Insurance** ✗ | **Commercial Insurance** ✔ | **Medicare Part D** ✗

For eligible patients with commercial insurance, program covers 100% of your eligible out-of-pocket Aldurazyme drug and infusion-related costs, up to the program maximum.

Charitable Access Program   1-800-745-4447   *www.aldurazyme.com*

Income Limits Call to Verify ? | Rx cost → | FREE $ | **No Medical Insurance** ✔ | **Commercial Insurance** ? | **Medicare Part D** ?

Program provides medications to patients who are uninsured or have inadequate insurance coverage for Aldurazyme and cannot afford their prescriptions. Call for specific income limits.

TIP: When in doubt... call the program and explain your situation. You may qualify for assistance.

ALECENSA® (alectinib)

GENENTECH, INC.

Co-pay Card Assistance Program　　1-855-692-6729　　*www.copayassistancenow.com*

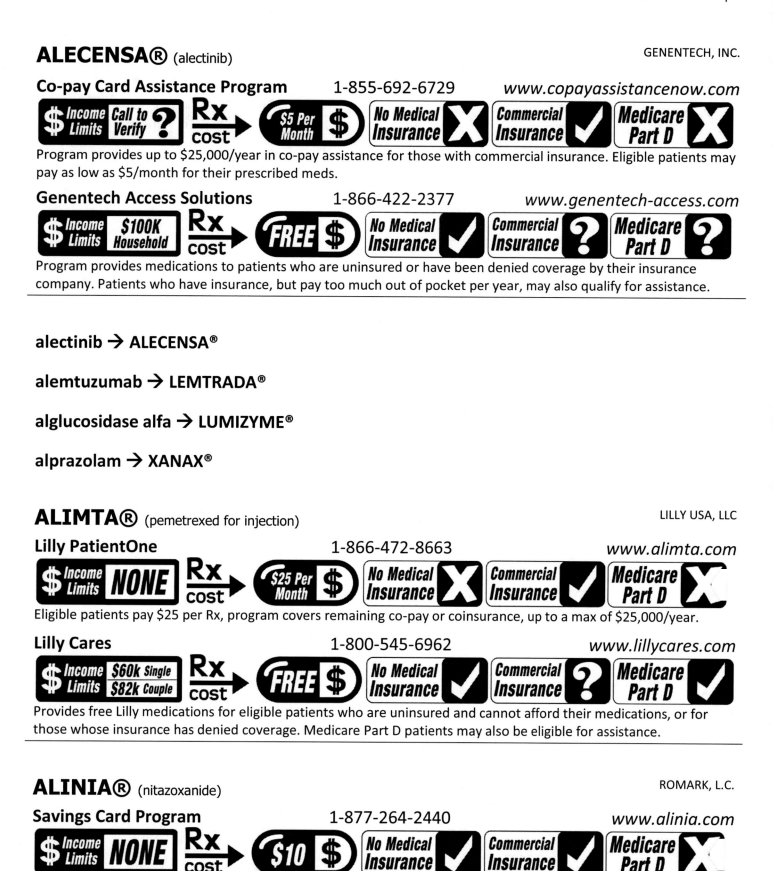

Program provides up to $25,000/year in co-pay assistance for those with commercial insurance. Eligible patients may pay as low as $5/month for their prescribed meds.

Genentech Access Solutions　　1-866-422-2377　　*www.genentech-access.com*

Program provides medications to patients who are uninsured or have been denied coverage by their insurance company. Patients who have insurance, but pay too much out of pocket per year, may also qualify for assistance.

---

alectinib → ALECENSA®

alemtuzumab → LEMTRADA®

alglucosidase alfa → LUMIZYME®

alprazolam → XANAX®

ALIMTA® (pemetrexed for injection)

LILLY USA, LLC

Lilly PatientOne　　1-866-472-8663　　*www.alimta.com*

Eligible patients pay $25 per Rx, program covers remaining co-pay or coinsurance, up to a max of $25,000/year.

Lilly Cares　　1-800-545-6962　　*www.lillycares.com*

Provides free Lilly medications for eligible patients who are uninsured and cannot afford their medications, or for those whose insurance has denied coverage. Medicare Part D patients may also be eligible for assistance.

ALINIA® (nitazoxanide)

ROMARK, L.C.

Savings Card Program　　1-877-264-2440　　*www.alinia.com*

Patient pays first $10 of Rx cost, program pays up to $150 in co-pays for tablets/$75 in co-pays for oral suspension.

ALINIA® (nitazoxanide)

ROMARK, L.C.

Romark Patient Assistance Program 1-813-282-8544 *www.alinia.com*

Program provides meds to patients who are uninsured or underinsured, and meet program guidelines. Patients with Medicare may be eligible, if they have been denied or are ineligible for Low Income Subsidy.

ALIQOPA™ (copanlisib)

BAYER HEALTHCARE PHARMACEUTICALS

Co-Pay Assistance Program 1-833-254-7672 *www.hcp.aliqopa-us.com*

Program covers up to 100% of co-pay/co-insurance for those with private insurance. Maximum benefit $25k per year.

Patient Assistance Program (PAP) 1-833-254-7672 *www.hcp.aliqopa-us.com*

Helps those who are uninsured (no insurance coverage at all) or underinsured (no prescription coverage, a benefits cap, denial of coverage, etc), and cannot afford medications.

alirocumab → **PRALUENT®**

alogliptin → **NESINA®**

alogliptin and metformin HCL → **KAZANO®**

alogliptin and pioglitazone → **OSENI®**

ALOMIDE® (lodoxamide tromethamine solution)

NOVARTIS PHARMACEUTICALS

Novartis Patient Assistance Foundation 1-800-277-2254 *www.pap.novartis.com*

Program assists those without insurance (or with limited/inadequate Rx coverage) and cannot afford their prescribed medication. Call for full details to see if you qualify for program assistance.

alosetron HCL → **LOTRONEX®**

alprazolam → **XANAX®**

ALPROLIX® [coagulation factor IX (recombinant),fc fusion protein]

BIOVERATIV

Bioverativ CoPay Assistance
1-855-692-5776   *www.alprolix.com*

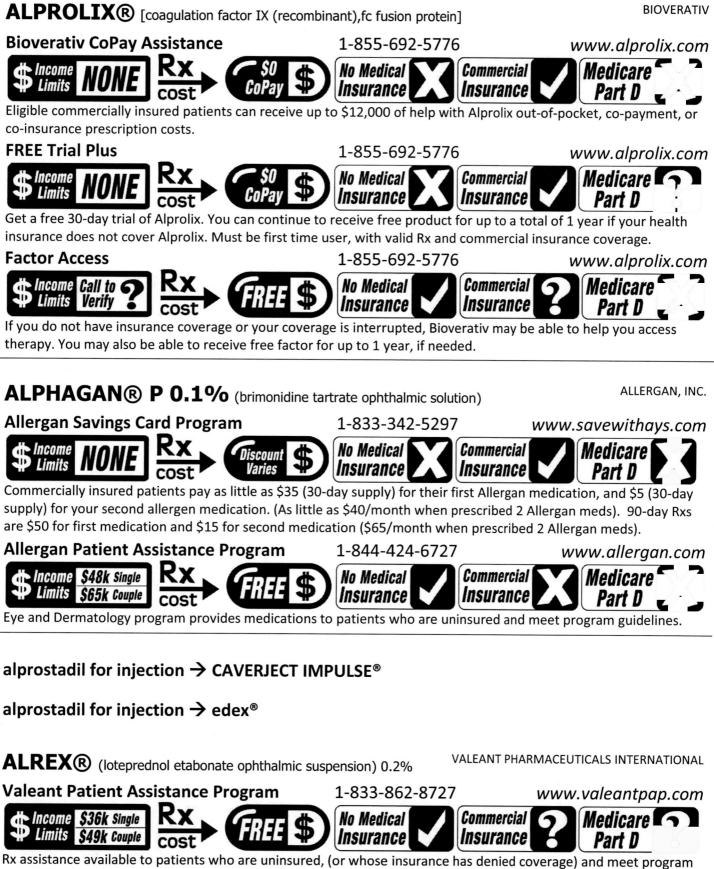

Eligible commercially insured patients can receive up to $12,000 of help with Alprolix out-of-pocket, co-payment, or co-insurance prescription costs.

FREE Trial Plus
1-855-692-5776   *www.alprolix.com*

Get a free 30-day trial of Alprolix. You can continue to receive free product for up to a total of 1 year if your health insurance does not cover Alprolix. Must be first time user, with valid Rx and commercial insurance coverage.

Factor Access
1-855-692-5776   *www.alprolix.com*

If you do not have insurance coverage or your coverage is interrupted, Bioverativ may be able to help you access therapy. You may also be able to receive free factor for up to 1 year, if needed.

ALPHAGAN® P 0.1% (brimonidine tartrate ophthalmic solution)

ALLERGAN, INC.

Allergan Savings Card Program
1-833-342-5297   *www.savewithays.com*

Commercially insured patients pay as little as $35 (30-day supply) for their first Allergan medication, and $5 (30-day supply) for your second allergen medication. (As little as $40/month when prescribed 2 Allergan meds). 90-day Rxs are $50 for first medication and $15 for second medication ($65/month when prescribed 2 Allergan meds).

Allergan Patient Assistance Program
1-844-424-6727   *www.allergan.com*

Eye and Dermatology program provides medications to patients who are uninsured and meet program guidelines.

alprostadil for injection → CAVERJECT IMPULSE®

alprostadil for injection → edex®

ALREX® (loteprednol etabonate ophthalmic suspension) 0.2%

VALEANT PHARMACEUTICALS INTERNATIONAL

Valeant Patient Assistance Program
1-833-862-8727   *www.valeantpap.com*

Rx assistance available to patients who are uninsured, (or whose insurance has denied coverage) and meet program eligibility requirements. Medicare Part D patients who cannot afford Rx can appeal for evaluation of eligibility.

ALTACE® (ramipril)
PFIZER, INC.

Pfizer Savings Program   1-866-706-2400   *www.pfizerrxpathways.com*

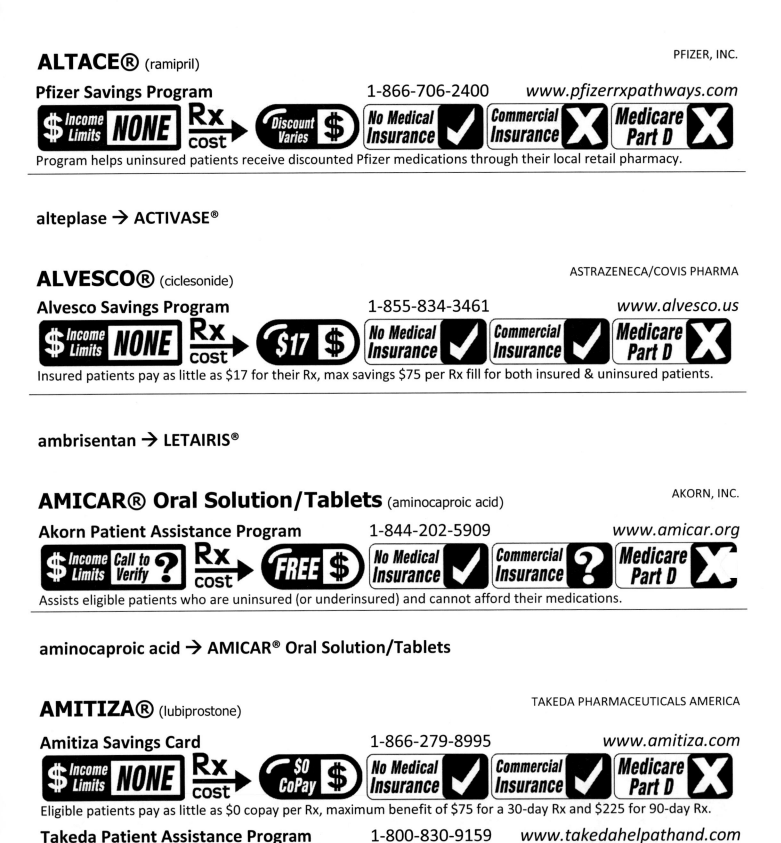

Income Limits NONE | **Rx cost** → Discount Varies $ | **No Medical Insurance** ✓ | **Commercial Insurance** ✗ | **Medicare Part D** ✗

Program helps uninsured patients receive discounted Pfizer medications through their local retail pharmacy.

---

alteplase → **ACTIVASE®**

ALVESCO® (ciclesonide)
ASTRAZENECA/COVIS PHARMA

Alvesco Savings Program   1-855-834-3461   *www.alvesco.us*

Income Limits NONE | **Rx cost** → $17 $ | **No Medical Insurance** ✓ | **Commercial Insurance** ✓ | **Medicare Part D** ✗

Insured patients pay as little as $17 for their Rx, max savings $75 per Rx fill for both insured & uninsured patients.

---

ambrisentan → **LETAIRIS®**

AMICAR® Oral Solution/Tablets (aminocaproic acid)
AKORN, INC.

Akorn Patient Assistance Program   1-844-202-5909   *www.amicar.org*

Income Limits Call to Verify ? | **Rx cost** → FREE $ | **No Medical Insurance** ✓ | **Commercial Insurance** ? | **Medicare Part D** ✗

Assists eligible patients who are uninsured (or underinsured) and cannot afford their medications.

---

aminocaproic acid → **AMICAR® Oral Solution/Tablets**

AMITIZA® (lubiprostone)
TAKEDA PHARMACEUTICALS AMERICA

Amitiza Savings Card   1-866-279-8995   *www.amitiza.com*

Income Limits NONE | **Rx cost** → $0 CoPay $ | **No Medical Insurance** ✓ | **Commercial Insurance** ✓ | **Medicare Part D** ✗

Eligible patients pay as little as $0 copay per Rx, maximum benefit of $75 for a 30-day Rx and $225 for 90-day Rx.

Takeda Patient Assistance Program   1-800-830-9159   *www.takedahelpathand.com*

Income Limits $60k Single / $82k Couple | **Rx cost** → FREE $ | **No Medical Insurance** ✓ | **Commercial Insurance** ? | **Medicare Part D** ?

Provides Amitiza at no cost to eligible patients who do not have insurance or not enough coverage to obtain meds.

amlodipine besylate → NORVASC®

amlodipine besylate/atorvastatin → CADUET®

amlodipine/olmesartan medoxomil → AZOR®

amphetamine → EVEKEO®

amphetamine → MYDAYIS®

amylase/lipase/pancrelipase/protease → PERTZYE®

ANAFRANIL™ (clomipramine hydrochloride)   MALLINCKRODT PHARMACEUTICALS

Mallinckrodt Patient Assistance Program   1-800-259-7765   www.mallinckrodt.com

| $ Income Limits $24k Single $32k Couple | Rx cost → | CALL TO VERIFY $ | No Medical Insurance ✓ | Commercial Insurance ✗ | Medicare Part D ✗ |

Program for uninsured patients who may not be able to afford their Mallinckrodt medications, call for application.

anakinra → KINERET®

ANALPRAM HC® (hydrocortisone/pramoxine)   SEBELA PHARMACEUTICALS, INC.

Instant Savings Offer   1-844-728-3459   www.analpram.com

| $ Income Limits NONE | Rx cost → | $30 $ | No Medical Insurance ✓ | Commercial Insurance ✓ | Medicare Part D ✗ |

Commercially insured patients pay as little as $30 copay for Analpram, uninsured patients receive $75 off per Rx.

Sebela Patient Assistance Program   1-866-562-7902   www.analpram.com

| $ Income Limits $12k Single $16k Couple | Rx cost → | FREE $ | No Medical Insurance ✓ | Commercial Insurance ✗ | Medicare Part D ? |

Program provides Analpram to qualified patients who are uninsured, or where Medicare does not cover treatment.

anastrozole → ARIMIDEX®

ANCOBON® (flucytosine) capsules   VALEANT PHARMACEUTICALS INTERNATIONAL

Valeant Patient Assistance Program   1-833-862-8727   www.valeantpap.com

| $ Income Limits $36k Single $49k Couple | Rx cost → | FREE $ | No Medical Insurance ✓ | Commercial Insurance ? | Medicare Part D ? |

Rx assistance available to patients who are uninsured, (or whose insurance has denied coverage) and meet program eligibility requirements. Medicare Part D patients who cannot afford Rx can appeal for evaluation of eligibility.

ANDROGEL® (testosterone gel) 1.62%

AbbVie, INC.

Restoration Program 1-855-498-0162 *www.androgel.com*

| $ Income Limits **NONE** | **Rx** cost → | $10 Per Month $ | No Medical Insurance ✗ | Commercial Insurance ✓ | Medicare Part D ✗ |

Eligible insured patients pay as little as $10 per month for their AndroGel Rx.

AbbVie Patient Assistance Foundation 1-800-222-6885 *www.abbviepaf.org*

| $ Income Limits $24k Single $32k Couple | **Rx** cost → | **FREE** $ | No Medical Insurance ✓ | Commercial Insurance ✓ | Medicare Part D |

Rx assistance available to patients who are uninsured and meet program eligibility requirements. Patients with Commercial Insurance or Medicare Part D, who are struggling to pay for their medications, are encouraged to apply.

ANDROID® (methyltestosterone) capsules

VALEANT PHARMACEUTICALS INTERNATIONAL

Valeant Patient Assistance Program 1-833-862-8727 *www.valeantpap.com*

| $ Income Limits $36k Single $49k Couple | **Rx** cost → | **FREE** $ | No Medical Insurance ✓ | Commercial Insurance ? | Medicare Part D |

Rx assistance available to patients who are uninsured, (or whose insurance has denied coverage) and meet program eligibility requirements. Medicare Part D patients who cannot afford Rx can appeal for evaluation of eligibility.

ANGELIQ® (drospirenone and estradiol)

BAYER HEALTHCARE PHARMACEUTICALS

Bayer Savings Card 1-866-203-3503 *www.savingscard.bayer.com*

| $ Income Limits **NONE** | **Rx** cost → | $30 Per Month $ | No Medical Insurance ✓ | Commercial Insurance ✓ | Medicare Part D ✗ |

Insured patients pay no more than $30 per month, (maximum savings of $125). If you pay cash for your monthly medications, you will receive up to $75 in savings on your out-of-pocket costs for each prescription.

Bayer Patient Assistance Program 1-866-575-5002 *Phone Only*

| $ Income Limits Call to Verify ? | **Rx** cost → | **FREE** $ | No Medical Insurance ✓ | Commercial Insurance ? | Medicare Part D ? |

Program provides medications to patients based on financial need. Application must be completed by both you and your healthcare provider. Before calling number, make sure you have your Doctor's office fax and phone number, as well as the contact name at the office. Eligibility determined on a case-by-case basis.

anidulafungin → ERAXIS®

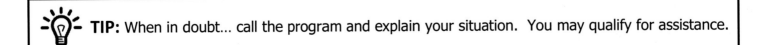

TIP: When in doubt... call the program and explain your situation. You may qualify for assistance.

ANORO® ELLIPTA® (umeclidinium and vilanterol inhalation powder)

ANORO Savings Offer

1-866-475-3678

www.anoro.com

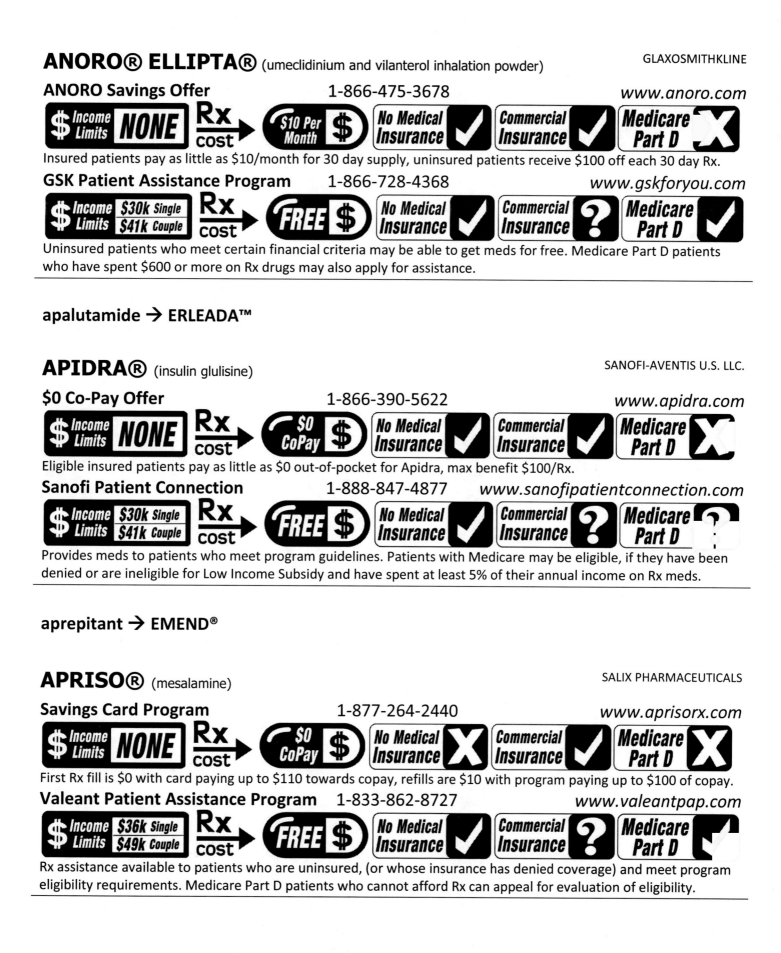

$ Income Limits **NONE** | **Rx** cost → | $10 Per Month $ | No Medical Insurance ✓ | Commercial Insurance ✓ | Medicare Part D ✗

Insured patients pay as little as $10/month for 30 day supply, uninsured patients receive $100 off each 30 day Rx.

GSK Patient Assistance Program

1-866-728-4368

www.gskforyou.com

$ Income Limits $30k Single $41k Couple | **Rx** cost → | **FREE** $ | No Medical Insurance ✓ | Commercial Insurance ? | Medicare Part D ✓

Uninsured patients who meet certain financial criteria may be able to get meds for free. Medicare Part D patients who have spent $600 or more on Rx drugs may also apply for assistance.

---

apalutamide → ERLEADA™

APIDRA® (insulin glulisine)

SANOFI-AVENTIS U.S. LLC.

$0 Co-Pay Offer

1-866-390-5622

www.apidra.com

$ Income Limits **NONE** | **Rx** cost → | $0 CoPay $ | No Medical Insurance ✓ | Commercial Insurance ✓ | Medicare Part D ✗

Eligible insured patients pay as little as $0 out-of-pocket for Apidra, max benefit $100/Rx.

Sanofi Patient Connection

1-888-847-4877

www.sanofipatientconnection.com

$ Income Limits $30k Single $41k Couple | **Rx** cost → | **FREE** $ | No Medical Insurance ✓ | Commercial Insurance ? | Medicare Part D ?

Provides meds to patients who meet program guidelines. Patients with Medicare may be eligible, if they have been denied or are ineligible for Low Income Subsidy and have spent at least 5% of their annual income on Rx meds.

---

aprepitant → EMEND®

APRISO® (mesalamine)

SALIX PHARMACEUTICALS

Savings Card Program

1-877-264-2440

www.aprisorx.com

$ Income Limits **NONE** | **Rx** cost → | $0 CoPay $ | No Medical Insurance ✗ | Commercial Insurance ✓ | Medicare Part D ✗

First Rx fill is $0 with card paying up to $110 towards copay, refills are $10 with program paying up to $100 of copay.

Valeant Patient Assistance Program

1-833-862-8727

www.valeantpap.com

$ Income Limits $36k Single $49k Couple | **Rx** cost → | **FREE** $ | No Medical Insurance ✓ | Commercial Insurance ? | Medicare Part D ✓

Rx assistance available to patients who are uninsured, (or whose insurance has denied coverage) and meet program eligibility requirements. Medicare Part D patients who cannot afford Rx can appeal for evaluation of eligibility.

APTIOM® (eslicarbazepine acetate) tablets

SUNOVION PHARMACEUTICALS, INC.

APTIOM Savings Card   1-844-427-8466   *www.aptiom.com*

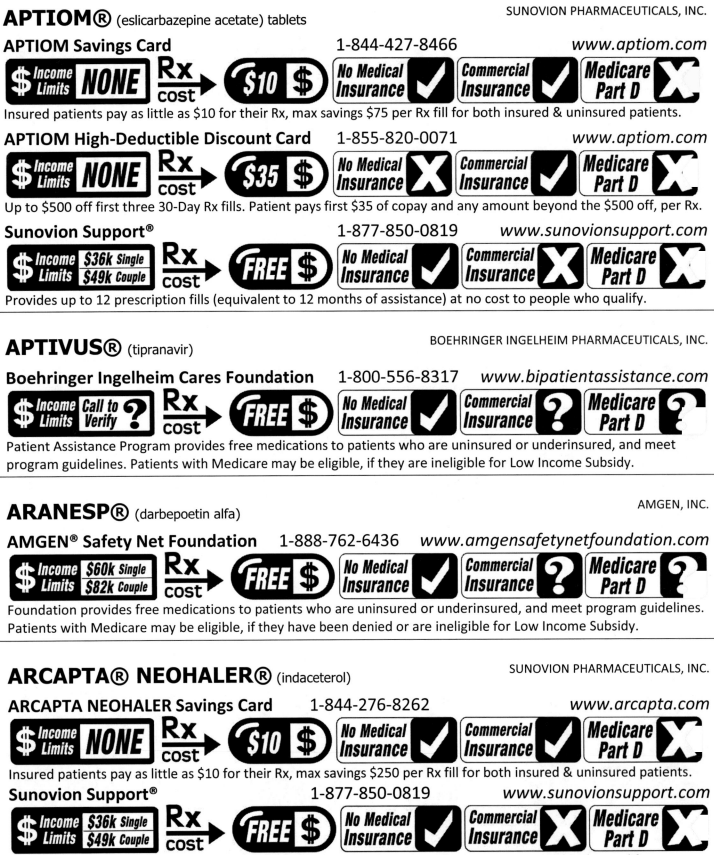

$ Income Limits NONE | **Rx cost →** $10 $ | No Medical Insurance ✓ | Commercial Insurance ✓ | Medicare Part D ✗

Insured patients pay as little as $10 for their Rx, max savings $75 per Rx fill for both insured & uninsured patients.

APTIOM High-Deductible Discount Card   1-855-820-0071   *www.aptiom.com*

$ Income Limits NONE | **Rx cost →** $35 $ | No Medical Insurance ✗ | Commercial Insurance ✓ | Medicare Part D ✗

Up to $500 off first three 30-Day Rx fills. Patient pays first $35 of copay and any amount beyond the $500 off, per Rx.

Sunovion Support®   1-877-850-0819   *www.sunovionsupport.com*

$ Income Limits $36k Single $49k Couple | **Rx cost →** FREE $ | No Medical Insurance ✓ | Commercial Insurance ✗ | Medicare Part D ✗

Provides up to 12 prescription fills (equivalent to 12 months of assistance) at no cost to people who qualify.

APTIVUS® (tipranavir)

BOEHRINGER INGELHEIM PHARMACEUTICALS, INC.

Boehringer Ingelheim Cares Foundation   1-800-556-8317   *www.bipatientassistance.com*

$ Income Limits Call to Verify ? | **Rx cost →** FREE $ | No Medical Insurance ✓ | Commercial Insurance ? | Medicare Part D ?

Patient Assistance Program provides free medications to patients who are uninsured or underinsured, and meet program guidelines. Patients with Medicare may be eligible, if they are ineligible for Low Income Subsidy.

ARANESP® (darbepoetin alfa)

AMGEN, INC.

AMGEN® Safety Net Foundation   1-888-762-6436   *www.amgensafetynetfoundation.com*

$ Income Limits $60k Single $82k Couple | **Rx cost →** FREE $ | No Medical Insurance ✓ | Commercial Insurance ? | Medicare Part D ?

Foundation provides free medications to patients who are uninsured or underinsured, and meet program guidelines. Patients with Medicare may be eligible, if they have been denied or are ineligible for Low Income Subsidy.

ARCAPTA® NEOHALER® (indaceterol)

SUNOVION PHARMACEUTICALS, INC.

ARCAPTA NEOHALER Savings Card   1-844-276-8262   *www.arcapta.com*

$ Income Limits NONE | **Rx cost →** $10 $ | No Medical Insurance ✓ | Commercial Insurance ✓ | Medicare Part D ✗

Insured patients pay as little as $10 for their Rx, max savings $250 per Rx fill for both insured & uninsured patients.

Sunovion Support®   1-877-850-0819   *www.sunovionsupport.com*

$ Income Limits $36k Single $49k Couple | **Rx cost →** FREE $ | No Medical Insurance ✓ | Commercial Insurance ✗ | Medicare Part D ✗

Provides up to 12 prescription fills (equivalent to 12 months of assistance) at no cost to people who qualify.

ARESTIN® (minocycline)

ORAPHARMA, INC.

Arestin Rx Access Co-Pay Assistance   1-855-684-7481   *www.arestin.com*

Insured patients may qualify for up to $1500 in Arestin Rx co-pay assistance, call for details.

---

arginine HCl injection → R-GENE® 10

ARIMIDEX® (anastrozole)

ASTRAZENECA PHARMACEUTICALS

ARIMIDEX Patient Direct   1-855-250-2483   *www.arimidex.com*

Program provides ARIMIDEX, shipped to your door, for only $1 per day, regardless of insurance status, with valid Rx.

AZ&ME™   1-800-292-6363   *www.azandmeapp.com*

Program provides free medications to patients who are uninsured and meet program guidelines. Patients with Medicare may be eligible, if they are not eligible for (or enrolled in) Limited Income Subsidy (LIS), and have spent at least 3% of their annual household income on Rx medications through their Medicare Part D plan in the current year.

---

aripiprazole → ABILIFY®

aripiprazole lauroxil → ARISTADA®

ARISTADA® (aripiprazole lauroxil)

ALKERMES, INC.

Aristada Co-pay Savings Program   1-866-274-7823   *www.aristadacaresupport.com*

Eligible patients with commercial insurance can receive Aristada for as little as $10 per month.

Aristada Patient Assistance Program   1-866-274-7823   *www.aristadacaresupport.com*

Program provides medications to patients who are uninsured or have been denied coverage for Aristada.

---

armodafinil → NUVIGIL®

ARMOUR® Thyroid Tablets (thyroid tablets)

ALLERGAN, INC.

Allergan Patient Assistance Program 1-844-424-6727 *www.allergan.com*

Program provides meds to patients who are uninsured or underinsured, and meet program guidelines. Patients with Medicare may be eligible, if they have been denied or are ineligible for Low Income Subsidy.

ARNUITY® ELLIPTA® (fluticasone furoate inhalation powder)

GLAXOSMITHKLINE

ARNUITY Savings Offer 1-866-475-3678 *www.arnuity.com*

Insured patients pay as little as $10/month for 30 day supply, uninsured patients receive $100 off each 30 day Rx.

GSK Patient Assistance Program 1-866-728-4368 *www.gskforyou.com*

Uninsured patients who meet certain financial criteria may be able to get meds for free. Medicare Part D patients who have spent $600 or more on Rx drugs may also apply for assistance.

AROMASIN® (exemestane tablets)

PFIZER, INC

Pfizer Savings Program 1-866-706-2400 *www.pfizerrxpathways.com*

Program helps uninsured patients receive discounted Pfizer medications through their local retail pharmacy.

Aromasin Co-Pay Savings Card 1-866-562-6151 *www.aromasin.com*

Eligible patients can save up to $3600 per year toward their co-pay, deductible, and coinsurance costs. Commercially insured patients pay as little as $4 per month.

Pfizer Patient Assistance Program 1-844-989-7284 *www.pfizerrxpathways.com*

Assists eligible patients who are uninsured (or have inadequate drug coverage) and cannot afford their medications.

TIP: Income limits are higher for households with three or more people. Call programs for details.

ARRANON® (nelarabine)

Novartis Patient Assistance Foundation   1-800-277-2254   *www.pap.novartis.com*

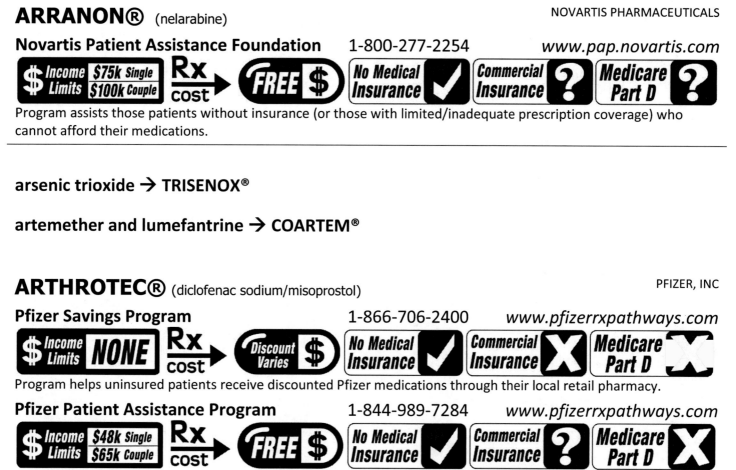

$ Income Limits $75k Single $100k Couple | **Rx cost** → **FREE $** | **No Medical Insurance** ✓ | **Commercial Insurance** ? | **Medicare Part D** ?

Program assists those patients without insurance (or those with limited/inadequate prescription coverage) who cannot afford their medications.

arsenic trioxide → TRISENOX®

artemether and lumefantrine → COARTEM®

ARTHROTEC® (diclofenac sodium/misoprostol)

Pfizer Savings Program   1-866-706-2400   *www.pfizerrxpathways.com*

$ Income Limits NONE | **Rx cost** → **Discount Varies $** | **No Medical Insurance** ✓ | **Commercial Insurance** ✗ | **Medicare Part D** ✗

Program helps uninsured patients receive discounted Pfizer medications through their local retail pharmacy.

Pfizer Patient Assistance Program   1-844-989-7284   *www.pfizerrxpathways.com*

$ Income Limits $48k Single $65k Couple | **Rx cost** → **FREE $** | **No Medical Insurance** ✓ | **Commercial Insurance** ? | **Medicare Part D** ✗

Assists eligible patients who are uninsured (or have inadequate drug coverage) and cannot afford their medications.

ARZERRA® (ofatumumab)

Novartis Patient Assistance Foundation   1-800-277-2254   *www.pap.novartis.com*

$ Income Limits $75k Single $100k Couple | **Rx cost** → **FREE $** | **No Medical Insurance** ✓ | **Commercial Insurance** ? | **Medicare Part D** ?

Program assists those patients without insurance (or with limited/inadequate Rx coverage) who are having trouble affording their prescribed medications.

asenapine maleate → SAPHRIS®

asfotase alfa → STRENSIQ®

TIP: When in doubt... call the program and explain your situation. You may qualify for assistance.

ASMANEX® HFA (mometasone furoate) Inhalation Aerosol
MERCK & COMPANY, INC.

Multiuse Savings Coupon — 1-800-672-6372 — www.asmanex.com

$ Income Limits **NONE** | Rx cost → | **$15** $ | No Medical Insurance ✗ | Commercial Insurance ✓ | Medicare Part D ✗

Commercially insured patients may pay as little as $15 per Rx, maximum savings is $90 per prescription.

Merck Patient Assistance Program — 1-800-727-5400 — www.merckhelps.com

$ Income Limits **$48k Single $65k Couple** | Rx cost → | **FREE** $ | No Medical Insurance ✓ | Commercial Insurance ? | Medicare Part D ?

Program is for patients who do not have Rx insurance coverage (or are underinsured) and cannot afford to pay for their prescribed medications.

ASMANEX® TWISTHALER® (mometasone furoate inhalation powder)
MERCK & COMPANY, INC.

Multiuse Savings Coupon — 1-800-672-6372 — www.asmanex.com

$ Income Limits **NONE** | Rx cost → | **$15** $ | No Medical Insurance ✗ | Commercial Insurance ✓ | Medicare Part D ✗

Commercially insured patients may pay as little as $15 per Rx, maximum savings is $90 per prescription.

Merck Patient Assistance Program — 1-800-727-5400 — www.merckhelps.com

$ Income Limits **$48k Single $65k Couple** | Rx cost → | **FREE** $ | No Medical Insurance ✓ | Commercial Insurance ? | Medicare Part D ?

Program is for patients who do not have Rx insurance coverage (or are underinsured) and cannot afford to pay for their prescribed medications.

ASTAGRAF® XL (tacrolimus extended release capsules)
ASTELLAS PHARMA, INC.

ASTAGRAF XL Co-Pay Card — 1-800-477-6472 — www.astellasaccess.com

$ Income Limits **NONE** | Rx cost → | **$0 CoPay** $ | No Medical Insurance ✗ | Commercial Insurance ✓ | Medicare Part D ✗

Provides up to $3000/year in co-pay assistance. Eligible patients pay as low as $0 out-of-pocket for prescribed meds.

Astellas Patient Assistance Program — 1-800-477-6472 — www.astellasaccess.com

$ Income Limits **$30k Single $41k Couple** | Rx cost → | **FREE** $ | No Medical Insurance ✓ | Commercial Insurance ? | Medicare Part D ✗

Provides medications for those uninsured or have insurance that excludes coverage for ASTAGRAF XL.

atazanavir → REYATAZ®

atazanavir/cobicistat → EVOTAZ®

atezolizumab → TECENTRIQ®

ATGAM® (lymphocyte immune globulin/anti-thymocyte globulin) PFIZER, INC

Pfizer Savings Program   1-866-706-2400   *www.pfizerrxpathways.com*

Program helps uninsured patients receive discounted Pfizer medications through their local retail pharmacy.

atomoxetine → **STRATTERA®**

atorvastatin calcium → LIPITOR®

atovaquone → **MEPRON®**

atovaquone and proguanil hydrochloride → MALARONE®

ATRIPLA® (efavirenx/emtricitabine/tenofovir disoproxil fumarate) GILEAD SCIENCES, INC

Co-Pay Assistance Card Program   1-800-226-2056   *www.atripla.com*

Program helps pay for the cost of prescription co-pays up to $6000 per product per year.

Gilead Advancing Access   1-800-226-2056   *www.gileadadvancingaccess.com*

Patient assistance program provides medications at no charge for eligible patients with no other insurance options.

ATROVENT HFA® (ipratropium bromide HFA)   BOEHRINGER INGELHEIM PHARMACEUTICALS, INC.

Boehringer Ingelheim Cares Foundation   1-800-556-8317   *www.bipatientassistance.com*

Patient Assistance Program provides free medications to patients who are uninsured or underinsured, and meet program guidelines. Patients with Medicare may be eligible, if they are ineligible for Low Income Subsidy.

AUBAGIO® (teriflunomide)   GENZYME CORPORATION

AUBAGIO Co-Pay Program   1-855-676-6326   *www.aubagio.com*

Covers 100% of your eligible out-of-pocket Aubagio drug costs up to the program maximum.

AUBAGIO® (teriflunomide)
GENZYME CORPORATION

Charitable Access Program   1-855-676-6326   *www.aubagio.com*

| $ Income Limits | Call to Verify ? | Rx cost → | FREE $ | No Medical Insurance ✓ | Commercial Insurance ? | Medicare Part D ? |

Program provides medications to patients who are uninsured or have inadequate insurance coverage for Aubagio

---

AURYXIA® (ferric citrate)
KERYX BIOPHARMACEUTICALS, INC.

AURYXIA CoPay Coupon   1-855-686-8601   *www.auryxia.com*

| $ Income Limits | NONE | Rx cost → | $0 CoPay $ | No Medical Insurance ✗ | Commercial Insurance ✓ | Medicare Part D ✗ |

Pay as little as $0, program pays the rest up to $500, on each 30-day Rx at your retail or mail order pharmacy.

Keryx Patient Plus   1-855-686-8601   *www.auryxia.org*

| $ Income Limits | $48k Single / $65k Couple | Rx cost → | FREE $ | No Medical Insurance ✓ | Commercial Insurance ✗ | Medicare Part D ✓ |

Provides meds free to those who are uninsured and Medicare Part D patients who cannot afford out-of-pocket costs.

Auvi-Q® (epinephrine injection, USP)
KALEO, INC.

Direct Delivery Service   1-877-302-8847   *www.auvi-q.com*

| $ Income Limits | NONE | Rx cost → | $0 CoPay $ | No Medical Insurance ✗ | Commercial Insurance ✓ | Medicare Part D ✗ |

Commercially insured patients pay absolutely nothing out of pocket for Auvi-Q.

KALÉO CARES Patient Assistance Program   1-877-302-8847   *www.auvi-q.org*

| $ Income Limits | $100K Household | Rx cost → | FREE $ | No Medical Insurance ✓ | Commercial Insurance ✗ | Medicare Part D ✗ |

Eligible patients who are experiencing financial difficulties may be able to receive Auvi-Q at no cost.

AVANDIA® (rosiglitazone maleate)
GLAXOSMITHKLINE

GSK Patient Assistance Program   1-866-728-4368   *www.gskforyou.com*

| $ Income Limits | $30k Single / $41k Couple | Rx cost → | FREE $ | No Medical Insurance ✓ | Commercial Insurance ? | Medicare Part D ✓ |

Uninsured patients who meet certain financial criteria may be able to get meds for free. Medicare Part D patients who have spent $600 or more on Rx drugs in calendar year may also apply for assistance.

💡 **TIP:** When in doubt... call the program and explain your situation. You may qualify for assistance.

AVASTIN® (bevacizumab)

Co-Pay Card Assistance Program — 1-855-692-6729 — www.copayassistancenow.com

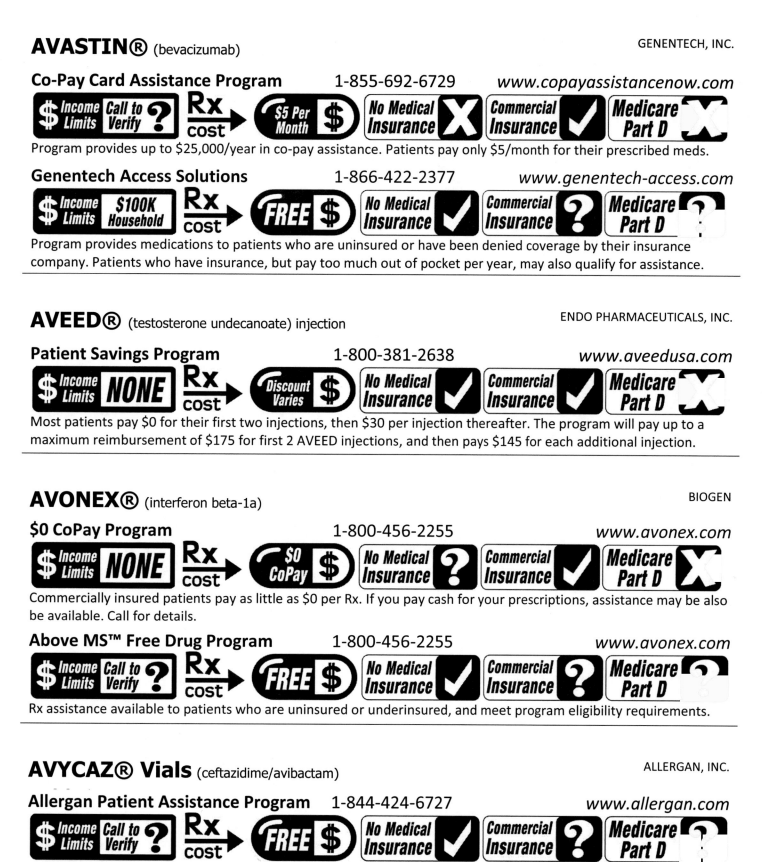

$ Income Limits — Call to Verify? | **Rx cost →** | **$5 Per Month $** | **No Medical Insurance ✗** | **Commercial Insurance ✓** | **Medicare Part D ✗**

Program provides up to $25,000/year in co-pay assistance. Patients pay only $5/month for their prescribed meds.

Genentech Access Solutions — 1-866-422-2377 — www.genentech-access.com

$ Income Limits — $100K Household | **Rx cost →** | **FREE $** | **No Medical Insurance ✓** | **Commercial Insurance ?** | **Medicare Part D ?**

Program provides medications to patients who are uninsured or have been denied coverage by their insurance company. Patients who have insurance, but pay too much out of pocket per year, may also qualify for assistance.

AVEED® (testosterone undecanoate) injection

ENDO PHARMACEUTICALS, INC.

Patient Savings Program — 1-800-381-2638 — www.aveedusa.com

$ Income Limits — NONE | **Rx cost →** | **Discount Varies $** | **No Medical Insurance ✓** | **Commercial Insurance ✓** | **Medicare Part D ✗**

Most patients pay $0 for their first two injections, then $30 per injection thereafter. The program will pay up to a maximum reimbursement of $175 for first 2 AVEED injections, and then pays $145 for each additional injection.

AVONEX® (interferon beta-1a)

BIOGEN

$0 CoPay Program — 1-800-456-2255 — www.avonex.com

$ Income Limits — NONE | **Rx cost →** | **$0 CoPay $** | **No Medical Insurance ?** | **Commercial Insurance ✓** | **Medicare Part D ✗**

Commercially insured patients pay as little as $0 per Rx. If you pay cash for your prescriptions, assistance may be also be available. Call for details.

Above MS™ Free Drug Program — 1-800-456-2255 — www.avonex.com

$ Income Limits — Call to Verify? | **Rx cost →** | **FREE $** | **No Medical Insurance ✓** | **Commercial Insurance ?** | **Medicare Part D ?**

Rx assistance available to patients who are uninsured or underinsured, and meet program eligibility requirements.

AVYCAZ® Vials (ceftazidime/avibactam)

ALLERGAN, INC.

Allergan Patient Assistance Program — 1-844-424-6727 — www.allergan.com

$ Income Limits — Call to Verify? | **Rx cost →** | **FREE $** | **No Medical Insurance ✓** | **Commercial Insurance ?** | **Medicare Part D ?**

Program provides meds to patients who are uninsured or underinsured, and meet program guidelines. Patients with Medicare may be eligible, if they have been denied or are ineligible for Low Income Subsidy.

axitinib tablets → INLYTA®

azacitidine for injection → VIDAZA®

azelaic acid → FINACEA®

azelastine/fluticasone propionate → DYMISTA® Nasal Spray

azilsartan medoxomil → EDARBI®

azilartan medoxomil/chlorthalidone → EDARBYCLOR®

azithromycin → ZITHROMAX®

azithromycin extended release → ZMAX®

AZOPT® (brinzolamide ophthalmic suspension) NOVARTIS PHARMACEUTICALS

OPENINGS® Program Savings Card   1-866-972-3008   *www.copay.novartispharma.com*

Commercially nsured patients pay as little as $30 for their prescription, the program pays the remaining Rx co-pay with maximuim benefit of $2,000/year.

Novartis Patient Assistance Foundation   1-800-277-2254   *www.pap.novartis.com*

Program assists those without insurance (or with limited/inadequate Rx coverage) and cannot afford their prescribed medication. Call for full details to see if you qualify for program assistance.

AZOR® (amlodipine/olmesartan medoxomil) DAIICHI SANKYO, INC.

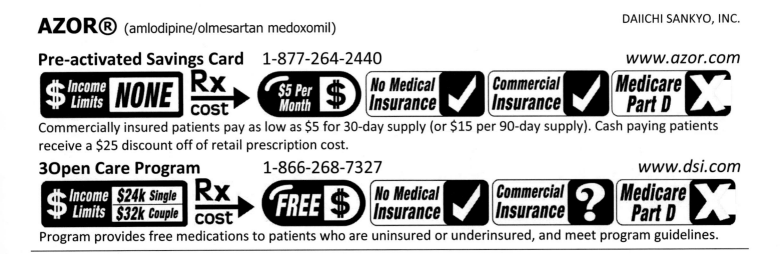

Pre-activated Savings Card   1-877-264-2440   *www.azor.com*

Commercially insured patients pay as low as $5 for 30-day supply (or $15 per 90-day supply). Cash paying patients receive a $25 discount off of retail prescription cost.

3Open Care Program   1-866-268-7327   *www.dsi.com*

Program provides free medications to patients who are uninsured or underinsured, and meet program guidelines.

aztreonam → CAYSTON®

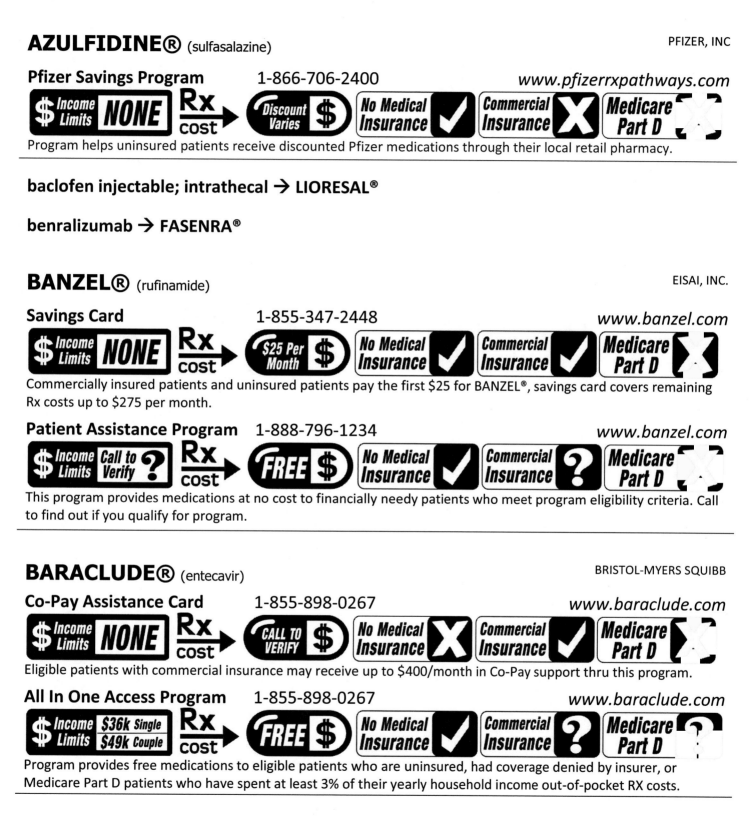

AZULFIDINE® (sulfasalazine)

PFIZER, INC

Pfizer Savings Program   1-866-706-2400   *www.pfizerrxpathways.com*

Income Limits **NONE** | **Rx** cost → | Discount Varies $ | No Medical Insurance ✓ | Commercial Insurance ✗ | Medicare Part D ✗

Program helps uninsured patients receive discounted Pfizer medications through their local retail pharmacy.

baclofen injectable; intrathecal → LIORESAL®

benralizumab → FASENRA®

BANZEL® (rufinamide)

EISAI, INC.

Savings Card   1-855-347-2448   *www.banzel.com*

Income Limits **NONE** | **Rx** cost → | $25 Per Month $ | No Medical Insurance ✓ | Commercial Insurance ✓ | Medicare Part D ✗

Commercially insured patients and uninsured patients pay the first $25 for BANZEL®, savings card covers remaining Rx costs up to $275 per month.

Patient Assistance Program   1-888-796-1234   *www.banzel.com*

Income Limits Call to Verify ? | **Rx** cost → | FREE $ | No Medical Insurance ✓ | Commercial Insurance ? | Medicare Part D ✗

This program provides medications at no cost to financially needy patients who meet program eligibility criteria. Call to find out if you qualify for program.

BARACLUDE® (entecavir)

BRISTOL-MYERS SQUIBB

Co-Pay Assistance Card   1-855-898-0267   *www.baraclude.com*

Income Limits **NONE** | **Rx** cost → | CALL TO VERIFY $ | No Medical Insurance ✗ | Commercial Insurance ✓ | Medicare Part D ✗

Eligible patients with commercial insurance may receive up to $400/month in Co-Pay support thru this program.

All In One Access Program   1-855-898-0267   *www.baraclude.com*

Income Limits $36k Single $49k Couple | **Rx** cost → | FREE $ | No Medical Insurance ✓ | Commercial Insurance ? | Medicare Part D ?

Program provides free medications to eligible patients who are uninsured, had coverage denied by insurer, or Medicare Part D patients who have spent at least 3% of their yearly household income out-of-pocket RX costs.

LILLY USA, LLC

baricitinib → OLUMIANT®

BASAGLAR® (insulin glargine injection)

Savings Program   1-800-545-5979   *www.basaglar.com*

$ Income Limits **NONE** | **Rx** cost → | $5 Per Month $ | **No Medical Insurance** ✗ | **Commercial Insurance** ✓ | **Medicare Part D** ✗

Provides co-pay assistance up to $150/month for your first 24 Rx's, insured patients pay as little as $5 out of pocket.

Lilly Cares   1-800-545-6962   *www.lillycares.com*

$ Income Limits $36k Single $49k Couple | **Rx** cost → | **FREE** $ | **No Medical Insurance** ✓ | **Commercial Insurance** ✗ | **Medicare Part D** ✓

Provides free Lilly medications for eligible patients who are uninsured and cannot afford their medications. Medicare Part D patients are eligible for assistance, after they have spent $1,100 on Rx meds in a calendar year.

BEBULIN® (factor IX complex)   BAXALTA, INC / SHIRE

Shire's CoPay Assistance Program   1-888-229-8379   *www.hematologysupport.com*

$ Income Limits **NONE** | **Rx** cost → | CALL TO VERIFY $ | **No Medical Insurance** ✗ | **Commercial Insurance** ✓ | **Medicare Part D** ✗

Patients with commercial insurance may be eligible to receive up to $12,000 in CoPay support thru this program.

beclomethasone dipropionate → BECONASE®

BECONASE® (beclomethasone dipropionate)   GLAXOSMITHKLINE

GSK Patient Assistance Program   1-866-728-4368   *www.gskforyou.com*

$ Income Limits $30k Single $41k Couple | **Rx** cost → | **FREE** $ | **No Medical Insurance** ✓ | **Commercial Insurance** ? | **Medicare Part D** ✓

Uninsured patients who meet certain financial criteria may be able to get meds for free. Medicare Part D patients who have spent $600 or more on Rx drugs may also apply for assistance.

beclomethasone dipropionate HFA inhalation powder → QVAR® RediHaler™

beclomethasone dipropionate nasal aerosol → QNASL®

bedaquiline → SIRTURO®

belatacept → NULOJIX®

💡 **TIP:** When in doubt... call the program and explain your situation. You may qualify for assistance.

BELEODAQ® (belinostat) for injection

SPECTRUM PHAMACEUTICALS, INC.

Co-Pay Assistance 1-888-537-8277 *www.spectrumpatientaccess.com*

| $ Income Limits | **NONE** | Rx cost → | **$25 $** | No Medical Insurance ✗ | Commercial Insurance ✓ | Medicare Part D ✗ |

Eligible patients pay $0 copay for first treatment, $25 for additional treatments with max savings $10,000/year.

Spectrum Therapy Access Resources 1-888-461-2255 *www.spectrumpatientaccess.com*

| $ Income Limits | Call to Verify ? | Rx cost → | **FREE $** | No Medical Insurance ✓ | Commercial Insurance ? | Medicare Part D ✗ |

Provides free Spectrum meds to patients who meet income, insurance, and citizenship/residency eligibility criteria.

---

belladonna alkaloids with phenobarbital → DONNATAL®

belimumab → BENLYSTA®

belinostat → BELEODAQ®

BELSOMRA® (suvorexant) tablets

MERCK & COMPANY, INC.

Multiuse Savings Coupon 1-800-672-6372 *www.belsomra.com*

| $ Income Limits | **NONE** | Rx cost → | **$30 $** | No Medical Insurance ✗ | Commercial Insurance ✓ | Medicare Part D ✗ |

Insured patients pay as little as $30 per Rx, maximum program savings is $4000 per patient.

Merck Patient Assistance Program 1-800-727-5400 *www.merckhelps.com*

| $ Income Limits | $48k Single $65k Couple | Rx cost → | **FREE $** | No Medical Insurance ✓ | Commercial Insurance ? | Medicare Part D ? |

Program is for patients who do not have Rx insurance coverage and cannot afford to pay for their medicine.

BELVIQ® / BELVIQ XR® (lorcaserin HCL)

EISAI, INC.

Savings Card 1-855-235-8471 *www.belviq.com*

| $ Income Limits | **NONE** | Rx cost → | **Discount Varies $** | No Medical Insurance ✓ | Commercial Insurance ✓ | Medicare Part D ✓ |

Eligible insured patients pay the first $30 for BELVIQ XR or $40 for BELVIQ, with max savings $160 off the patient's out-of-pocket costs per covered prescription. Patients paying cash receive $195 off cash price per 30 day fill.

Patient Assistance Program 1-866-613-4724 *www.belviq.com*

| $ Income Limits | Call to Verify ? | Rx cost → | **FREE $** | No Medical Insurance ✓ | Commercial Insurance ? | Medicare Part D ✗ |

This program provides medications at no cost to financially needy patients who meet program eligibility criteria.

bendamustine HCL → BENDEKA™

bendamustine HCl → TREANDA®

BENDEKA™ (bendamustine HCL)

TEVA PHARMACEUTICALS

Teva Cares Foundation Patient Assistance Program   1-877-237-4881   *www.tevacares.org*

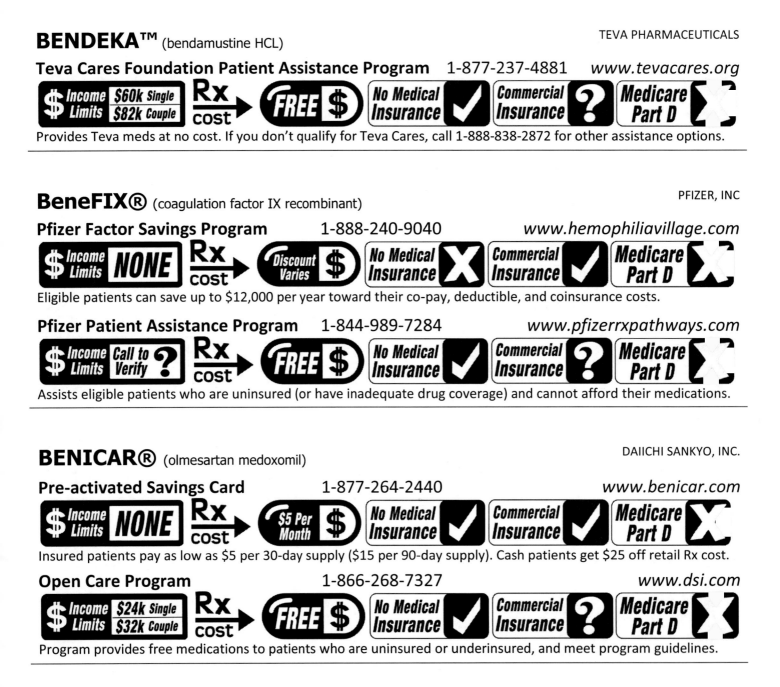

$ Income Limits $60k Single $82k Couple | Rx cost → | FREE $ | No Medical Insurance ✓ | Commercial Insurance ? | Medicare Part D ✗

Provides Teva meds at no cost. If you don't qualify for Teva Cares, call 1-888-838-2872 for other assistance options.

BeneFIX® (coagulation factor IX recombinant)

PFIZER, INC

Pfizer Factor Savings Program   1-888-240-9040   *www.hemophiliavillage.com*

$ Income Limits NONE | Rx cost → | Discount Varies $ | No Medical Insurance ✗ | Commercial Insurance ✓ | Medicare Part D ✗

Eligible patients can save up to $12,000 per year toward their co-pay, deductible, and coinsurance costs.

Pfizer Patient Assistance Program   1-844-989-7284   *www.pfizerrxpathways.com*

$ Income Limits Call to Verify ? | Rx cost → | FREE $ | No Medical Insurance ✓ | Commercial Insurance ? | Medicare Part D ✗

Assists eligible patients who are uninsured (or have inadequate drug coverage) and cannot afford their medications.

BENICAR® (olmesartan medoxomil)

DAIICHI SANKYO, INC.

Pre-activated Savings Card   1-877-264-2440   *www.benicar.com*

$ Income Limits NONE | Rx cost → | $5 Per Month $ | No Medical Insurance ✓ | Commercial Insurance ✓ | Medicare Part D ✗

Insured patients pay as low as $5 per 30-day supply ($15 per 90-day supply). Cash patients get $25 off retail Rx cost.

Open Care Program   1-866-268-7327   *www.dsi.com*

$ Income Limits $24k Single $32k Couple | Rx cost → | FREE $ | No Medical Insurance ✓ | Commercial Insurance ? | Medicare Part D ✗

Program provides free medications to patients who are uninsured or underinsured, and meet program guidelines.

💡 **TIP:** Income limits are higher for households with three or more people. Call programs for details.

DAIICHI SANKYO, INC.

BENICAR HCT® (olmesartan medoxomil /hydrocholorothiazide)

Pre-activated Savings Card   1-877-264-2440   *www.benicar.com*

Income Limits **NONE** | Rx cost → | **$5 Per Month** $ | **No Medical Insurance** ✓ | **Commercial Insurance** ✓ | **Medicare Part D** ›

Commercially insured patients pay as low as $5 for a 30-day supply ($15 for 90-day supply). Cash patients receive a $25 discount off of the retail Rx cost.

Open Care Program   1-866-268-7327   *www.dsi.com*

Income Limits **$24k Single $32k Couple** | Rx cost → | **FREE** $ | **No Medical Insurance** ✓ | **Commercial Insurance** ? | **Medicare Part D** ✗

Program provides free medications to patients who are uninsured or underinsured, and meet program guidelines.

BENLYSTA® (belimumab)

GLAXOSMITHKLINE

BENLYSTA Co-Pay Program   1-877-423-6597   *www.benlysta.com*

Income Limits **NONE** | Rx cost → | **$0 CoPay** $ | **No Medical Insurance** ✗ | **Commercial Insurance** ✓ | **Medicare Part D** ›

This program covers the co-pay/co-insurance amount for Benlysta, for those with commercial insurance. Maximum benefit is $11,000 per year.

Patient Assistance Program (PAP)   1-877-423-6597   *www.benlysta.com*

Income Limits **$60k Single $82k Couple** | Rx cost → | **FREE** $ | **No Medical Insurance** ✓ | **Commercial Insurance** ✗ | **Medicare Part D** ✗

Uninsured patients who meet certain financial criteria may be able to get BENLYSTA for free.

benzonatate → TESSALON®

bepotastine besilate ophthalmic solution 1.5% → BEPREVE®

BEPREVE® (bepotastine besilate ophthalmic solution) 1.5%   VALEANT PHARMACEUTICALS INTERNATIONAL

Valeant Patient Assistance Program   1-833-862-8727   *www.valeantpap.com*

Income Limits **$36k Single $49k Couple** | Rx cost → | **FREE** $ | **No Medical Insurance** ✓ | **Commercial Insurance** ? | **Medicare Part D** ↰

Rx assistance available to patients who are uninsured, (or whose insurance has denied coverage) and meet program eligibility requirements. Medicare Part D patients who cannot afford Rx can appeal for evaluation of eligibility.

TIP: When in doubt... call the program and explain your situation. You may qualify for assistance.

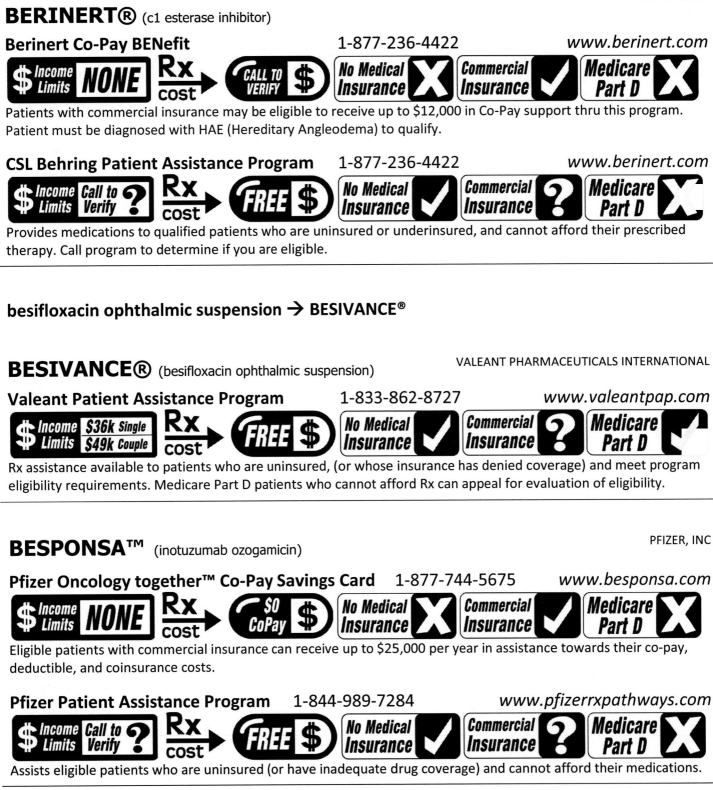

CSL BEHRING

BERINERT® (c1 esterase inhibitor)

Berinert Co-Pay BENefit 1-877-236-4422 *www.berinert.com*

| $ Income Limits **NONE** | Rx cost → | **CALL TO VERIFY** $ | No Medical Insurance **X** | Commercial Insurance ✔ | Medicare Part D **X** |

Patients with commercial insurance may be eligible to receive up to $12,000 in Co-Pay support thru this program. Patient must be diagnosed with HAE (Hereditary Angleodema) to qualify.

CSL Behring Patient Assistance Program 1-877-236-4422 *www.berinert.com*

| $ Income Limits Call to Verify **?** | Rx cost → | **FREE** $ | No Medical Insurance ✔ | Commercial Insurance **?** | Medicare Part D **X** |

Provides medications to qualified patients who are uninsured or underinsured, and cannot afford their prescribed therapy. Call program to determine if you are eligible.

---

besifloxacin ophthalmic suspension → BESIVANCE®

BESIVANCE® (besifloxacin ophthalmic suspension)

VALEANT PHARMACEUTICALS INTERNATIONAL

Valeant Patient Assistance Program 1-833-862-8727 *www.valeantpap.com*

| $ Income Limits **$36k Single / $49k Couple** | Rx cost → | **FREE** $ | No Medical Insurance ✔ | Commercial Insurance **?** | Medicare Part D ✔ |

Rx assistance available to patients who are uninsured, (or whose insurance has denied coverage) and meet program eligibility requirements. Medicare Part D patients who cannot afford Rx can appeal for evaluation of eligibility.

BESPONSA™ (inotuzumab ozogamicin)

PFIZER, INC

Pfizer Oncology together™ Co-Pay Savings Card 1-877-744-5675 *www.besponsa.com*

| $ Income Limits **NONE** | Rx cost → | **$0 CoPay** $ | No Medical Insurance **X** | Commercial Insurance ✔ | Medicare Part D **X** |

Eligible patients with commercial insurance can receive up to $25,000 per year in assistance towards their co-pay, deductible, and coinsurance costs.

Pfizer Patient Assistance Program 1-844-989-7284 *www.pfizerrxpathways.com*

| $ Income Limits Call to Verify **?** | Rx cost → | **FREE** $ | No Medical Insurance ✔ | Commercial Insurance **?** | Medicare Part D **X** |

Assists eligible patients who are uninsured (or have inadequate drug coverage) and cannot afford their medications.

---

betaine anhydrous oral solution → CYSTADANE®

BETAPACE® / BETAPACE AF® (sotalol HCL)

BAYER HEALTHCARE PHARMACEUTICALS

Bayer Patient Assistance Program   1-866-575-5002

Phone Only

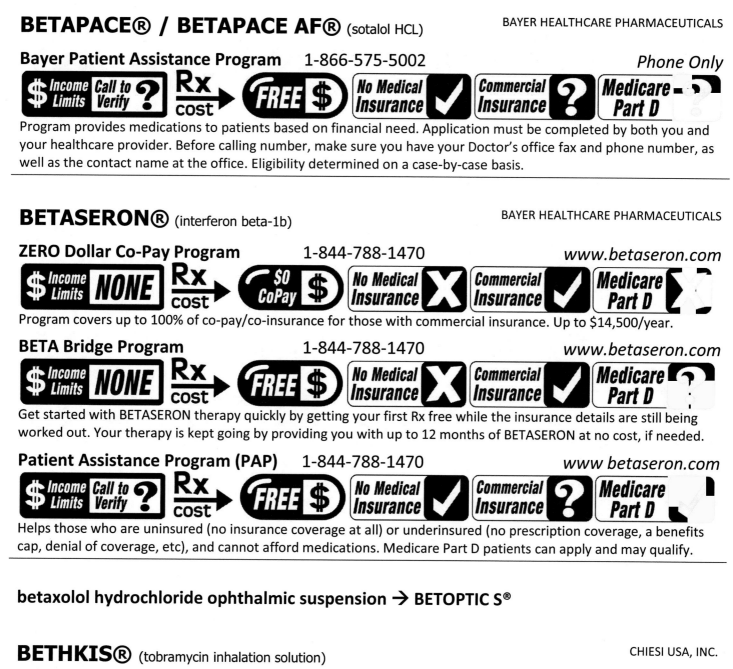

Program provides medications to patients based on financial need. Application must be completed by both you and your healthcare provider. Before calling number, make sure you have your Doctor's office fax and phone number, as well as the contact name at the office. Eligibility determined on a case-by-case basis.

BETASERON® (interferon beta-1b)

BAYER HEALTHCARE PHARMACEUTICALS

ZERO Dollar Co-Pay Program   1-844-788-1470

www.betaseron.com

Program covers up to 100% of co-pay/co-insurance for those with commercial insurance. Up to $14,500/year.

BETA Bridge Program   1-844-788-1470

www.betaseron.com

Get started with BETASERON therapy quickly by getting your first Rx free while the insurance details are still being worked out. Your therapy is kept going by providing you with up to 12 months of BETASERON at no cost, if needed.

Patient Assistance Program (PAP)   1-844-788-1470

www.betaseron.com

Helps those who are uninsured (no insurance coverage at all) or underinsured (no prescription coverage, a benefits cap, denial of coverage, etc), and cannot afford medications. Medicare Part D patients can apply and may qualify.

betaxolol hydrochloride ophthalmic suspension → BETOPTIC S®

BETHKIS® (tobramycin inhalation solution)

CHIESI USA, INC.

BETHKIS $0 Copay Assistance Program   1-888-865-1222

www.bethkis.com

Provides up to $1,400/month in co-pay assistance. Eligible patients pay as low as $0 out-of-pocket for BETHKIS.

Chiesi CAREDIRECT®   1-888-865-1222

www.bethkis.com

Rx assistance available to patients who are uninsured or underinsured, and meet program eligibility requirements.

BETIMOL® (timolol ophthalmic solution)

AKORN, INC.

Akorn Patient Assistance Program   1-844-202-5909   *www.betimol.com*

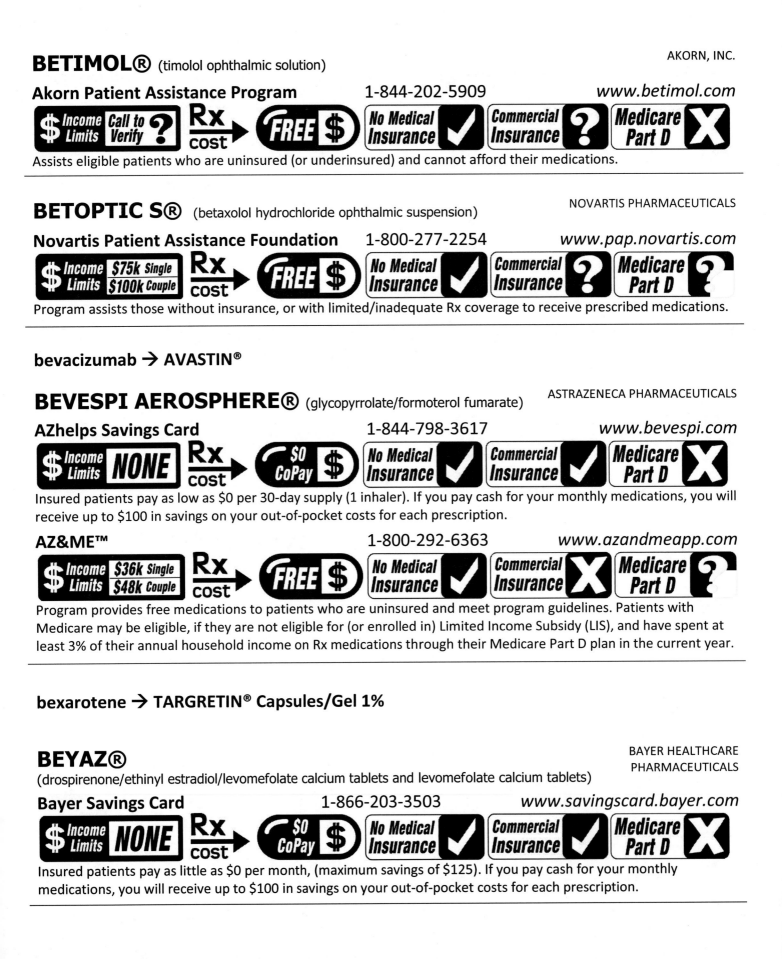

$ Income Limits — Call to Verify **?** | **Rx cost →** FREE **$** | **No Medical Insurance** ✓ | **Commercial Insurance** **?** | **Medicare Part D** **X**

Assists eligible patients who are uninsured (or underinsured) and cannot afford their medications.

BETOPTIC S® (betaxolol hydrochloride ophthalmic suspension)

NOVARTIS PHARMACEUTICALS

Novartis Patient Assistance Foundation   1-800-277-2254   *www.pap.novartis.com*

$ Income Limits — $75k Single / $100k Couple | **Rx cost →** FREE **$** | **No Medical Insurance** ✓ | **Commercial Insurance** **?** | **Medicare Part D** **?**

Program assists those without insurance, or with limited/inadequate Rx coverage to receive prescribed medications.

---

bevacizumab → AVASTIN®

BEVESPI AEROSPHERE® (glycopyrrolate/formoterol fumarate)

ASTRAZENECA PHARMACEUTICALS

AZhelps Savings Card   1-844-798-3617   *www.bevespi.com*

$ Income Limits — NONE | **Rx cost →** $0 CoPay **$** | **No Medical Insurance** ✓ | **Commercial Insurance** ✓ | **Medicare Part D** **X**

Insured patients pay as low as $0 per 30-day supply (1 inhaler). If you pay cash for your monthly medications, you will receive up to $100 in savings on your out-of-pocket costs for each prescription.

AZ&ME™   1-800-292-6363   *www.azandmeapp.com*

$ Income Limits — $36k Single / $48k Couple | **Rx cost →** FREE **$** | **No Medical Insurance** ✓ | **Commercial Insurance** **X** | **Medicare Part D** **?**

Program provides free medications to patients who are uninsured and meet program guidelines. Patients with Medicare may be eligible, if they are not eligible for (or enrolled in) Limited Income Subsidy (LIS), and have spent at least 3% of their annual household income on Rx medications through their Medicare Part D plan in the current year.

---

bexarotene → TARGRETIN® Capsules/Gel 1%

BEYAZ®

BAYER HEALTHCARE PHARMACEUTICALS

(drospirenone/ethinyl estradiol/levomefolate calcium tablets and levomefolate calcium tablets)

Bayer Savings Card   1-866-203-3503   *www.savingscard.bayer.com*

$ Income Limits — NONE | **Rx cost →** $0 CoPay **$** | **No Medical Insurance** ✓ | **Commercial Insurance** ✓ | **Medicare Part D** **X**

Insured patients pay as little as $0 per month, (maximum savings of $125). If you pay cash for your monthly medications, you will receive up to $100 in savings on your out-of-pocket costs for each prescription.

bezlotoxumab injection → ZINPLAVA™

bictegravir/emtricitabine/tenofovir alafenamide → BIKTARVY®

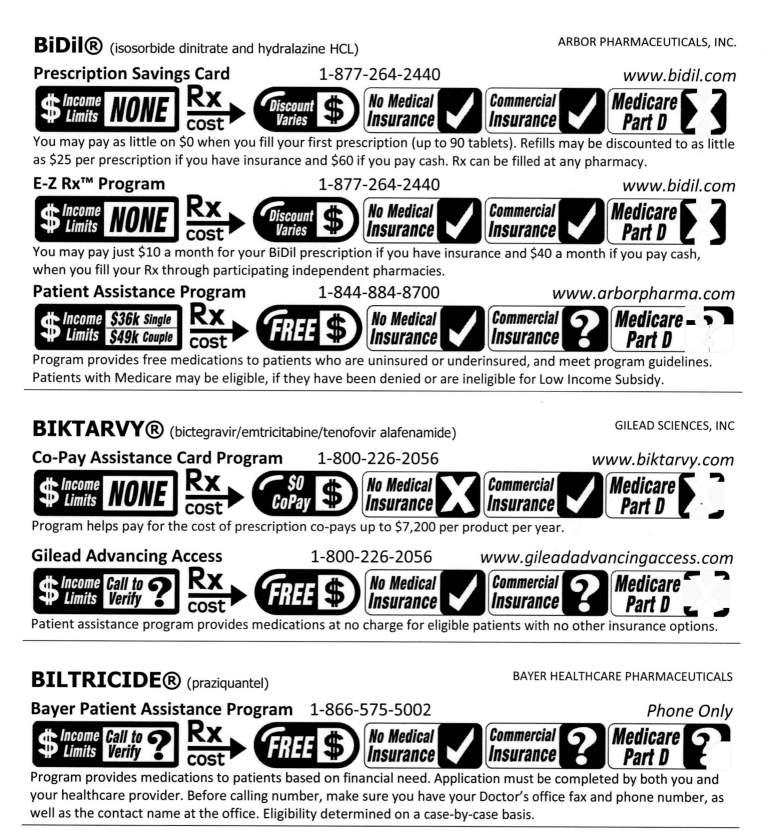

BiDil® (isosorbide dinitrate and hydralazine HCL)   ARBOR PHARMACEUTICALS, INC.

Prescription Savings Card   1-877-264-2440   *www.bidil.com*

$ **Income Limits NONE** | **Rx cost** → | **Discount Varies $** | **No Medical Insurance** ✓ | **Commercial Insurance** ✓ | **Medicare Part D** ✗

You may pay as little on $0 when you fill your first prescription (up to 90 tablets). Refills may be discounted to as little as $25 per prescription if you have insurance and $60 if you pay cash. Rx can be filled at any pharmacy.

E-Z Rx™ Program   1-877-264-2440   *www.bidil.com*

$ **Income Limits NONE** | **Rx cost** → | **Discount Varies $** | **No Medical Insurance** ✓ | **Commercial Insurance** ✓ | **Medicare Part D** ✗

You may pay just $10 a month for your BiDil prescription if you have insurance and $40 a month if you pay cash, when you fill your Rx through participating independent pharmacies.

Patient Assistance Program   1-844-884-8700   *www.arborpharma.com*

$ **Income Limits $36k Single $49k Couple** | **Rx cost** → | **FREE $** | **No Medical Insurance** ✓ | **Commercial Insurance ?** | **Medicare Part D** —?

Program provides free medications to patients who are uninsured or underinsured, and meet program guidelines. Patients with Medicare may be eligible, if they have been denied or are ineligible for Low Income Subsidy.

BIKTARVY® (bictegravir/emtricitabine/tenofovir alafenamide)   GILEAD SCIENCES, INC

Co-Pay Assistance Card Program   1-800-226-2056   *www.biktarvy.com*

$ **Income Limits NONE** | **Rx cost** → | **$0 CoPay $** | **No Medical Insurance** ✗ | **Commercial Insurance** ✓ | **Medicare Part D** ✗

Program helps pay for the cost of prescription co-pays up to $7,200 per product per year.

Gilead Advancing Access   1-800-226-2056   *www.gileadadvancingaccess.com*

$ **Income Limits Call to Verify ?** | **Rx cost** → | **FREE $** | **No Medical Insurance** ✓ | **Commercial Insurance ?** | **Medicare Part D** ✗

Patient assistance program provides medications at no charge for eligible patients with no other insurance options.

BILTRICIDE® (praziquantel)   BAYER HEALTHCARE PHARMACEUTICALS

Bayer Patient Assistance Program   1-866-575-5002   *Phone Only*

$ **Income Limits Call to Verify ?** | **Rx cost** → | **FREE $** | **No Medical Insurance** ✓ | **Commercial Insurance ?** | **Medicare Part D ?**

Program provides medications to patients based on financial need. Application must be completed by both you and your healthcare provider. Before calling number, make sure you have your Doctor's office fax and phone number, as well as the contact name at the office. Eligibility determined on a case-by-case basis.

bimatoprost ophthalmic solution → LUMIGAN® 0.01%

bismuth subcitrate potassium, metronidazole, tetracycline HCl → PYLERA® Capsules

blinatumomab → BLINCYTO®

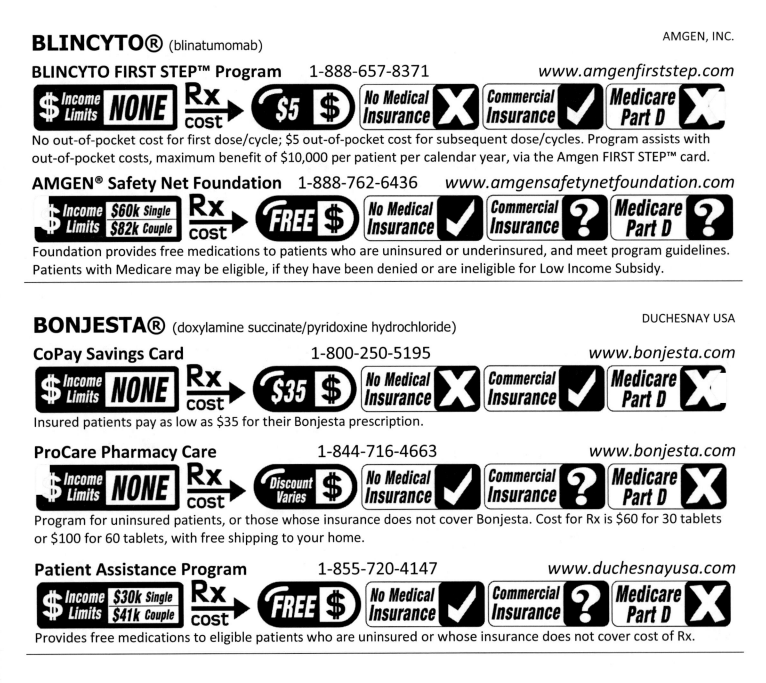

BLINCYTO® (blinatumomab)   AMGEN, INC.

BLINCYTO FIRST STEP™ Program   1-888-657-8371   *www.amgenfirststep.com*

| $ Income Limits NONE | Rx cost → | $5 $ | No Medical Insurance X | Commercial Insurance ✓ | Medicare Part D X |

No out-of-pocket cost for first dose/cycle; $5 out-of-pocket cost for subsequent dose/cycles. Program assists with out-of-pocket costs, maximum benefit of $10,000 per patient per calendar year, via the Amgen FIRST STEP™ card.

AMGEN® Safety Net Foundation   1-888-762-6436   *www.amgensafetynetfoundation.com*

| $ Income Limits $60k Single $82k Couple | Rx cost → | FREE $ | No Medical Insurance ✓ | Commercial Insurance ? | Medicare Part D ? |

Foundation provides free medications to patients who are uninsured or underinsured, and meet program guidelines. Patients with Medicare may be eligible, if they have been denied or are ineligible for Low Income Subsidy.

BONJESTA® (doxylamine succinate/pyridoxine hydrochloride)   DUCHESNAY USA

CoPay Savings Card   1-800-250-5195   *www.bonjesta.com*

| $ Income Limits NONE | Rx cost → | $35 $ | No Medical Insurance X | Commercial Insurance ✓ | Medicare Part D X |

Insured patients pay as low as $35 for their Bonjesta prescription.

ProCare Pharmacy Care   1-844-716-4663   *www.bonjesta.com*

| $ Income Limits NONE | Rx cost → | Discount Varies $ | No Medical Insurance ✓ | Commercial Insurance ? | Medicare Part D X |

Program for uninsured patients, or those whose insurance does not cover Bonjesta. Cost for Rx is $60 for 30 tablets or $100 for 60 tablets, with free shipping to your home.

Patient Assistance Program   1-855-720-4147   *www.duchesnayusa.com*

| $ Income Limits $30k Single $41k Couple | Rx cost → | FREE $ | No Medical Insurance ✓ | Commercial Insurance ? | Medicare Part D X |

Provides free medications to eligible patients who are uninsured or whose insurance does not cover cost of Rx.

---

bortezomib → VELCADE®

bosentan → TRACLEER®

BOSULIF® (bosutinib)

PFIZER, INC

Pfizer Savings Program   1-866-706-2400   *www.pfizerrxpathways.com*

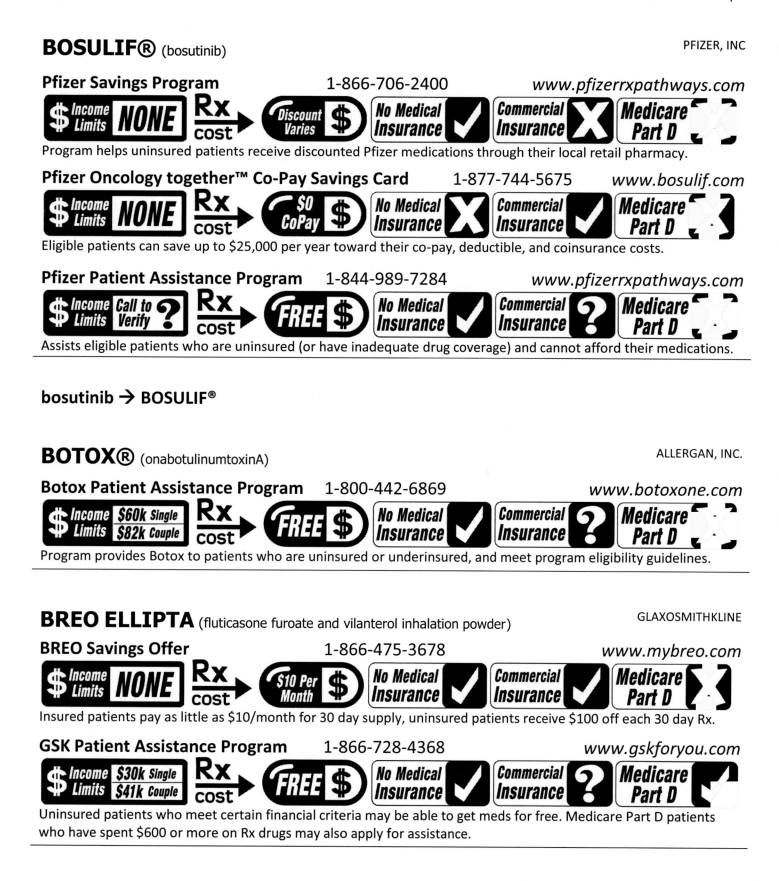

Income Limits	Rx cost		No Medical Insurance	Commercial Insurance	Medicare Part D
NONE		Discount Varies $	✓	✗	

Program helps uninsured patients receive discounted Pfizer medications through their local retail pharmacy.

Pfizer Oncology together™ Co-Pay Savings Card   1-877-744-5675   *www.bosulif.com*

Income Limits	Rx cost		No Medical Insurance	Commercial Insurance	Medicare Part D
NONE		$0 CoPay $	✗	✓	

Eligible patients can save up to $25,000 per year toward their co-pay, deductible, and coinsurance costs.

Pfizer Patient Assistance Program   1-844-989-7284   *www.pfizerrxpathways.com*

Income Limits	Rx cost		No Medical Insurance	Commercial Insurance	Medicare Part D
Call to Verify ?		FREE $	✓	?	

Assists eligible patients who are uninsured (or have inadequate drug coverage) and cannot afford their medications.

bosutinib → BOSULIF®

BOTOX® (onabotulinumtoxinA)

ALLERGAN, INC.

Botox Patient Assistance Program   1-800-442-6869   *www.botoxone.com*

Income Limits	Rx cost		No Medical Insurance	Commercial Insurance	Medicare Part D
$60k Single $82k Couple		FREE $	✓	?	

Program provides Botox to patients who are uninsured or underinsured, and meet program eligibility guidelines.

BREO ELLIPTA (fluticasone furoate and vilanterol inhalation powder)

GLAXOSMITHKLINE

BREO Savings Offer   1-866-475-3678   *www.mybreo.com*

Income Limits	Rx cost		No Medical Insurance	Commercial Insurance	Medicare Part D
NONE		$10 Per Month $	✓	✓	✗

Insured patients pay as little as $10/month for 30 day supply, uninsured patients receive $100 off each 30 day Rx.

GSK Patient Assistance Program   1-866-728-4368   *www.gskforyou.com*

Income Limits	Rx cost		No Medical Insurance	Commercial Insurance	Medicare Part D
$30k Single $41k Couple		FREE $	✓	?	✓

Uninsured patients who meet certain financial criteria may be able to get meds for free. Medicare Part D patients who have spent $600 or more on Rx drugs may also apply for assistance.

brexpiprazole tablet → REXULTI®

BRILINTA® Tablets (ticagrelor)

ASTRAZENECA PHARMACEUTICALS

BRILINTA $18 Savings Card   1-888-512-7454   *www.brilinta.com*

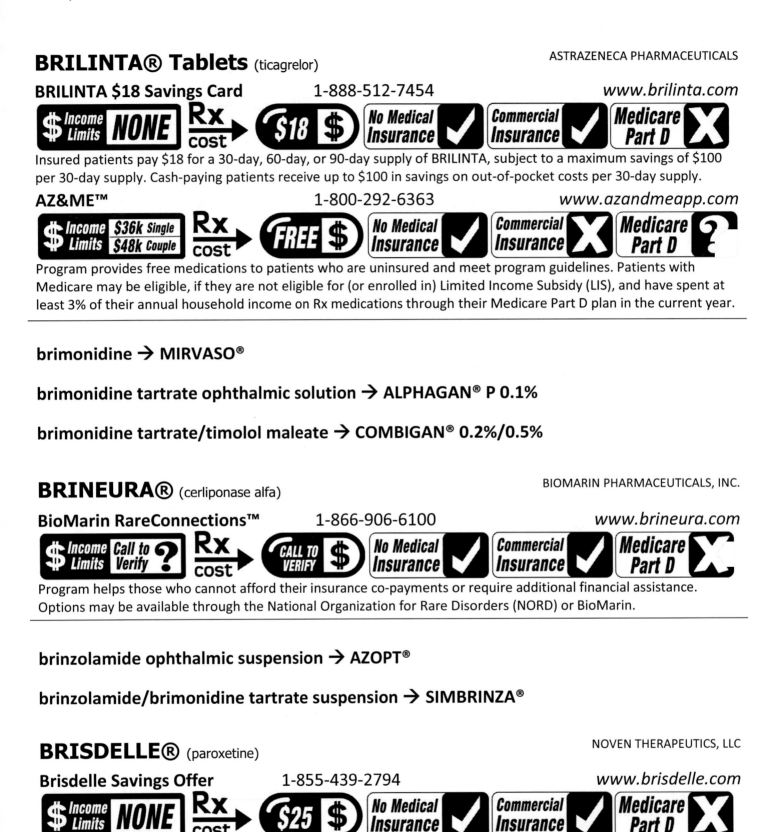

$ Income Limits NONE | **Rx cost** → | **$18 $** | **No Medical Insurance ✔** | **Commercial Insurance ✔** | **Medicare Part D ✘**

Insured patients pay $18 for a 30-day, 60-day, or 90-day supply of BRILINTA, subject to a maximum savings of $100 per 30-day supply. Cash-paying patients receive up to $100 in savings on out-of-pocket costs per 30-day supply.

AZ&ME™   1-800-292-6363   *www.azandmeapp.com*

$ Income Limits $36k Single $48k Couple | **Rx cost** → | **FREE $** | **No Medical Insurance ✔** | **Commercial Insurance ✘** | **Medicare Part D ?**

Program provides free medications to patients who are uninsured and meet program guidelines. Patients with Medicare may be eligible, if they are not eligible for (or enrolled in) Limited Income Subsidy (LIS), and have spent at least 3% of their annual household income on Rx medications through their Medicare Part D plan in the current year.

---

brimonidine → MIRVASO®

brimonidine tartrate ophthalmic solution → ALPHAGAN® P 0.1%

brimonidine tartrate/timolol maleate → COMBIGAN® 0.2%/0.5%

BRINEURA® (cerliponase alfa)

BIOMARIN PHARMACEUTICALS, INC.

BioMarin RareConnections™   1-866-906-6100   *www.brineura.com*

$ Income Limits Call to Verify ? | **Rx cost** → | **CALL TO VERIFY $** | **No Medical Insurance ✔** | **Commercial Insurance ✔** | **Medicare Part D ✘**

Program helps those who cannot afford their insurance co-payments or require additional financial assistance. Options may be available through the National Organization for Rare Disorders (NORD) or BioMarin.

---

brinzolamide ophthalmic suspension → AZOPT®

brinzolamide/brimonidine tartrate suspension → SIMBRINZA®

BRISDELLE® (paroxetine)

NOVEN THERAPEUTICS, LLC

Brisdelle Savings Offer   1-855-439-2794   *www.brisdelle.com*

$ Income Limits NONE | **Rx cost** → | **$25 $** | **No Medical Insurance ✔** | **Commercial Insurance ✔** | **Medicare Part D ✘**

Insured patients pay as little as $25 per 30 or 90 day Rx. Insured and uninsured patients receive $125 off 30 day Rx after they pay first $25, $250 off 60 day Rx after they pay first $50, or $400 off 90 day supply after they pay $25.

brivaracetam → BRIVIACT®

BRIVIACT® (brivaracetam)

UCB PHARMA, INC.

Briviact Patient Savings Program　　　1-888-786-5879　　　*www.briviact.com*

Commercially insured patients pay as little as $20 per month, maximum savings $100 per Rx, $1300 per year.

UCBCares Patient Assistance Program　　　1-877-785-8906　　　*www.askucbcares.com*

Provides medication free of charge to those who are uninsured or underinsured, and cannot afford their Rx.

---

brodalumab → SILIQ®

bromfenac sodium solution 0.07% → PROLENSA®

bromocriptine mesylate tablets → CYCLOSET®

budesonide inhalation powder → PULMICORT FLEXHALER®

budesonide → UCERIS®

budesonide/formoterol fumarate dihydrate → SYMBICORT®

BUPHENYL® (sodium phenylbutyrate)

HORIZON PHARMA USA, INC.

TranscendRare™ Program　　　1-855-823-7878　　　*www.buphenyl.com*

Program provides copay, reimbursement, and financial assistance for insured/uninsured patients with valid BUPHENYL Rx. Call for complete details and eligibility criteria.

---

buprenorphine → BUTRANS®

buprenorphine/naloxone → SUBOXONE® Sublingual Film

buprenorphine/naloxone → ZUBSOLV®

bupropion HCL → FORFIVO XL®

BUTRANS® (buprenorphine)

PURDUE PHARMA, L.P.

Purdue Patient Assistance Program   1-800-599-6070   *www.purduepharma.com*

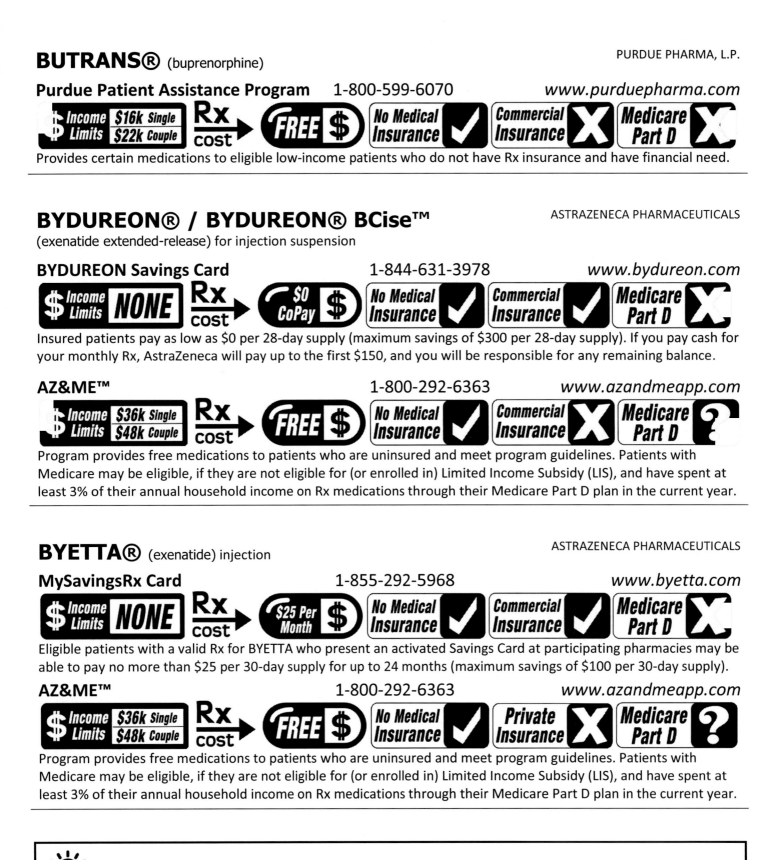

| Income Limits | $16k Single / $22k Couple | Rx cost → | FREE $ | No Medical Insurance ✓ | Commercial Insurance ✗ | Medicare Part D ✗ |

Provides certain medications to eligible low-income patients who do not have Rx insurance and have financial need.

BYDUREON® / BYDUREON® BCise™

ASTRAZENECA PHARMACEUTICALS

(exenatide extended-release) for injection suspension

BYDUREON Savings Card   1-844-631-3978   *www.bydureon.com*

| Income Limits | NONE | Rx cost → | $0 CoPay $ | No Medical Insurance ✓ | Commercial Insurance ✓ | Medicare Part D ✗ |

Insured patients pay as low as $0 per 28-day supply (maximum savings of $300 per 28-day supply). If you pay cash for your monthly Rx, AstraZeneca will pay up to the first $150, and you will be responsible for any remaining balance.

AZ&ME™   1-800-292-6363   *www.azandmeapp.com*

| Income Limits | $36k Single / $48k Couple | Rx cost → | FREE $ | No Medical Insurance ✓ | Commercial Insurance ✗ | Medicare Part D ? |

Program provides free medications to patients who are uninsured and meet program guidelines. Patients with Medicare may be eligible, if they are not eligible for (or enrolled in) Limited Income Subsidy (LIS), and have spent at least 3% of their annual household income on Rx medications through their Medicare Part D plan in the current year.

BYETTA® (exenatide) injection

ASTRAZENECA PHARMACEUTICALS

MySavingsRx Card   1-855-292-5968   *www.byetta.com*

| Income Limits | NONE | Rx cost → | $25 Per Month $ | No Medical Insurance ✓ | Commercial Insurance ✓ | Medicare Part D ✗ |

Eligible patients with a valid Rx for BYETTA who present an activated Savings Card at participating pharmacies may be able to pay no more than $25 per 30-day supply for up to 24 months (maximum savings of $100 per 30-day supply).

AZ&ME™   1-800-292-6363   *www.azandmeapp.com*

| Income Limits | $36k Single / $48k Couple | Rx cost → | FREE $ | No Medical Insurance ✓ | Private Insurance ✗ | Medicare Part D ? |

Program provides free medications to patients who are uninsured and meet program guidelines. Patients with Medicare may be eligible, if they are not eligible for (or enrolled in) Limited Income Subsidy (LIS), and have spent at least 3% of their annual household income on Rx medications through their Medicare Part D plan in the current year.

TIP: Income limits are higher for households with three or more people. Call programs for details.

BYSTOLIC® TABLETS (nebivolol)

ALLERGAN, INC.

Allergan Patient Assistance Program   1-844-424-6727   *www.allergan.com*

Program provides meds to patients who are uninsured or underinsured, and meet program guidelines. Patients with Medicare may be eligible, if they have been denied or are ineligible for Low Income Subsidy.

BYVALSON™ (nebivolol and valsartan)

ALLERGAN, INC.

Allergan Patient Assistance Program   1-844-424-6727   *www.allergan.com*

Program provides meds to patients who are uninsured or underinsured, and meet program guidelines. Patients with Medicare may be eligible, if they have been denied or are ineligible for Low Income Subsidy.

cabazitaxel → JEVTANA®

CABOMETYX® (cabozantinib s-malate)

EXELIXIS, INC.

$10 Co-pay Card   1-844-900-3273   *www.cabometyx.com*

Eligible commercially insured patients pay no more than $10 per month for CABOMETYX. The program covers the remaining out-of-pocket drug costs, up to a $25,000 yearly limit.

EASE Patient Assistance Program   1-844-900-3273   *www.cabometyx.com*

Provides those who are uninsured (or insured but cannot afford their medications) with CABOMETYX free of charge.

cabozantinib s-malate → CABOMETYX®

CADUET® (amlodipine besylate/atorvastatin)

PFIZER, INC

Pfizer Savings Program   1-866-706-2400   *www.pfizerrxpathways.com*

Program helps uninsured patients receive discounted Pfizer medications through their local retail pharmacy.

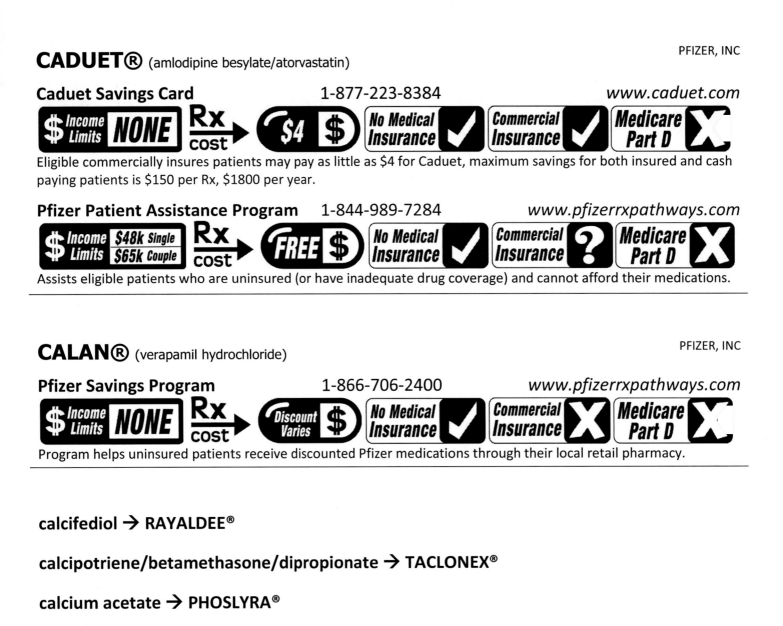

CADUET® (amlodipine besylate/atorvastatin)   PFIZER, INC

Caduet Savings Card   1-877-223-8384   *www.caduet.com*

| $ Income Limits **NONE** | **Rx** cost → | **$4 $** | **No Medical Insurance** ✔ | **Commercial Insurance** ✔ | **Medicare Part D** ✗ |

Eligible commercially insures patients may pay as little as $4 for Caduet, maximum savings for both insured and cash paying patients is $150 per Rx, $1800 per year.

Pfizer Patient Assistance Program   1-844-989-7284   *www.pfizerrxpathways.com*

| $ Income Limits **$48k Single $65k Couple** | **Rx** cost → | **FREE $** | **No Medical Insurance** ✔ | **Commercial Insurance** ? | **Medicare Part D** ✗ |

Assists eligible patients who are uninsured (or have inadequate drug coverage) and cannot afford their medications.

CALAN® (verapamil hydrochloride)   PFIZER, INC

Pfizer Savings Program   1-866-706-2400   *www.pfizerrxpathways.com*

| $ Income Limits **NONE** | **Rx** cost → | **Discount Varies $** | **No Medical Insurance** ✔ | **Commercial Insurance** ✗ | **Medicare Part D** ✗ |

Program helps uninsured patients receive discounted Pfizer medications through their local retail pharmacy.

---

calcifediol → **RAYALDEE®**

calcipotriene/betamethasone/dipropionate → **TACLONEX®**

calcium acetate → **PHOSLYRA®**

CALQUENCE® (acalabrutinib)   ASTRAZENECA PHARMACEUTICALS

AstraZeneca Access 360   1-844-275-2360   *www.astrazenecaspecialtysavings.com*

| $ Income Limits **NONE** | **Rx** cost → | **$0 CoPay $** | **No Medical Insurance** ✗ | **Commercial Insurance** ✔ | **Medicare Part D** ✗ |

Patient pays $0 per 30-day supply, program pays remaining out-of-pocket costs up to a max of $26,000 per year.

AZ&ME™   1-800-292-6363   *www.azandmeapp.com*

| $ Income Limits **$36k Single $48k Couple** | **Rx** cost → | **FREE $** | **No Medical Insurance** ✔ | **Commercial Insurance** ✗ | **Medicare Part D** ? |

Program provides free medications to patients who are uninsured and meet program guidelines. Patients with Medicare may be eligible, if they are not eligible for (or enrolled in) Limited Income Subsidy (LIS), and have spent at least 3% of their annual household income on Rx medications through their Medicare Part D plan in the current year.

CAMBIA® (diclofenac potassium)
DEPOMED, INC.

Cambia Savings Program   1-844-546-8634   *www.cambiarx.com*

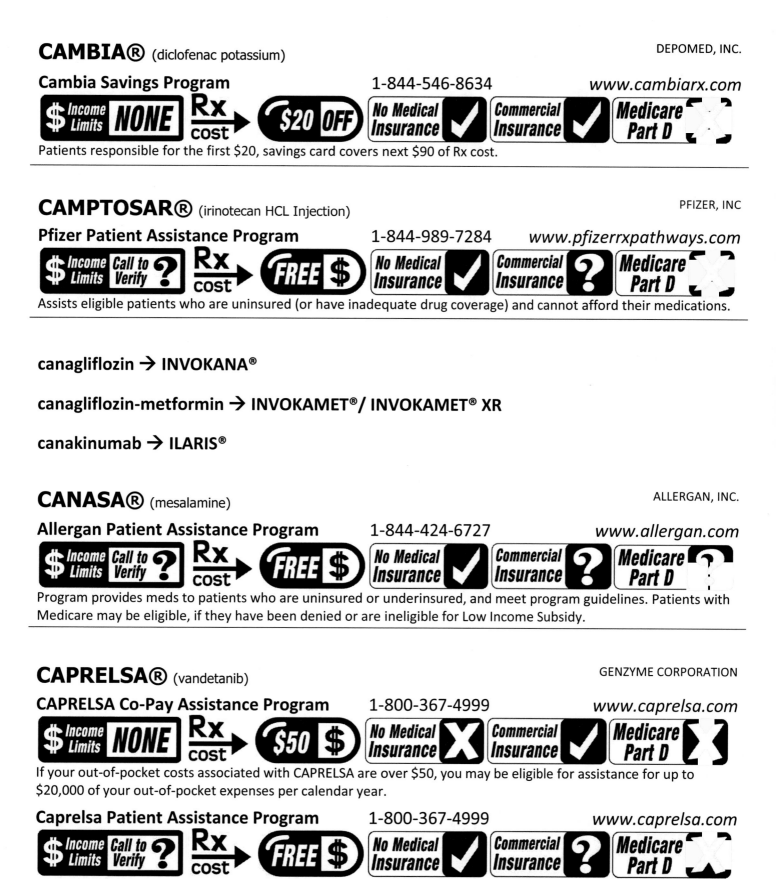

Patients responsible for the first $20, savings card covers next $90 of Rx cost.

CAMPTOSAR® (irinotecan HCL Injection)
PFIZER, INC

Pfizer Patient Assistance Program   1-844-989-7284   *www.pfizerrxpathways.com*

Assists eligible patients who are uninsured (or have inadequate drug coverage) and cannot afford their medications.

canagliflozin → **INVOKANA®**

canagliflozin-metformin → **INVOKAMET®/ INVOKAMET® XR**

canakinumab → **ILARIS®**

CANASA® (mesalamine)
ALLERGAN, INC.

Allergan Patient Assistance Program   1-844-424-6727   *www.allergan.com*

Program provides meds to patients who are uninsured or underinsured, and meet program guidelines. Patients with Medicare may be eligible, if they have been denied or are ineligible for Low Income Subsidy.

CAPRELSA® (vandetanib)
GENZYME CORPORATION

CAPRELSA Co-Pay Assistance Program   1-800-367-4999   *www.caprelsa.com*

If your out-of-pocket costs associated with CAPRELSA are over $50, you may be eligible for assistance for up to $20,000 of your out-of-pocket expenses per calendar year.

Caprelsa Patient Assistance Program   1-800-367-4999   *www.caprelsa.com*

Program provides medications to patients who are uninsured or have inadequate insurance coverage for Caprelsa

CARAC® (fluorouracil cream) 0.5%

VALEANT PHARMACEUTICALS INTERNATIONAL

Valeant Patient Assistance Program   1-833-862-8727   *www.valeantpap.com*

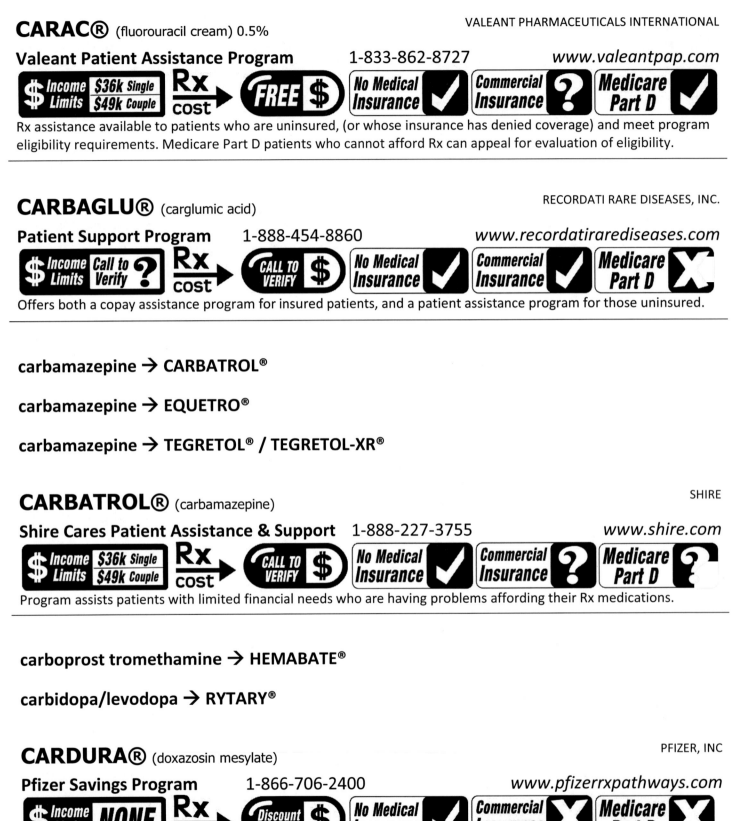

Rx assistance available to patients who are uninsured, (or whose insurance has denied coverage) and meet program eligibility requirements. Medicare Part D patients who cannot afford Rx can appeal for evaluation of eligibility.

CARBAGLU® (carglumic acid)

RECORDATI RARE DISEASES, INC.

Patient Support Program   1-888-454-8860   *www.recordatirarediseases.com*

Offers both a copay assistance program for insured patients, and a patient assistance program for those uninsured.

carbamazepine → CARBATROL®

carbamazepine → EQUETRO®

carbamazepine → TEGRETOL® / TEGRETOL-XR®

CARBATROL® (carbamazepine)

SHIRE

Shire Cares Patient Assistance & Support   1-888-227-3755   *www.shire.com*

Program assists patients with limited financial needs who are having problems affording their Rx medications.

carboprost tromethamine → HEMABATE®

carbidopa/levodopa → RYTARY®

CARDURA® (doxazosin mesylate)

PFIZER, INC

Pfizer Savings Program   1-866-706-2400   *www.pfizerrxpathways.com*

Program helps uninsured patients receive discounted Pfizer medications through their local retail pharmacy.

carfilzomib → KYPROLIS®

carglumic acid → CARBAGLU®

CARIMUNE® [nanofiltered immune globulin intravenous (human)]

CSL BEHRING

CSL Behring Patient Assistance Program   1-877-236-4422   *www.cslbehring.com*

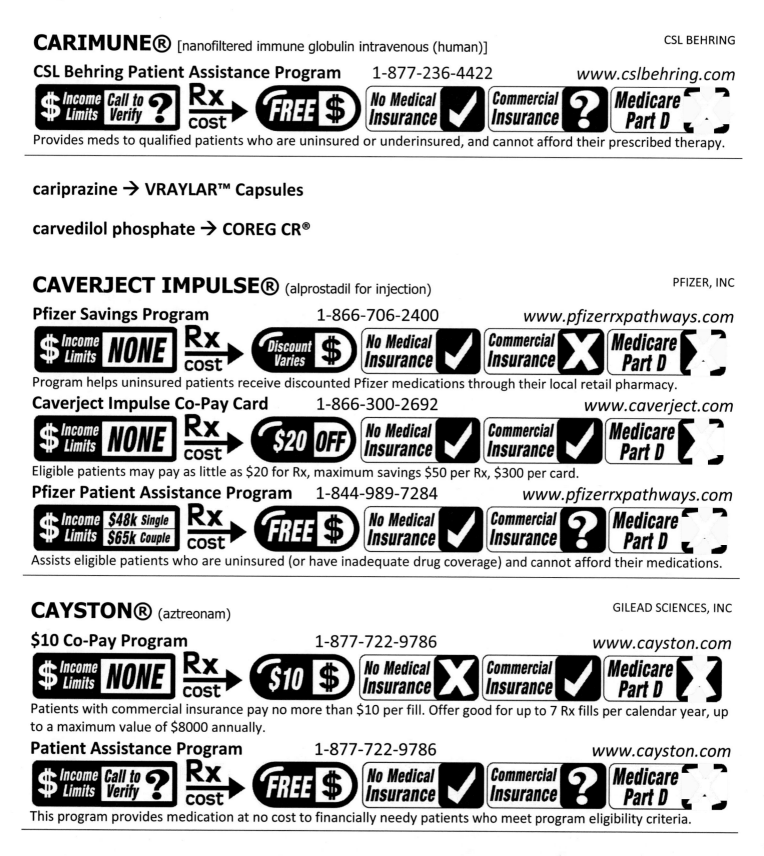

| $ Income Limits | Call to Verify ? | Rx cost → | FREE $ | No Medical Insurance ✓ | Commercial Insurance ? | Medicare Part D |

Provides meds to qualified patients who are uninsured or underinsured, and cannot afford their prescribed therapy.

cariprazine → VRAYLAR™ Capsules

carvedilol phosphate → COREG CR®

CAVERJECT IMPULSE® (alprostadil for injection)

PFIZER, INC

Pfizer Savings Program   1-866-706-2400   *www.pfizerrxpathways.com*

| $ Income Limits | NONE | Rx cost → | Discount Varies $ | No Medical Insurance ✓ | Commercial Insurance ✗ | Medicare Part D ✗ |

Program helps uninsured patients receive discounted Pfizer medications through their local retail pharmacy.

Caverject Impulse Co-Pay Card   1-866-300-2692   *www.caverject.com*

| $ Income Limits | NONE | Rx cost → | $20 OFF | No Medical Insurance ✓ | Commercial Insurance ✓ | Medicare Part D |

Eligible patients may pay as little as $20 for Rx, maximum savings $50 per Rx, $300 per card.

Pfizer Patient Assistance Program   1-844-989-7284   *www.pfizerrxpathways.com*

| $ Income Limits | $48k Single / $65k Couple | Rx cost → | FREE $ | No Medical Insurance ✓ | Commercial Insurance ? | Medicare Part D ✗ |

Assists eligible patients who are uninsured (or have inadequate drug coverage) and cannot afford their medications.

CAYSTON® (aztreonam)

GILEAD SCIENCES, INC

$10 Co-Pay Program   1-877-722-9786   *www.cayston.com*

| $ Income Limits | NONE | Rx cost → | $10 $ | No Medical Insurance ✗ | Commercial Insurance ✓ | Medicare Part D ✗ |

Patients with commercial insurance pay no more than $10 per fill. Offer good for up to 7 Rx fills per calendar year, up to a maximum value of $8000 annually.

Patient Assistance Program   1-877-722-9786   *www.cayston.com*

| $ Income Limits | Call to Verify ? | Rx cost → | FREE $ | No Medical Insurance ✓ | Commercial Insurance ? | Medicare Part D |

This program provides medication at no cost to financially needy patients who meet program eligibility criteria.

ceftaroline fosamil for injection → TEFLARO®

ceftazidime/avibactam → AVYCAZ®

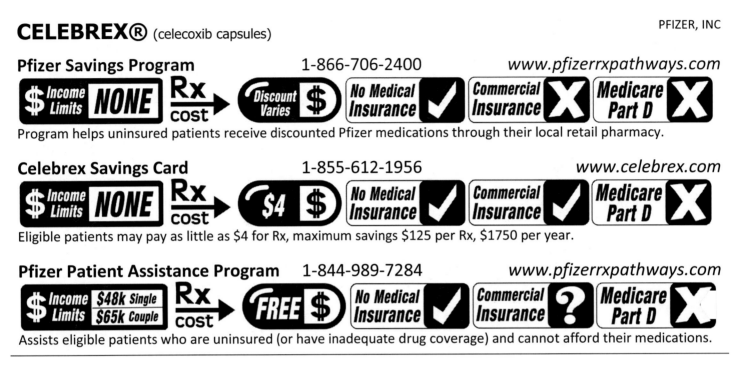

PFIZER, INC

CELEBREX® (celecoxib capsules)

Pfizer Savings Program 1-866-706-2400 www.pfizerrxpathways.com

$ Income Limits **NONE** | **Rx** cost → | Discount Varies $ | No Medical Insurance ✔ | Commercial Insurance ✗ | Medicare Part D ✗

Program helps uninsured patients receive discounted Pfizer medications through their local retail pharmacy.

Celebrex Savings Card 1-855-612-1956 www.celebrex.com

$ Income Limits **NONE** | **Rx** cost → | $4 $ | No Medical Insurance ✔ | Commercial Insurance ✔ | Medicare Part D ✗

Eligible patients may pay as little as $4 for Rx, maximum savings $125 per Rx, $1750 per year.

Pfizer Patient Assistance Program 1-844-989-7284 www.pfizerrxpathways.com

$ Income Limits $48k Single $65k Couple | **Rx** cost → | FREE $ | No Medical Insurance ✔ | Commercial Insurance ? | Medicare Part D ✗

Assists eligible patients who are uninsured (or have inadequate drug coverage) and cannot afford their medications.

celecoxib capsules → CELEBREX®

PFIZER, INC

CELONTIN® (methsuximide capsules)

Pfizer Savings Program 1-866-706-2400 www.pfizerrxpathways.com

$ Income Limits **NONE** | **Rx** cost → | Discount Varies $ | No Medical Insurance ✔ | Commercial Insurance ✗ | Medicare Part D ✗

Program helps uninsured patients receive discounted Pfizer medications through their local retail pharmacy.

Pfizer Patient Assistance Program 1-844-989-7284 www.pfizerrxpathways.com

$ Income Limits $48k Single $65k Couple | **Rx** cost → | FREE $ | No Medical Insurance ✔ | Commercial Insurance ? | Medicare Part D ✗

Assists eligible patients who are uninsured (or have inadequate drug coverage) and cannot afford their medications.

TIP: When in doubt... call the program and explain your situation. You may qualify for assistance.

CERDELGA® (eliglustat)

Sanofi Genzyme Co-Pay Assistance Program   1-800-745-4447   *www.cerdelga.com*

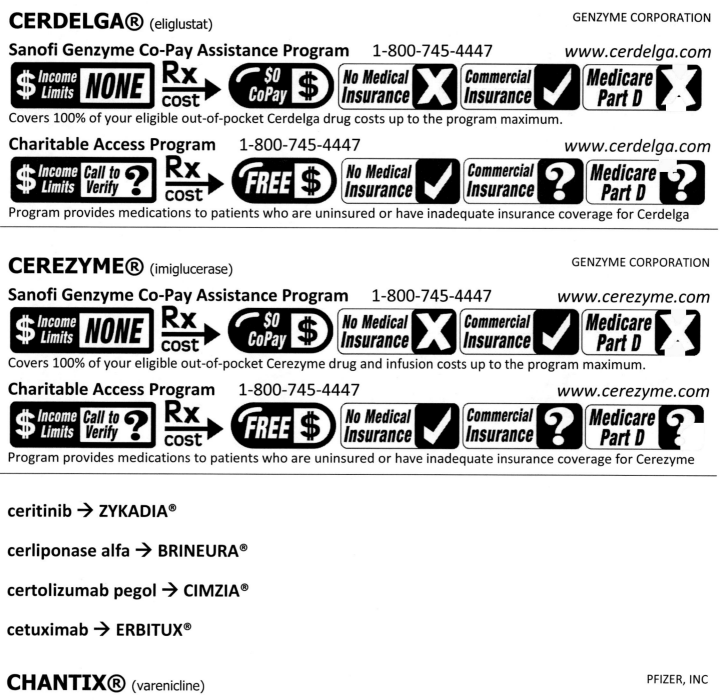

Covers 100% of your eligible out-of-pocket Cerdelga drug costs up to the program maximum.

Charitable Access Program   1-800-745-4447   *www.cerdelga.com*

Program provides medications to patients who are uninsured or have inadequate insurance coverage for Cerdelga

CEREZYME® (imiglucerase)

GENZYME CORPORATION

Sanofi Genzyme Co-Pay Assistance Program   1-800-745-4447   *www.cerezyme.com*

Covers 100% of your eligible out-of-pocket Cerezyme drug and infusion costs up to the program maximum.

Charitable Access Program   1-800-745-4447   *www.cerezyme.com*

Program provides medications to patients who are uninsured or have inadequate insurance coverage for Cerezyme

ceritinib → ZYKADIA®

cerliponase alfa → BRINEURA®

certolizumab pegol → CIMZIA®

cetuximab → ERBITUX®

CHANTIX® (varenicline)

PFIZER, INC

Pfizer Savings Program   1-866-706-2400   *www.pfizerrxpathways.com*

Program helps uninsured patients receive discounted Pfizer medications through their local retail pharmacy.

Chantix Savings Card   1-800-746-4678   *www.chantix.com*

Eligible patients pay as little as $40 for RX, maximum savings $75 per Rx, savings card can be used 6 times per year.

CHANTIX® (varenicline)
PFIZER, INC

Pfizer Patient Assistance Program 1-844-989-7284 *www.pfizerrxpathways.com*

$ Income Limits $48k Single $65k Couple | **Rx cost →** | **FREE $** | **No Medical Insurance** ✓ | **Commercial Insurance** ? | **Medicare Part D** X

Assists eligible patients who are uninsured (or have inadequate drug coverage) and cannot afford their medications.

CHEMET® Capsules (succimer)
RECORDATI RARE DISEASES, INC.

Patient Support Program 1-888-454-8860 *www.recordatirarediseases.com*

$ Income Limits Call to Verify ? | **Rx cost →** | **CALL TO VERIFY $** | **No Medical Insurance** ✓ | **Commercial Insurance** ✓ | **Medicare Part D** X

Offers both a copay assistance program for insured patients, and a patient assistance program for those uninsured.

CIALIS® (tadalafil)
LILLY USA, LLC

Lilly Cares 1-800-545-6962 *www.lillycares.com*

$ Income Limits $36k Single $49k Couple | **Rx cost →** | **FREE $** | **No Medical Insurance** ✓ | **Commercial Insurance** X | **Medicare Part D** ✓

Provides free Lilly medications for eligible patients who are uninsured and cannot afford their medications. Medicare Part D patients are eligible for assistance, after they have spent $1,100 on Rx meds in a calendar year.

ciclesonide → ALVESCO®

CIMZIA® (certolizumab pegol)
UCB PHARMA, INC.

$0 CIMplicity® Savings Program 1-866-424-6942 *www.cimzia.com*

$ Income Limits NONE | **Rx cost →** | **$0 CoPay $** | **No Medical Insurance** X | **Commercial Insurance** ✓ | **Medicare Part D** X

Covers out-of-pocket costs (co-pay, co-insurance, and/or deductible) up to $15,000 per year for insured patients.

UCBCares Patient Assistance Program 1-877-785-8906 *www.askucbcares.com*

$ Income Limits $36k Single $49k Couple | **Rx cost →** | **FREE $** | **No Medical Insurance** ✓ | **Commercial Insurance** ? | **Medicare Part D** ?

Provides medication free of charge to those who are uninsured or underinsured, and cannot afford their Rx.

cinacalcet HCl → SENSIPAR®

💡 **TIP:** When in doubt... call the program and explain your situation. You may qualify for assistance.

CINRYZE® (c1 esterase inhibitor)
SHIRE

OnePath Co-Pay Assistance Program 1-866-888-0660 *www.cinryze.com*

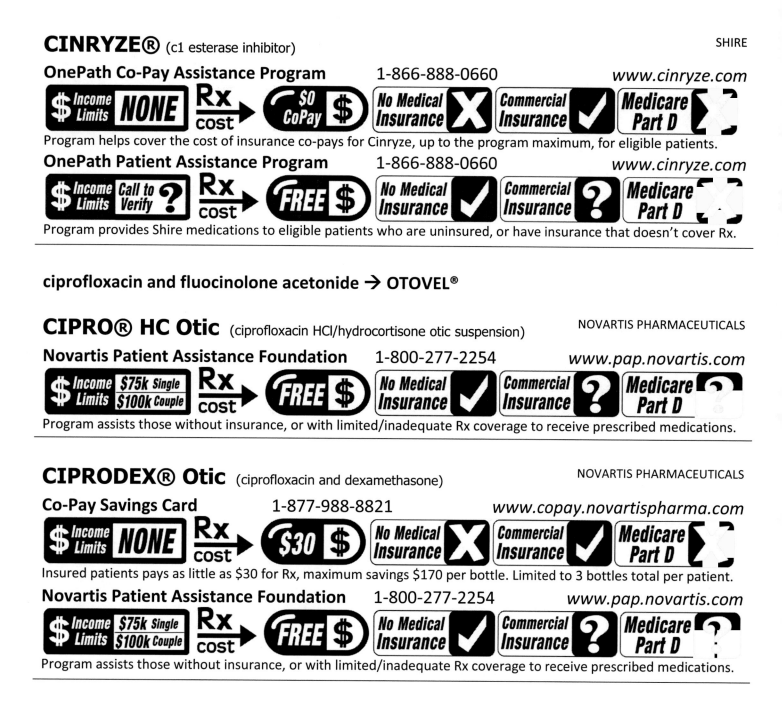

Program helps cover the cost of insurance co-pays for Cinryze, up to the program maximum, for eligible patients.

OnePath Patient Assistance Program 1-866-888-0660 *www.cinryze.com*

Program provides Shire medications to eligible patients who are uninsured, or have insurance that doesn't cover Rx.

---

ciprofloxacin and fluocinolone acetonide → OTOVEL®

CIPRO® HC Otic (ciprofloxacin HCl/hydrocortisone otic suspension)
NOVARTIS PHARMACEUTICALS

Novartis Patient Assistance Foundation 1-800-277-2254 *www.pap.novartis.com*

Program assists those without insurance, or with limited/inadequate Rx coverage to receive prescribed medications.

CIPRODEX® Otic (ciprofloxacin and dexamethasone)
NOVARTIS PHARMACEUTICALS

Co-Pay Savings Card 1-877-988-8821 *www.copay.novartispharma.com*

Insured patients pays as little as $30 for Rx, maximum savings $170 per bottle. Limited to 3 bottles total per patient.

Novartis Patient Assistance Foundation 1-800-277-2254 *www.pap.novartis.com*

Program assists those without insurance, or with limited/inadequate Rx coverage to receive prescribed medications.

---

ciprofloxacin and dexamethasone → CIPRODEX® Otic

ciprofloxacin HCL/hydrocortisone otic suspension → CIPRO® HC Otic

---

CLEOCIN® (clindamycin)
PFIZER, INC

Pfizer Savings Program 1-866-706-2400 *www.pfizerrxpathways.com*

Program helps uninsured patients receive discounted Pfizer medications through their local retail pharmacy.

CLEOCIN® (clindamycin)
PFIZER, INC

Pfizer Patient Assistance Program   1-844-989-7284   *www.pfizerrxpathways.com*

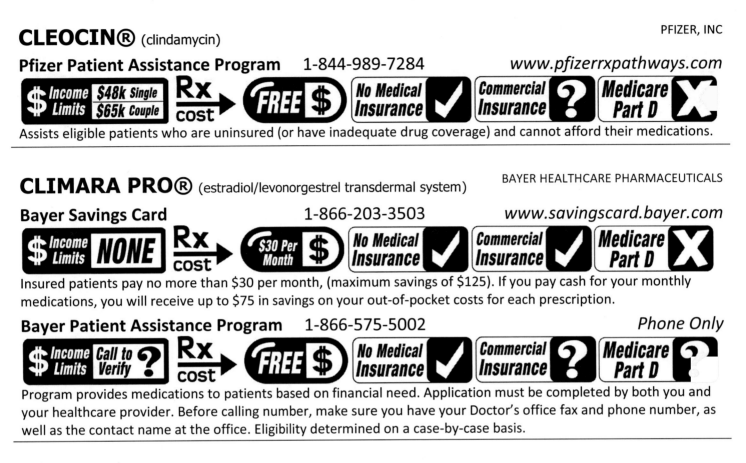

| Income Limits $48k Single $65k Couple | Rx cost → FREE $ | No Medical Insurance ✓ | Commercial Insurance ? | Medicare Part D ✗ |

Assists eligible patients who are uninsured (or have inadequate drug coverage) and cannot afford their medications.

CLIMARA PRO® (estradiol/levonorgestrel transdermal system)
BAYER HEALTHCARE PHARMACEUTICALS

Bayer Savings Card   1-866-203-3503   *www.savingscard.bayer.com*

| Income Limits NONE | Rx cost → $30 Per Month $ | No Medical Insurance ✓ | Commercial Insurance ✓ | Medicare Part D ✗ |

Insured patients pay no more than $30 per month, (maximum savings of $125). If you pay cash for your monthly medications, you will receive up to $75 in savings on your out-of-pocket costs for each prescription.

Bayer Patient Assistance Program   1-866-575-5002   *Phone Only*

| Income Limits Call to Verify ? | Rx cost → FREE $ | No Medical Insurance ✓ | Commercial Insurance ? | Medicare Part D ? |

Program provides medications to patients based on financial need. Application must be completed by both you and your healthcare provider. Before calling number, make sure you have your Doctor's office fax and phone number, as well as the contact name at the office. Eligibility determined on a case-by-case basis.

clinclamycin phosphate gel 1%→ **CLINDAGEL®**

clindamycin → **CLEOCIN®**

clindamycin phosphate and benzoyl peroxide → **ACANYA®**

clindamycin phosphate/benzoyl peroxide gel → **ONEXTON®**

CLINDAGEL® (clinclamycin phosphate gel) 1%
VALEANT PHARMACEUTICALS INTERNATIONAL

Ortho Dermatologics Rx Access Program   1-855-202-3279   *www.orthorxaccess.com*

| Income Limits NONE | Rx cost → $40 $ | No Medical Insurance ✓ | Commercial Insurance ✓ | Medicare Part D ✗ |

Most commercially insured patients pay as little as $40 per Rx, once deductible has been met. Those with insurance where drug is not covered pay $75 per Rx, and uninsured patients pay just $100 per Rx.

Valeant Patient Assistance Program   1-833-862-8727   *www.valeantpap.com*

| Income Limits $36k Single $49k Couple | Rx cost → FREE $ | No Medical Insurance ✓ | Commercial Insurance ? | Medicare Part D ✓ |

Rx assistance available to patients who are uninsured, (or whose insurance has denied coverage) and meet program eligibility requirements. Medicare Part D patients who cannot afford Rx can appeal for evaluation of eligibility.

clobazam → ONFI®

clomipramine hydrochloride → ANAFRANIL™

clorazepate dipotassium → TRAXENE®

clotrimazole and betamethasone dipropionate cream → LOTRISONE®

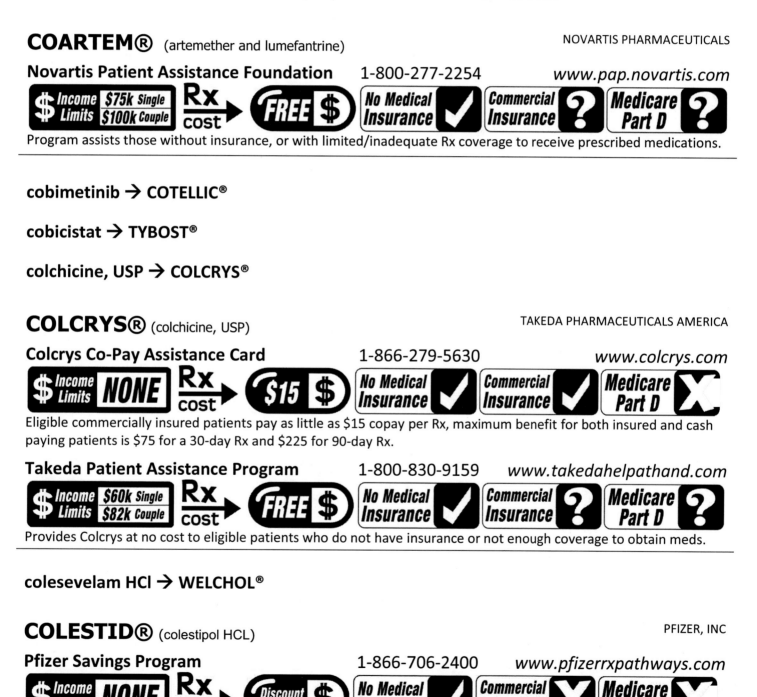

COARTEM® (artemether and lumefantrine) — NOVARTIS PHARMACEUTICALS

Novartis Patient Assistance Foundation — 1-800-277-2254 — www.pap.novartis.com

$ Income Limits $75k Single / $100k Couple | Rx cost → FREE $ | No Medical Insurance ✔ | Commercial Insurance ? | Medicare Part D ?

Program assists those without insurance, or with limited/inadequate Rx coverage to receive prescribed medications.

cobimetinib → COTELLIC®

cobicistat → TYBOST®

colchicine, USP → COLCRYS®

COLCRYS® (colchicine, USP) — TAKEDA PHARMACEUTICALS AMERICA

Colcrys Co-Pay Assistance Card — 1-866-279-5630 — www.colcrys.com

$ Income Limits NONE | Rx cost → $15 $ | No Medical Insurance ✔ | Commercial Insurance ✔ | Medicare Part D X

Eligible commercially insured patients pay as little as $15 copay per Rx, maximum benefit for both insured and cash paying patients is $75 for a 30-day Rx and $225 for 90-day Rx.

Takeda Patient Assistance Program — 1-800-830-9159 — www.takedahelpathand.com

$ Income Limits $60k Single / $82k Couple | Rx cost → FREE $ | No Medical Insurance ✔ | Commercial Insurance ? | Medicare Part D ?

Provides Colcrys at no cost to eligible patients who do not have insurance or not enough coverage to obtain meds.

colesevelam HCl → WELCHOL®

COLESTID® (colestipol HCL) — PFIZER, INC

Pfizer Savings Program — 1-866-706-2400 — www.pfizerrxpathways.com

$ Income Limits NONE | Rx cost → Discount Varies $ | No Medical Insurance ✔ | Commercial Insurance X | Medicare Part D X

Program helps uninsured patients receive discounted Pfizer medications through their local retail pharmacy.

colestipol HCL → COLESTID®

collagenase clostridium histolyticum → XIAFLEX®

COMBIGAN® 0.2%/0.5% (brimonidine tartrate/timolol maleate)

ALLERGAN, INC.

Allergan Savings Card Program   1-833-342-5297   *www.savewithays.com*

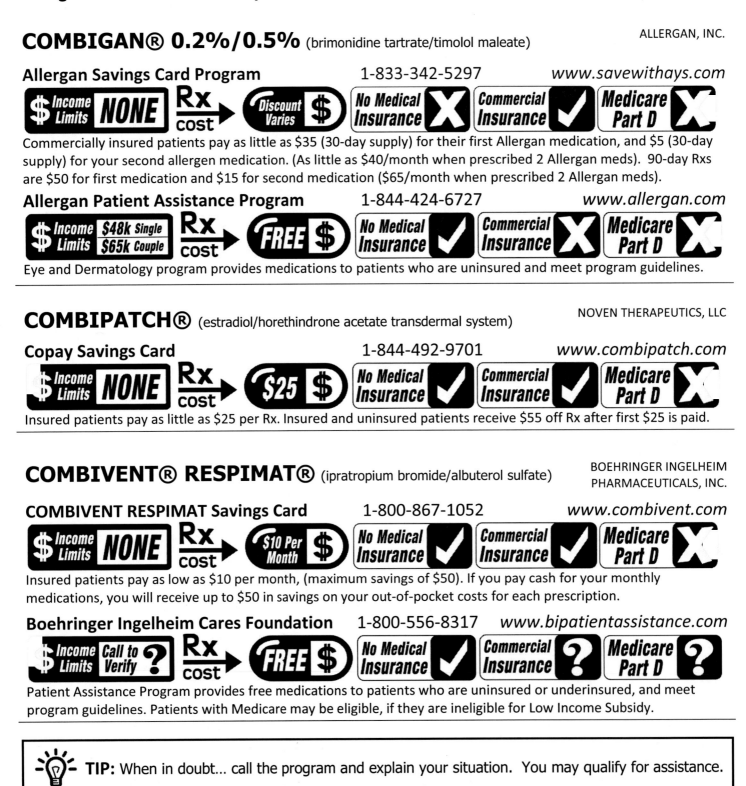

Income Limits **NONE** | Rx cost → | Discount Varies $ | No Medical Insurance **X** | Commercial Insurance ✔ | Medicare Part D **X**

Commercially insured patients pay as little as $35 (30-day supply) for their first Allergan medication, and $5 (30-day supply) for your second allergen medication. (As little as $40/month when prescribed 2 Allergan meds). 90-day Rxs are $50 for first medication and $15 for second medication ($65/month when prescribed 2 Allergan meds).

Allergan Patient Assistance Program   1-844-424-6727   *www.allergan.com*

Income Limits $48k Single $65k Couple | Rx cost → | FREE $ | No Medical Insurance ✔ | Commercial Insurance **X** | Medicare Part D **X**

Eye and Dermatology program provides medications to patients who are uninsured and meet program guidelines.

COMBIPATCH® (estradiol/horethindrone acetate transdermal system)

NOVEN THERAPEUTICS, LLC

Copay Savings Card   1-844-492-9701   *www.combipatch.com*

Income Limits **NONE** | Rx cost → | $25 $ | No Medical Insurance ✔ | Commercial Insurance ✔ | Medicare Part D **X**

Insured patients pay as little as $25 per Rx. Insured and uninsured patients receive $55 off Rx after first $25 is paid.

COMBIVENT® RESPIMAT® (ipratropium bromide/albuterol sulfate)

BOEHRINGER INGELHEIM PHARMACEUTICALS, INC.

COMBIVENT RESPIMAT Savings Card   1-800-867-1052   *www.combivent.com*

Income Limits **NONE** | Rx cost → | $10 Per Month $ | No Medical Insurance ✔ | Commercial Insurance ✔ | Medicare Part D **X**

Insured patients pay as low as $10 per month, (maximum savings of $50). If you pay cash for your monthly medications, you will receive up to $50 in savings on your out-of-pocket costs for each prescription.

Boehringer Ingelheim Cares Foundation   1-800-556-8317   *www.bipatientassistance.com*

Income Limits Call to Verify **?** | Rx cost → | FREE $ | No Medical Insurance ✔ | Commercial Insurance **?** | Medicare Part D **?**

Patient Assistance Program provides free medications to patients who are uninsured or underinsured, and meet program guidelines. Patients with Medicare may be eligible, if they are ineligible for Low Income Subsidy.

TIP: When in doubt... call the program and explain your situation. You may qualify for assistance.

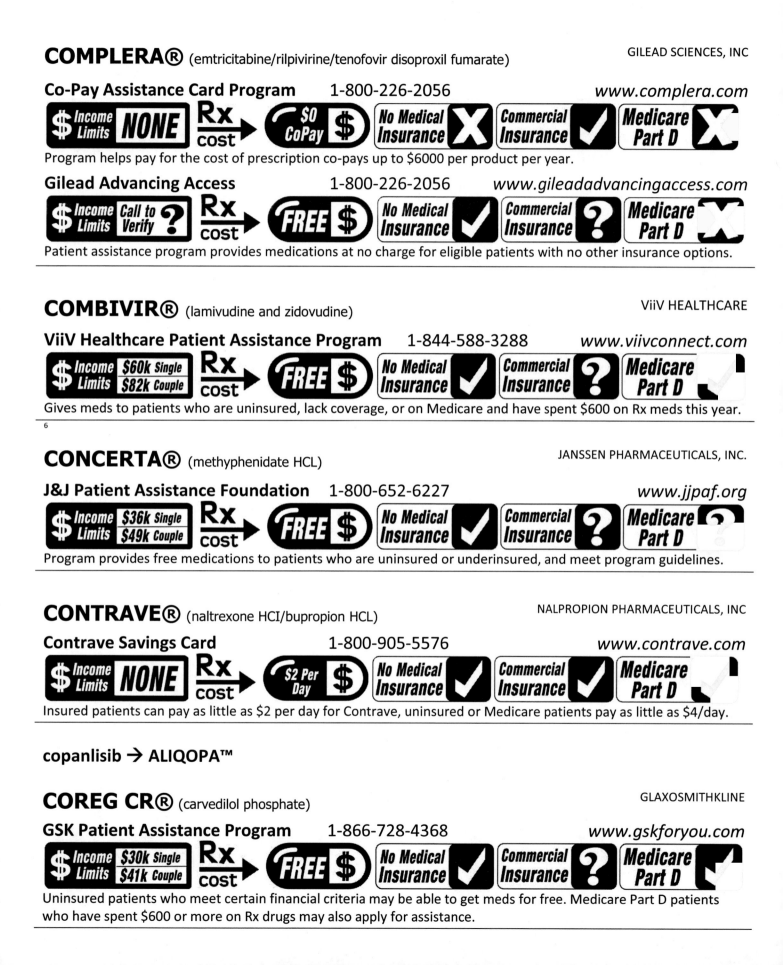

COMPLERA® (emtricitabine/rilpivirine/tenofovir disoproxil fumarate)   GILEAD SCIENCES, INC

Co-Pay Assistance Card Program   1-800-226-2056   www.complera.com

$ Income Limits **NONE** | Rx cost → | $0 CoPay $ | No Medical Insurance ✗ | Commercial Insurance ✓ | Medicare Part D ✗

Program helps pay for the cost of prescription co-pays up to $6000 per product per year.

Gilead Advancing Access   1-800-226-2056   www.gileadadvancingaccess.com

$ Income Limits Call to Verify ? | Rx cost → | FREE $ | No Medical Insurance ✓ | Commercial Insurance ? | Medicare Part D ✗

Patient assistance program provides medications at no charge for eligible patients with no other insurance options.

COMBIVIR® (lamivudine and zidovudine)   ViiV HEALTHCARE

ViiV Healthcare Patient Assistance Program   1-844-588-3288   www.viivconnect.com

$ Income Limits $60k Single $82k Couple | Rx cost → | FREE $ | No Medical Insurance ✓ | Commercial Insurance ? | Medicare Part D ✓

Gives meds to patients who are uninsured, lack coverage, or on Medicare and have spent $600 on Rx meds this year.

CONCERTA® (methyphenidate HCL)   JANSSEN PHARMACEUTICALS, INC.

J&J Patient Assistance Foundation   1-800-652-6227   www.jjpaf.org

$ Income Limits $36k Single $49k Couple | Rx cost → | FREE $ | No Medical Insurance ✓ | Commercial Insurance ? | Medicare Part D ?

Program provides free medications to patients who are uninsured or underinsured, and meet program guidelines.

CONTRAVE® (naltrexone HCI/bupropion HCL)   NALPROPION PHARMACEUTICALS, INC

Contrave Savings Card   1-800-905-5576   www.contrave.com

$ Income Limits **NONE** | Rx cost → | $2 Per Day $ | No Medical Insurance ✓ | Commercial Insurance ✓ | Medicare Part D ✓

Insured patients can pay as little as $2 per day for Contrave, uninsured or Medicare patients pay as little as $4/day.

copanlisib → ALIQOPA™

COREG CR® (carvedilol phosphate)   GLAXOSMITHKLINE

GSK Patient Assistance Program   1-866-728-4368   www.gskforyou.com

$ Income Limits $30k Single $41k Couple | Rx cost → | FREE $ | No Medical Insurance ✓ | Commercial Insurance ? | Medicare Part D ✓

Uninsured patients who meet certain financial criteria may be able to get meds for free. Medicare Part D patients who have spent $600 or more on Rx drugs may also apply for assistance.

CORIFACT® [factor xiii concentrate (human)]

CSL BEHRING

CSL Behring Patient Assistance Program   1-844-727-2752   *www.corifact.com*

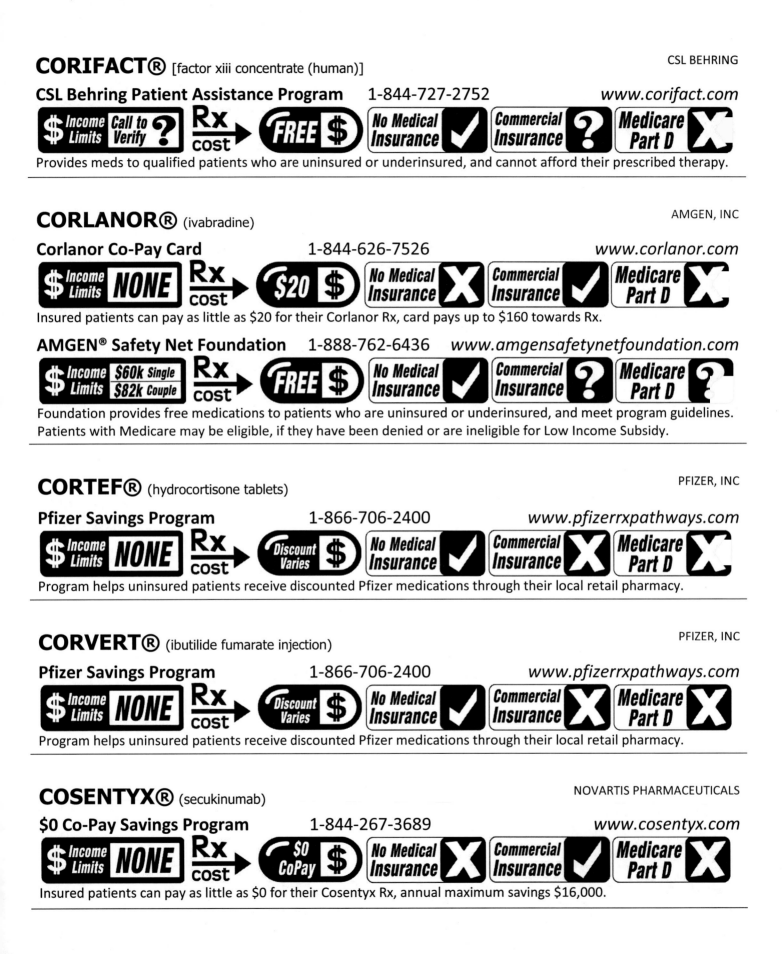

$ Income Limits — Call to Verify ?   Rx cost →   FREE $ No Medical Insurance ✓   Commercial Insurance ?   Medicare Part D ✗

Provides meds to qualified patients who are uninsured or underinsured, and cannot afford their prescribed therapy.

CORLANOR® (ivabradine)

AMGEN, INC

Corlanor Co-Pay Card   1-844-626-7526   *www.corlanor.com*

$ Income Limits — NONE   Rx cost → $20 $ No Medical Insurance ✗   Commercial Insurance ✓   Medicare Part D ✗

Insured patients can pay as little as $20 for their Corlanor Rx, card pays up to $160 towards Rx.

AMGEN® Safety Net Foundation   1-888-762-6436   *www.amgensafetynetfoundation.com*

$ Income Limits — $60k Single / $82k Couple   Rx cost →   FREE $ No Medical Insurance ✓   Commercial Insurance ?   Medicare Part D ?

Foundation provides free medications to patients who are uninsured or underinsured, and meet program guidelines. Patients with Medicare may be eligible, if they have been denied or are ineligible for Low Income Subsidy.

CORTEF® (hydrocortisone tablets)

PFIZER, INC

Pfizer Savings Program   1-866-706-2400   *www.pfizerrxpathways.com*

$ Income Limits — NONE   Rx cost →   Discount Varies $ No Medical Insurance ✓   Commercial Insurance ✗   Medicare Part D ✗

Program helps uninsured patients receive discounted Pfizer medications through their local retail pharmacy.

CORVERT® (ibutilide fumarate injection)

PFIZER, INC

Pfizer Savings Program   1-866-706-2400   *www.pfizerrxpathways.com*

$ Income Limits — NONE   Rx cost →   Discount Varies $ No Medical Insurance ✓   Commercial Insurance ✗   Medicare Part D ✗

Program helps uninsured patients receive discounted Pfizer medications through their local retail pharmacy.

COSENTYX® (secukinumab)

NOVARTIS PHARMACEUTICALS

$0 Co-Pay Savings Program   1-844-267-3689   *www.cosentyx.com*

$ Income Limits — NONE   Rx cost → $0 CoPay $ No Medical Insurance ✗   Commercial Insurance ✓   Medicare Part D ✗

Insured patients can pay as little as $0 for their Cosentyx Rx, annual maximum savings $16,000.

COSENTYX® (secukinumab)

Novartis Patient Assistance Foundation　1-800-277-2254　*www.pap.novartis.com*

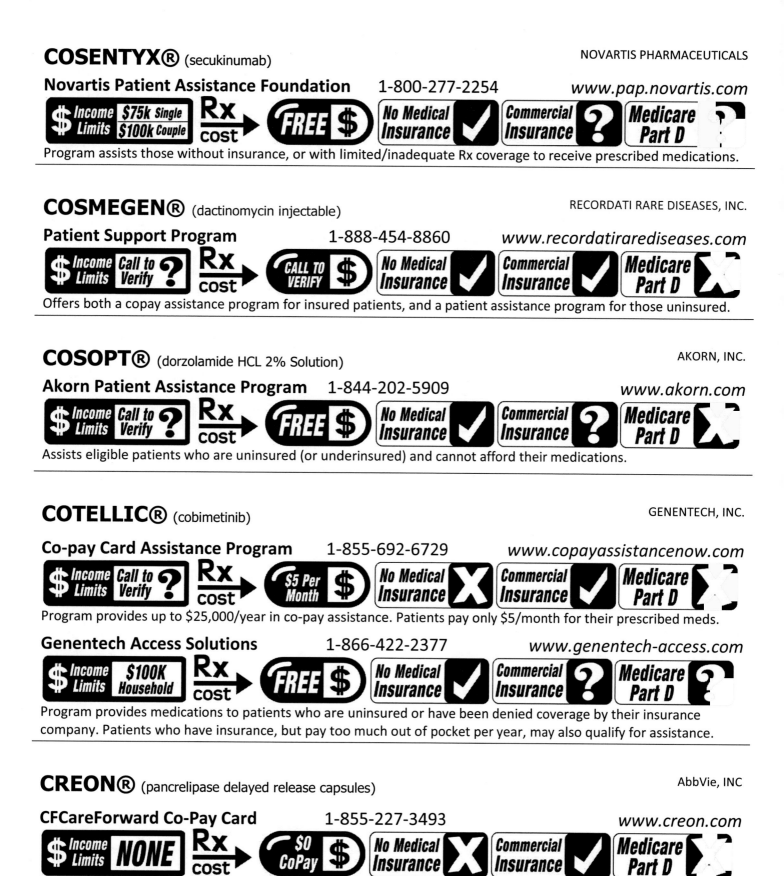

| $ Income Limits | $75k Single / $100k Couple | Rx cost → | FREE $ | No Medical Insurance ✓ | Commercial Insurance ? | Medicare Part D ? |

Program assists those without insurance, or with limited/inadequate Rx coverage to receive prescribed medications.

COSMEGEN® (dactinomycin injectable)
RECORDATI RARE DISEASES, INC.

Patient Support Program　1-888-454-8860　*www.recordatirarediseases.com*

| $ Income Limits | Call to Verify ? | Rx cost → | CALL TO VERIFY $ | No Medical Insurance ✓ | Commercial Insurance ✓ | Medicare Part D ✗ |

Offers both a copay assistance program for insured patients, and a patient assistance program for those uninsured.

COSOPT® (dorzolamide HCL 2% Solution)
AKORN, INC.

Akorn Patient Assistance Program　1-844-202-5909　*www.akorn.com*

| $ Income Limits | Call to Verify ? | Rx cost → | FREE $ | No Medical Insurance ✓ | Commercial Insurance ? | Medicare Part D ✗ |

Assists eligible patients who are uninsured (or underinsured) and cannot afford their medications.

COTELLIC® (cobimetinib)
GENENTECH, INC.

Co-pay Card Assistance Program　1-855-692-6729　*www.copayassistancenow.com*

| $ Income Limits | Call to Verify ? | Rx cost → | $5 Per Month $ | No Medical Insurance ✗ | Commercial Insurance ✓ | Medicare Part D ✗ |

Program provides up to $25,000/year in co-pay assistance. Patients pay only $5/month for their prescribed meds.

Genentech Access Solutions　1-866-422-2377　*www.genentech-access.com*

| $ Income Limits | $100K Household | Rx cost → | FREE $ | No Medical Insurance ✓ | Commercial Insurance ? | Medicare Part D ? |

Program provides medications to patients who are uninsured or have been denied coverage by their insurance company. Patients who have insurance, but pay too much out of pocket per year, may also qualify for assistance.

CREON® (pancrelipase delayed release capsules)
AbbVie, INC

CFCareForward Co-Pay Card　1-855-227-3493　*www.creon.com*

| $ Income Limits | NONE | Rx cost → | $0 CoPay $ | No Medical Insurance ✗ | Commercial Insurance ✓ | Medicare Part D ✗ |

Eligible insured patients with Exocrine Pancreatic Insufficiency (EPI) **due to Cyststic Fibrosis** pay as little as $0 when their Rx is $100 or less, and pay $5 when their Rx is $105 or more.

CREON® (pancrelipase delayed release capsules)

AbbVie, INC

CREON On Course Co-Pay Card   1-844-662-7366   *www.creon.com*

Income Limits **NONE** | Rx cost → | **$5 Per Month** $ | No Medical Insurance **X** | Commercial Insurance **✓** | Medicare Part D **X**

Eligible insured patients with Exocrine Pancreatic Insufficiency (EPI) pay as little as $5 per month for their Creon Rx.

AbbVie Patient Assistance Foundation   1-800-222-6885   *www.abbviepaf.org*

Income Limits **$36k Single $49k Couple** | Rx cost → | **FREE** $ | No Medical Insurance **✓** | Commercial Insurance **✓** | Medicare Part D **✓**

Rx assistance available to patients who are uninsured and meet program eligibility requirements. Patients with Commercial Insurance or Medicare Part D, who are struggling to pay for their medications, are encouraged to apply.

CRESEMBA® (isavuconazonium sulfate)

ASTELLAS PHARMA, INC.

CRESEMBA Patient Savings Program   1-855-898-2634   *www.astellasaccess.com*

Income Limits **NONE** | Rx cost → | **$25 Per Month** $ | No Medical Insurance **X** | Commercial Insurance **✓** | Medicare Part D **X**

Provides up to $4,000/year in co-pay assistance. Eligible patients pay as low as $25 out-of-pocket for Rx meds.

Astellas Patient Assistance Program   1-800-477-6472   *www.astellasaccess.com*

Income Limits **$60k Single $82k Couple** | Rx cost → | **FREE** $ | No Medical Insurance **✓** | Commercial Insurance **?** | Medicare Part D **X**

Provides medications for those uninsured or have insurance that excludes coverage for CRESEMBA.

CRINONE® (progesterone gel)

ALLERGAN, INC.

Allergan Patient Assistance Program   1-844-424-6727   *www.allergan.com*

Income Limits **Call to Verify ?** | Rx cost → | **FREE** $ | No Medical Insurance **✓** | Commercial Insurance **?** | Medicare Part D **?**

Program provides meds to patients who are uninsured or underinsured, and meet program guidelines. Patients with Medicare may be eligible, if they have been denied or are ineligible for Low Income Subsidy.

crisaborole ointment 2%→ EUCRISA®

crizotinib → XALKORI®

crofelemer → MYTESI®

TIP: When in doubt... call the program and explain your situation. You may qualify for assistance.

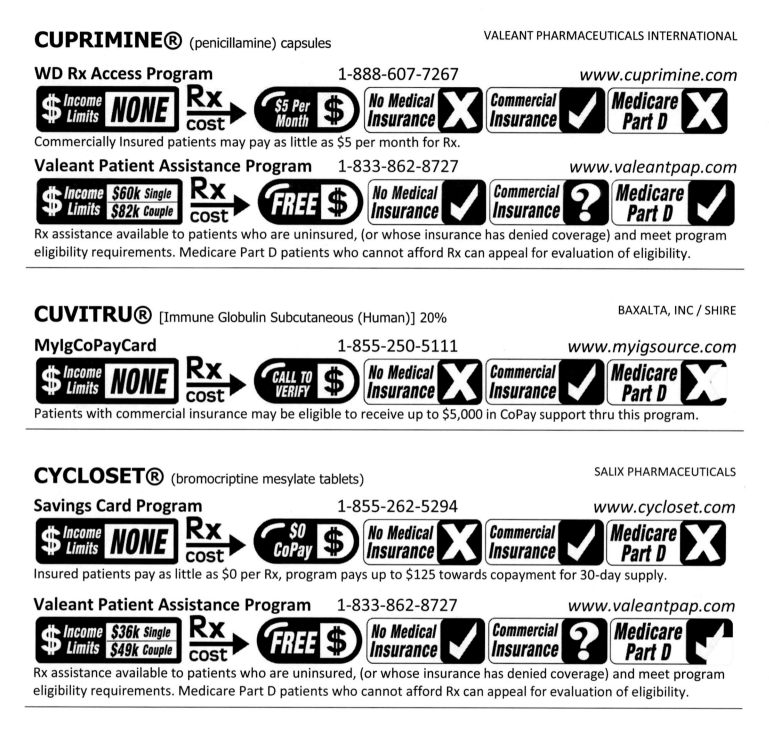

CUPRIMINE® (penicillamine) capsules

VALEANT PHARMACEUTICALS INTERNATIONAL

WD Rx Access Program   1-888-607-7267   *www.cuprimine.com*

$ Income Limits **NONE** | **Rx** cost → | **$5 Per Month** $ | **No Medical Insurance** X | **Commercial Insurance** ✓ | **Medicare Part D** X

Commercially Insured patients may pay as little as $5 per month for Rx.

Valeant Patient Assistance Program   1-833-862-8727   *www.valeantpap.com*

$ Income Limits **$60k Single $82k Couple** | **Rx** cost → | **FREE** $ | **No Medical Insurance** ✓ | **Commercial Insurance** ? | **Medicare Part D** ✓

Rx assistance available to patients who are uninsured, (or whose insurance has denied coverage) and meet program eligibility requirements. Medicare Part D patients who cannot afford Rx can appeal for evaluation of eligibility.

CUVITRU® [Immune Globulin Subcutaneous (Human)] 20%

BAXALTA, INC / SHIRE

MyIgCoPayCard   1-855-250-5111   *www.myigsource.com*

$ Income Limits **NONE** | **Rx** cost → | **CALL TO VERIFY** $ | **No Medical Insurance** X | **Commercial Insurance** ✓ | **Medicare Part D** X

Patients with commercial insurance may be eligible to receive up to $5,000 in CoPay support thru this program.

CYCLOSET® (bromocriptine mesylate tablets)

SALIX PHARMACEUTICALS

Savings Card Program   1-855-262-5294   *www.cycloset.com*

$ Income Limits **NONE** | **Rx** cost → | **$0 CoPay** $ | **No Medical Insurance** X | **Commercial Insurance** ✓ | **Medicare Part D** X

Insured patients pay as little as $0 per Rx, program pays up to $125 towards copayment for 30-day supply.

Valeant Patient Assistance Program   1-833-862-8727   *www.valeantpap.com*

$ Income Limits **$36k Single $49k Couple** | **Rx** cost → | **FREE** $ | **No Medical Insurance** ✓ | **Commercial Insurance** ? | **Medicare Part D** ✓

Rx assistance available to patients who are uninsured, (or whose insurance has denied coverage) and meet program eligibility requirements. Medicare Part D patients who cannot afford Rx can appeal for evaluation of eligibility.

cyclosporine → **GENGRAF®**

cyclosporine → **NEORAL®**

cyclosporine → **SANDIMMUNE®**

cyclosporine opthalmic emulsion → **RESTASIS® 0.05%**

CYKLOKAPRON® (tranexamic acid)

PFIZER, INC

Pfizer Savings Program   1-866-706-2400   www.pfizerrxpathways.com

Income Limits NONE | **Rx cost** → | **Discount Varies** $ | **No Medical Insurance** ✓ | **Commercial Insurance** ✗ | **Medicare Part D** ✗

Program helps uninsured patients receive discounted Pfizer medications through their local retail pharmacy.

CYMBALTA® (duloxetine)

LILLY USA, LLC

Lilly Cares   1-800-545-6962   www.lillycares.com

Income Limits $36k Single / $49k Couple | **Rx cost** → | **FREE** $ | **No Medical Insurance** ✓ | **Commercial Insurance** ? | **Medicare Part D** ✓

Provides free Lilly medications for eligible patients who are uninsured and cannot afford their medications. Medicare Part D patients are eligible for assistance, after they have spent $1,100 on Rx meds in a calendar year.

CYRAMZA® (ramucirumab)

LILLY USA, LLC

Lilly PatientOne   1-866-472-8663   www.cyramza.com

Income Limits NONE | **Rx cost** → | **$25 Per Month** $ | **No Medical Insurance** ✗ | **Commercial Insurance** ✓ | **Medicare Part D** ✗

Eligible patients pay $25 per Rx, program covers remaining co-pay or coinsurance, up to a max of $25,000/year.

Lilly Cares   1-800-545-6962   www.lillycares.com

Income Limits $60k Single / $82k Couple | **Rx cost** → | **FREE** $ | **No Medical Insurance** ✓ | **Commercial Insurance** ? | **Medicare Part D** ✓

Provides free Lilly medications for eligible patients who are uninsured and cannot afford their medications, or for those whose insurance has denied coverage. Medicare Part D patients may also be eligible for assistance.

CYSTADANE® (betaine anhydrous) oral solution

RECORDATI RARE DISEASES, INC.

Anovo Specialty Pharmacy   1-888-487-4703   www.cystadane.com

Income Limits Call to Verify ? | **Rx cost** → | **CALL TO VERIFY** $ | **No Medical Insurance** ✓ | **Commercial Insurance** ✓ | **Medicare Part D** ✗

Offers both a copay assistance program for insured patients, and a patient assistance program for those uninsured.

cysteamine bitartrate → PROCYSBI®

CYTOMEL® (liothyronine sodium)

PFIZER, INC

Pfizer Savings Program   1-866-706-2400   www.pfizerrxpathways.com

Income Limits NONE | **Rx cost** → | **Discount Varies** $ | **No Medical Insurance** ✓ | **Commercial Insurance** ✗ | **Medicare Part D** ✗

Program helps uninsured patients receive discounted Pfizer medications through their local retail pharmacy.

CYTOTEC® (misoprostol)

PFIZER, INC

Pfizer Savings Program   1-866-706-2400   *www.pfizerrxpathways.com*

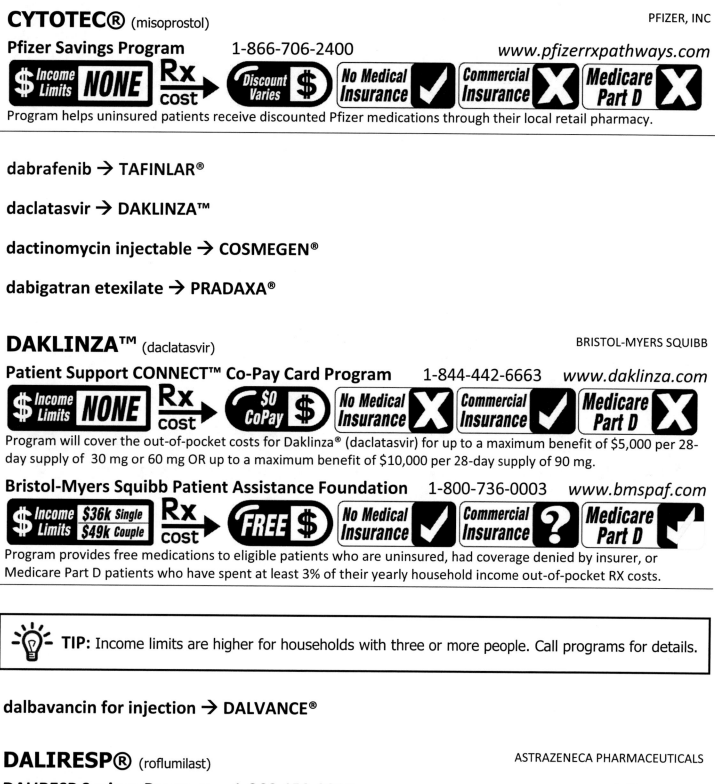

| $ Income Limits **NONE** | **Rx** cost → | Discount Varies $ | No Medical Insurance ✓ | Commercial Insurance ✗ | Medicare Part D ✗ |

Program helps uninsured patients receive discounted Pfizer medications through their local retail pharmacy.

---

dabrafenib → **TAFINLAR®**

daclatasvir → **DAKLINZA™**

dactinomycin injectable → **COSMEGEN®**

dabigatran etexilate → **PRADAXA®**

DAKLINZA™ (daclatasvir)

BRISTOL-MYERS SQUIBB

Patient Support CONNECT™ Co-Pay Card Program   1-844-442-6663   *www.daklinza.com*

| $ Income Limits **NONE** | **Rx** cost → | $0 CoPay $ | No Medical Insurance ✗ | Commercial Insurance ✓ | Medicare Part D ✗ |

Program will cover the out-of-pocket costs for Daklinza® (daclatasvir) for up to a maximum benefit of $5,000 per 28-day supply of 30 mg or 60 mg OR up to a maximum benefit of $10,000 per 28-day supply of 90 mg.

Bristol-Myers Squibb Patient Assistance Foundation   1-800-736-0003   *www.bmspaf.com*

| $ Income Limits $36k Single $49k Couple | **Rx** cost → | FREE $ | No Medical Insurance ✓ | Commercial Insurance ? | Medicare Part D ✓ |

Program provides free medications to eligible patients who are uninsured, had coverage denied by insurer, or Medicare Part D patients who have spent at least 3% of their yearly household income out-of-pocket RX costs.

TIP: Income limits are higher for households with three or more people. Call programs for details.

---

dalbavancin for injection → **DALVANCE®**

DALIRESP® (roflumilast)

ASTRAZENECA PHARMACEUTICALS

DALIRESP Savings Program   1-866-459-2015   *www.daliresp.com*

| $ Income Limits **NONE** | **Rx** cost → | $25 Per Month $ | No Medical Insurance ✓ | Commercial Insurance ✓ | Medicare Part D ✗ |

Insured patients with a valid Rx for DALIRESP pay as low as $25 per 30-day supply. If you pay cash for your monthly prescription, you will receive up to $100 in savings on your out-of-pocket costs that exceed $25 for each prescription.

DALIRESP® (roflumilast)

AZ&ME™   1-800-292-6363   *www.azandmeapp.com*

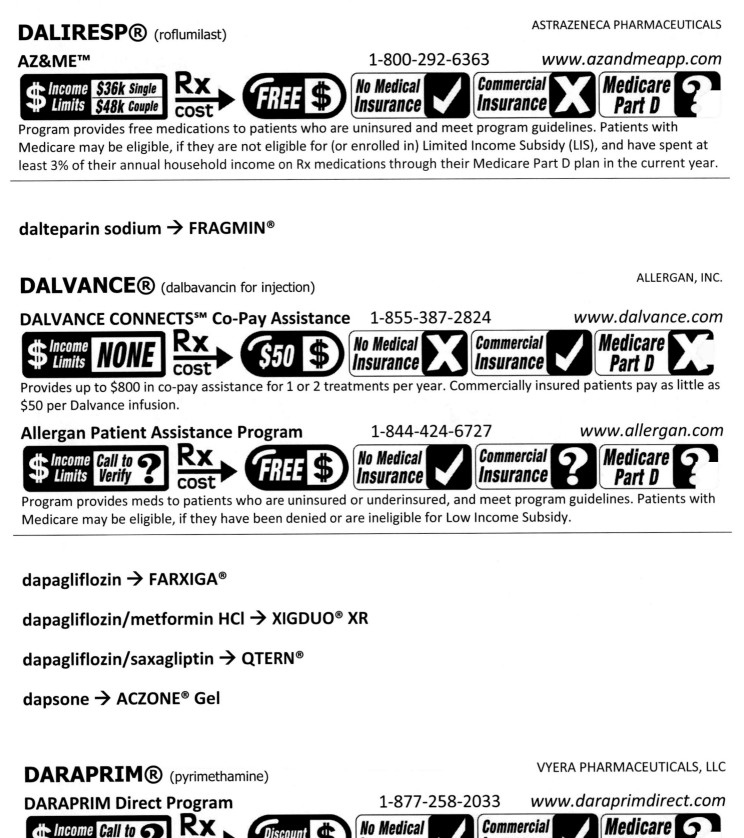

Income Limits $36k Single $48k Couple	**Rx cost** → **FREE $**	**No Medical Insurance** ✓ **Commercial Insurance** ✗ **Medicare Part D** ?

Program provides free medications to patients who are uninsured and meet program guidelines. Patients with Medicare may be eligible, if they are not eligible for (or enrolled in) Limited Income Subsidy (LIS), and have spent at least 3% of their annual household income on Rx medications through their Medicare Part D plan in the current year.

---

dalteparin sodium → FRAGMIN®

DALVANCE® (dalbavancin for injection)

ALLERGAN, INC.

DALVANCE CONNECTS℠ Co-Pay Assistance   1-855-387-2824   *www.dalvance.com*

Income Limits NONE	**Rx cost** → **$50 $**	**No Medical Insurance** ✗ **Commercial Insurance** ✓ **Medicare Part D** ✗

Provides up to $800 in co-pay assistance for 1 or 2 treatments per year. Commercially insured patients pay as little as $50 per Dalvance infusion.

Allergan Patient Assistance Program   1-844-424-6727   *www.allergan.com*

Income Limits Call to Verify ?	**Rx cost** → **FREE $**	**No Medical Insurance** ✓ **Commercial Insurance** ? **Medicare Part D** ?

Program provides meds to patients who are uninsured or underinsured, and meet program guidelines. Patients with Medicare may be eligible, if they have been denied or are ineligible for Low Income Subsidy.

---

dapagliflozin → FARXIGA®

dapagliflozin/metformin HCl → XIGDUO® XR

dapagliflozin/saxagliptin → QTERN®

dapsone → ACZONE® Gel

DARAPRIM® (pyrimethamine)

VYERA PHARMACEUTICALS, LLC

DARAPRIM Direct Program   1-877-258-2033   *www.daraprimdirect.com*

Income Limits Call to Verify ?	**Rx cost** → **Discount Varies $**	**No Medical Insurance** ✓ **Commercial Insurance** ✓ **Medicare Part D** ?

Insured patients pay as little as $10 per Rx, program also provides meds at no cost to qualified uninsured patients.

daratumumab → DARZALEX®

darbepoetin alfa → ARANESP®

darunavir → PREZISTA®

darunavir/cobicistat → PREZCOBIX®

DARZALEX® (daratumumab)

JANSSEN PHARMACEUTICALS INC.

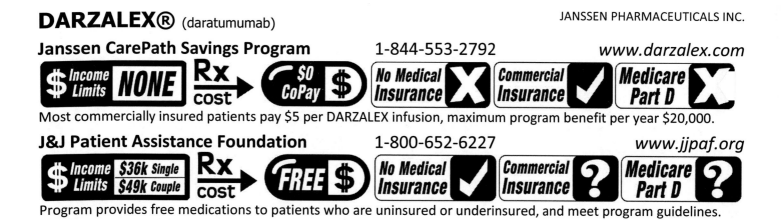

Janssen CarePath Savings Program   1-844-553-2792   *www.darzalex.com*

Most commercially insured patients pay $5 per DARZALEX infusion, maximum program benefit per year $20,000.

J&J Patient Assistance Foundation   1-800-652-6227   *www.jjpaf.org*

Program provides free medications to patients who are uninsured or underinsured, and meet program guidelines.

dasatinib → SPRYCEL®

DAYPRO® (oxaprozin)

PFIZER, INC

Pfizer Savings Program   1-866-706-2400   *www.pfizerrxpathways.com*

Program helps uninsured patients receive discounted Pfizer medications through their local retail pharmacy.

DAYTRANA® (methylphenidate transdermal system)

NOVEN THERAPEUTICS, LLC

Copay Savings Card   1-866-849-4512   *www.datrana.com*

Insured patients pay as little as $20 per Rx. Insured and uninsured patients receive $80 off Rx after first $20 is paid.

deferasirox → EXJADE®

deferasirox → JADENU®

deflazacort → EMFLAZA®

delavirdine mesylate → RESCRIPTOR®

DELZICOL® DR Capsules (mesalamine)

ALLERGAN, INC.

Allergan Patient Assistance Program   1-844-424-6727   *www.allergan.com*

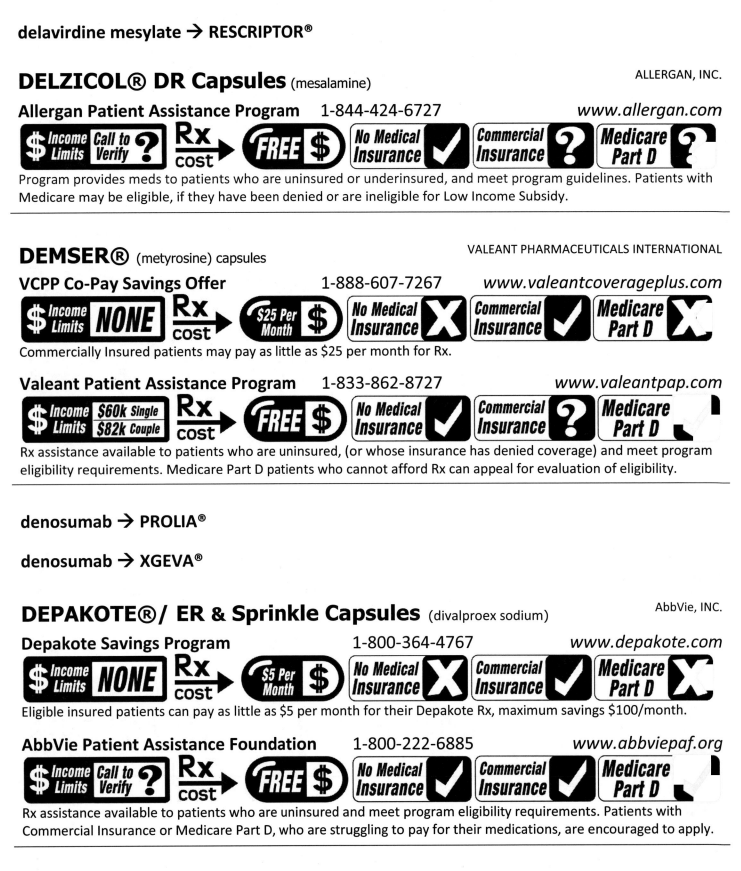

Program provides meds to patients who are uninsured or underinsured, and meet program guidelines. Patients with Medicare may be eligible, if they have been denied or are ineligible for Low Income Subsidy.

DEMSER® (metyrosine) capsules

VALEANT PHARMACEUTICALS INTERNATIONAL

VCPP Co-Pay Savings Offer   1-888-607-7267   *www.valeantcoverageplus.com*

Commercially Insured patients may pay as little as $25 per month for Rx.

Valeant Patient Assistance Program   1-833-862-8727   *www.valeantpap.com*

Rx assistance available to patients who are uninsured, (or whose insurance has denied coverage) and meet program eligibility requirements. Medicare Part D patients who cannot afford Rx can appeal for evaluation of eligibility.

denosumab → PROLIA®

denosumab → XGEVA®

DEPAKOTE®/ ER & Sprinkle Capsules (divalproex sodium)

AbbVie, INC.

Depakote Savings Program   1-800-364-4767   *www.depakote.com*

Eligible insured patients can pay as little as $5 per month for their Depakote Rx, maximum savings $100/month.

AbbVie Patient Assistance Foundation   1-800-222-6885   *www.abbviepaf.org*

Rx assistance available to patients who are uninsured and meet program eligibility requirements. Patients with Commercial Insurance or Medicare Part D, who are struggling to pay for their medications, are encouraged to apply.

denosumab → XGEVA®

DEPO®-ESTRADIOL (estradiol cypionate)
PFIZER, INC

Pfizer Savings Program   1-866-706-2400   *www.pfizerrxpathways.com*

$ Income Limits **NONE** | **Rx** cost → | *Discount Varies* $ | **No Medical Insurance** ✓ | **Commercial Insurance** ✗ | **Medicare Part D** ✗

Program helps uninsured patients receive discounted Pfizer medications through their local retail pharmacy.

Pfizer Patient Assistance Program   1-844-989-7284   *www.pfizerrxpathways.com*

$ Income Limits **$48k Single / $65k Couple** | **Rx** cost → | **FREE** $ | **No Medical Insurance** ✓ | **Commercial Insurance** ? | **Medicare Part D** ✗

Assists eligible patients who are uninsured (or have inadequate drug coverage) and cannot afford their medications.

DEPO-MEDROL® (methylprednisolone acetate)
PFIZER, INC

Pfizer Savings Program   1-866-706-2400   *www.pfizerrxpathways.com*

$ Income Limits **NONE** | **Rx** cost → | *Discount Varies* $ | **No Medical Insurance** ✓ | **Commercial Insurance** ✗ | **Medicare Part D** ✗

Program helps uninsured patients receive discounted Pfizer medications through their local retail pharmacy.

DEPO-PROVERA® (medroxyprogesterone acetate)
PFIZER, INC

Pfizer Savings Program   1-866-706-2400   *www.pfizerrxpathways.com*

$ Income Limits **NONE** | **Rx** cost → | *Discount Varies* $ | **No Medical Insurance** ✓ | **Commercial Insurance** ✗ | **Medicare Part D** ✗

Program helps uninsured patients receive discounted Pfizer medications through their local retail pharmacy.

Pfizer Patient Assistance Program   1-844-989-7284   *www.pfizerrxpathways.com*

$ Income Limits **$48k Single / $65k Couple** | **Rx** cost → | **FREE** $ | **No Medical Insurance** ✓ | **Commercial Insurance** ? | **Medicare Part D** ✗

Assists eligible patients who are uninsured (or have inadequate drug coverage) and cannot afford their medications.

DEPO-SUBQ PROVERA 104® (medroxyprogesterone acetate)
PFIZER, INC

Pfizer Savings Program   1-866-706-2400   *www.pfizerrxpathways.com*

$ Income Limits **NONE** | **Rx** cost → | *Discount Varies* $ | **No Medical Insurance** ✓ | **Commercial Insurance** ✗ | **Medicare Part D** ✗

Program helps uninsured patients receive discounted Pfizer medications through their local retail pharmacy.

Pfizer Patient Assistance Program   1-844-989-7284   *www.pfizerrxpathways.com*

$ Income Limits **$48k Single / $65k Couple** | **Rx** cost → | **FREE** $ | **No Medical Insurance** ✓ | **Commercial Insurance** ? | **Medicare Part D** ✗

Assists eligible patients who are uninsured (or have inadequate drug coverage) and cannot afford their medications.

DEPO®-TESTOSTERONE (testosterone cypionate)

PFIZER, INC

Pfizer Savings Program   1-866-706-2400   *www.pfizerrxpathways.com*

| $ Income Limits **NONE** | **Rx** cost → | *Discount Varies* $ | *No Medical* **Insurance** ✔ | *Commercial* **Insurance** ✘ | *Medicare* **Part D** ✘ |

Program helps uninsured patients receive discounted Pfizer medications through their local retail pharmacy.

DESCOVY® (emtricitabine/tenofovir alafenamide)

GILEAD SCIENCES, INC

Co-Pay Assistance Card Program   1-800-226-2056   *www.descovy.com*

| $ Income Limits **NONE** | **Rx** cost → | *$0 CoPay* $ | *No Medical* **Insurance** ✘ | *Commercial* **Insurance** ✔ | *Medicare* **Part D** ✘ |

Program helps pay for the cost of prescription co-pays up to $4,800 per product per year.

Gilead Advancing Access   1-800-226-2056   *www.gileadadvancingaccess.com*

| $ Income Limits *Call to Verify* ? | **Rx** cost → | *FREE* $ | *No Medical* **Insurance** ✔ | *Commercial* **Insurance** ? | *Medicare* **Part D** ✘ |

Patient assistance program provides medications at no charge for eligible patients with no other insurance options.

desmopressin acetate → STIMATE®

desvenlafaxine → PRISTIQ®

DESONATE® (desonide)

BAYER HEALTHCARE PHARMACEUTICALS

Bayer Patient Assistance Program   1-866-575-5002   *Phone Only*

| $ Income Limits *Call to Verify* ? | **Rx** cost → | *FREE* $ | *No Medical* **Insurance** ✔ | *Commercial* **Insurance** ? | *Medicare* **Part D** ? |

Program provides medications to patients based on financial need. Application must be completed by both you and your healthcare provider. Before calling number, make sure you have your Doctor's office fax and phone number, as well as the contact name at the office. Eligibility determined on a case-by-case basis.

desonide → DESONATE®

DESOXYN® (methamphetamine hydrochloride)

RECORDATI RARE DISEASES, INC.

Patient Support Program   1-866-209-7604   *www.recordatirarediseases.com*

| $ Income Limits *Call to Verify* ? | **Rx** cost → | *CALL TO VERIFY* $ | *No Medical* **Insurance** ✔ | *Commercial* **Insurance** ✔ | *Medicare* **Part D** ✘ |

Offers both a copay assistance program for insured patients, and a patient assistance program for those uninsured.

DETROL® /DETROL® LA (tolterodine tartrate)

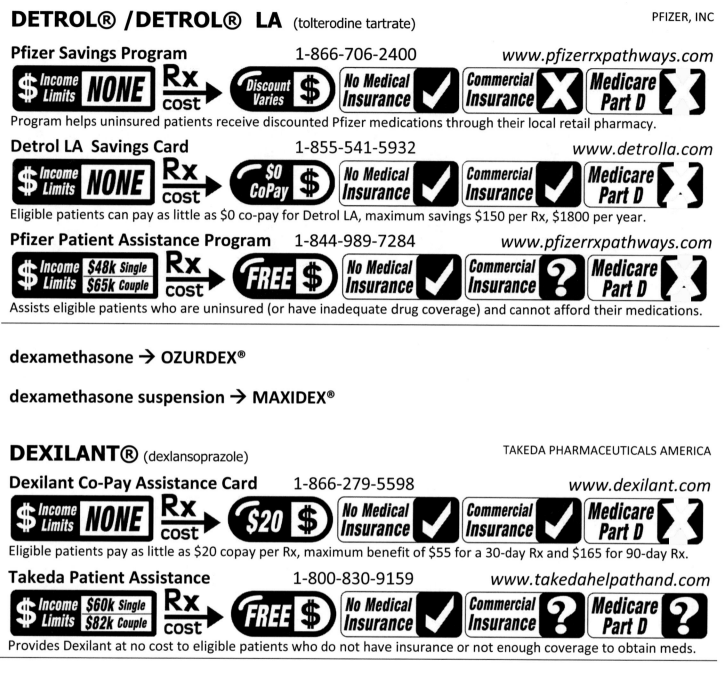

Pfizer Savings Program   1-866-706-2400   *www.pfizerrxpathways.com*

$ Income Limits **NONE** | **Rx** cost → | Discount Varies $ | No Medical Insurance ✓ | Commercial Insurance ✗ | Medicare Part D ✗

Program helps uninsured patients receive discounted Pfizer medications through their local retail pharmacy.

Detrol LA Savings Card   1-855-541-5932   *www.detrolla.com*

$ Income Limits **NONE** | **Rx** cost → | $0 CoPay $ | No Medical Insurance ✓ | Commercial Insurance ✓ | Medicare Part D ✗

Eligible patients can pay as little as $0 co-pay for Detrol LA, maximum savings $150 per Rx, $1800 per year.

Pfizer Patient Assistance Program   1-844-989-7284   *www.pfizerrxpathways.com*

$ Income Limits $48k Single $65k Couple | **Rx** cost → | FREE $ | No Medical Insurance ✓ | Commercial Insurance ? | Medicare Part D ✗

Assists eligible patients who are uninsured (or have inadequate drug coverage) and cannot afford their medications.

---

dexamethasone → OZURDEX®

dexamethasone suspension → MAXIDEX®

DEXILANT® (dexlansoprazole)

Dexilant Co-Pay Assistance Card   1-866-279-5598   *www.dexilant.com*

$ Income Limits **NONE** | **Rx** cost → | $20 $ | No Medical Insurance ✓ | Commercial Insurance ✓ | Medicare Part D ✗

Eligible patients pay as little as $20 copay per Rx, maximum benefit of $55 for a 30-day Rx and $165 for 90-day Rx.

Takeda Patient Assistance   1-800-830-9159   *www.takedahelpathand.com*

$ Income Limits $60k Single $82k Couple | **Rx** cost → | FREE $ | No Medical Insurance ✓ | Commercial Insurance ? | Medicare Part D ?

Provides Dexilant at no cost to eligible patients who do not have insurance or not enough coverage to obtain meds.

---

dexlansoprazole → DEXILANT®

dexmethylphenidate HCL → FOCALIN® XR

dexrazoxane for injection → ZINECARD®

dextroamphetamine sulfate tablets → ZENZEDI®

dextromethorphan HBr and quinidine sulfate → NUEDEXTA®

diazoxide → PROGLYCEM®

DICLEGIS® (doxylamine succinate/pyridoxine hydrochloride)

DUCHESNAY USA

CoPay Savings Card   1-800-250-5195   *www.diclegis.com*

| **$ Income Limits** NONE | Rx cost → | $40 $ | No Medical Insurance ✗ | Commercial Insurance ✓ | Medicare Part D ✗ |

Insured patients pay as low as $40 for their Diclegis prescription

ProCare Pharmacy Care   1-844-716-4663   *www.diclegis.com*

| **$ Income Limits** NONE | Rx cost → | Discount Varies $ | No Medical Insurance ✓ | Commercial Insurance ? | Medicare Part D ✗ |

Program for uninsured patients, or those whose insurance does not cover Diclegis. Cost for Rx is $60 for 60 tablets, $90 for 90 tablets, or $120 for 120 tablets, all with free shipping to your home.

Patient Assistance Program   1-855-720-4147   *www.duchesnayusa.com*

| **$ Income Limits** $30k Single $41k Couple | Rx cost → | FREE $ | No Medical Insurance ✓ | Commercial Insurance ? | Medicare Part D ✗ |

Provides free medications to eligible patients who are uninsured or whose insurance does not cover cost of Rx.

diclofenac epolamine → FLECTOR® PATCH

diclofenac sodium solution → PENNSAID® 2%

diclofenac sodium/misoprostol → ARTHROTEC®

diclofenac potassium → CAMBIA®

diclofenac potassium → ZIPSOR®

DIFICID® (fidaxomicin) tablets

MERCK & COMPANY, INC.

Multiuse Savings Coupon   1-800-672-6372   *www.dificid.com*

| **$ Income Limits** NONE | Rx cost → | $50 $ | No Medical Insurance ✗ | Commercial Insurance ✓ | Medicare Part D ✗ |

Insured patients pay as little as $50 per Rx, maximum savings is $3,400 per prescription.

Merck Patient Assistance Program   1-800-727-5400   *www.merckhelps.com*

| **$ Income Limits** $48k Single $65k Couple | Rx cost → | FREE $ | No Medical Insurance ✓ | Commercial Insurance ? | Medicare Part D ? |

Program is for patients who do not have Rx insurance coverage and cannot afford to pay for their medicine.

DIFLUCAN® (fluconazole)

PFIZER, INC

Pfizer Savings Program 1-866-706-2400 *www.pfizerrxpathways.com*

Program helps uninsured patients receive discounted Pfizer medications through their local retail pharmacy.

---

difluprednate ophthalmic emulsion → DUREZOL®

DILANTIN® (phenytoin sodium)

PFIZER, INC

Pfizer Savings Program 1-866-706-2400 *www.pfizerrxpathways.com*

Program helps uninsured patients receive discounted Pfizer medications through their local retail pharmacy.

Dilantin Savings Card 1-866-590-9400 *www.dilantin.com*

Eligible patients save up to $20 off their Dilantin Rx, maximum savings $240/year.

Pfizer Patient Assistance Program 1-844-989-7284 *www.pfizerrxpathways.com*

Assists eligible patients who are uninsured (or have inadequate drug coverage) and cannot afford their medications.

---

dimethyl fumarate → TECFIDERA®

DIOVAN® (valsartan)

NOVARTIS PHARMACEUTICALS

Co-Pay Savings Card 1-844-685-3406 *www.copay.novartispharma.com*

Patients pay as little as $10, max savings $75 per Rx. If total Rx exceeds $85, pt. pays $10 plus amount over $85.

DIOVAN HCT® (valsartan and hydrochlorothiazide USP)

NOVARTIS PHARMACEUTICALS

Co-Pay Savings Card 1-844-685-3406 *www.copay.novartispharma.com*

Patients pay as little as $10, max savings $75 per Rx. If total Rx exceeds $85, pt. pays $10 plus amount over $85.

diphenoxylate HCL / atropine → LOMOTIL®

disopyramide phosphate → NORPACE® / NORPACE® CR

divalproex sodium → DEPAKOTE®

docusate sodium → ENEMEEZ®

dofetilide → TIKOSYN®

dolutegravir → TIVICAY®

dolutegravir and rilpivirine → JULUCA®

DONNATAL® (belladonna alkaloids with phenobarbital)

CONCORDIA HEALTHCARE USA, INC.

Donnatal Patient Assistance Program   1-800-858-4006   *www.donnatal.com*

Rx assistance available to patients who are uninsured or underinsured, and meet program eligibility requirements.

dornase alfa → PULMOZYME®

dorzolamide HCL 2% Solution → COSOPT®

dorzolamide hydrochloride ophthalmic solution 2% → TRUSOPT®

doxazosin mesylate → CARDURA®

doxepin → SILENOR®

doxycycline, USP → ORACEA®

doxylamine succinate/pyridoxine hydrochloride → BONJESTA®

doxylamine succinate/pyridoxine hydrochloride → DICLEGIS®

dronedarone → MULTAQ®

drospirenone and estradiol → ANGELIQ®

drospirenone/ethinyl estradiol → YASMIN®

drospirenone/ethinyl estradiol → YAZ®

drospirenone/ethinyl estradiol/levomefolate calcium tablets → BEYAZ®

drospirenone/ethinyl estradiol/levomefolate calcium → SAFYRAL®

DROXIA® (hydroxyurea)

BRISTOL-MYERS SQUIBB

Access Support Program for Oncology 1-800-861-0048 www.bmsaccesssupport.com

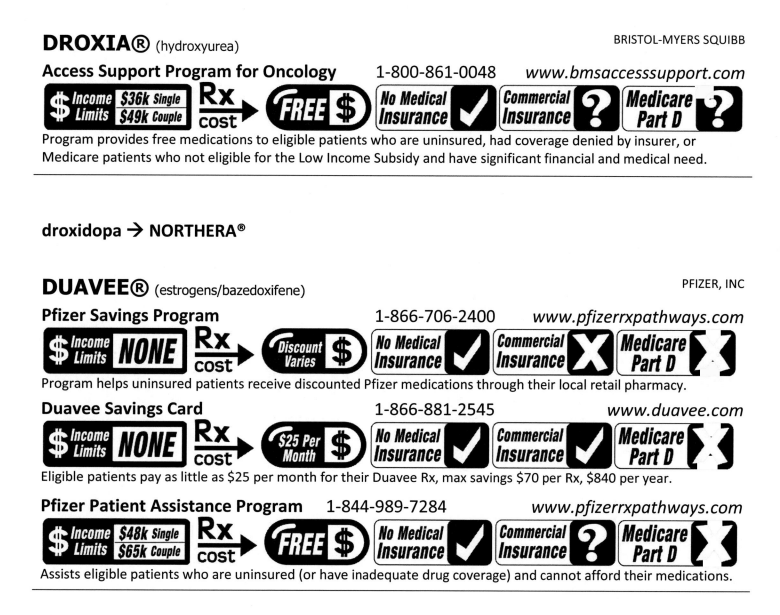

Program provides free medications to eligible patients who are uninsured, had coverage denied by insurer, or Medicare patients who not eligible for the Low Income Subsidy and have significant financial and medical need.

droxidopa → NORTHERA®

DUAVEE® (estrogens/bazedoxifene)

PFIZER, INC

Pfizer Savings Program 1-866-706-2400 www.pfizerrxpathways.com

Program helps uninsured patients receive discounted Pfizer medications through their local retail pharmacy.

Duavee Savings Card 1-866-881-2545 www.duavee.com

Eligible patients pay as little as $25 per month for their Duavee Rx, max savings $70 per Rx, $840 per year.

Pfizer Patient Assistance Program 1-844-989-7284 www.pfizerrxpathways.com

Assists eligible patients who are uninsured (or have inadequate drug coverage) and cannot afford their medications.

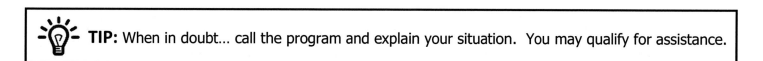

TIP: When in doubt... call the program and explain your situation. You may qualify for assistance.

DUEXIS® (ibuprofen/famotidine)

HORIZON PHARMA USA, INC.

HorizonCares™ Prescription Savings Program   1-855-250-6335   *www.duexis.com*

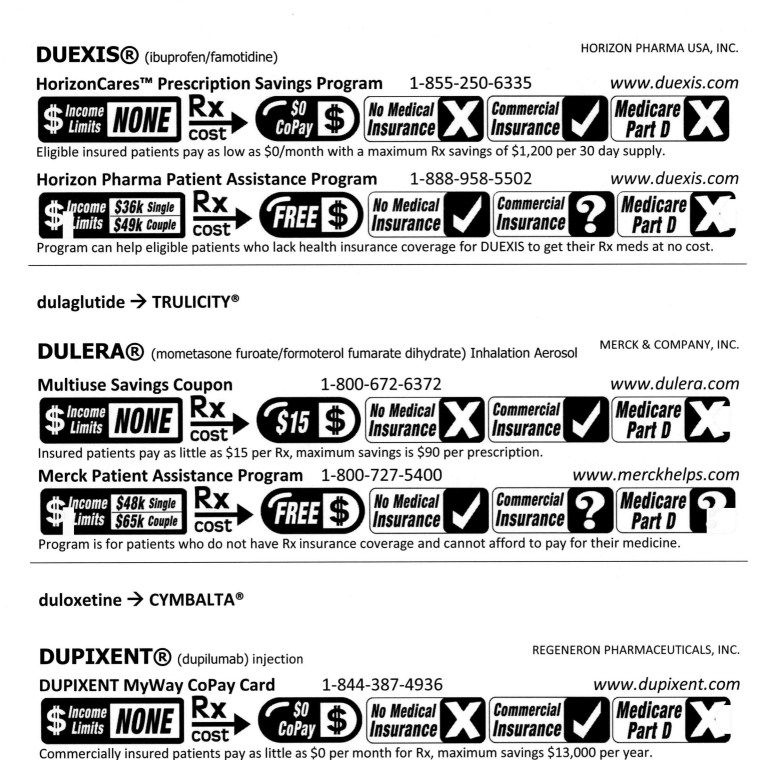

Eligible insured patients pay as low as $0/month with a maximum Rx savings of $1,200 per 30 day supply.

Horizon Pharma Patient Assistance Program   1-888-958-5502   *www.duexis.com*

Program can help eligible patients who lack health insurance coverage for DUEXIS to get their Rx meds at no cost.

---

dulaglutide → TRULICITY®

DULERA® (mometasone furoate/formoterol fumarate dihydrate) Inhalation Aerosol

MERCK & COMPANY, INC.

Multiuse Savings Coupon   1-800-672-6372   *www.dulera.com*

Insured patients pay as little as $15 per Rx, maximum savings is $90 per prescription.

Merck Patient Assistance Program   1-800-727-5400   *www.merckhelps.com*

Program is for patients who do not have Rx insurance coverage and cannot afford to pay for their medicine.

---

duloxetine → CYMBALTA®

DUPIXENT® (dupilumab) injection

REGENERON PHARMACEUTICALS, INC.

DUPIXENT MyWay CoPay Card   1-844-387-4936   *www.dupixent.com*

Commercially insured patients pay as little as $0 per month for Rx, maximum savings $13,000 per year.

Patient Assistance Program   1-844-387-4936   *www.dupixent.com*

Program provides medications to patients who are uninsured or denied coverage for Dupixent.

dupilumab → DUPIXENT®

DUREZOL® (difluprednate ophthalmic emulsion)

NOVARTIS PHARMACEUTICALS

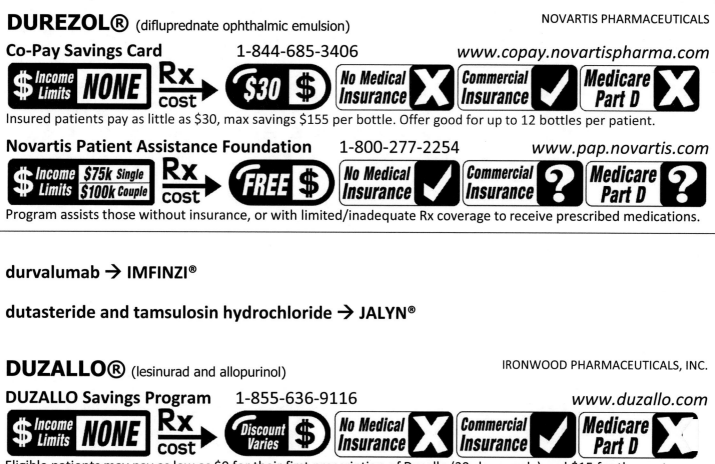

Co-Pay Savings Card　　　1-844-685-3406　　　*www.copay.novartispharma.com*

| $ Income Limits **NONE** | Rx cost → | **$30** $ | **No Medical Insurance** ✕ | **Commercial Insurance** ✓ | **Medicare Part D** ✕ |

Insured patients pay as little as $30, max savings $155 per bottle. Offer good for up to 12 bottles per patient.

Novartis Patient Assistance Foundation　　　1-800-277-2254　　　*www.pap.novartis.com*

| $ Income Limits **$75k Single $100k Couple** | Rx cost → | **FREE** $ | **No Medical Insurance** ✓ | **Commercial Insurance** ? | **Medicare Part D** ? |

Program assists those without insurance, or with limited/inadequate Rx coverage to receive prescribed medications.

---

durvalumab → IMFINZI®

dutasteride and tamsulosin hydrochloride → JALYN®

DUZALLO® (lesinurad and allopurinol)

IRONWOOD PHARMACEUTICALS, INC.

DUZALLO Savings Program　　　1-855-636-9116　　　*www.duzallo.com*

| $ Income Limits **NONE** | Rx cost → | **Discount Varies** $ | **No Medical Insurance** ✕ | **Commercial Insurance** ✓ | **Medicare Part D** ✕ |

Eligible patients may pay as low as $0 for their first prescription of Duzallo (30-day supply) and $15 for the next eleven 30-day supply prescription fills, or receive a total of four 90-day prescription fills for $30 each time.

Ironwood Patient Assistance Program　　　1-833-557-2413　　　*www.duzallo.com*

| $ Income Limits **$36k Single $49k Couple** | Rx cost → | **FREE** $ | **No Medical Insurance** ✓ | **Commercial Insurance** ? | **Medicare Part D** ? |

Program provides free medications to patients who are uninsured or underinsured, and meet program guidelines. Patients with Medicare may be eligible, if meds are not covered and they are ineligible for Low Income Subsidy.

DYMISTA® Nasal Spray (azelastine/fluticasone propionate)

MEDA PHARMACEUTICALS, INC.

Dymista Copay Card Program　　　1-888-939-6478　　　*www.dymista.com*

| $ Income Limits **NONE** | Rx cost → | **$29 Per Month** $ | **No Medical Insurance** ✕ | **Commercial Insurance** ✓ | **Medicare Part D** ✕ |

Program provides up to $1800/year in co-pay assistance. Patients pay as little as $29/month for Dymista.

TIP: When in doubt... call the program and explain your situation. You may qualify for assistance.

DYSPORT® (abobotulinumtoxinA)

IPSEN BIOPHARMACEUTICALS, INC.

DYSPORT® Copay Savings 1-866-435-5677 *www.ipsencares.com*

Income Limits **NONE** | **Rx** cost → | Discount Varies $ | No Medical Insurance ✔ | Commercial Insurance ✔ | Medicare Part D ✗

Program provides copay assistance, with maximum assistance of $1250/per injection treatment ($5,000/yr max)

DYSPORT® Patient Assistance 1-866-435-5677 *www.ipsencares.com*

Income Limits **Call to Verify ?** | **Rx** cost → | **FREE** $ | No Medical Insurance ✔ | Commercial Insurance ✗ | Medicare Part D ✗

Eligible patients without insurance coverage and who are experiencing financial hardship, may receive Dysport free.

---

ecallantide → KALBITOR®

echothiophate iodide ophthalmic solution → PHOSPHOLINE IODIDE®

eculizumab → SOLIRIS®

EDARBI® (azilsartan medoxomil)

ARBOR PHARMACEUTICALS, INC.

Instant Savings Card 1-877-264-2440 *www.edarbi.com*

Income Limits **NONE** | **Rx** cost → | Discount Varies $ | No Medical Insurance ✔ | Commercial Insurance ✔ | Medicare Part D ✗

Insured patients pay as little as $25, cash patients pay $60. Rx can be filled at any pharmacy.

E-Z Rx™ Program 1-877-264-2440 *www.edarbi.com*

Income Limits **NONE** | **Rx** cost → | Discount Varies $ | No Medical Insurance ✔ | Commercial Insurance ✔ | Medicare Part D ✗

You may pay just $10 a month for your BiDil prescription if you have insurance and $40 a month if you pay cash, when you fill your Rx through participating independent pharmacies.

Patient Assistance Program 1-844-884-8700 *www.arborpharma.com*

Income Limits **$24k Single $32k Couple** | **Rx** cost → | **FREE** $ | No Medical Insurance ✔ | Commercial Insurance ? | Medicare Part D ?

Program provides free medications to patients who are uninsured or underinsured, and meet program guidelines. Patients with Medicare may be eligible, if they have been denied or are ineligible for Low Income Subsidy.

EDARBYCLOR® (azilartan medoxomil/chlorthalidone)

ARBOR PHARMACEUTICALS, INC.

Instant Savings Card 1-877-264-2440 *www.edarbi.com*

Income Limits **NONE** | **Rx** cost → | Discount Varies $ | No Medical Insurance ✔ | Commercial Insurance ✔ | Medicare Part D ✗

Insured patients pay as little as $25, cash patients pay $60. Rx can be filled at any pharmacy.

EDARBYCLOR® (azilartan medoxomil/chlorthalidone)

ARBOR PHARMACEUTICALS, INC.

E-Z Rx™ Program

1-877-264-2440   *www.edarbi.com*

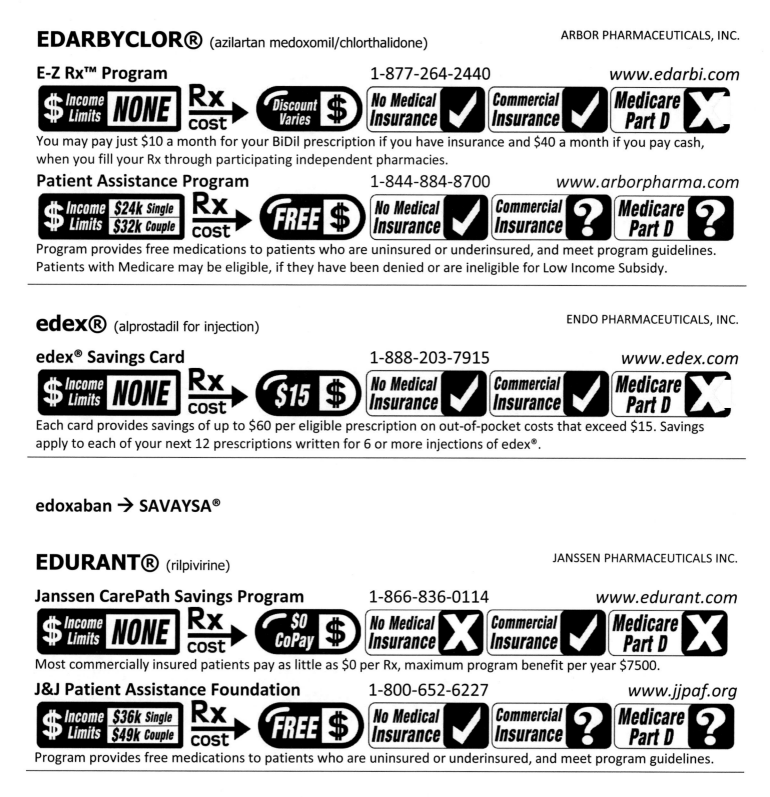

$ Income Limits **NONE** | **Rx** cost → | Discount Varies $ | No Medical Insurance ✓ | Commercial Insurance ✓ | Medicare Part D ✗

You may pay just $10 a month for your BiDil prescription if you have insurance and $40 a month if you pay cash, when you fill your Rx through participating independent pharmacies.

Patient Assistance Program

1-844-884-8700   *www.arborpharma.com*

$ Income Limits $24k Single / $32k Couple | **Rx** cost → | FREE $ | No Medical Insurance ✓ | Commercial Insurance ? | Medicare Part D ?

Program provides free medications to patients who are uninsured or underinsured, and meet program guidelines. Patients with Medicare may be eligible, if they have been denied or are ineligible for Low Income Subsidy.

---

edex® (alprostadil for injection)

ENDO PHARMACEUTICALS, INC.

edex® Savings Card

1-888-203-7915   *www.edex.com*

$ Income Limits **NONE** | **Rx** cost → | $15 $ | No Medical Insurance ✓ | Commercial Insurance ✓ | Medicare Part D ✗

Each card provides savings of up to $60 per eligible prescription on out-of-pocket costs that exceed $15. Savings apply to each of your next 12 prescriptions written for 6 or more injections of edex®.

---

edoxaban → SAVAYSA®

EDURANT® (rilpivirine)

JANSSEN PHARMACEUTICALS INC.

Janssen CarePath Savings Program

1-866-836-0114   *www.edurant.com*

$ Income Limits **NONE** | **Rx** cost → | $0 CoPay $ | No Medical Insurance ✗ | Commercial Insurance ✓ | Medicare Part D ✗

Most commercially insured patients pay as little as $0 per Rx, maximum program benefit per year $7500.

J&J Patient Assistance Foundation

1-800-652-6227   *www.jjpaf.org*

$ Income Limits $36k Single / $49k Couple | **Rx** cost → | FREE $ | No Medical Insurance ✓ | Commercial Insurance ? | Medicare Part D ?

Program provides free medications to patients who are uninsured or underinsured, and meet program guidelines.

---

efavirenx/emtricitabine/tenofovir disoproxil fumarate → ATRIPLA®

💡 **TIP:** Income limits are higher for households with three or more people. Call programs for details.

EFFEXOR XR® (venlafaxine hydrochloride)

PFIZER, INC

Pfizer Savings Program

1-866-706-2400   *www.pfizerrxpathways.com*

| $ Income Limits **NONE** | **Rx cost** → | Discount Varies $ | No Medical Insurance ✓ | Commercial Insurance ✗ | Medicare Part D ✗ |

Program helps uninsured patients receive discounted Pfizer medications through their local retail pharmacy.

Effexor XR Savings Card

1-855-488-0749   *www.effexorxr.com*

| $ Income Limits **NONE** | **Rx cost** → | $4 Per Month $ | No Medical Insurance ✓ | Commercial Insurance ✓ | Medicare Part D ✗ |

Pay as little as $4 per month for Rx, maximum savings $150 per Rx, $1800 per year.

---

efinaconazole topical solution 10% → JUBLIA®

ELAPRASE® (idsulfase)

SHIRE

OnePath Co-Pay Assistance Program

1-866-888-0660   *www.elaprase.com*

| $ Income Limits **NONE** | **Rx cost** → | $0 CoPay $ | No Medical Insurance ✗ | Commercial Insurance ✓ | Medicare Part D ✗ |

Program helps cover the cost of insurance co-pays for Elaprase, up to the program maximum, for eligible patients.

OnePath Patient Assistance Program

1-866-888-0660   *www.elaprase.com*

| $ Income Limits Call to Verify ? | **Rx cost** → | FREE $ | No Medical Insurance ✓ | Commercial Insurance ? | Medicare Part D ✗ |

Program provides Shire medications to eligible patients who are uninsured, or have insurance that doesn't cover Rx.

---

elbasvir and grazoprevir → ZEPATIER®

ELELYSO® (taliglucerase alfa)

PFIZER, INC

Pfizer Gaucher Personal Support

1-855-353-5976   *www.elelyso.com*

| $ Income Limits Call to Verify ? | **Rx cost** → | Discount Varies $ | No Medical Insurance ✓ | Commercial Insurance ✓ | Medicare Part D ✗ |

Eligible insured patients can pay as little as $0 out-of-pocket cost for ELELYSO infusions, maximum savings $15,000/year. ELELYSO and supplies may also be available at no cost to qualified uninsured or underinsured patients.

---

eletriptan HBr → RELPAX®

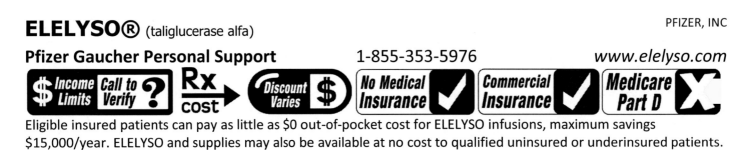

TIP: When in doubt... call the program and explain your situation. You may qualify for assistance.

ELIDEL® (pimecrolimus) cream 1%   VALEANT PHARMACEUTICALS INTERNATIONAL

Ortho Dermatologics Rx Access Program   1-855-202-3279   www.orthorxaccess.com

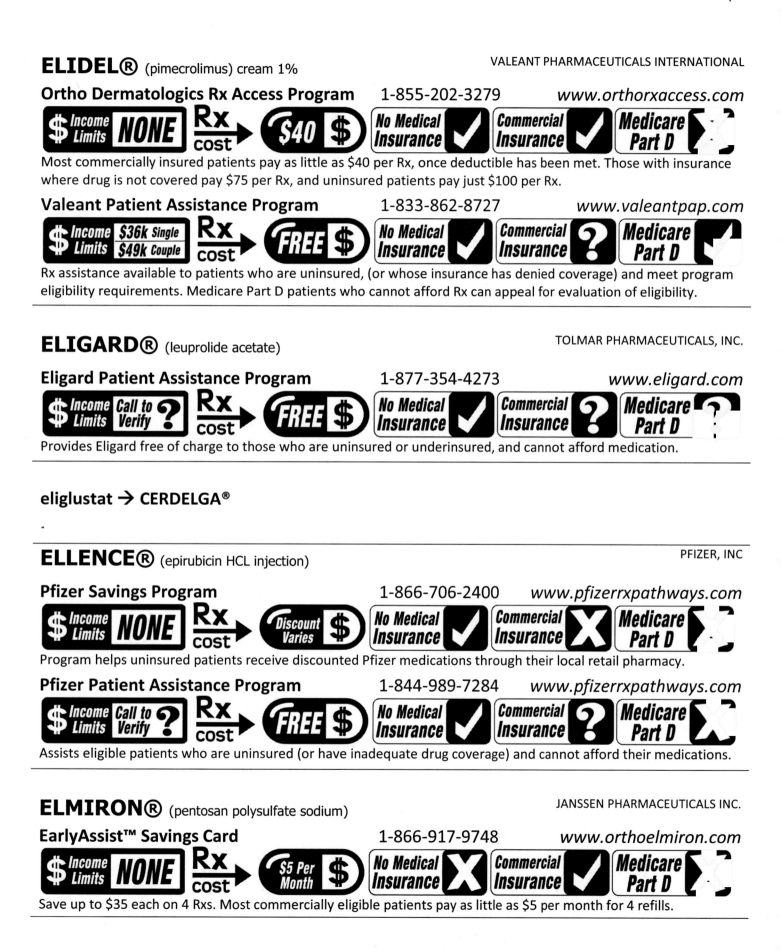

| $ Income Limits | **NONE** | Rx cost → | **$40 $** | No Medical Insurance ✓ | Commercial Insurance ✓ | Medicare Part D ✗ |

Most commercially insured patients pay as little as $40 per Rx, once deductible has been met. Those with insurance where drug is not covered pay $75 per Rx, and uninsured patients pay just $100 per Rx.

Valeant Patient Assistance Program   1-833-862-8727   www.valeantpap.com

| $ Income Limits | $36k Single / $49k Couple | Rx cost → | **FREE $** | No Medical Insurance ✓ | Commercial Insurance ? | Medicare Part D ✓ |

Rx assistance available to patients who are uninsured, (or whose insurance has denied coverage) and meet program eligibility requirements. Medicare Part D patients who cannot afford Rx can appeal for evaluation of eligibility.

ELIGARD® (leuprolide acetate)   TOLMAR PHARMACEUTICALS, INC.

Eligard Patient Assistance Program   1-877-354-4273   www.eligard.com

| $ Income Limits | Call to Verify ? | Rx cost → | **FREE $** | No Medical Insurance ✓ | Commercial Insurance ? | Medicare Part D ? |

Provides Eligard free of charge to those who are uninsured or underinsured, and cannot afford medication.

---

eliglustat → CERDELGA®

-

ELLENCE® (epirubicin HCL injection)   PFIZER, INC

Pfizer Savings Program   1-866-706-2400   www.pfizerrxpathways.com

| $ Income Limits | **NONE** | Rx cost → | Discount Varies $ | No Medical Insurance ✓ | Commercial Insurance ✗ | Medicare Part D ✗ |

Program helps uninsured patients receive discounted Pfizer medications through their local retail pharmacy.

Pfizer Patient Assistance Program   1-844-989-7284   www.pfizerrxpathways.com

| $ Income Limits | Call to Verify ? | Rx cost → | **FREE $** | No Medical Insurance ✓ | Commercial Insurance ? | Medicare Part D ✗ |

Assists eligible patients who are uninsured (or have inadequate drug coverage) and cannot afford their medications.

ELMIRON® (pentosan polysulfate sodium)   JANSSEN PHARMACEUTICALS INC.

EarlyAssist™ Savings Card   1-866-917-9748   www.orthoelmiron.com

| $ Income Limits | **NONE** | Rx cost → | $5 Per Month $ | No Medical Insurance ✗ | Commercial Insurance ✓ | Medicare Part D ✗ |

Save up to $35 each on 4 Rxs. Most commercially eligible patients pay as little as $5 per month for 4 refills.

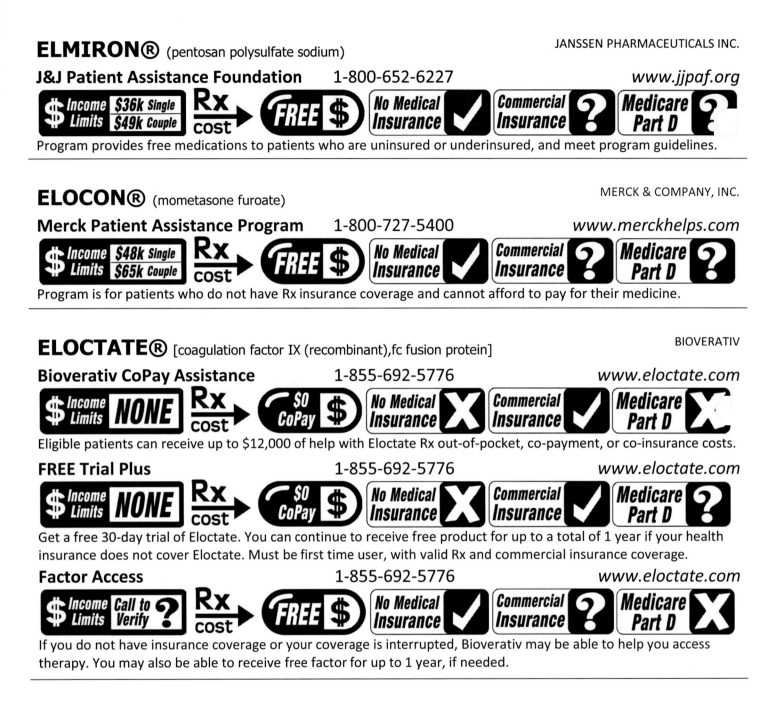

ELMIRON® (pentosan polysulfate sodium)

JANSSEN PHARMACEUTICALS INC.

J&J Patient Assistance Foundation   1-800-652-6227   *www.jjpaf.org*

$ Income Limits | $36k Single / $49k Couple | Rx cost → | FREE $ | No Medical Insurance ✓ | Commercial Insurance ? | Medicare Part D ?

Program provides free medications to patients who are uninsured or underinsured, and meet program guidelines.

ELOCON® (mometasone furoate)

MERCK & COMPANY, INC.

Merck Patient Assistance Program   1-800-727-5400   *www.merckhelps.com*

$ Income Limits | $48k Single / $65k Couple | Rx cost → | FREE $ | No Medical Insurance ✓ | Commercial Insurance ? | Medicare Part D ?

Program is for patients who do not have Rx insurance coverage and cannot afford to pay for their medicine.

ELOCTATE® [coagulation factor IX (recombinant),fc fusion protein]

BIOVERATIV

Bioverativ CoPay Assistance   1-855-692-5776   *www.eloctate.com*

$ Income Limits | NONE | Rx cost → | $0 CoPay $ | No Medical Insurance X | Commercial Insurance ✓ | Medicare Part D X

Eligible patients can receive up to $12,000 of help with Eloctate Rx out-of-pocket, co-payment, or co-insurance costs.

FREE Trial Plus   1-855-692-5776   *www.eloctate.com*

$ Income Limits | NONE | Rx cost → | $0 CoPay $ | No Medical Insurance X | Commercial Insurance ✓ | Medicare Part D ?

Get a free 30-day trial of Eloctate. You can continue to receive free product for up to a total of 1 year if your health insurance does not cover Eloctate. Must be first time user, with valid Rx and commercial insurance coverage.

Factor Access   1-855-692-5776   *www.eloctate.com*

$ Income Limits | Call to Verify ? | Rx cost → | FREE $ | No Medical Insurance ✓ | Commercial Insurance ? | Medicare Part D X

If you do not have insurance coverage or your coverage is interrupted, Bioverativ may be able to help you access therapy. You may also be able to receive free factor for up to 1 year, if needed.

elotuzumab → EMPLICITI™

eltrombopag → PROMACTA®

eluxadoline → VIBERZI® Tablets

elvitegravir/cobicistat/emtricitabine/tenofovir alafenamide → GENVOYA®

elvitegravir/cobicistat/emtricitabine/tenofovir disoproxil fumarate → STRIBILD®

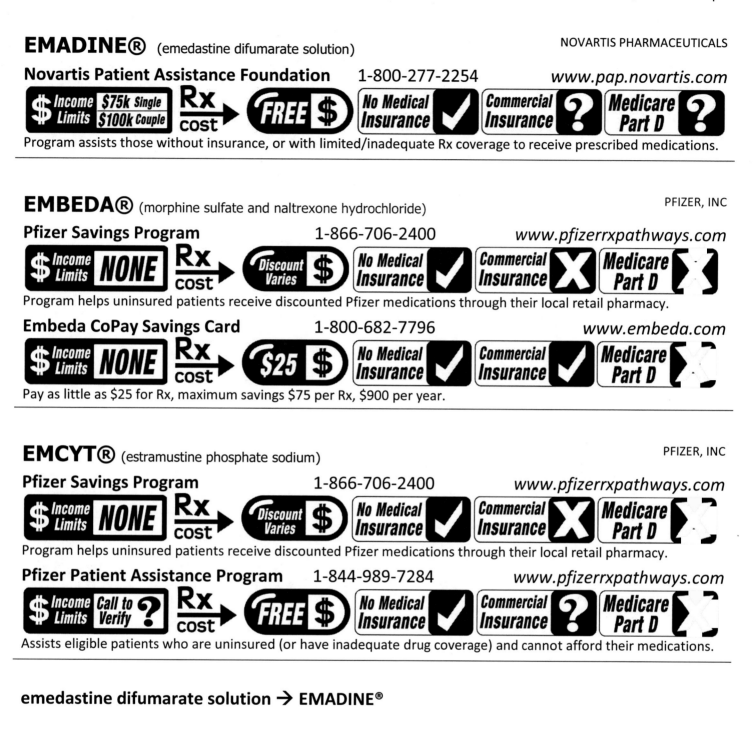

EMADINE® (emedastine difumarate solution)   NOVARTIS PHARMACEUTICALS

Novartis Patient Assistance Foundation   1-800-277-2254   *www.pap.novartis.com*

$ Income Limits $75k Single $100k Couple | Rx cost → | FREE $ | No Medical Insurance ✓ | Commercial Insurance ? | Medicare Part D ?

Program assists those without insurance, or with limited/inadequate Rx coverage to receive prescribed medications.

EMBEDA® (morphine sulfate and naltrexone hydrochloride)   PFIZER, INC

Pfizer Savings Program   1-866-706-2400   *www.pfizerrxpathways.com*

$ Income Limits NONE | Rx cost → | Discount Varies $ | No Medical Insurance ✓ | Commercial Insurance X | Medicare Part D X

Program helps uninsured patients receive discounted Pfizer medications through their local retail pharmacy.

Embeda CoPay Savings Card   1-800-682-7796   *www.embeda.com*

$ Income Limits NONE | Rx cost → | $25 $ | No Medical Insurance ✓ | Commercial Insurance ✓ | Medicare Part D X

Pay as little as $25 for Rx, maximum savings $75 per Rx, $900 per year.

EMCYT® (estramustine phosphate sodium)   PFIZER, INC

Pfizer Savings Program   1-866-706-2400   *www.pfizerrxpathways.com*

$ Income Limits NONE | Rx cost → | Discount Varies $ | No Medical Insurance ✓ | Commercial Insurance X | Medicare Part D X

Program helps uninsured patients receive discounted Pfizer medications through their local retail pharmacy.

Pfizer Patient Assistance Program   1-844-989-7284   *www.pfizerrxpathways.com*

$ Income Limits Call to Verify ? | Rx cost → | FREE $ | No Medical Insurance ✓ | Commercial Insurance ? | Medicare Part D X

Assists eligible patients who are uninsured (or have inadequate drug coverage) and cannot afford their medications.

emedastine difumarate solution → EMADINE®

EMEND® (aprepitant)   MERCK & COMPANY, INC.

Merck Patient Assistance Program   1-800-727-5400   *www.merckhelps.com*

$ Income Limits $48k Single $65k Couple | Rx cost → | FREE $ | No Medical Insurance ✓ | Commercial Insurance ? | Medicare Part D ?

Program is for patients who do not have Rx insurance coverage and cannot afford to pay for their medicine.

EMFLAZA® (deflazacort)

PTC THERAPEUTICS, INC.

EmflazaCares Patient Support Program   1-844-478-2227   *www.emflaza.com*

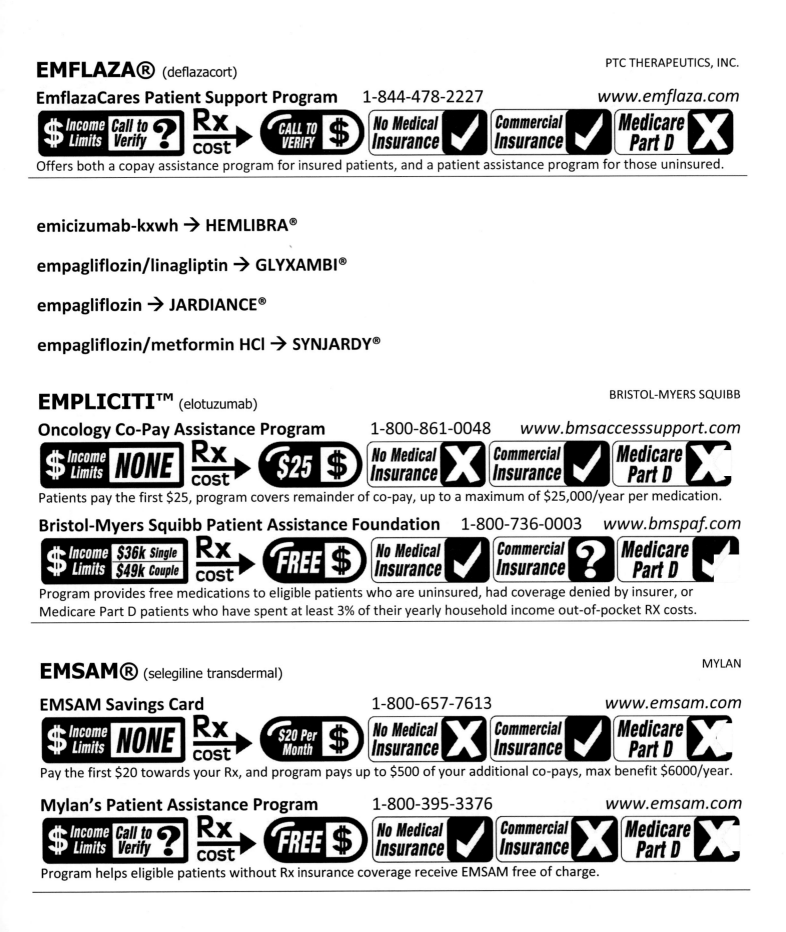

Offers both a copay assistance program for insured patients, and a patient assistance program for those uninsured.

emicizumab-kxwh → HEMLIBRA®

empagliflozin/linagliptin → GLYXAMBI®

empagliflozin → JARDIANCE®

empagliflozin/metformin HCl → SYNJARDY®

EMPLICITI™ (elotuzumab)

BRISTOL-MYERS SQUIBB

Oncology Co-Pay Assistance Program   1-800-861-0048   *www.bmsaccesssupport.com*

Patients pay the first $25, program covers remainder of co-pay, up to a maximum of $25,000/year per medication.

Bristol-Myers Squibb Patient Assistance Foundation   1-800-736-0003   *www.bmspaf.com*

Program provides free medications to eligible patients who are uninsured, had coverage denied by insurer, or Medicare Part D patients who have spent at least 3% of their yearly household income out-of-pocket RX costs.

EMSAM® (selegiline transdermal)

MYLAN

EMSAM Savings Card   1-800-657-7613   *www.emsam.com*

Pay the first $20 towards your Rx, and program pays up to $500 of your additional co-pays, max benefit $6000/year.

Mylan's Patient Assistance Program   1-800-395-3376   *www.emsam.com*

Program helps eligible patients without Rx insurance coverage receive EMSAM free of charge.

emtricitabine → EMTRIVA®

emtricitabine/rilpivirine/tenofovir alafenamide → ODEFSEY®

emtricitabine/rilpivirine/tenofovir disoproxil fumarate → COMPLERA®

emtricitabine/tenofovir alafenamide → DESCOVY®

emtricitabine/tenofovir disoproxil fumarate → TRUVADA®

EMTRIVA® (emtricitabine)

GILEAD SCIENCES, INC

Co-Pay Assistance Card Program   1-800-226-2056   www.gileadadvancingaccess.com

Program covers up to $3,600 in co-pays per year, with a monthly maximum of $300.

Gilead Advancing Access   1-800-226-2056   www.gileadadvancingaccess.com

Patient assistance program provides medications at no charge for eligible patients with no other insurance options.

EMVERM® (mebendazole)

IMPAX LABORATORIES, INC.

EMVERM Savings Card   1-866-325-7153   www.emverm.com

Patient pays first $20, next $60 is covered by savings card, and pt. pays any remaining costs above $80 total for Rx.

Impax Patient Assistance Program   1-877-764-9021   www.emverm.com

Provides free meds for qualified patients that do not have affordable coverage for the Rx. Medicare Part D patients must have spent at least 3% of annual household income out-of-pocket on prescription medicines to qualify.

emicizumab-kxwh → HEMLIBRA®

empagliflozin/linagliptin → GLYXAMBI®

empagliflozin → JARDIANCE®

enasidenib → OTEZLA®

ENBREL® (etanercept)

AMGEN, INC.

Enbrel Support Card 1-888-436-2735 *www.enbrel.com*

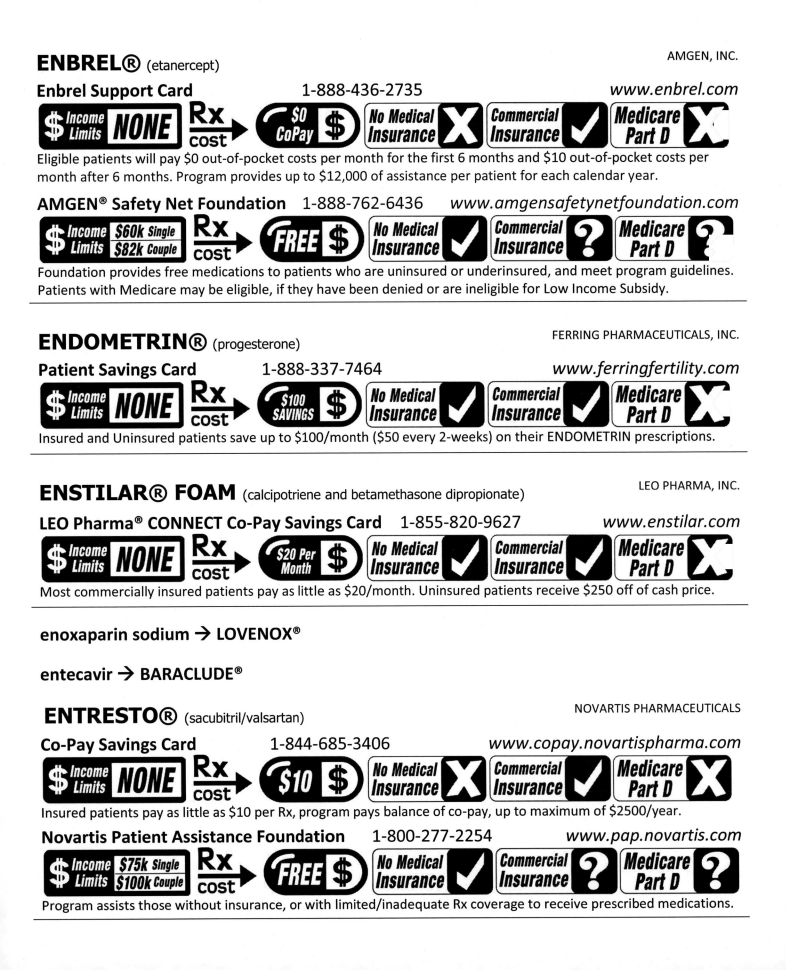

| $ Income Limits **NONE** | **Rx** cost → | $0 CoPay $ | No Medical Insurance ✗ | Commercial Insurance ✓ | Medicare Part D ✗ |

Eligible patients will pay $0 out-of-pocket costs per month for the first 6 months and $10 out-of-pocket costs per month after 6 months. Program provides up to $12,000 of assistance per patient for each calendar year.

AMGEN® Safety Net Foundation 1-888-762-6436 *www.amgensafetynetfoundation.com*

| $ Income Limits **$60k Single / $82k Couple** | **Rx** cost → | FREE $ | No Medical Insurance ✓ | Commercial Insurance ? | Medicare Part D ? |

Foundation provides free medications to patients who are uninsured or underinsured, and meet program guidelines. Patients with Medicare may be eligible, if they have been denied or are ineligible for Low Income Subsidy.

ENDOMETRIN® (progesterone)

FERRING PHARMACEUTICALS, INC.

Patient Savings Card 1-888-337-7464 *www.ferringfertility.com*

| $ Income Limits **NONE** | **Rx** cost → | $100 SAVINGS $ | No Medical Insurance ✓ | Commercial Insurance ✓ | Medicare Part D ✗ |

Insured and Uninsured patients save up to $100/month ($50 every 2-weeks) on their ENDOMETRIN prescriptions.

ENSTILAR® FOAM (calcipotriene and betamethasone dipropionate)

LEO PHARMA, INC.

LEO Pharma® CONNECT Co-Pay Savings Card 1-855-820-9627 *www.enstilar.com*

| $ Income Limits **NONE** | **Rx** cost → | $20 Per Month $ | No Medical Insurance ✓ | Commercial Insurance ✓ | Medicare Part D ✗ |

Most commercially insured patients pay as little as $20/month. Uninsured patients receive $250 off of cash price.

enoxaparin sodium → LOVENOX®

entecavir → BARACLUDE®

ENTRESTO® (sacubitril/valsartan)

NOVARTIS PHARMACEUTICALS

Co-Pay Savings Card 1-844-685-3406 *www.copay.novartispharma.com*

| $ Income Limits **NONE** | **Rx** cost → | $10 $ | No Medical Insurance ✗ | Commercial Insurance ✓ | Medicare Part D ✗ |

Insured patients pay as little as $10 per Rx, program pays balance of co-pay, up to maximum of $2500/year.

Novartis Patient Assistance Foundation 1-800-277-2254 *www.pap.novartis.com*

| $ Income Limits **$75k Single / $100k Couple** | **Rx** cost → | FREE $ | No Medical Insurance ✓ | Commercial Insurance ? | Medicare Part D ? |

Program assists those without insurance, or with limited/inadequate Rx coverage to receive prescribed medications.

ENTYVIO® (vedolizumab)
TAKEDA PHARMACEUTICALS AMERICA

EntyvioConnect Co-Pay Assistance Program   1-844-368-9846   www.entyvio.com

| $ Income Limits **NONE** | Rx cost → | **$5** $ | No Medical Insurance ✗ | Commercial Insurance ✓ | Medicare Part D ✗ |

Eligible patients with commercial insurance coverage can pay as little as $5 per dose of Entyvio.

EntyvioConnect Patient Assistance Program   1-844-368-9846   www.entyvio.com

| $ Income Limits **Call to Verify ?** | Rx cost → | **FREE** $ | No Medical Insurance ✓ | Commercial Insurance **?** | Medicare Part D ✗ |

Provides Entyvio at no cost to eligible patients who do not have insurance or are functionally uninsured.

ENEMEEZ® (docusate sodium)
ALLIANCE LABS

Enemeez Patient Assistance Program   1-888-273-9734   www.enemeezprovider.com

| $ Income Limits **$23k Single $31k Couple** | Rx cost → | **Discount Varies** $ | No Medical Insurance ✓ | Commercial Insurance **?** | Medicare Part D **?** |

Individuals who qualify will receive the medication for $42. Those with yearly income less than $10k will receive the medication for $26. If your insurance or Medicare plan does not cover Enemeez, you may also qualify.

ENVARSUS XR® (tacrolimus extended-release tablets)
VELOXIS PHARMACEUTICALS

$0 Co-Pay Savings Card   1-844-415-0673   www.envarsusxr.com

| $ Income Limits **NONE** | Rx cost → | **$0 CoPay** $ | No Medical Insurance ✗ | Commercial Insurance ✓ | Medicare Part D ✗ |

Patients can save up to a max benefit of $5,000 annually off their co-pay or out-of-pocket Envarsus XR expenses.

Patient Assistance Program   1-844-835-6947   www.envarsusxr.com

| $ Income Limits **Call to Verify ?** | Rx cost → | **FREE** $ | No Medical Insurance ✓ | Commercial Insurance ✗ | Medicare Part D ✗ |

Veloxis Transplant Support sends medications to eligible patients free of charge, who qualify for assistance.

enzalutamide → XTANDI®

EPCLUSA® (sofosbuvir/velpatasvir)
GILEAD SCIENCES, INC

EPCLUSA Co-pay Coupon Program   1-855-769-7284   www.epclusa.com

| $ Income Limits **NONE** | Rx cost → | **$5 Per Month** $ | No Medical Insurance ✗ | Commercial Insurance ✓ | Medicare Part D ✗ |

Covers cost over $5, up to a maximum of 25% of the catalog price of a 12-week regimen of EPCLUSA.

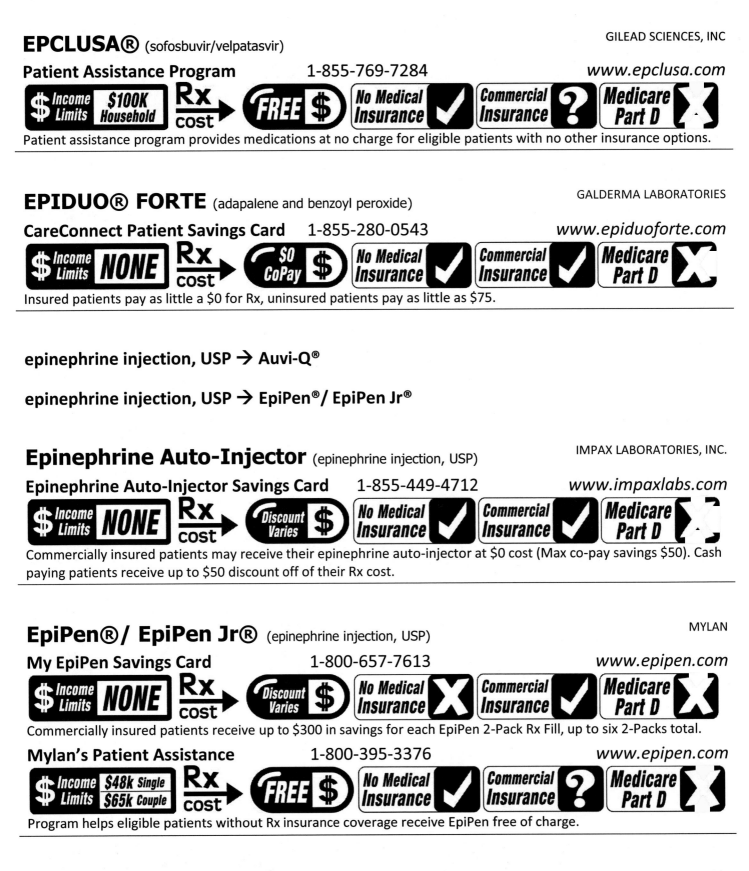

EPCLUSA® (sofosbuvir/velpatasvir)

GILEAD SCIENCES, INC

Patient Assistance Program   1-855-769-7284   www.epclusa.com

$ Income Limits **$100K Household** | Rx cost → | **FREE** $ | **No Medical Insurance** ✓ | **Commercial Insurance** ? | **Medicare Part D** ✗

Patient assistance program provides medications at no charge for eligible patients with no other insurance options.

EPIDUO® FORTE (adapalene and benzoyl peroxide)

GALDERMA LABORATORIES

CareConnect Patient Savings Card   1-855-280-0543   www.epiduoforte.com

$ Income Limits **NONE** | Rx cost → | **$0 CoPay** $ | **No Medical Insurance** ✓ | **Commercial Insurance** ✓ | **Medicare Part D** ✗

Insured patients pay as little a $0 for Rx, uninsured patients pay as little as $75.

epinephrine injection, USP → Auvi-Q®

epinephrine injection, USP → EpiPen®/ EpiPen Jr®

Epinephrine Auto-Injector (epinephrine injection, USP)

IMPAX LABORATORIES, INC.

Epinephrine Auto-Injector Savings Card   1-855-449-4712   www.impaxlabs.com

$ Income Limits **NONE** | Rx cost → | **Discount Varies** $ | **No Medical Insurance** ✓ | **Commercial Insurance** ✓ | **Medicare Part D** ✗

Commercially insured patients may receive their epinephrine auto-injector at $0 cost (Max co-pay savings $50). Cash paying patients receive up to $50 discount off of their Rx cost.

EpiPen®/ EpiPen Jr® (epinephrine injection, USP)

MYLAN

My EpiPen Savings Card   1-800-657-7613   www.epipen.com

$ Income Limits **NONE** | Rx cost → | **Discount Varies** $ | **No Medical Insurance** ✗ | **Commercial Insurance** ✓ | **Medicare Part D** ✗

Commercially insured patients receive up to $300 in savings for each EpiPen 2-Pack Rx Fill, up to six 2-Packs total.

Mylan's Patient Assistance   1-800-395-3376   www.epipen.com

$ Income Limits **$48k Single $65k Couple** | Rx cost → | **FREE** $ | **No Medical Insurance** ✓ | **Commercial Insurance** ? | **Medicare Part D** ✗

Program helps eligible patients without Rx insurance coverage receive EpiPen free of charge.

epirubicin HCL injection → ELLENCE®

EPIVIR® (lamivudine)

ViiV HEALTHCARE

ViiV Healthcare Patient Assistance Program   1-844-588-3288   *www.viivconnect.com*

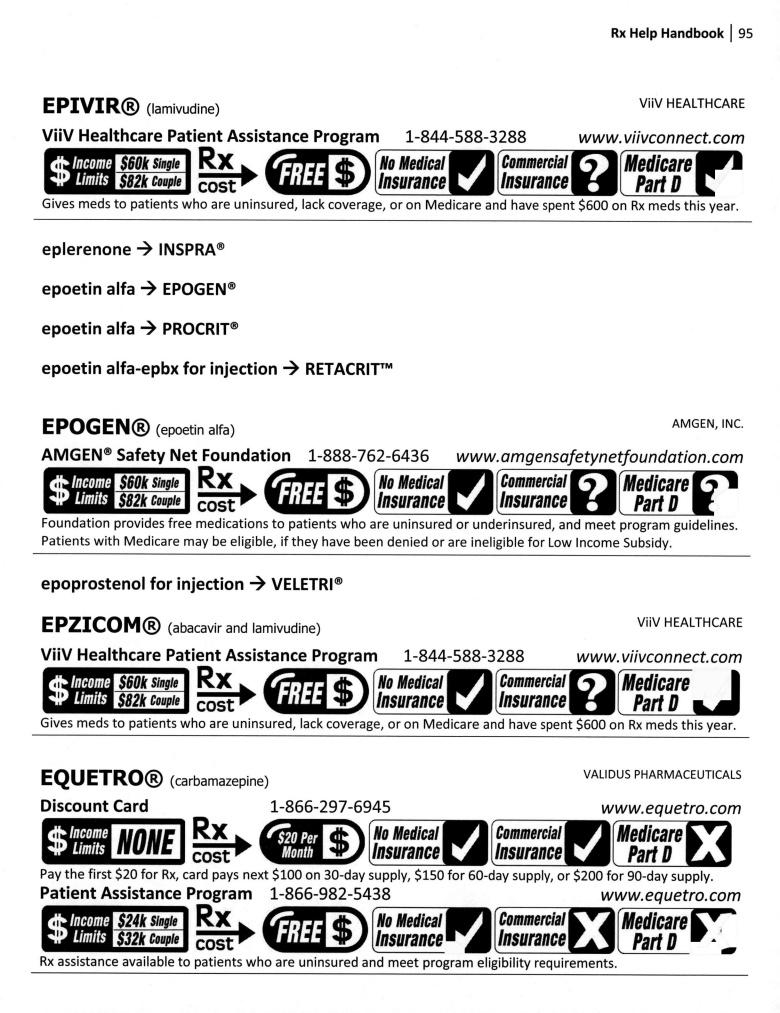

| $ Income Limits $60k Single $82k Couple | Rx cost → | FREE $ | No Medical Insurance ✓ | Commercial Insurance ? | Medicare Part D ✓ |

Gives meds to patients who are uninsured, lack coverage, or on Medicare and have spent $600 on Rx meds this year.

---

eplerenone → INSPRA®

epoetin alfa → EPOGEN®

epoetin alfa → PROCRIT®

epoetin alfa-epbx for injection → RETACRIT™

EPOGEN® (epoetin alfa)

AMGEN, INC.

AMGEN® Safety Net Foundation   1-888-762-6436   *www.amgensafetynetfoundation.com*

| $ Income Limits $60k Single $82k Couple | Rx cost → | FREE $ | No Medical Insurance ✓ | Commercial Insurance ? | Medicare Part D ? |

Foundation provides free medications to patients who are uninsured or underinsured, and meet program guidelines. Patients with Medicare may be eligible, if they have been denied or are ineligible for Low Income Subsidy.

---

epoprostenol for injection → VELETRI®

EPZICOM® (abacavir and lamivudine)

ViiV HEALTHCARE

ViiV Healthcare Patient Assistance Program   1-844-588-3288   *www.viivconnect.com*

| $ Income Limits $60k Single $82k Couple | Rx cost → | FREE $ | No Medical Insurance ✓ | Commercial Insurance ? | Medicare Part D ✓ |

Gives meds to patients who are uninsured, lack coverage, or on Medicare and have spent $600 on Rx meds this year.

EQUETRO® (carbamazepine)

VALIDUS PHARMACEUTICALS

Discount Card   1-866-297-6945   *www.equetro.com*

| $ Income Limits NONE | Rx cost → | $20 Per Month $ | No Medical Insurance ✓ | Commercial Insurance ✓ | Medicare Part D X |

Pay the first $20 for Rx, card pays next $100 on 30-day supply, $150 for 60-day supply, or $200 for 90-day supply.

Patient Assistance Program   1-866-982-5438   *www.equetro.com*

| $ Income Limits $24k Single $32k Couple | Rx cost → | FREE $ | No Medical Insurance ✓ | Commercial Insurance X | Medicare Part D X |

Rx assistance available to patients who are uninsured and meet program eligibility requirements.

ERAXIS® (anidulafungin)

PFIZER, INC

Pfizer Savings Program　　　1-866-706-2400　　　*www.pfizerrxpathways.com*

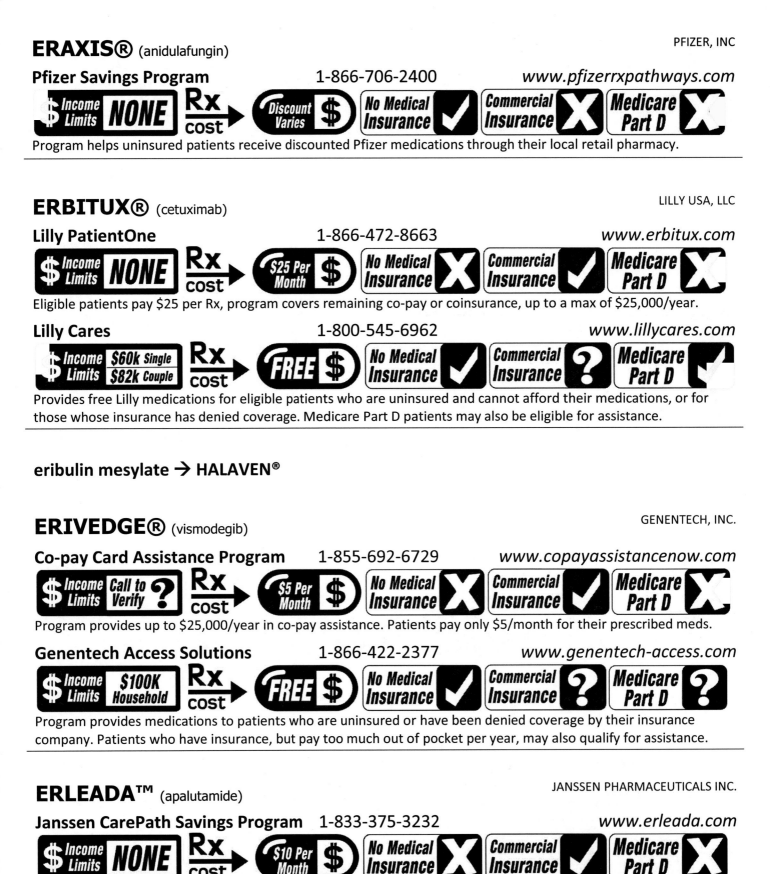

Income Limits **NONE** | Rx cost → | Discount Varies $ | **No Medical Insurance** ✓ | **Commercial Insurance** X | **Medicare Part D** X

Program helps uninsured patients receive discounted Pfizer medications through their local retail pharmacy.

ERBITUX® (cetuximab)

LILLY USA, LLC

Lilly PatientOne　　　1-866-472-8663　　　*www.erbitux.com*

Income Limits **NONE** | Rx cost → | $25 Per Month $ | **No Medical Insurance** X | **Commercial Insurance** ✓ | **Medicare Part D** X

Eligible patients pay $25 per Rx, program covers remaining co-pay or coinsurance, up to a max of $25,000/year.

Lilly Cares　　　1-800-545-6962　　　*www.lillycares.com*

Income Limits **$60k Single $82k Couple** | Rx cost → | **FREE** $ | **No Medical Insurance** ✓ | **Commercial Insurance** ? | **Medicare Part D** ✓

Provides free Lilly medications for eligible patients who are uninsured and cannot afford their medications, or for those whose insurance has denied coverage. Medicare Part D patients may also be eligible for assistance.

eribulin mesylate → HALAVEN®

ERIVEDGE® (vismodegib)

GENENTECH, INC.

Co-pay Card Assistance Program　　　1-855-692-6729　　　*www.copayassistancenow.com*

Income Limits **Call to Verify** ? | Rx cost → | $5 Per Month $ | **No Medical Insurance** X | **Commercial Insurance** ✓ | **Medicare Part D** X

Program provides up to $25,000/year in co-pay assistance. Patients pay only $5/month for their prescribed meds.

Genentech Access Solutions　　　1-866-422-2377　　　*www.genentech-access.com*

Income Limits **$100K Household** | Rx cost → | **FREE** $ | **No Medical Insurance** ✓ | **Commercial Insurance** ? | **Medicare Part D** ?

Program provides medications to patients who are uninsured or have been denied coverage by their insurance company. Patients who have insurance, but pay too much out of pocket per year, may also qualify for assistance.

ERLEADA™ (apalutamide)

JANSSEN PHARMACEUTICALS INC.

Janssen CarePath Savings Program　　　1-833-375-3232　　　*www.erleada.com*

Income Limits **NONE** | Rx cost → | $10 Per Month $ | **No Medical Insurance** X | **Commercial Insurance** ✓ | **Medicare Part D** X

Most commercially insured patients pay as little as $10 per month, maximum program benefit per year $15,000.

ERLEADA™ (apalutamide)

JANSSEN PHARMACEUTICALS INC.

J&J Patient Assistance Foundation   1-800-652-6227   *www.jjpaf.org*

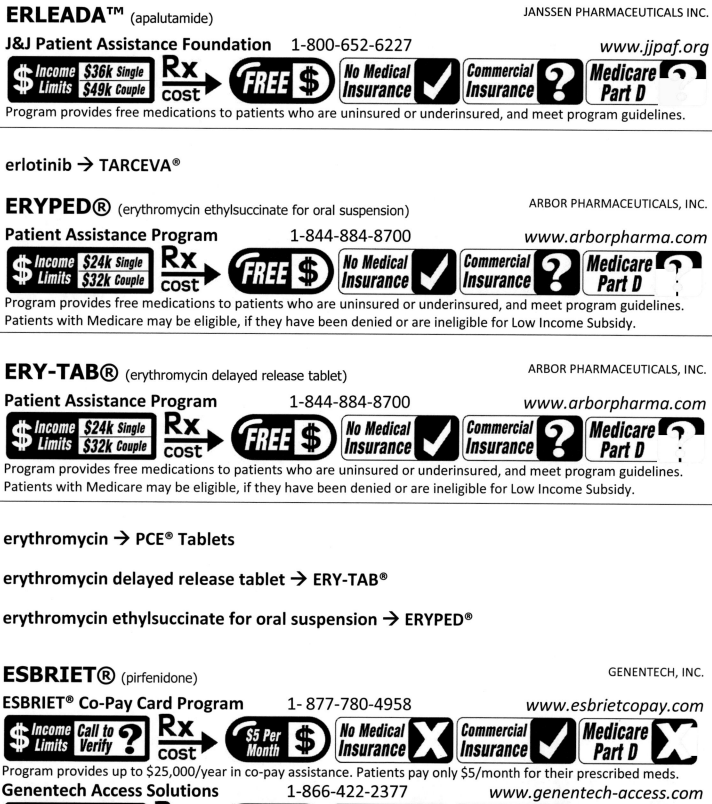

| $ Income Limits | $36k Single / $49k Couple | Rx cost → | FREE $ | No Medical Insurance ✓ | Commercial Insurance ? | Medicare Part D ? |

Program provides free medications to patients who are uninsured or underinsured, and meet program guidelines.

---

erlotinib → TARCEVA®

ERYPED® (erythromycin ethylsuccinate for oral suspension)

ARBOR PHARMACEUTICALS, INC.

Patient Assistance Program   1-844-884-8700   *www.arborpharma.com*

| $ Income Limits | $24k Single / $32k Couple | Rx cost → | FREE $ | No Medical Insurance ✓ | Commercial Insurance ? | Medicare Part D ? |

Program provides free medications to patients who are uninsured or underinsured, and meet program guidelines. Patients with Medicare may be eligible, if they have been denied or are ineligible for Low Income Subsidy.

ERY-TAB® (erythromycin delayed release tablet)

ARBOR PHARMACEUTICALS, INC.

Patient Assistance Program   1-844-884-8700   *www.arborpharma.com*

| $ Income Limits | $24k Single / $32k Couple | Rx cost → | FREE $ | No Medical Insurance ✓ | Commercial Insurance ? | Medicare Part D ? |

Program provides free medications to patients who are uninsured or underinsured, and meet program guidelines. Patients with Medicare may be eligible, if they have been denied or are ineligible for Low Income Subsidy.

---

erythromycin → PCE® Tablets

erythromycin delayed release tablet → ERY-TAB®

erythromycin ethylsuccinate for oral suspension → ERYPED®

ESBRIET® (pirfenidone)

GENENTECH, INC.

ESBRIET® Co-Pay Card Program   1- 877-780-4958   *www.esbrietcopay.com*

| $ Income Limits | Call to Verify ? | Rx cost → | $5 Per Month $ | No Medical Insurance ✗ | Commercial Insurance ✓ | Medicare Part D ✗ |

Program provides up to $25,000/year in co-pay assistance. Patients pay only $5/month for their prescribed meds.

Genentech Access Solutions   1-866-422-2377   *www.genentech-access.com*

| $ Income Limits | $100K Household | Rx cost → | FREE $ | No Medical Insurance ✓ | Commercial Insurance ? | Medicare Part D ? |

Program provides medications to patients who are uninsured or have been denied coverage by their insurance company. Patients who have insurance, but pay too much out of pocket per year, may also qualify for assistance.

eslicarbazepine acetate → APTIOM®

esomeprazole magnesium → NEXIUM®

esterified estrogens → MENEST®

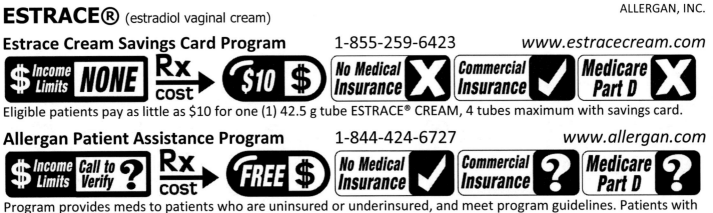

ESTRACE® (estradiol vaginal cream)   ALLERGAN, INC.

Estrace Cream Savings Card Program   1-855-259-6423   *www.estracecream.com*

$ Income Limits **NONE** | **Rx** cost → **$10** $ | **No Medical Insurance** X | **Commercial Insurance** ✓ | **Medicare Part D** X

Eligible patients pay as little as $10 for one (1) 42.5 g tube ESTRACE® CREAM, 4 tubes maximum with savings card.

Allergan Patient Assistance Program   1-844-424-6727   *www.allergan.com*

$ Income Limits **Call to Verify** ? | **Rx** cost → **FREE** $ | **No Medical Insurance** ✓ | **Commercial Insurance** ? | **Medicare Part D** ?

Program provides meds to patients who are uninsured or underinsured, and meet program guidelines. Patients with Medicare may be eligible, if they have been denied or are ineligible for Low Income Subsidy.

estradiol cypionate → DEPO®-ESTRADIOL

estradiol/horethindrone acetate transdermal system → COMBIPATCH®

estradiol/levonorgestrel transdermal system → CLIMARA PRO®

estradiol transdermal system → MENOSTAR®

estradiol transdermal system → MINIVELLE®

estradiol vaginal cream → ESTRACE®

estradiol vaginal inserts → VAGIFEM®

estradiol vaginal ring → ESTRING®

estradiol valerate and estradiol valerate/dienogest → NATAZIA®

estramustine phosphate sodium → EMCYT®

TIP: When in doubt... call the program and explain your situation. You may qualify for assistance.

ESTRING® (estradiol vaginal ring)

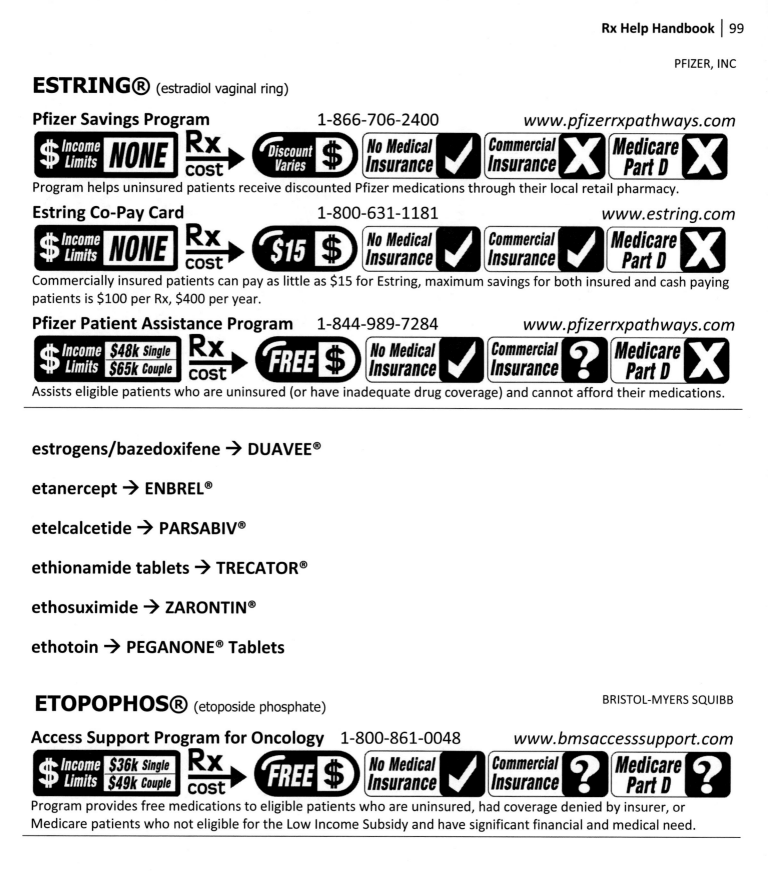

Pfizer Savings Program   1-866-706-2400   *www.pfizerrxpathways.com*

| $ Income Limits **NONE** | **Rx** cost → | Discount Varies $ | No Medical Insurance ✓ | Commercial Insurance ✗ | Medicare Part D ✗ |

Program helps uninsured patients receive discounted Pfizer medications through their local retail pharmacy.

Estring Co-Pay Card   1-800-631-1181   *www.estring.com*

| $ Income Limits **NONE** | **Rx** cost → | $15 $ | No Medical Insurance ✓ | Commercial Insurance ✓ | Medicare Part D ✗ |

Commercially insured patients can pay as little as $15 for Estring, maximum savings for both insured and cash paying patients is $100 per Rx, $400 per year.

Pfizer Patient Assistance Program   1-844-989-7284   *www.pfizerrxpathways.com*

| $ Income Limits $48k Single $65k Couple | **Rx** cost → | FREE $ | No Medical Insurance ✓ | Commercial Insurance ? | Medicare Part D ✗ |

Assists eligible patients who are uninsured (or have inadequate drug coverage) and cannot afford their medications.

---

estrogens/bazedoxifene → DUAVEE®

etanercept → ENBREL®

etelcalcetide → PARSABIV®

ethionamide tablets → TRECATOR®

ethosuximide → ZARONTIN®

ethotoin → PEGANONE® Tablets

ETOPOPHOS® (etoposide phosphate)

Access Support Program for Oncology   1-800-861-0048   *www.bmsaccesssupport.com*

| $ Income Limits $36k Single $49k Couple | **Rx** cost → | FREE $ | No Medical Insurance ✓ | Commercial Insurance ? | Medicare Part D ? |

Program provides free medications to eligible patients who are uninsured, had coverage denied by insurer, or Medicare patients who not eligible for the Low Income Subsidy and have significant financial and medical need.

---

etoposide phosphate → ETOPOPHOS®

etravirine → INTELENCE®

EUCRISA® (crisaborole) ointment, 2%

PFIZER, INC

EUCRISA Co-Pay Savings Card   1-866-382-7472   *www.eucrisa.com*

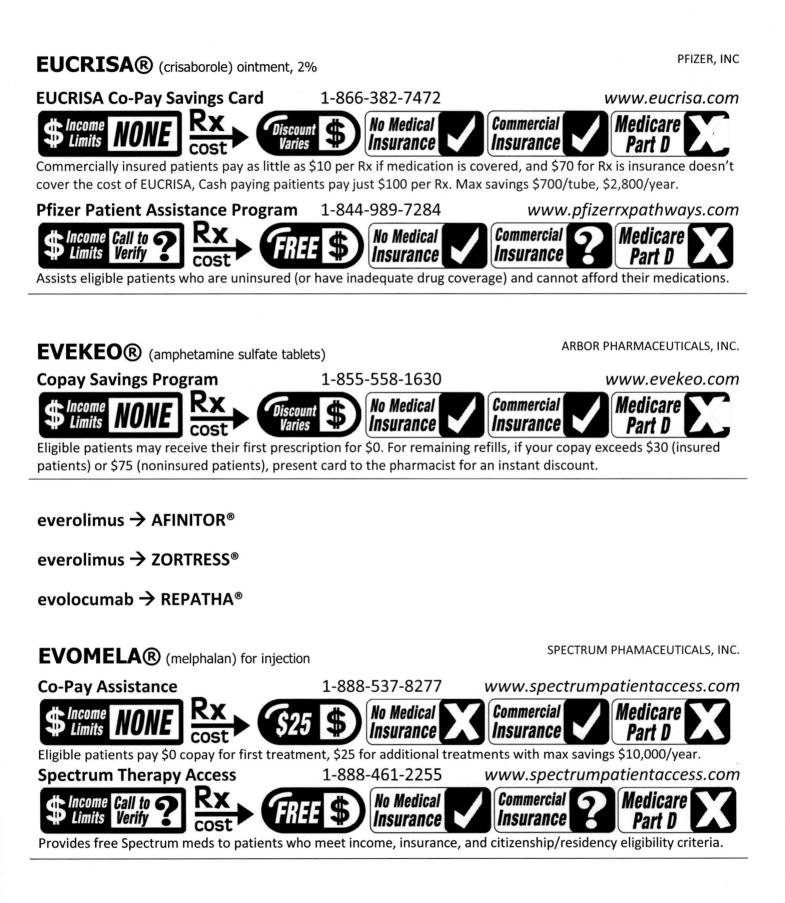

Commercially insured patients pay as little as $10 per Rx if medication is covered, and $70 for Rx is insurance doesn't cover the cost of EUCRISA, Cash paying paitients pay just $100 per Rx. Max savings $700/tube, $2,800/year.

Pfizer Patient Assistance Program   1-844-989-7284   *www.pfizerrxpathways.com*

Assists eligible patients who are uninsured (or have inadequate drug coverage) and cannot afford their medications.

EVEKEO® (amphetamine sulfate tablets)

ARBOR PHARMACEUTICALS, INC.

Copay Savings Program   1-855-558-1630   *www.evekeo.com*

Eligible patients may receive their first prescription for $0. For remaining refills, if your copay exceeds $30 (insured patients) or $75 (noninsured patients), present card to the pharmacist for an instant discount.

everolimus → AFINITOR®

everolimus → ZORTRESS®

evolocumab → REPATHA®

EVOMELA® (melphalan) for injection

SPECTRUM PHAMACEUTICALS, INC.

Co-Pay Assistance   1-888-537-8277   *www.spectrumpatientaccess.com*

Eligible patients pay $0 copay for first treatment, $25 for additional treatments with max savings $10,000/year.

Spectrum Therapy Access   1-888-461-2255   *www.spectrumpatientaccess.com*

Provides free Spectrum meds to patients who meet income, insurance, and citizenship/residency eligibility criteria.

EVOTAZ® (atazanavir/cobicistat)
BRISTOL-MYERS SQUIBB

Co-Pay Assist Card   1-888-281-8981   *www.bmscustomerconnect.com*

Helps pay your out-of-pocket Rx expenses (co-pay, co-insurance, deductibles), up to a maximum of $7.500/year.

BMS3assist Program   1-888-281-8981   *www.bmscustomerconnect.com*

Program provides free medications to eligible patients who are uninsured, had coverage denied by insurer, or Medicare Part D patients who have spent at least 3% of their yearly household income out-of-pocket RX costs.

EVZIO® (naloxone HCL injection)
KALEO, INC.

EVZIO2YOU   1-855-773-8946   *www.evzio.com*

Commercially insured patients pay absolutely nothing out of pocket for EVZIO.

KALÉO CARES Patient Assistance   1-502-213-7601   *www.evzio.org*

Eligible patients who are experiencing financial difficulties may be able to receive EVZIO at no cost.

EXALGO® (hydromorphone HCL)
MALLINCKRODT PHARMACEUTICALS

Mallinckrodt Patient Assistance   1-800-259-7765   *www.mallinckrodt.com*

Program for uninsured patients who may not be able to afford their Mallinckrodt medications, call for application.

exemestane tablets → AROMASIN®

exenatide injection → BYETTA®

exenatide extended-release for injection → BYDUREON® / BYDUREON® BCise™

EXJADE® (deferasirox)
NOVARTIS PHARMACEUTICALS

Universal Co-Pay Card   1-877-577-7756   *www.copay.novartisoncology.com*

Patients pay the first $25, the program pays the remaining co-pay or coinsurance to max benefit of $15,000/year.

EXJADE® (deferasirox)

NOVARTIS PHARMACEUTICALS

Novartis Patient Assistance   1-800-277-2254   *www.pap.novartis.com*

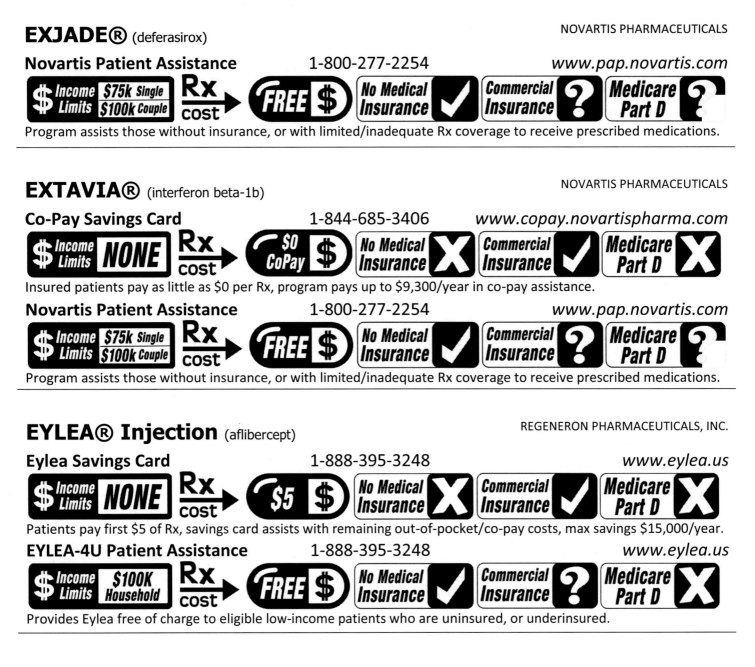

Program assists those without insurance, or with limited/inadequate Rx coverage to receive prescribed medications.

EXTAVIA® (interferon beta-1b)

NOVARTIS PHARMACEUTICALS

Co-Pay Savings Card   1-844-685-3406   *www.copay.novartispharma.com*

Insured patients pay as little as $0 per Rx, program pays up to $9,300/year in co-pay assistance.

Novartis Patient Assistance   1-800-277-2254   *www.pap.novartis.com*

Program assists those without insurance, or with limited/inadequate Rx coverage to receive prescribed medications.

EYLEA® Injection (aflibercept)

REGENERON PHARMACEUTICALS, INC.

Eylea Savings Card   1-888-395-3248   *www.eylea.us*

Patients pay first $5 of Rx, savings card assists with remaining out-of-pocket/co-pay costs, max savings $15,000/year.

EYLEA-4U Patient Assistance   1-888-395-3248   *www.eylea.us*

Provides Eylea free of charge to eligible low-income patients who are uninsured, or underinsured.

ezetimibe tablets → ZETIA®

ezetimibe and simvastatin → VYTORIN®

FABRAZYME® (agalsidase beta)

GENZYME CORPORATION

Sanofi Genzyme Co-Pay Assistance   1-800-745-4447   *www.fabrazyme.com*

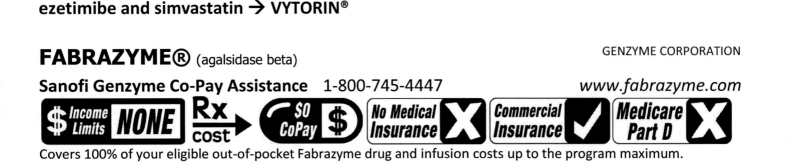

Covers 100% of your eligible out-of-pocket Fabrazyme drug and infusion costs up to the program maximum.

FABRAZYME® (agalsidase beta)

GENZYME CORPORATION

Charitable Access Program   1-800-745-4447   www.fabrazyme.com

$ Income Limits **Call to Verify** ? | **Rx** cost → | **FREE** $ | **No Medical Insurance** ✔ | **Commercial Insurance** ? | **Medicare Part D** ?

Program provides medications to patients who are uninsured or have inadequate insurance coverage for Fabrazyme

FANAPT® (iloperidone) tablets

VANDA PHARMCEUTICALS, INC.

Fanapt Savings Card   1-844-690-3770   www.fanapt.com

$ Income Limits **NONE** | **Rx** cost → | **$0 CoPay** $ | **No Medical Insurance** ✔ | **Commercial Insurance** ✔ | **Medicare Part D** X

Card pays up to $200 of Rx cost, insured patients can pay as little as $0 copay.

FARESTON® (toremifene citrate)

KYOWA KIRIN, INC.

Copay Assistance Program   1-800-676-5884   www.fareston.com

$ Income Limits **NONE** | **Rx** cost → | **$20 Per Month** $ | **No Medical Insurance** ✔ | **Commercial Insurance** ✔ | **Medicare Part D** X

Eligible patients pay the first $20 for Fareston Rx, remaining out-of-pocket costs reduced by $150 by program.

Fareston Patient Assistance   1-866-325-8231   www.patientrxsolutions.com

$ Income Limits **$36k Single $48k Couple** | **Rx** cost → | **FREE** $ | **No Medical Insurance** ✔ | **Commercial Insurance** X | **Medicare Part D** ✔

Provides Fareston to eligible patients who are uninsured or have been denied by Medicare, and have financial need.

FARXIGA® (dapagliflozin)

ASTRAZENECA PHARMACEUTICALS

FARXIGA Savings Card   1-844-631-3978   www.farxiga.com

$ Income Limits **NONE** | **Rx** cost → | **$0 CoPay** $ | **No Medical Insurance** ✔ | **Commercial Insurance** ✔ | **Medicare Part D** X

Insured patients pay as low as $0 per 30-day supply (maximum savings of $435 per 30-day supply). If you pay cash for your monthly Rx, AstraZeneca will pay up to the first $150, and you will be responsible for any remaining balance.

AZ&ME™   1-800-292-6363   www.azandmeapp.com

$ Income Limits **$36k Single $48k Couple** | **Rx** cost → | **FREE** $ | **No Medical Insurance** ✔ | **Commercial Insurance** X | **Medicare Part D** ?

Program provides free medications to patients who are uninsured and meet program guidelines. Patients with Medicare may be eligible, if they are not eligible for (or enrolled in) Limited Income Subsidy (LIS), and have spent at least 3% of their annual household income on Rx medications through their Medicare Part D plan in the current year.

FARYDAK® (panobinostat)

Universal Co-Pay Card   1-877-577-7756   www.copay.novartisoncology.com

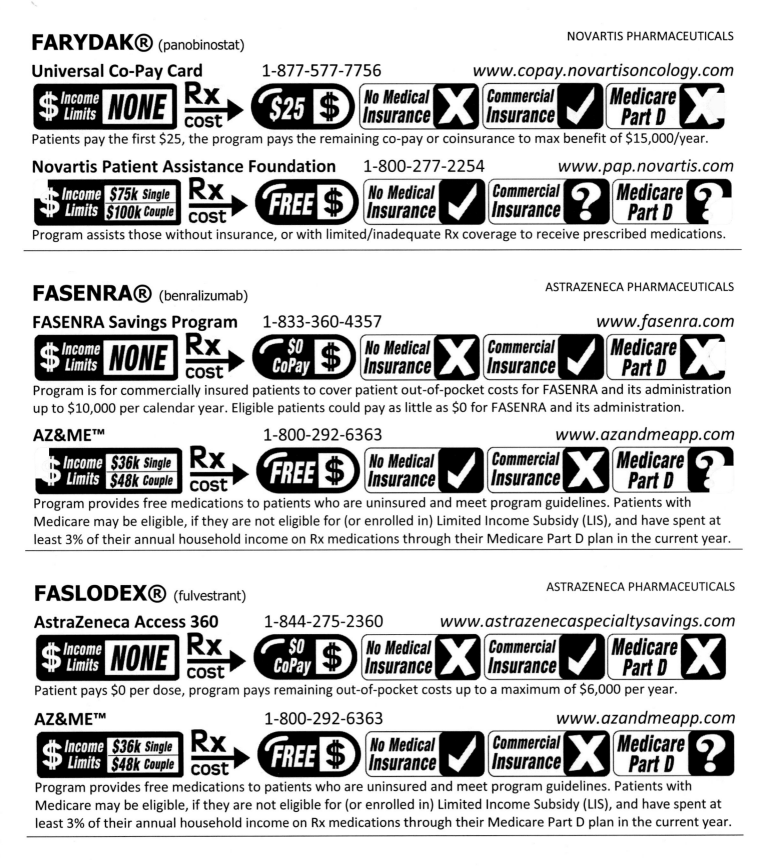

Income Limits NONE — **Rx cost** → $25 — **No Medical Insurance** ✗ — **Commercial Insurance** ✓ — **Medicare Part D** ✗

Patients pay the first $25, the program pays the remaining co-pay or coinsurance to max benefit of $15,000/year.

Novartis Patient Assistance Foundation   1-800-277-2254   www.pap.novartis.com

Income Limits $75k Single / $100k Couple — **Rx cost** → FREE — **No Medical Insurance** ✓ — **Commercial Insurance** ? — **Medicare Part D** ?

Program assists those without insurance, or with limited/inadequate Rx coverage to receive prescribed medications.

FASENRA® (benralizumab)

FASENRA Savings Program   1-833-360-4357   www.fasenra.com

Income Limits NONE — **Rx cost** → $0 CoPay — **No Medical Insurance** ✗ — **Commercial Insurance** ✓ — **Medicare Part D** ✗

Program is for commercially insured patients to cover patient out-of-pocket costs for FASENRA and its administration up to $10,000 per calendar year. Eligible patients could pay as little as $0 for FASENRA and its administration.

AZ&ME™   1-800-292-6363   www.azandmeapp.com

Income Limits $36k Single / $48k Couple — **Rx cost** → FREE — **No Medical Insurance** ✓ — **Commercial Insurance** ✗ — **Medicare Part D** ?

Program provides free medications to patients who are uninsured and meet program guidelines. Patients with Medicare may be eligible, if they are not eligible for (or enrolled in) Limited Income Subsidy (LIS), and have spent at least 3% of their annual household income on Rx medications through their Medicare Part D plan in the current year.

FASLODEX® (fulvestrant)

AstraZeneca Access 360   1-844-275-2360   www.astrazenecaspecialtysavings.com

Income Limits NONE — **Rx cost** → $0 CoPay — **No Medical Insurance** ✗ — **Commercial Insurance** ✓ — **Medicare Part D** ✗

Patient pays $0 per dose, program pays remaining out-of-pocket costs up to a maximum of $6,000 per year.

AZ&ME™   1-800-292-6363   www.azandmeapp.com

Income Limits $36k Single / $48k Couple — **Rx cost** → FREE — **No Medical Insurance** ✓ — **Commercial Insurance** ✗ — **Medicare Part D** ?

Program provides free medications to patients who are uninsured and meet program guidelines. Patients with Medicare may be eligible, if they are not eligible for (or enrolled in) Limited Income Subsidy (LIS), and have spent at least 3% of their annual household income on Rx medications through their Medicare Part D plan in the current year.

FEIBA® (Anti-Inhibitor Coagulant Complex)
BAXALTA, INC / SHIRE

Shire's CoPay Assistance Program   1-888-229-8379   *www.hematologysupport.com*

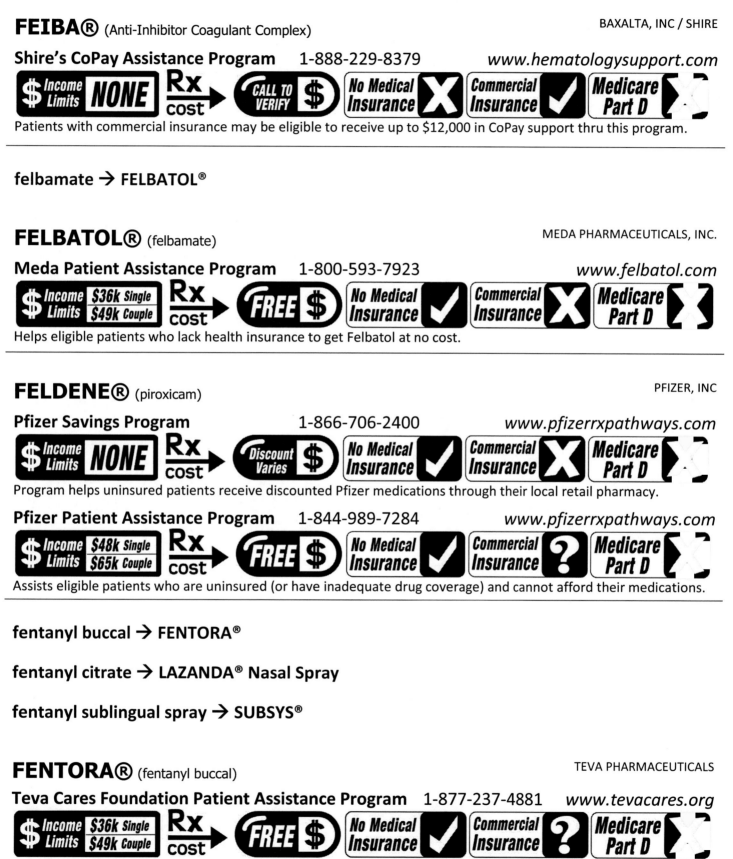

$ Income Limits NONE | **Rx cost** → | **CALL TO VERIFY $** | **No Medical Insurance X** | **Commercial Insurance ✓** | **Medicare Part D >**

Patients with commercial insurance may be eligible to receive up to $12,000 in CoPay support thru this program.

---

felbamate → FELBATOL®

FELBATOL® (felbamate)
MEDA PHARMACEUTICALS, INC.

Meda Patient Assistance Program   1-800-593-7923   *www.felbatol.com*

$ Income Limits $36k Single $49k Couple | **Rx cost** → | **FREE $** | **No Medical Insurance ✓** | **Commercial Insurance X** | **Medicare Part D >>**

Helps eligible patients who lack health insurance to get Felbatol at no cost.

FELDENE® (piroxicam)
PFIZER, INC

Pfizer Savings Program   1-866-706-2400   *www.pfizerrxpathways.com*

$ Income Limits NONE | **Rx cost** → | **Discount Varies $** | **No Medical Insurance ✓** | **Commercial Insurance X** | **Medicare Part D >**

Program helps uninsured patients receive discounted Pfizer medications through their local retail pharmacy.

Pfizer Patient Assistance Program   1-844-989-7284   *www.pfizerrxpathways.com*

$ Income Limits $48k Single $65k Couple | **Rx cost** → | **FREE $** | **No Medical Insurance ✓** | **Commercial Insurance ?** | **Medicare Part D >**

Assists eligible patients who are uninsured (or have inadequate drug coverage) and cannot afford their medications.

---

fentanyl buccal → FENTORA®

fentanyl citrate → LAZANDA® Nasal Spray

fentanyl sublingual spray → SUBSYS®

FENTORA® (fentanyl buccal)
TEVA PHARMACEUTICALS

Teva Cares Foundation Patient Assistance Program   1-877-237-4881   *www.tevacares.org*

$ Income Limits $36k Single $49k Couple | **Rx cost** → | **FREE $** | **No Medical Insurance ✓** | **Commercial Insurance ?** | **Medicare Part D >**

Provides Teva meds at no cost. If you don't qualify for Teva Cares, call 1-888-838-2872 for other assistance options.

ferric carboxymaltose injection → INJECTAFER®

ferric citrate → AURYXIA®

fesoterodine fumarate → TOVIAZ®

FETZIMA® Capsules & Titration Pack (levomilnacipran)

ALLERGAN, INC.

Allergan Patient Assistance Program   1-844-424-6727   *www.allergan.com*

Program provides meds to patients who are uninsured or underinsured, and meet program guidelines. Patients with Medicare may be eligible, if they have been denied or are ineligible for Low Income Subsidy.

FIASP® (insulin aspart injection)

NOVO NORDISK, INC.

Novo Nordisk Savings Card   1-877-304-6855   *www.novocare.com*

Pay as little as $25 per 30-day, $50 per 60-day, or $75 per 90-day supply for up to 24 months from the date of Savings Card activation, subject to a max savings of $100 per 30-day, $200 per 60-day, or $300 per 90-day supply.

Patient Access Program   1-866-310-7549   *www.novocare.com*

For patients who are uninsured. Also for Medicare patients who have spent more than $1000 this year on Rx meds.

fidaxomicin → DIFICID®

filgrastim → NEUPOGEN®

filgrastim-sndz → ZARXIO®

FINACEA® (azelaic acid)

BAYER HEALTHCARE PHARMACEUTICALS

Bayer Patient Assistance Program   1-866-575-5002   *Phone Only*

Program provides medications to patients based on financial need. Application must be completed by both you and your healthcare provider. Before calling number, make sure you have your Doctor's office fax and phone number, as well as the contact name at the office. Eligibility determined on a case-by-case basis.

fingolimod → GILENYA®

FIRAZYR® (icatibant injection)
SHIRE

OnePath Co-Pay Assistance Program   1-866-888-0660   *www.firazyr.com*

$ Income Limits NONE | **Rx cost** → | **$0 CoPay $** | **No Medical Insurance ✗** | **Commercial Insurance ✓** | **Medicare Part D ✗**

Program helps cover the cost of insurance co-pays for Firazyr, up to the program maximum, for eligible patients.

OnePath Patient Assistance Program   1-866-888-0660   *www.firazyr.com*

$ Income Limits Call to Verify ? | **Rx cost** → | **FREE $** | **No Medical Insurance ✓** | **Commercial Insurance ?** | **Medicare Part D ✗**

Program provides Shire medications to eligible patients who are uninsured, or have insurance that doesn't cover Rx.

FLAGYL® (metronidazole)
PFIZER, INC

Pfizer Savings Program   1-866-706-2400   *www.pfizerrxpathways.com*

$ Income Limits NONE | **Rx cost** → | **Discount Varies $** | **No Medical Insurance ✓** | **Commercial Insurance ✗** | **Medicare Part D ✗**

Program helps uninsured patients receive discounted Pfizer medications through their local retail pharmacy.

FLAREX® (fluorometholone acetate suspension)
NOVARTIS PHARMACEUTICALS

Novartis Patient Assistance Foundation   1-800-277-2254   *www.pap.novartis.com*

$ Income Limits $75k Single $100k Couple | **Rx cost** → | **FREE $** | **No Medical Insurance ✓** | **Commercial Insurance ?** | **Medicare Part D ?**

Program assists those without insurance, or with limited/inadequate Rx coverage to receive prescribed medications.

FLECTOR® PATCH (diclofenac epolamine)
PFIZER, INC

Pfizer Savings Program   1-866-706-2400   *www.pfizerrxpathways.com*

$ Income Limits NONE | **Rx cost** → | **Discount Varies $** | **No Medical Insurance ✓** | **Commercial Insurance ✗** | **Medicare Part D ✗**

Program helps uninsured patients receive discounted Pfizer medications through their local retail pharmacy.

Flector Patch Savings Card   1-877-620-1400   *www.flectorpatch.com*

$ Income Limits NONE | **Rx cost** → | **$4 $** | **No Medical Insurance ✓** | **Commercial Insurance ✓** | **Medicare Part D ✗**

Pay as little as $4 for Rx, maximum savings $120 per Rx, $360 per year.

Pfizer Patient Assistance Program   1-844-989-7284   *www.pfizerrxpathways.com*

$ Income Limits $48k Single $65k Couple | **Rx cost** → | **FREE $** | **No Medical Insurance ✓** | **Commercial Insurance ?** | **Medicare Part D ✗**

Assists eligible patients who are uninsured (or have inadequate drug coverage) and cannot afford their medications.

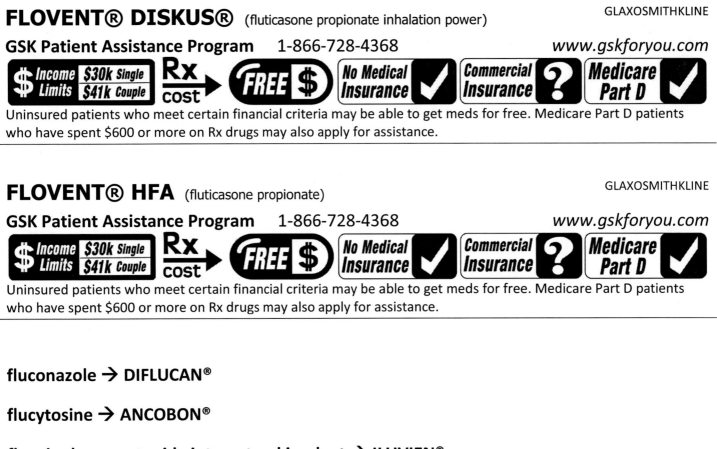

FLOVENT® DISKUS® (fluticasone propionate inhalation power) GLAXOSMITHKLINE

GSK Patient Assistance Program   1-866-728-4368   *www.gskforyou.com*

$ Income Limits $30k Single $41k Couple | Rx cost → | FREE $ | No Medical Insurance ✓ | Commercial Insurance ? | Medicare Part D ✓

Uninsured patients who meet certain financial criteria may be able to get meds for free. Medicare Part D patients who have spent $600 or more on Rx drugs may also apply for assistance.

FLOVENT® HFA (fluticasone propionate) GLAXOSMITHKLINE

GSK Patient Assistance Program   1-866-728-4368   *www.gskforyou.com*

$ Income Limits $30k Single $41k Couple | Rx cost → | FREE $ | No Medical Insurance ✓ | Commercial Insurance ? | Medicare Part D ✓

Uninsured patients who meet certain financial criteria may be able to get meds for free. Medicare Part D patients who have spent $600 or more on Rx drugs may also apply for assistance.

fluconazole → DIFLUCAN®

flucytosine → ANCOBON®

fluocinolone acetonide intravetreal implant → ILUVIEN®

fluocinolone acetonide 0.01%/hydroquinone 4%/tretinoin 0.05% → TRI-LUMA®

fluorometholone acetate suspension → FLAREX®

fluoxetine HCl → PROZAC®

fluticasone propionate inhalation power → FLOVENT® DISKUS®

fluticasone furoate inhalation powder → ARNUITY® ELLIPTA®

fluticasone furoate, umeclidinium, and vilanterol → TRELEGY ELLIPTA

fluticasone furoate and vilanterol inhalation powder → BREO ELLIPTA

fluticasone propionate → FLOVENT® HFA

fluticasone propionate and salmeterol → ADVAIR DISKUS®/ADVAIR HFA®

fluorouracil cream 0.5% → CARAC®

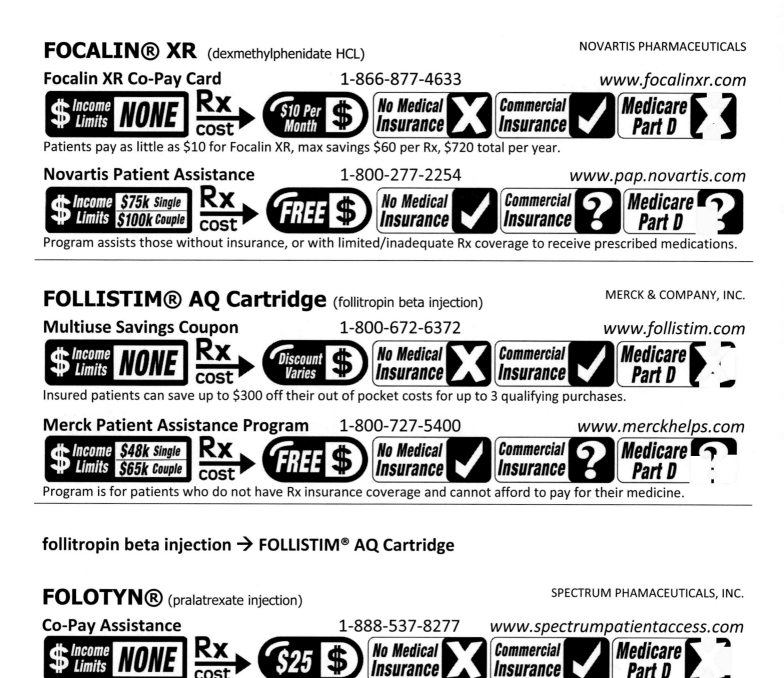

FOCALIN® XR (dexmethylphenidate HCL)   NOVARTIS PHARMACEUTICALS

Focalin XR Co-Pay Card   1-866-877-4633   www.focalinxr.com

$ Income Limits **NONE** | Rx cost → | $10 Per Month $ | No Medical Insurance **X** | Commercial Insurance ✓ | Medicare Part D **X**

Patients pay as little as $10 for Focalin XR, max savings $60 per Rx, $720 total per year.

Novartis Patient Assistance   1-800-277-2254   www.pap.novartis.com

$ Income Limits **$75k Single / $100k Couple** | Rx cost → | **FREE** $ | No Medical Insurance ✓ | Commercial Insurance **?** | Medicare Part D **?**

Program assists those without insurance, or with limited/inadequate Rx coverage to receive prescribed medications.

FOLLISTIM® AQ Cartridge (follitropin beta injection)   MERCK & COMPANY, INC.

Multiuse Savings Coupon   1-800-672-6372   www.follistim.com

$ Income Limits **NONE** | Rx cost → | Discount Varies $ | No Medical Insurance **X** | Commercial Insurance ✓ | Medicare Part D **X**

Insured patients can save up to $300 off their out of pocket costs for up to 3 qualifying purchases.

Merck Patient Assistance Program   1-800-727-5400   www.merckhelps.com

$ Income Limits **$48k Single / $65k Couple** | Rx cost → | **FREE** $ | No Medical Insurance ✓ | Commercial Insurance **?** | Medicare Part D **?**

Program is for patients who do not have Rx insurance coverage and cannot afford to pay for their medicine.

follitropin beta injection → FOLLISTIM® AQ Cartridge

FOLOTYN® (pralatrexate injection)   SPECTRUM PHAMACEUTICALS, INC.

Co-Pay Assistance   1-888-537-8277   www.spectrumpatientaccess.com

$ Income Limits **NONE** | Rx cost → | $25 $ | No Medical Insurance **X** | Commercial Insurance ✓ | Medicare Part D **X**

Eligible patients pay $0 copay for first treatment, $25 for additional treatments with max savings $10,000/year.

Spectrum Therapy Access Resources   1-888-461-2255   www.spectrumpatientaccess.com

$ Income Limits **Call to Verify ?** | Rx cost → | **FREE** $ | No Medical Insurance ✓ | Commercial Insurance **?** | Medicare Part D **X**

Provides free Spectrum meds to patients who meet income, insurance, and citizenship/residency eligibility criteria.

TIP: When in doubt... call the program and explain your situation. You may qualify for assistance.

FORFIVO XL® (bupropion HCL)

INTELGENX CORP/ALMATICA PHARMA, INC.

Forfivo XL Savings Program   1-877-447-7979   *www.forfivoxl.com*

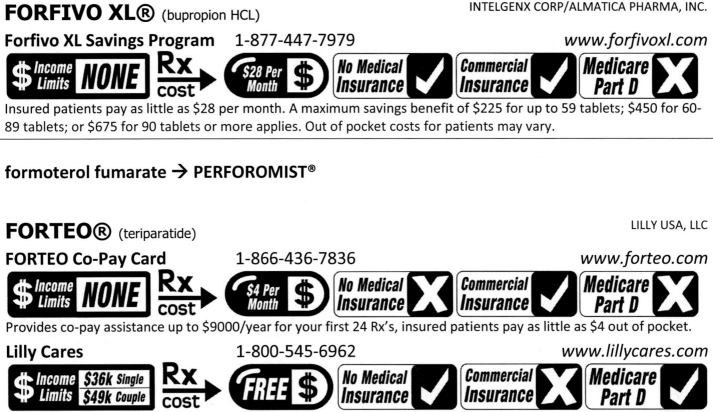

Insured patients pay as little as $28 per month. A maximum savings benefit of $225 for up to 59 tablets; $450 for 60-89 tablets; or $675 for 90 tablets or more applies. Out of pocket costs for patients may vary.

---

formoterol fumarate → PERFOROMIST®

FORTEO® (teriparatide)

LILLY USA, LLC

FORTEO Co-Pay Card   1-866-436-7836   *www.forteo.com*

Provides co-pay assistance up to $9000/year for your first 24 Rx's, insured patients pay as little as $4 out of pocket.

Lilly Cares   1-800-545-6962   *www.lillycares.com*

Provides free Lilly medications for eligible patients who are uninsured and cannot afford their medications. Medicare Part D patients are eligible for assistance, after they have spent $1,100 on Rx meds in a calendar year.

---

fosamprenavir calcium → LEXIVA®

---

fosfomycin → MONUROL® Powder

FOSRENOL® (lanthanum carbonate)

SHIRE

Shire Cares Patient Assistance & Support   1-888-227-3755   *www.shire.com*

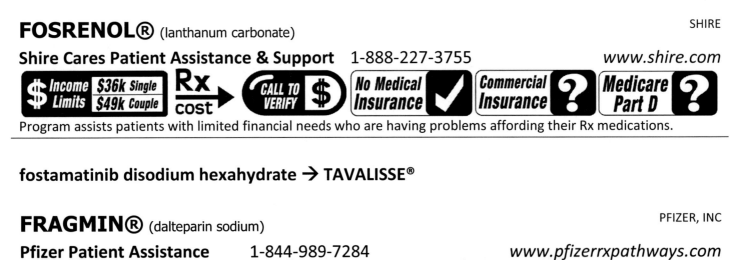

Program assists patients with limited financial needs who are having problems affording their Rx medications.

---

fostamatinib disodium hexahydrate → TAVALISSE®

FRAGMIN® (dalteparin sodium)

PFIZER, INC

Pfizer Patient Assistance   1-844-989-7284   *www.pfizerrxpathways.com*

Assists eligible patients who are uninsured (or have inadequate drug coverage) and cannot afford their medications.

fulvestrant → FASLODEX®

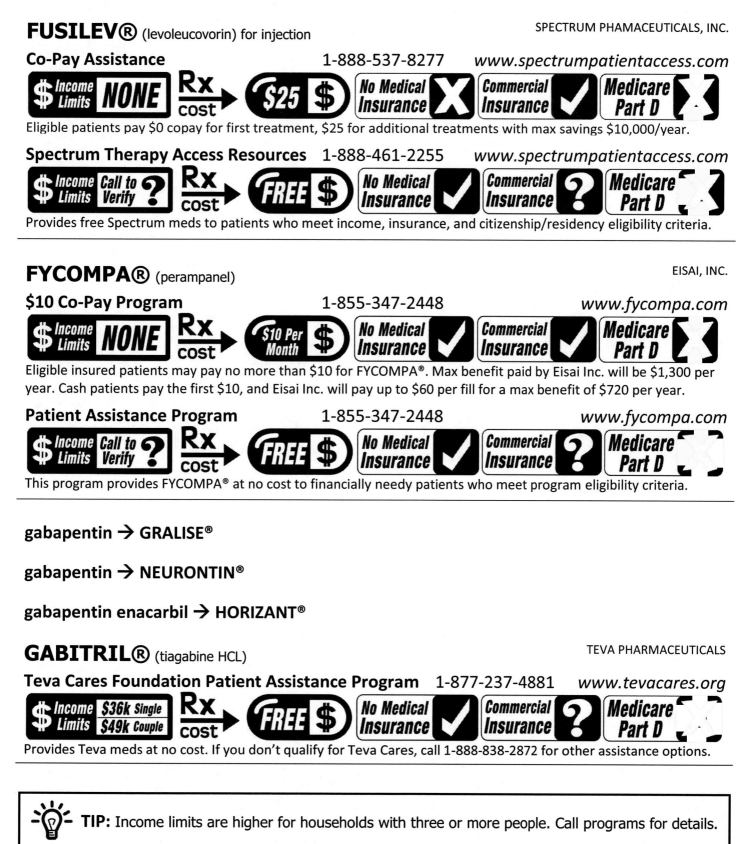

FUSILEV® (levoleucovorin) for injection   SPECTRUM PHAMACEUTICALS, INC.

Co-Pay Assistance   1-888-537-8277   *www.spectrumpatientaccess.com*

$ Income Limits **NONE** | Rx cost → | **$25** $ | **No Medical Insurance** ✗ | **Commercial Insurance** ✓ | **Medicare Part D** ✗

Eligible patients pay $0 copay for first treatment, $25 for additional treatments with max savings $10,000/year.

Spectrum Therapy Access Resources   1-888-461-2255   *www.spectrumpatientaccess.com*

$ Income Limits | Call to Verify **?** | Rx cost → | **FREE** $ | **No Medical Insurance** ✓ | **Commercial Insurance ?** | **Medicare Part D** ✗

Provides free Spectrum meds to patients who meet income, insurance, and citizenship/residency eligibility criteria.

FYCOMPA® (perampanel)   EISAI, INC.

$10 Co-Pay Program   1-855-347-2448   *www.fycompa.com*

$ Income Limits **NONE** | Rx cost → | **$10 Per Month** $ | **No Medical Insurance** ✓ | **Commercial Insurance** ✓ | **Medicare Part D** ✗

Eligible insured patients may pay no more than $10 for FYCOMPA®. Max benefit paid by Eisai Inc. will be $1,300 per year. Cash patients pay the first $10, and Eisai Inc. will pay up to $60 per fill for a max benefit of $720 per year.

Patient Assistance Program   1-855-347-2448   *www.fycompa.com*

$ Income Limits | Call to Verify **?** | Rx cost → | **FREE** $ | **No Medical Insurance** ✓ | **Commercial Insurance ?** | **Medicare Part D**

This program provides FYCOMPA® at no cost to financially needy patients who meet program eligibility criteria.

---

gabapentin → GRALISE®

gabapentin → NEURONTIN®

gabapentin enacarbil → HORIZANT®

GABITRIL® (tiagabine HCL)   TEVA PHARMACEUTICALS

Teva Cares Foundation Patient Assistance Program   1-877-237-4881   *www.tevacares.org*

$ Income Limits **$36k Single / $49k Couple** | Rx cost → | **FREE** $ | **No Medical Insurance** ✓ | **Commercial Insurance ?** | **Medicare Part D** ✗

Provides Teva meds at no cost. If you don't qualify for Teva Cares, call 1-888-838-2872 for other assistance options.

💡 **TIP:** Income limits are higher for households with three or more people. Call programs for details.

GALZIN® (zinc acetate)

Teva Cares Foundation Patient Assistance Program   1-877-237-4881   *www.tevacares.org*

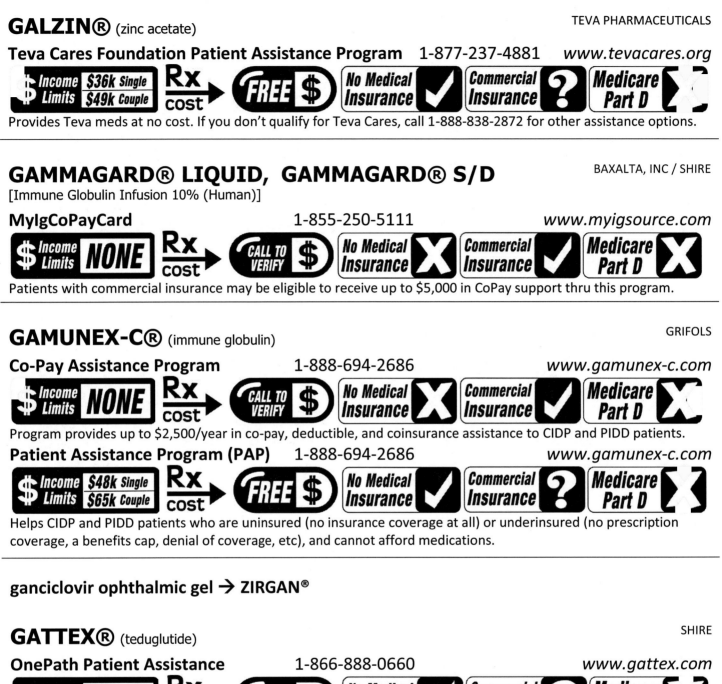

Provides Teva meds at no cost. If you don't qualify for Teva Cares, call 1-888-838-2872 for other assistance options.

GAMMAGARD® LIQUID, GAMMAGARD® S/D

[Immune Globulin Infusion 10% (Human)]

MyIgCoPayCard   1-855-250-5111   *www.myigsource.com*

Patients with commercial insurance may be eligible to receive up to $5,000 in CoPay support thru this program.

GAMUNEX-C® (immune globulin)

Co-Pay Assistance Program   1-888-694-2686   *www.gamunex-c.com*

Program provides up to $2,500/year in co-pay, deductible, and coinsurance assistance to CIDP and PIDD patients.

Patient Assistance Program (PAP)   1-888-694-2686   *www.gamunex-c.com*

Helps CIDP and PIDD patients who are uninsured (no insurance coverage at all) or underinsured (no prescription coverage, a benefits cap, denial of coverage, etc), and cannot afford medications.

ganciclovir ophthalmic gel → ZIRGAN®

GATTEX® (teduglutide)

OnePath Patient Assistance   1-866-888-0660   *www.gattex.com*

Program provides Shire medications to eligible patients who are uninsured, or have insurance that doesn't cover Rx.

GAZYVA® (obinutuzumab)

Co-pay Card Assistance Program   1-855-692-6729   *www.copayassistancenow.com*

Program provides up to $25,000/year in co-pay assistance. Patients pay only $5/month for their prescribed meds.

GAZYVA® (obinutuzumab)

GENENTECH, INC.

Genentech Access Solutions   1-866-422-2377   *www.genentech-access.com*

Program provides medications to patients who are uninsured or have been denied coverage by their insurance company. Patients who have insurance, but pay too much out of pocket per year, may also qualify for assistance.

GELNIQUE® (oxybutynin chloride 10% gel)

ALLERGAN, INC.

Allergan Patient Assistance Program   1-844-424-6727   *www.allergan.com*

Program provides meds to patients who are uninsured or underinsured, and meet program guidelines. Patients with Medicare may be eligible, if they have been denied or are ineligible for Low Income Subsidy.

gemfibrozil → LOPID®

gemtuzumab ozogamicin → MYLOTARG®

GENGRAF® CAPSULES (cyclosporine capsules)

AbbVie, INC.

AbbVie Patient Assistance Foundation   1-800-222-6885   *www.abbviepaf.org*

Rx assistance available to patients who are uninsured and meet program eligibility requirements. Patients with Commercial Insurance or Medicare Part D, who are struggling to pay for their medications, are encouraged to apply.

GENOTROPIN® (somatropin) for injection

PFIZER, INC

Genotropin Savings Program   1-800-645-1280   *www.genotropin.com*

Eligible patients pay as little as $0 CoPay for Rx, maximum savings $5000 per year.

Pfizer Patient Assistance Program   1-844-989-7284   *www.pfizerrxpathways.com*

Assists eligible patients who are uninsured (or have inadequate drug coverage) and cannot afford their medications.

GENVOYA® (elvitegravir/cobicistat/emtricitabine/tenofovir alafenamide)

GILEAD SCIENCES, INC

Co-Pay Assistance Card Program   1-800-226-2056   www.genvoya.com

Income Limits **NONE** | **Rx** cost → | $0 CoPay $ | No Medical Insurance **X** | Commercial Insurance ✔ | Medicare Part D **X**

Program helps pay for the cost of prescription co-pays up to $7,200 per product per year.

Gilead Advancing Access   1-800-226-2056   www.gileadadvancingaccess.com

Income Limits Call to Verify **?** | **Rx** cost → | FREE $ | No Medical Insurance ✔ | Commercial Insurance **?** | Medicare Part D **X**

Patient assistance program provides medications at no charge for eligible patients with no other insurance options.

GEODON® (ziprasidone HCL)

PFIZER, INC

Pfizer Savings Program   1-866-706-2400   www.pfizerrxpathways.com

Income Limits **NONE** | **Rx** cost → | Discount Varies $ | No Medical Insurance ✔ | Commercial Insurance **X** | Medicare Part D **X**

Program helps uninsured patients receive discounted Pfizer medications through their local retail pharmacy.

Geodon Savings Card   1-800-725-9655   www.geodon.com

Income Limits **NONE** | **Rx** cost → | $4 Per Month $ | No Medical Insurance ✔ | Commercial Insurance ✔ | Medicare Part D **X**

Eligible patients pay as little as $4 per month for Rx, maximum savings $250/month, $3000/year.

getfitinib → IRESSA® Tablets

GILENYA® (fingolimod)

NOVARTIS PHARMACEUTICALS

Co-Pay Savings Card   1-844-685-3406   www.copay.novartispharma.com

Income Limits **NONE** | **Rx** cost → | $0 CoPay $ | No Medical Insurance **X** | Commercial Insurance ✔ | Medicare Part D **X**

Insured patients pay as little as $0 per Rx, call 1-800-GILENYA for info/details.

Novartis Patient Assistance Foundation   1-800-277-2254   www.pap.novartis.com

Income Limits $75k Single $100k Couple | **Rx** cost → | FREE $ | No Medical Insurance ✔ | Commercial Insurance **?** | Medicare Part D **?**

Program assists those without insurance, or with limited/inadequate Rx coverage to receive prescribed medications.

💡 **TIP:** When in doubt... call the program and explain your situation. You may qualify for assistance.

GILOTRIF® (afatinib)

BOEHRINGER INGELHEIM PHARMACEUTICALS, INC.

Solutions Plus Co-Pay Assistance Program   1-877-814-3915   *www.gilotrif.com*

Program allows eligible, commercially insured patients to pay no more than $25 co-pay per month for their medicine.

Boehringer Ingelheim Cares Foundation   1-877-814-3915   *www.gilotrif.com*

Helps uninsured patients get treatment with GILOTRIF, those underinsured and on Medicare may also apply.

---

glatiramer acetate → GLATOPA®

GLATOPA® (glatiramer acetate)

NOVARTIS PHARMACEUTICALS

Glatopa Co-Pay Program   1-855-452-8672   *www.glatopa.com*

Commercially insured patients canpay as little as $0 for their Glatopa prescription, the program pays the remaining co-pay to a maximum benefit of $9,000/year.

Novartis Patient Assistance Foundation   1-800-277-2254   *www.pap.novartis.com*

Program assists qualified patients without insurance (or with limited/inadequate Rx coverage) who cannot afford their prescribed medications. Call program for complete details

---

glecaprevir and pibrentasvir → MAVYRET®

GLEEVEC® (imatinib mesylate)

NOVARTIS PHARMACEUTICALS

Gleevec Savings Card   1-866-453-3832   *www.gleevec.com*

Commercially insured patients pay a $10 co-pay, program will pay remaining out-of-pocket costs up to $10,630 per 30-day supply, up to an annual maximum assistance of $30,000.

Novartis Patient Assistance Foundation   1-800-277-2254   *www.pap.novartis.com*

Program assists those without insurance, or with limited/inadequate Rx coverage to receive prescribed medications.

glipizide → GLUCOTROL®

glycerol phenylbutyrate → RAVICTI®

glycopyrrolate → SEEBRI® NEOHALER®

GLUCAGEN® HYPOKIT® (glucagon (rDNA) for injection)   NOVO NORDISK, INC.

Patient Access Program   1-866-310-7549   *www.glucagenhypokit.com*

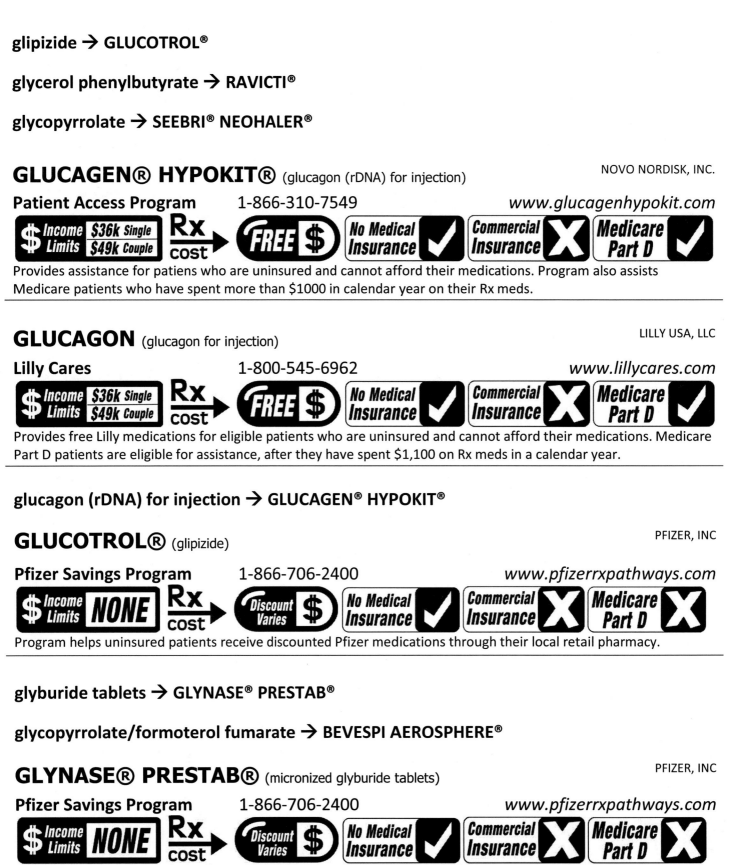

$ Income Limits **$36k Single / $49k Couple**   **Rx cost →** FREE **$**   No Medical Insurance ✓   Commercial Insurance ✗   Medicare Part D ✓

Provides assistance for patiens who are uninsured and cannot afford their medications. Program also assists Medicare patients who have spent more than $1000 in calendar year on their Rx meds.

GLUCAGON (glucagon for injection)   LILLY USA, LLC

Lilly Cares   1-800-545-6962   *www.lillycares.com*

$ Income Limits **$36k Single / $49k Couple**   **Rx cost →** FREE **$**   No Medical Insurance ✓   Commercial Insurance ✗   Medicare Part D ✓

Provides free Lilly medications for eligible patients who are uninsured and cannot afford their medications. Medicare Part D patients are eligible for assistance, after they have spent $1,100 on Rx meds in a calendar year.

---

glucagon (rDNA) for injection → GLUCAGEN® HYPOKIT®

GLUCOTROL® (glipizide)   PFIZER, INC

Pfizer Savings Program   1-866-706-2400   *www.pfizerrxpathways.com*

$ Income Limits **NONE**   **Rx cost →** Discount Varies **$**   No Medical Insurance ✓   Commercial Insurance ✗   Medicare Part D ✗

Program helps uninsured patients receive discounted Pfizer medications through their local retail pharmacy.

---

glyburide tablets → GLYNASE® PRESTAB®

glycopyrrolate/formoterol fumarate → BEVESPI AEROSPHERE®

GLYNASE® PRESTAB® (micronized glyburide tablets)   PFIZER, INC

Pfizer Savings Program   1-866-706-2400   *www.pfizerrxpathways.com*

$ Income Limits **NONE**   **Rx cost →** Discount Varies **$**   No Medical Insurance ✓   Commercial Insurance ✗   Medicare Part D ✗

Program helps uninsured patients receive discounted Pfizer medications through their local retail pharmacy.

GLYSET® (miglitol)

PFIZER, INC

Pfizer Savings Program   1-866-706-2400   *www.pfizerrxpathways.com*

Income Limits **NONE** | Rx cost → Discount Varies $ | No Medical Insurance ✓ | Commercial Insurance ✗ | Medicare Part D ❯

Program helps uninsured patients receive discounted Pfizer medications through their local retail pharmacy.

Pfizer Patient Assistance Program   1-844-989-7284   *www.pfizerrxpathways.com*

Income Limits **$48k Single / $65k Couple** | Rx cost → FREE $ | No Medical Insurance ✓ | Commercial Insurance ? | Medicare Part D ✗

Assists eligible patients who are uninsured (or have inadequate drug coverage) and cannot afford their medications.

GLYXAMBI® (empagliflozin/linagliptin)

BOEHRINGER INGELHEIM PHARMACEUTICALS, INC.

GLYXAMBI Savings Card   1-855-459-9262   *www.glyxambi.com*

Income Limits **NONE** | Rx cost → $0 CoPay $ | No Medical Insurance ✗ | Commercial Insurance ✓ | Medicare Part D ❯

Eligible insured patients pay as low as $0 per month for GLYXAMBI (maximum savings of $400/monthly prescription).

Boehringer Ingelheim Cares Foundation   1-800-556-8317   *www.bipatientassistance.com*

Income Limits **Call to Verify** ? | Rx cost → FREE $ | No Medical Insurance ✓ | Commercial Insurance ? | Medicare Part D ?

Patient Assistance Program provides free medications to patients who are uninsured or underinsured, and meet program guidelines. Patients with Medicare may be eligible, if they are ineligible for Low Income Subsidy.

golimumab → SIMPONI®

GRALISE® (gabapentin)

DEPOMED, INC.

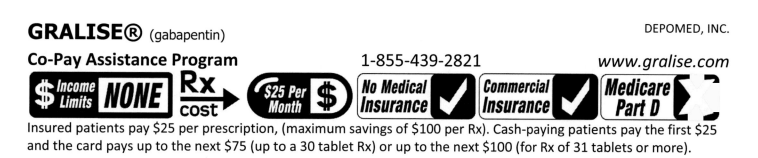

Co-Pay Assistance Program   1-855-439-2821   *www.gralise.com*

Income Limits **NONE** | Rx cost → $25 Per Month $ | No Medical Insurance ✓ | Commercial Insurance ✓ | Medicare Part D ❯

Insured patients pay $25 per prescription, (maximum savings of $100 per Rx). Cash-paying patients pay the first $25 and the card pays up to the next $75 (up to a 30 tablet Rx) or up to the next $100 (for Rx of 31 tablets or more).

granisetron transdermal system → SANCUSO®

TIP: When in doubt... call the program and explain your situation. You may qualify for assistance.

GRANIX® (tbo-filgrastim)

Granix Patient Savings Program   1-888-587-3263   *www.granixrx.com*

Eligible patients pay as little as $0 Copay/Coinsurance, with max savings of $14,000/year.

Teva Cares Foundation Patient Assistance Program   1-877-237-4881   *www.tevacares.org*

Provides Teva meds at no cost. If you don't qualify for Teva Cares, call 1-888-838-2872 for other assistance options.

guanfacine → INTUNIV®

guselkumab → TREMFYA®

HALAVEN® (eribulin mesylate)

EISAI, INC.

$0 Co-Pay Program   1-866-613-4724   *www.halaven.com*

Eligible patients may pay no more than $0 for HALAVEN®. Max benefit paid by Eisai Inc. will be $18,000 per year.

Patient Assistance Program   1-866-613-4724   *www.halaven.com*

This program provides HALAVEN® at no cost to financially needy patients who meet program eligibility criteria.

HALCION® (triazolam)

PFIZER, INC

Pfizer Savings Program   1-866-706-2400   *www.pfizerrxpathways.com*

Program helps uninsured patients receive discounted Pfizer medications through their local retail pharmacy.

HALDOL® (haloperidol)

JANSSEN PHARMACEUTICALS INC.

J&J Patient Assistance Foundation   1-800-652-6227   *www.jjpaf.org*

Program provides free medications to eligible patients who are uninsured or underinsured, and meet program guidelines. Call for complete details and eligibility criteria.

haloperidol → HALDOL®

HARVONI® (ledipasvir/sofosbuvir)

GILEAD SCIENCES, INC

HARVONI Co-pay Coupon Program   1-855-769-7284   *www.harvoni.com*

Covers monthly costs over $5 (up to a maximum of 25% of the catalog price) for a 12-week regimen of HARVONI.

Patient Assistance Program   1-855-769-7284   *www.harvoni.com*

Patient assistance program provides medications at no charge for eligible patients with no other insurance options.

HELIXATE® FS [Antihemophilic factor (recombinant)]

CSL BEHRING

CSL Behring Patient Assistance Program   1-844-727-2752   *www.helixatefs.com*

Provides meds to qualified patients who are uninsured or underinsured, and cannot afford their prescribed therapy.

HEMABATE® (carboprost tromethamine)

PFIZER, INC

Pfizer Savings Program   1-866-706-2400   *www.pfizerrxpathways.com*

Program helps uninsured patients receive discounted Pfizer medications through their local retail pharmacy.

hemin → PANHEMATIN® Injection

HEMLIBRA® (emicizumab-kxwh)

GENENTECH, INC.

HEMLIBRA® Co-Pay Card Program   1- 844-436-2672   *www.hemlibracopay.com*

Program provides up to $15,000/year in co-pay assistance. Patients pay $5/month for HEMLIBRA®.

Genentech Access Solutions   1-866-422-2377   *www.genentech-access.com*

Program provides medications to patients who are uninsured or have been denied coverage by their insurance company. Patients who have insurance, but pay too much out of pocket per year, may also qualify for assistance.

HEMOFIL® M (antihemophilic factor)   BAXALTA, INC / SHIRE

Shire's CoPay Assistance Program   1-888-229-8379   *www.hematologysupport.com*

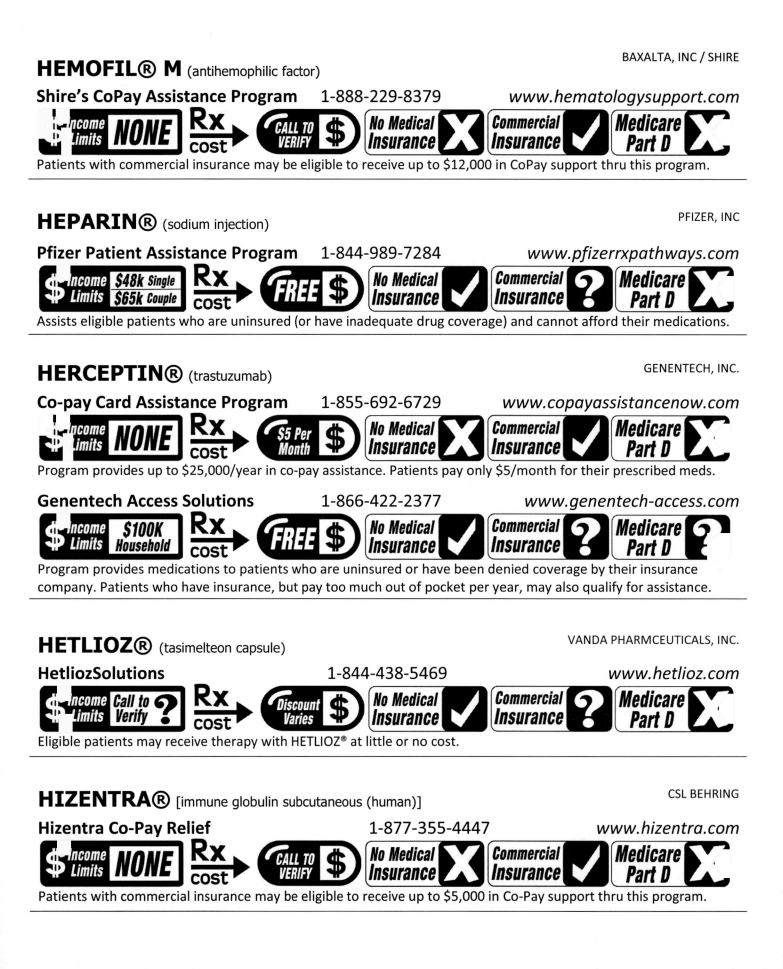

Income Limits **NONE** | **Rx** cost → | **CALL TO VERIFY** $ | No Medical Insurance **X** | Commercial Insurance ✔ | Medicare Part D **X**

Patients with commercial insurance may be eligible to receive up to $12,000 in CoPay support thru this program.

HEPARIN® (sodium injection)   PFIZER, INC

Pfizer Patient Assistance Program   1-844-989-7284   *www.pfizerrxpathways.com*

Income Limits **$48k Single** **$65k Couple** | **Rx** cost → | **FREE** $ | No Medical Insurance ✔ | Commercial Insurance **?** | Medicare Part D **X**

Assists eligible patients who are uninsured (or have inadequate drug coverage) and cannot afford their medications.

HERCEPTIN® (trastuzumab)   GENENTECH, INC.

Co-pay Card Assistance Program   1-855-692-6729   *www.copayassistancenow.com*

Income Limits **NONE** | **Rx** cost → | **$5 Per Month** $ | No Medical Insurance **X** | Commercial Insurance ✔ | Medicare Part D **X**

Program provides up to $25,000/year in co-pay assistance. Patients pay only $5/month for their prescribed meds.

Genentech Access Solutions   1-866-422-2377   *www.genentech-access.com*

Income Limits **$100K Household** | **Rx** cost → | **FREE** $ | No Medical Insurance ✔ | Commercial Insurance **?** | Medicare Part D **?**

Program provides medications to patients who are uninsured or have been denied coverage by their insurance company. Patients who have insurance, but pay too much out of pocket per year, may also qualify for assistance.

HETLIOZ® (tasimelteon capsule)   VANDA PHARMCEUTICALS, INC.

HetliozSolutions   1-844-438-5469   *www.hetlioz.com*

Income Limits **Call to Verify ?** | **Rx** cost → | **Discount Varies** $ | No Medical Insurance ✔ | Commercial Insurance **?** | Medicare Part D **X**

Eligible patients may receive therapy with HETLIOZ® at little or no cost.

HIZENTRA® [immune globulin subcutaneous (human)]   CSL BEHRING

Hizentra Co-Pay Relief   1-877-355-4447   *www.hizentra.com*

Income Limits **NONE** | **Rx** cost → | **CALL TO VERIFY** $ | No Medical Insurance **X** | Commercial Insurance ✔ | Medicare Part D **X**

Patients with commercial insurance may be eligible to receive up to $5,000 in Co-Pay support thru this program.

HIZENTRA® [immune globulin subcutaneous (human)]
CSL BEHRING

CSL Behring Patient Assistance Program 1-877-355-4447 *www.hizentra.com*

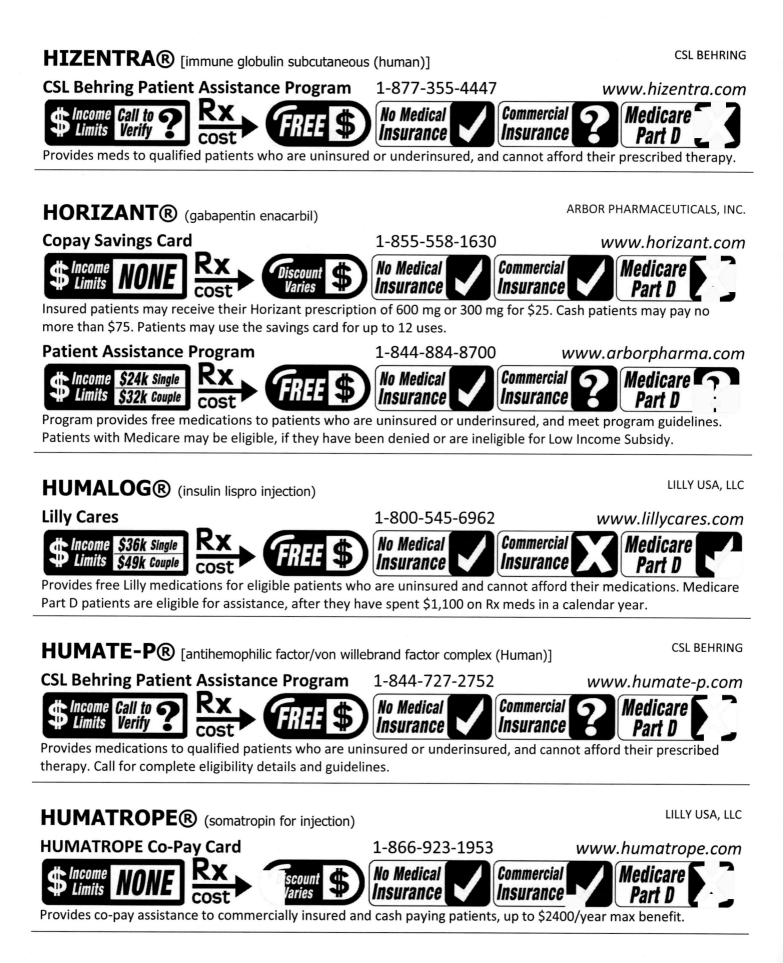

$ Income Limits | Call to Verify **?** | **Rx cost** → | FREE **$** | No Medical Insurance ✓ | Commercial Insurance **?** | Medicare Part D ✗

Provides meds to qualified patients who are uninsured or underinsured, and cannot afford their prescribed therapy.

HORIZANT® (gabapentin enacarbil)
ARBOR PHARMACEUTICALS, INC.

Copay Savings Card 1-855-558-1630 *www.horizant.com*

$ Income Limits | NONE | **Rx cost** → | Discount Varies **$** | No Medical Insurance ✓ | Commercial Insurance ✓ | Medicare Part D ✗

Insured patients may receive their Horizant prescription of 600 mg or 300 mg for $25. Cash patients may pay no more than $75. Patients may use the savings card for up to 12 uses.

Patient Assistance Program 1-844-884-8700 *www.arborpharma.com*

$ Income Limits | $24k Single / $32k Couple | **Rx cost** → | FREE **$** | No Medical Insurance ✓ | Commercial Insurance **?** | Medicare Part D **?**

Program provides free medications to patients who are uninsured or underinsured, and meet program guidelines. Patients with Medicare may be eligible, if they have been denied or are ineligible for Low Income Subsidy.

HUMALOG® (insulin lispro injection)
LILLY USA, LLC

Lilly Cares 1-800-545-6962 *www.lillycares.com*

$ Income Limits | $36k Single / $49k Couple | **Rx cost** → | FREE **$** | No Medical Insurance ✓ | Commercial Insurance ✗ | Medicare Part D ✓

Provides free Lilly medications for eligible patients who are uninsured and cannot afford their medications. Medicare Part D patients are eligible for assistance, after they have spent $1,100 on Rx meds in a calendar year.

HUMATE-P® [antihemophilic factor/von willebrand factor complex (Human)]
CSL BEHRING

CSL Behring Patient Assistance Program 1-844-727-2752 *www.humate-p.com*

$ Income Limits | Call to Verify **?** | **Rx cost** → | FREE **$** | No Medical Insurance ✓ | Commercial Insurance **?** | Medicare Part D ✗

Provides medications to qualified patients who are uninsured or underinsured, and cannot afford their prescribed therapy. Call for complete eligibility details and guidelines.

HUMATROPE® (somatropin for injection)
LILLY USA, LLC

HUMATROPE Co-Pay Card 1-866-923-1953 *www.humatrope.com*

$ Income Limits | NONE | **Rx cost** → | Discount Varies **$** | No Medical Insurance ✓ | Commercial Insurance ✓ | Medicare Part D ✗

Provides co-pay assistance to commercially insured and cash paying patients, up to $2400/year max benefit.

HUMATROPE® <small>(somatropin for injection)</small>

<small>LILLY USA, LLC</small>

Lilly Cares   1-800-545-6962   *www.lillycares.com*

Provides free Lilly medications for eligible patients who are uninsured and cannot afford their medications, or for those whose insurance has denied coverage. Medicare Part D patients may also be eligible for assistance.

HUMIRA® <small>(adalimumab)</small>

<small>AbbVie, INC.</small>

HUMIRA® Complete Savings Card   1-800-448-6472   *www.humira.com*

Eligible patients with commercial insurance pay as little as $5/month for their HUMIRA® Rx.

AbbVie Patient Assistance Foundation   1-800-222-6885   *www.abbviepaf.org*

Rx assistance available to patients who are uninsured and meet program eligibility requirements. Patients with Commercial Insurance or Medicare Part D, who are struggling to pay for their medications, are encouraged to apply.

HYALGAN® <small>(hyaluronate sodium)</small>

<small>FIDIA PHARMA USA, INC.</small>

Patient Assistance Program   1-866-749-2542   *www.hyalgan.com*

Provides access to HYALGAN® for eligible under-insured or uninsured patients who cannot afford their Rx costs.

hyaluronate sodium → HYALGAN®

HYCAMTIN® Capsules <small>(topotecan)</small>

<small>NOVARTIS PHARMACEUTICALS</small>

Novartis Patient Assistance Foundation   1-800-277-2254   *www.pap.novartis.com*

Program assists those without insurance, or with limited/inadequate Rx coverage to receive prescribed medications.

TIP: When in doubt... call the program and explain your situation. You may qualify for assistance.

HYCAMTIN® for Injection (topotecan hydrochloride)

NOVARTIS PHARMACEUTICALS

Novartis Patient Assistance Foundation   1-800-277-2254   *www.pap.novartis.com*

Program assists those without insurance, or with limited/inadequate Rx coverage to receive prescribed medications.

---

hydrocodone bitartrate → HYSINGLA® ER

hydrocodone bitartrate → ZOHYDRO® ER

hydrocortisone → CORTEF®

hydrocortisone butyrate lotion 0.1% → LOCOID®

hydrocortisone/pramoxine → ANALPRAM HC®

hydromorphone HCL → EXALGO®

hydroxyprogesterone caproate → MAKENA® Injection

hydroxyurea → DROXIA®

hydroxyzine pamoate → VISTARIL®

HYMOVIS® (high molecular weight viscoelastic hyaluronan)

FIDIA PHARMA USA, INC.

Patient Assistance Program   1-866-749-2542   *www.hymovis.com*

Provides access to HYMOVIS® for eligible under-insured or uninsured patients who cannot afford their Rx costs.

HYQVIA® Solution

BAXALTA, INC / SHIRE

[Immune Globulin Infusion 10% (Human) with Recombinant Human Hyaluronidase]

MyIgCoPayCard   1-855-250-5111   *www.myigsource.com*

Patients with commercial insurance may be eligible to receive up to $5,000 in CoPay support thru this program.

HYSINGLA® ER (hydrocodone bitartrate)

PURDUE PHARMA, L.P.

Hysingla ER Co-Pay Savings Card   1-855-396-2622   *www.hysingla.com*

Income Limits **NONE** | **Rx** cost → **$25** $ | **No Medical Insurance** ✓ | **Commercial Insurance** ✓ | **Medicare Part D** ✗

Patients pay the first $25 of Rx, co-pay card assists with up to $170 of remaining out-of-pocket/co-pay costs.

Purdue Patient Assistance Program   1-800-599-6070   *www.purduepharma.com*

Income Limits **$16k Single / $22k Couple** | **Rx** cost → **FREE** $ | **No Medical Insurance** ✓ | **Commercial Insurance** ✗ | **Medicare Part D** ✗

Provides certain medications to eligible low-income patients who do not have Rx insurance and have financial need.

IBRANCE® (palbociclib)

PFIZER, INC

Pfizer Savings Program   1-866-706-2400   *www.pfizerrxpathways.com*

Income Limits **NONE** | **Rx** cost → **Discount Varies** $ | **No Medical Insurance** ✓ | **Commercial Insurance** ✗ | **Medicare Part D** ✗

Program helps uninsured patients receive discounted Pfizer medications through their local retail pharmacy.

Pfizer Oncology together™ Co-Pay Savings Card   1-877-744-5675   *www.ibrance.com*

Income Limits **NONE** | **Rx** cost → **$0 CoPay** $ | **No Medical Insurance** ✗ | **Commercial Insurance** ✓ | **Medicare Part D** ✗

Eligible patients can save up to $25,000 per year toward their co-pay, deductible, and coinsurance costs.

Pfizer Patient Assistance Program   1-844-989-7284   *www.pfizerrxpathways.com*

Income Limits **Call to Verify** ? | **Rx** cost → **FREE** $ | **No Medical Insurance** ✓ | **Commercial Insurance** ? | **Medicare Part D** ✗

Assists eligible patients who are uninsured (or have inadequate drug coverage) and cannot afford their medications.

ibritumomab tiuxetan → ZEVALIN®

ibrutinib → IMBRUVICA®

ibuprofen/famotidine → DUEXIS®

ibuprofen lysine → NEOPROFEN® Injection

ibutilide fumarate injection → CORVERT®

icatibant injection → FIRAZYR®

ICLUSIG® (ponatinib)
TAKEDA ONCOLOGY

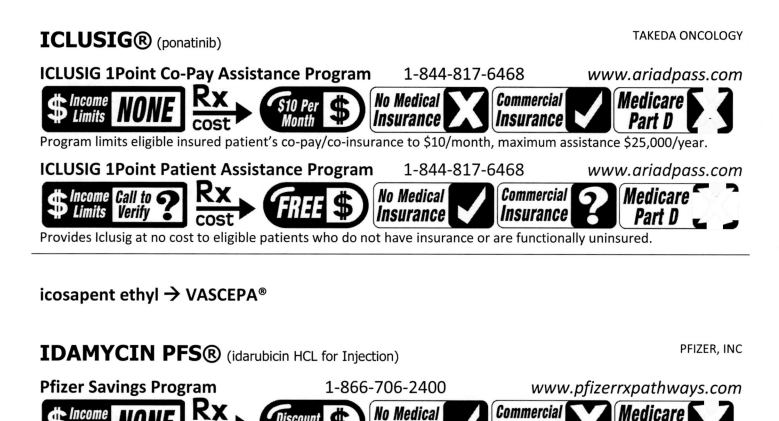

ICLUSIG 1Point Co-Pay Assistance Program　　1-844-817-6468　　*www.ariadpass.com*

Program limits eligible insured patient's co-pay/co-insurance to $10/month, maximum assistance $25,000/year.

ICLUSIG 1Point Patient Assistance Program　　1-844-817-6468　　*www.ariadpass.com*

Provides Iclusig at no cost to eligible patients who do not have insurance or are functionally uninsured.

---

icosapent ethyl → VASCEPA®

IDAMYCIN PFS® (idarubicin HCL for Injection)
PFIZER, INC

Pfizer Savings Program　　1-866-706-2400　　*www.pfizerrxpathways.com*

Program helps uninsured patients receive discounted Pfizer medications through their local retail pharmacy.

Pfizer Patient Assistance Program　　1-844-989-7284　　*www.pfizerrxpathways.com*

Assists eligible patients who are uninsured (or have inadequate drug coverage) and cannot afford their medications.

---

idarubicin HCL for Injection → IDAMYCIN PFS®

idelalisib → ZYDELIG®

IDELVION® [coagulation factor IX (recombinant),albumin fusion protein]
CSL BEHRING

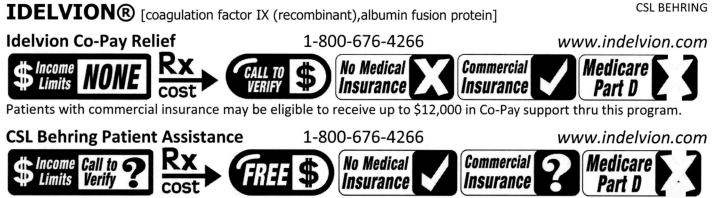

Idelvion Co-Pay Relief　　1-800-676-4266　　*www.indelvion.com*

Patients with commercial insurance may be eligible to receive up to $12,000 in Co-Pay support thru this program.

CSL Behring Patient Assistance　　1-800-676-4266　　*www.indelvion.com*

Provides meds to qualified patients who are uninsured or underinsured, and cannot afford their prescribed therapy.

IDHIFA® (enasidenib)

CELGENE CORPORATION

Celgene Co-Pay Assistance Program 1-800-931-8691 *www.celgenepatientsupport.com*

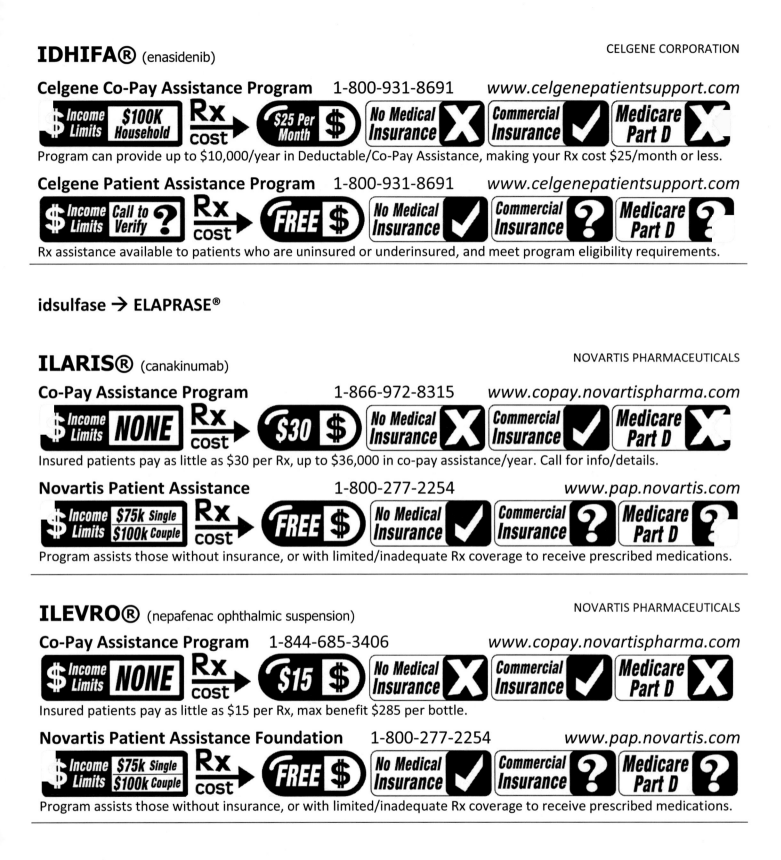

Income Limits **$100K Household** | Rx cost → **$25 Per Month** $ | **No Medical Insurance** ✗ | **Commercial Insurance** ✓ | **Medicare Part D** ✗

Program can provide up to $10,000/year in Deductable/Co-Pay Assistance, making your Rx cost $25/month or less.

Celgene Patient Assistance Program 1-800-931-8691 *www.celgenepatientsupport.com*

Income Limits **Call to Verify** ? | Rx cost → **FREE** $ | **No Medical Insurance** ✓ | **Commercial Insurance** ? | **Medicare Part D** ?

Rx assistance available to patients who are uninsured or underinsured, and meet program eligibility requirements.

---

idsulfase → **ELAPRASE®**

ILARIS® (canakinumab)

NOVARTIS PHARMACEUTICALS

Co-Pay Assistance Program 1-866-972-8315 *www.copay.novartispharma.com*

Income Limits **NONE** | Rx cost → **$30** $ | **No Medical Insurance** ✗ | **Commercial Insurance** ✓ | **Medicare Part D** ✗

Insured patients pay as little as $30 per Rx, up to $36,000 in co-pay assistance/year. Call for info/details.

Novartis Patient Assistance 1-800-277-2254 *www.pap.novartis.com*

Income Limits **$75k Single $100k Couple** | Rx cost → **FREE** $ | **No Medical Insurance** ✓ | **Commercial Insurance** ? | **Medicare Part D** ?

Program assists those without insurance, or with limited/inadequate Rx coverage to receive prescribed medications.

ILEVRO® (nepafenac ophthalmic suspension)

NOVARTIS PHARMACEUTICALS

Co-Pay Assistance Program 1-844-685-3406 *www.copay.novartispharma.com*

Income Limits **NONE** | Rx cost → **$15** $ | **No Medical Insurance** ✗ | **Commercial Insurance** ✓ | **Medicare Part D** ✗

Insured patients pay as little as $15 per Rx, max benefit $285 per bottle.

Novartis Patient Assistance Foundation 1-800-277-2254 *www.pap.novartis.com*

Income Limits **$75k Single $100k Couple** | Rx cost → **FREE** $ | **No Medical Insurance** ✓ | **Commercial Insurance** ? | **Medicare Part D** ?

Program assists those without insurance, or with limited/inadequate Rx coverage to receive prescribed medications.

---

iloperidone → **FANAPT®**

iloprost inhalation solution → **VENTAVIS®**

ILUVIEN® (fluocinolone acetonide intravetreal implant)

ALIMERA SCIENCES,INC

ILUVIEN® Co-Pay Program
1-844-445-8843 — www.iluvien.com

Income Limits: NONE | Rx cost → $25 Per Month | No Medical Insurance ✗ | Commercial Insurance ✓ | Medicare Part D ✗

Provides Co-Pay assistance to qualified patient, your Rx cost $25/month or less.

ILUVIEN® Patient Assistance Program
1-844-445-8843 — www.iluvien.com

Income Limits: $60k Single / $82k Couple | Rx cost → FREE | No Medical Insurance ✓ | Commercial Insurance ? | Medicare Part D ✗

Assists eligible patients who are uninsured (or whose insurance will not cover ILUVIEN®).

IMATINIB (imatinib) tablets

SUN PHARMACEUTICAL INDUSTRIES INC.

Imatinib Savings Card
1-844-502-5950 — www.imatinibrx.com

Income Limits: NONE | Rx cost → $0 CoPay | No Medical Insurance ✗ | Commercial Insurance ✓ | Medicare Part D ✗

Eligible insured patients pay $0 copay for their Imatinib Rx, max savings $250 per fill.

Patient Assistance Program (PAP)
1-844-502-5950 — www.imatinibrx.com

Income Limits: $60k Single / $82k Couple | Rx cost → FREE | No Medical Insurance ✓ | Commercial Insurance ✗ | Medicare Part D ✗

Provides free Imatinib to patients who meet income and citizenship/residency eligibility criteria.

imatinib mesylate → GLEEVEC®

IMBRUVICA® (ibrutinib)

PHARMACYCLICS LLC/JANSSEN PHARMACEUTICALS INC.

You&I™ Instant Savings Program
1-877-877-3536 — www.imbruvica.com

Income Limits: NONE | Rx cost → $10 | No Medical Insurance ✗ | Commercial Insurance ✓ | Medicare Part D ✗

Eligible patients may qualify for $10 per Rx of IMBRUVICA® until the maximum limit of $24,600/year is reached. Program applies to commercial insurance co-pay, deductible, and coinsurance medication costs for IMBRUVICA®

J&J Patient Assistance Foundation
1-800-652-6227 — www.jjpaf.org

Income Limits: NONE | Rx cost → FREE | No Medical Insurance ✓ | Commercial Insurance ? | Medicare Part D ?

Program provides free medications to patients who are uninsured or underinsured, and meet program guidelines.

💡 **TIP:** Income limits are higher for households with three or more people. Call programs for details.

IMFINZI® (durvalumab) for infusion

ASTRAZENECA PHARMACEUTICALS

AZ&ME™   1-800-292-6363   *www.azandmeapp.com*

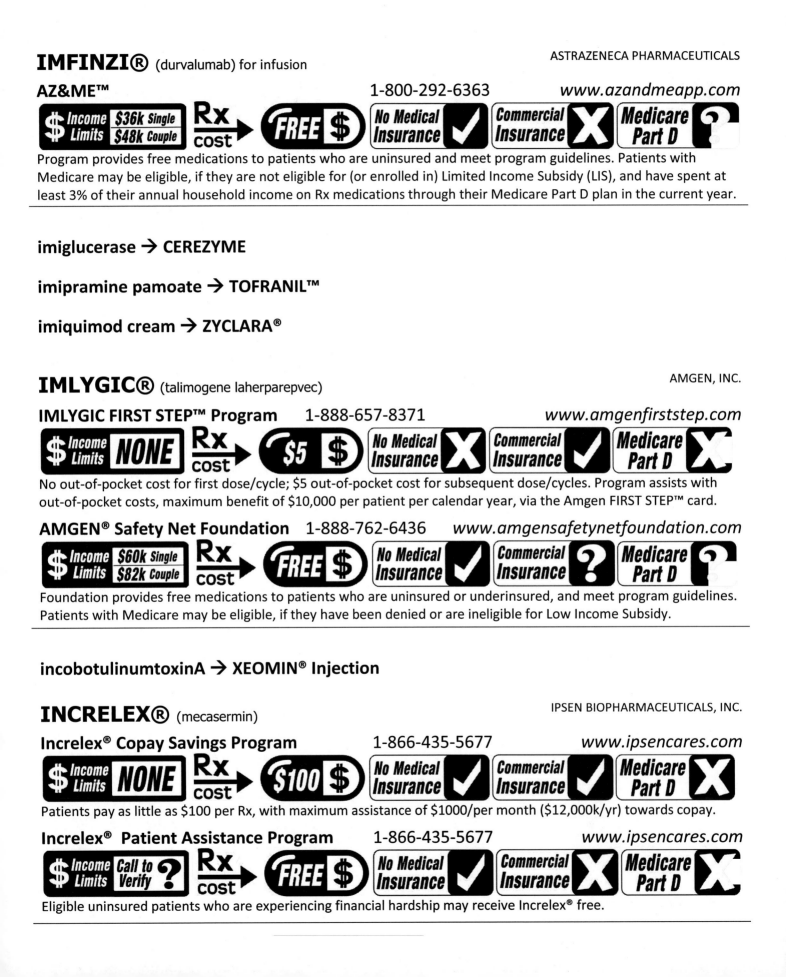

Program provides free medications to patients who are uninsured and meet program guidelines. Patients with Medicare may be eligible, if they are not eligible for (or enrolled in) Limited Income Subsidy (LIS), and have spent at least 3% of their annual household income on Rx medications through their Medicare Part D plan in the current year.

---

imiglucerase → CEREZYME

imipramine pamoate → TOFRANIL™

imiquimod cream → ZYCLARA®

IMLYGIC® (talimogene laherparepvec)

AMGEN, INC.

IMLYGIC FIRST STEP™ Program   1-888-657-8371   *www.amgenfirststep.com*

No out-of-pocket cost for first dose/cycle; $5 out-of-pocket cost for subsequent dose/cycles. Program assists with out-of-pocket costs, maximum benefit of $10,000 per patient per calendar year, via the Amgen FIRST STEP™ card.

AMGEN® Safety Net Foundation   1-888-762-6436   *www.amgensafetynetfoundation.com*

Foundation provides free medications to patients who are uninsured or underinsured, and meet program guidelines. Patients with Medicare may be eligible, if they have been denied or are ineligible for Low Income Subsidy.

---

incobotulinumtoxinA → XEOMIN® Injection

INCRELEX® (mecasermin)

IPSEN BIOPHARMACEUTICALS, INC.

Increlex® Copay Savings Program   1-866-435-5677   *www.ipsencares.com*

Patients pay as little as $100 per Rx, with maximum assistance of $1000/per month ($12,000k/yr) towards copay.

Increlex® Patient Assistance Program   1-866-435-5677   *www.ipsencares.com*

Eligible uninsured patients who are experiencing financial hardship may receive Increlex® free.

INCRUSE ELLIPTA (umeclidinium inhalation powder)

INCRUSE Savings Offer   1-866-475-3678   *www.mybreo.com*

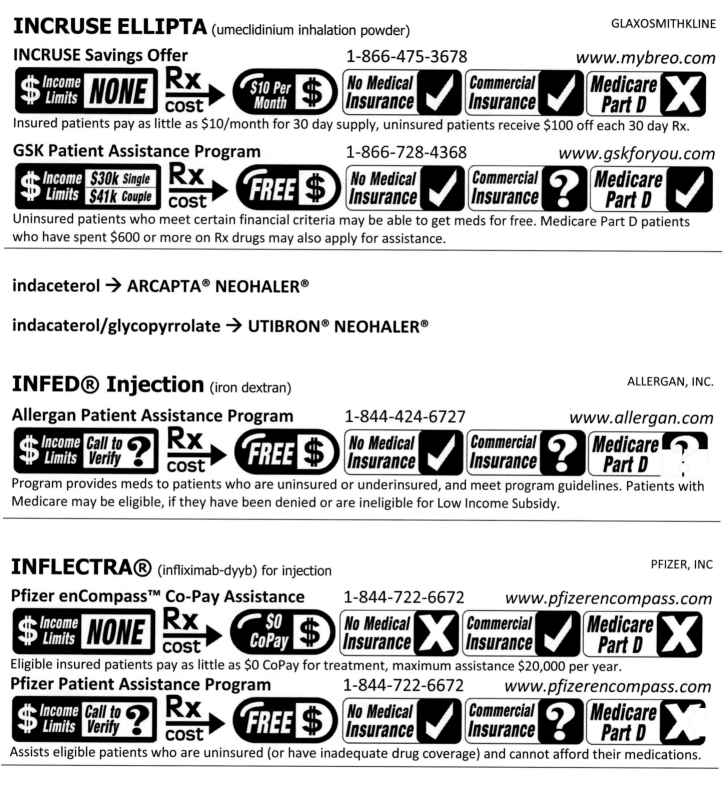

$ Income Limits **NONE** | **Rx** cost → | $10 Per Month $ | No Medical Insurance ✓ | Commercial Insurance ✓ | Medicare Part D ✗

Insured patients pay as little as $10/month for 30 day supply, uninsured patients receive $100 off each 30 day Rx.

GSK Patient Assistance Program   1-866-728-4368   *www.gskforyou.com*

$ Income Limits **$30k Single $41k Couple** | **Rx** cost → | **FREE** $ | No Medical Insurance ✓ | Commercial Insurance ? | Medicare Part D ✓

Uninsured patients who meet certain financial criteria may be able to get meds for free. Medicare Part D patients who have spent $600 or more on Rx drugs may also apply for assistance.

---

indaceterol → **ARCAPTA® NEOHALER®**

indacaterol/glycopyrrolate → **UTIBRON® NEOHALER®**

INFED® Injection (iron dextran)

ALLERGAN, INC.

Allergan Patient Assistance Program   1-844-424-6727   *www.allergan.com*

$ Income Limits **Call to Verify** ? | **Rx** cost → | **FREE** $ | No Medical Insurance ✓ | Commercial Insurance ? | Medicare Part D ?

Program provides meds to patients who are uninsured or underinsured, and meet program guidelines. Patients with Medicare may be eligible, if they have been denied or are ineligible for Low Income Subsidy.

INFLECTRA® (infliximab-dyyb) for injection

PFIZER, INC

Pfizer enCompass™ Co-Pay Assistance   1-844-722-6672   *www.pfizerencompass.com*

$ Income Limits **NONE** | **Rx** cost → | $0 CoPay $ | No Medical Insurance ✗ | Commercial Insurance ✓ | Medicare Part D ✗

Eligible insured patients pay as little as $0 CoPay for treatment, maximum assistance $20,000 per year.

Pfizer Patient Assistance Program   1-844-722-6672   *www.pfizerencompass.com*

$ Income Limits **Call to Verify** ? | **Rx** cost → | **FREE** $ | No Medical Insurance ✓ | Commercial Insurance ? | Medicare Part D ✗

Assists eligible patients who are uninsured (or have inadequate drug coverage) and cannot afford their medications.

---

infliximab → **REMICADE®**

infliximab-dyyb → **INFLECTRA®**

ingenol mebutate → **PICATO® GEL**

INGREZZA® (valbenazine)

NEUROCRINE BIOSCIENCES, INC.

Ingrezza Support Program 1-844-647-3992 *www.ingrezza.com*

$ **Income Limits** NONE | **Rx cost** → | $0 CoPay $ | **No Medical Insurance** X | **Commercial Insurance** ✔ | **Medicare Part D** X

Insured patients can pay as little as $0 for their Ingrezza Rx.

Ingrezza Patient Assistance Program 1-844-647-3992 *www.ingrezza.com*

$ **Income Limits** Call to Verify ? | **Rx cost** → | FREE $ | **No Medical Insurance** ✔ | **Commercial Insurance** X | **Medicare Part D** X

Program assists those without insurance and limited income to receive Ingrezza.

INJECTAFER® (ferric carboxymaltose injection)

AMERICAN REGENT

Injectafer Savings Card 1-877-448-4766 *www.injectafer.com*

$ **Income Limits** NONE | **Rx cost** → | Discount Varies $ | **No Medical Insurance** ✔ | **Commercial Insurance** ✔ | **Medicare Part D** X

Eligible insured patients may pay no more than $50 for the first dose and $0 for the second dose of Injectafer, up to a maximum savings limit of $500 per dose ($1,000 max/year). Patient out-of-pocket expense may vary, call for info.

INLYTA® (axitinib tablets)

PFIZER, INC

Pfizer Savings Program 1-866-706-2400 *www.pfizerrxpathways.com*

$ **Income Limits** NONE | **Rx cost** → | Discount Varies $ | **No Medical Insurance** ✔ | **Commercial Insurance** X | **Medicare Part D** X

Program helps uninsured patients receive discounted Pfizer medications through their local retail pharmacy.

Pfizer Oncology together™ Co-Pay Savings Card 1-877-744-5675 *www.inlyta.com*

$ **Income Limits** NONE | **Rx cost** → | $0 CoPay $ | **No Medical Insurance** X | **Commercial Insurance** ✔ | **Medicare Part D** X

Eligible patients can save up to $25,000 per year toward their co-pay, deductible, and coinsurance costs.

Pfizer Patient Assistance Program 1-844-989-7284 *www.pfizerrxpathways.com*

$ **Income Limits** Call to Verify ? | **Rx cost** → | FREE $ | **No Medical Insurance** ✔ | **Commercial Insurance** ? | **Medicare Part D** X

Assists eligible patients who are uninsured (or have inadequate drug coverage) and cannot afford their medications.

INNOPRAN® XL (propranolol hydrochloride)

AKRIMAX PHARMACEUTICALS

Akrimax Patient Assistance Program 1-855-856-6915 *www.akrimaxpap.com*

$ **Income Limits** $24k Single / $32k Couple | **Rx cost** → | FREE $ | **No Medical Insurance** ✔ | **Commercial Insurance** X | **Medicare Part D** X

Program provides Akrimax brand name medications free of charge, to individuals who meet eligibility requirements.

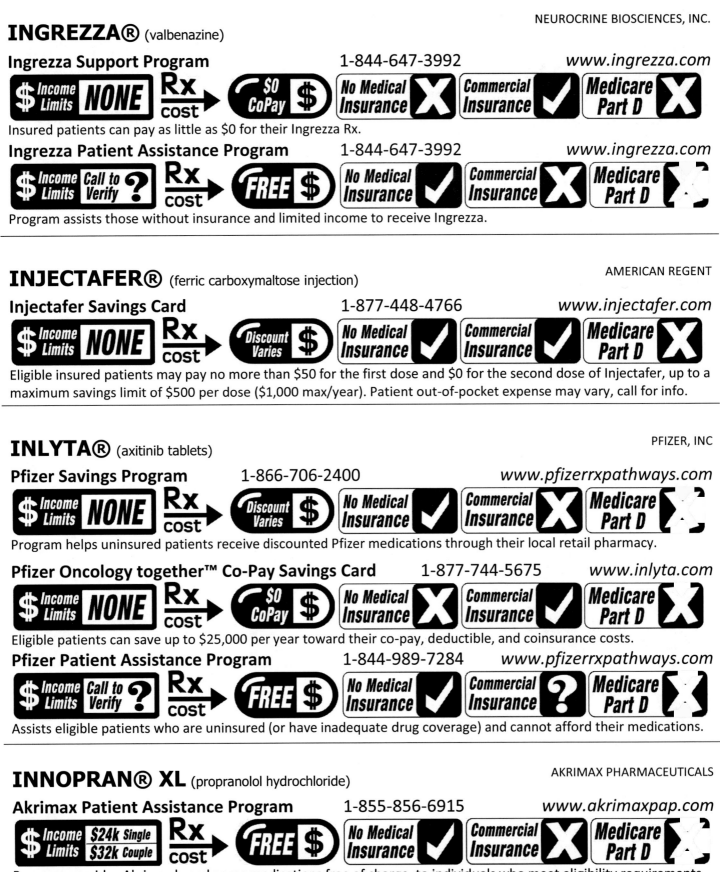

inotuzumab ozogamicin → BESPONSA™

INSPRA® (eplerenone)

PFIZER, INC

Pfizer Savings Program   1-866-706-2400   *www.pfizerrxpathways.com*

Program helps uninsured patients receive discounted Pfizer medications through their local retail pharmacy.

Pfizer Patient Assistance Program   1-844-989-7284   *www.pfizerrxpathways.com*

Assists eligible patients who are uninsured (or have inadequate drug coverage) and cannot afford their medications.

---

insulin aspart injection → FIASP®

insulin aspart injection → NOVOLOG®

insulin degludec injection → TRESIBA®

insulin degludec/liraglutide injection → XULTOPHY® 100/3.6

insulin detemir [rDNA origin] injection → LEVEMIR®

insulin glargine → BASAGLAR®

insulin glargine → LANTUS®/Lantus® SoloStar® Pen

insulin glargine → TOUJEO®

insulin glargine and lixisenatide injection → SOLIQUA® 100/33

insulin glulisine → APIDRA®

insulin lispro → ADMELOG®

insulin lispro → HUMALOG®

TIP: Income limits are higher for households with three or more people. Call programs for details.

INTELENCE® (etravirine)

JANSSEN PHARMACEUTICALS INC.

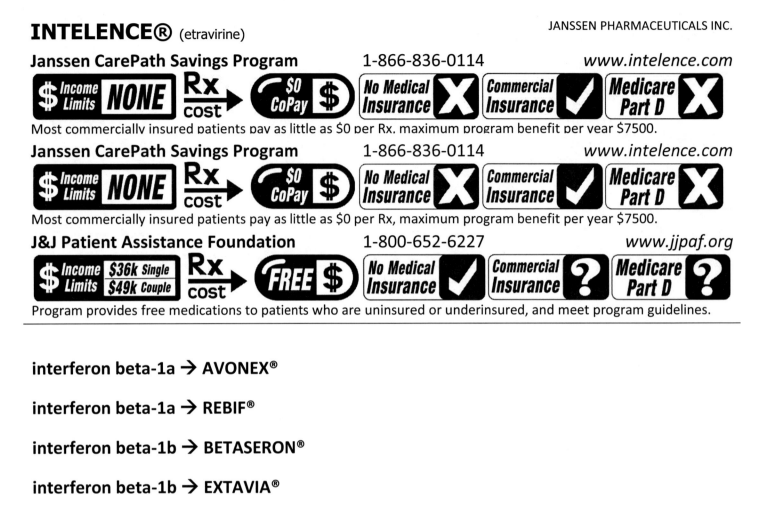

Janssen CarePath Savings Program   1-866-836-0114   *www.intelence.com*

$ Income Limits NONE | Rx cost → | $0 CoPay $ | No Medical Insurance ✗ | Commercial Insurance ✓ | Medicare Part D ✗

Most commercially insured patients pay as little as $0 per Rx, maximum program benefit per year $7500.

Janssen CarePath Savings Program   1-866-836-0114   *www.intelence.com*

$ Income Limits NONE | Rx cost → | $0 CoPay $ | No Medical Insurance ✗ | Commercial Insurance ✓ | Medicare Part D ✗

Most commercially insured patients pay as little as $0 per Rx, maximum program benefit per year $7500.

J&J Patient Assistance Foundation   1-800-652-6227   *www.jjpaf.org*

$ Income Limits $36k Single $49k Couple | Rx cost → | FREE $ | No Medical Insurance ✓ | Commercial Insurance ? | Medicare Part D ?

Program provides free medications to patients who are uninsured or underinsured, and meet program guidelines.

---

interferon beta-1a → AVONEX®

interferon beta-1a → REBIF®

interferon beta-1b → BETASERON®

interferon beta-1b → EXTAVIA®

interferon gamma-1b → ACTIMMUNE®

INTUNIV® (guanfacine)

SHIRE

Shire Cares Patient Assistance & Support   1-888-227-3755   *www.shire.com*

$ Income Limits $36k Single $49k Couple | Rx cost → | CALL TO VERIFY $ | No Medical Insurance ✓ | Commercial Insurance ? | Medicare Part D ?

Program assists patients with limited financial needs who are having problems affording their Rx medications.

INVEGA® SUSTENNA/TRINZA (paliperidone palmitate)

JANSSEN PHARMACEUTICALS INC.

J&J Patient Assistance Foundation   1-800-652-6227   *www.jjpaf.org*

$ Income Limits $36k Single $49k Couple | Rx cost → | FREE $ | No Medical Insurance ✓ | Commercial Insurance ? | Medicare Part D ?

Program provides free medications to patients who are uninsured or underinsured, and meet program guidelines.

INVOKAMET®/ INVOKAMET® XR (canagliflozin-metformin)

JANSSEN PHARMACEUTICALS

Janssen CarePath Savings Program   1-877-468-6526   *www.invokana.com*

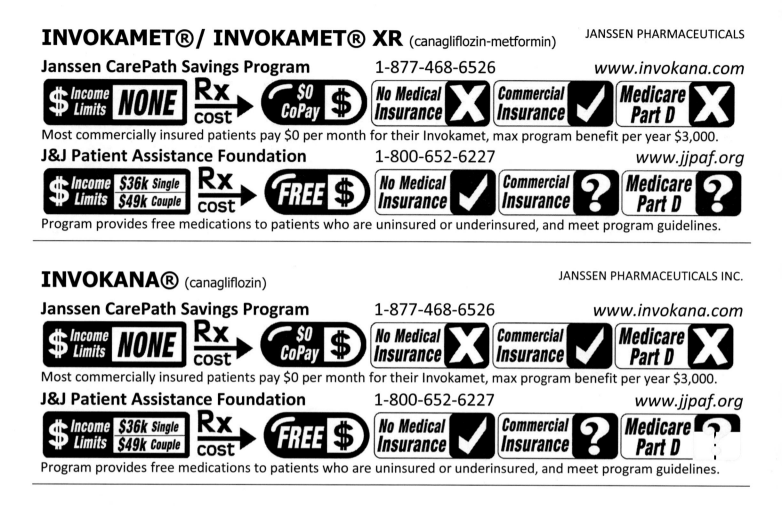

$ Income Limits NONE | **Rx cost** → | **$0 CoPay $** | **No Medical Insurance X** | **Commercial Insurance ✓** | **Medicare Part D X**

Most commercially insured patients pay $0 per month for their Invokamet, max program benefit per year $3,000.

J&J Patient Assistance Foundation   1-800-652-6227   *www.jjpaf.org*

$ Income Limits $36k Single $49k Couple | **Rx cost** → | **FREE $** | **No Medical Insurance ✓** | **Commercial Insurance ?** | **Medicare Part D ?**

Program provides free medications to patients who are uninsured or underinsured, and meet program guidelines.

INVOKANA® (canagliflozin)

JANSSEN PHARMACEUTICALS INC.

Janssen CarePath Savings Program   1-877-468-6526   *www.invokana.com*

$ Income Limits NONE | **Rx cost** → | **$0 CoPay $** | **No Medical Insurance X** | **Commercial Insurance ✓** | **Medicare Part D X**

Most commercially insured patients pay $0 per month for their Invokamet, max program benefit per year $3,000.

J&J Patient Assistance Foundation   1-800-652-6227   *www.jjpaf.org*

$ Income Limits $36k Single $49k Couple | **Rx cost** → | **FREE $** | **No Medical Insurance ✓** | **Commercial Insurance ?** | **Medicare Part D ?**

Program provides free medications to patients who are uninsured or underinsured, and meet program guidelines.

ipilimumab → **YERVOY®**

ipratropium bromide → **ATROVENT HFA®**

ipratropium bromide/albuterol sulfate → **COMBIVENT® RESPIMAT®**

IRESSA® Tablets (getfitinib)

ASTRAZENECA PHARMACEUTICALS

AZ&ME™   1-800-292-6363   *www.azandmeapp.com*

$ Income Limits $36k Single $48k Couple | **Rx cost** → | **FREE $** | **No Medical Insurance ✓** | **Commercial Insurance X** | **Medicare Part D ?**

Program provides free medications to patients who are uninsured and meet program guidelines. Patients with Medicare may be eligible, if they are not eligible for (or enrolled in) Limited Income Subsidy (LIS), and have spent at least 3% of their annual household income on Rx medications through their Medicare Part D plan in the current year.

irinotecan HCL Injection → **CAMPTOSAR®**

irinotecan liposome → **ONIVYDE®**

isavuconazonium sulfate → CRESEMBA®

ISENTRESS®/ ISENTRESS® HD (raltegravir)

MERCK & COMPANY, INC.

Multiuse Savings Coupon 1-800-672-6372 *www.isentress.com*

Income Limits **NONE** | Rx cost → | Discount Varies $ | No Medical Insurance **X** | Commercial Insurance ✓ | Medicare Part D **X**

Insured patients can save on their out of pocket costs, up to $6,800 maximum total program savings.

Merck Patient Assistance Program 1-800-727-5400 *www.merckhelps.com*

Income Limits **$48k Single $65k Couple** | Rx cost → | **FREE** $ | No Medical Insurance ✓ | Commercial Insurance **?** | Medicare Part D **?**

Program is for patients who do not have Rx insurance coverage and cannot afford to pay for their medicine.

isocarboxazid → MARPLAN®

isosorbide dinitrate and hydralazine HCL → BiDil®

ISTODAX® (romidepsin)

CELGENE CORPORATION

Celgene Co-Pay Assistance Program 1-800-931-8691 *www.celgenepatientsupport.com*

Income Limits **$100K Household** | Rx cost → | $0 CoPay $ | No Medical Insurance **X** | Commercial Insurance ✓ | Medicare Part D **X**

Program can provide up to $10,000/year in Deductible/Co-Pay Assistance, making your Rx cost as low as $0/month.

Celgene Patient Assistance Program 1-800-931-8691 *www.celgenepatientsupport.com*

Income Limits **Call to Verify ?** | Rx cost → | **FREE** $ | No Medical Insurance ✓ | Commercial Insurance **?** | Medicare Part D **?**

Rx assistance available to patients who are uninsured or underinsured, and meet program eligibility requirements.

itraconazole → SPORANOX®

ivabradine → CORLANOR®

ivacaftor → KALYDECO®

ivermectin → SOOLANTRA®

ivermectin lotion → SKLICE®

ivermectin tablets → STROMECTOL®

ixabepilone → IXEMPRA®

ixazomib → NINLARO®

ixekizumab → TALTZ®

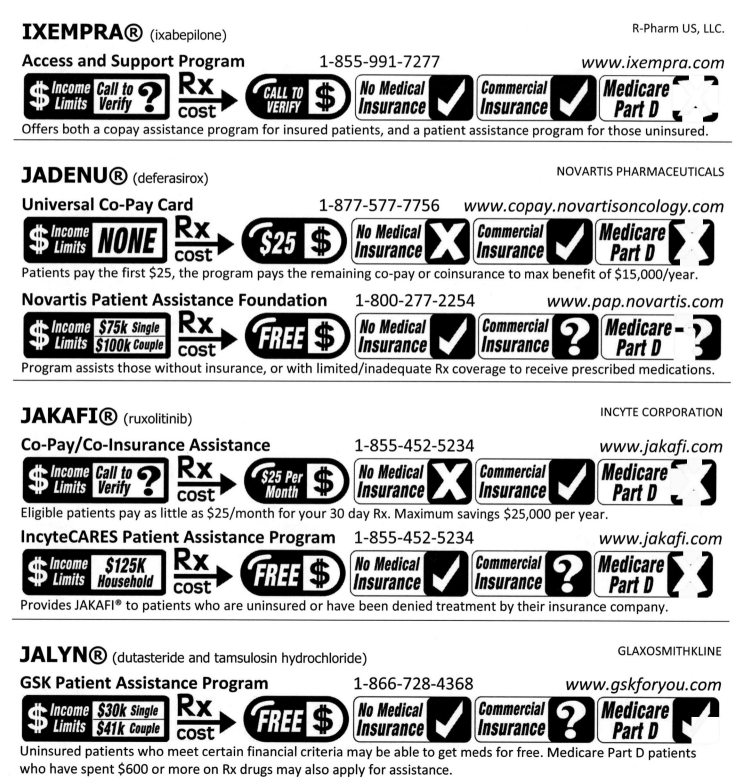

IXEMPRA® (ixabepilone)
R-Pharm US, LLC.

Access and Support Program   1-855-991-7277   www.ixempra.com

| $ Income Limits | Call to Verify ? | Rx cost → | CALL TO VERIFY $ | No Medical Insurance ✓ | Commercial Insurance ✓ | Medicare Part D ✗ |

Offers both a copay assistance program for insured patients, and a patient assistance program for those uninsured.

JADENU® (deferasirox)
NOVARTIS PHARMACEUTICALS

Universal Co-Pay Card   1-877-577-7756   www.copay.novartisoncology.com

| $ Income Limits | NONE | Rx cost → | $25 $ | No Medical Insurance ✗ | Commercial Insurance ✓ | Medicare Part D ✗ |

Patients pay the first $25, the program pays the remaining co-pay or coinsurance to max benefit of $15,000/year.

Novartis Patient Assistance Foundation   1-800-277-2254   www.pap.novartis.com

| $ Income Limits | $75k Single $100k Couple | Rx cost → | FREE $ | No Medical Insurance ✓ | Commercial Insurance ? | Medicare Part D ? |

Program assists those without insurance, or with limited/inadequate Rx coverage to receive prescribed medications.

JAKAFI® (ruxolitinib)
INCYTE CORPORATION

Co-Pay/Co-Insurance Assistance   1-855-452-5234   www.jakafi.com

| $ Income Limits | Call to Verify ? | Rx cost → | $25 Per Month $ | No Medical Insurance ✗ | Commercial Insurance ✓ | Medicare Part D ✗ |

Eligible patients pay as little as $25/month for your 30 day Rx. Maximum savings $25,000 per year.

IncyteCARES Patient Assistance Program   1-855-452-5234   www.jakafi.com

| $ Income Limits | $125K Household | Rx cost → | FREE $ | No Medical Insurance ✓ | Commercial Insurance ? | Medicare Part D ✗ |

Provides JAKAFI® to patients who are uninsured or have been denied treatment by their insurance company.

JALYN® (dutasteride and tamsulosin hydrochloride)
GLAXOSMITHKLINE

GSK Patient Assistance Program   1-866-728-4368   www.gskforyou.com

| $ Income Limits | $30k Single $41k Couple | Rx cost → | FREE $ | No Medical Insurance ✓ | Commercial Insurance ? | Medicare Part D ✓ |

Uninsured patients who meet certain financial criteria may be able to get meds for free. Medicare Part D patients who have spent $600 or more on Rx drugs may also apply for assistance.

JANUMET®/ JANUMET® XR (sitagliptin and metformin HCL) tablets   MERCK & COMPANY, INC.

Multiuse Savings Coupon   1-800-672-6372   *www.jamumetxr.com*

| $ Income Limits | NONE | Rx→cost | $5 $ | No Medical Insurance ✗ | Commercial Insurance ✓ | Medicare Part D ✗ |

Insured patients pay as little as $5 per Rx, maximum savings is $150 per prescription.

Merck Patient Assistance Program   1-800-727-5400   *www.merckhelps.com*

| $ Income Limits | $48k Single / $65k Couple | Rx→cost | FREE $ | No Medical Insurance ✓ | Commercial Insurance ? | Medicare Part D ? |

Program is for patients who do not have Rx insurance coverage and cannot afford to pay for their medicine.

JANUVIA® (sitagliptin) tablets   MERCK & COMPANY, INC.

Multiuse Savings Coupon   1-800-672-6372   *www.januvia.com*

| $ Income Limits | NONE | Rx→cost | $5 $ | No Medical Insurance ✗ | Commercial Insurance ✓ | Medicare Part D ✗ |

Insured patients pay as little as $5 per Rx, maximum savings is $150 per prescription.

Merck Patient Assistance Program   1-800-727-5400   *www.merckhelps.com*

| $ Income Limits | $48k Single / $65k Couple | Rx→cost | FREE $ | No Medical Insurance ✓ | Commercial Insurance ? | Medicare Part D ? |

Program is for patients who do not have Rx insurance coverage and cannot afford to pay for their medicine.

JARDIANCE® (empagliflozin)   BOEHRINGER INGELHEIM PHARMACEUTICALS, INC.

JARDIANCE Savings Card   1-866-279-8990   *www.jardiance.com*

| $ Income Limits | NONE | Rx→cost | $0 CoPay $ | No Medical Insurance ✗ | Commercial Insurance ✓ | Medicare Part D ✗ |

Eligible insured patients pay as low as $0 per month for JARDIANCE (max savings of $250/monthly prescription).

Boehringer Ingelheim Cares Foundation   1-800-556-8317   *www.bipatientassistance.com*

| $ Income Limits | Call to Verify ? | Rx→cost | FREE $ | No Medical Insurance ✓ | Commercial Insurance ? | Medicare Part D ? |

Patient Assistance Program provides free medications to patients who are uninsured or underinsured, and meet program guidelines. Patients with Medicare may be eligible, if they are ineligible for Low Income Subsidy.

JENTADUETO® (linagliptin/metformin HCL)   BOEHRINGER INGELHEIM PHARMACEUTICALS, INC.

JENTADUETO Savings Card   1-888-879-0466   *www.jentadueto.com*

| $ Income Limits | NONE | Rx→cost | $10 Per Month $ | No Medical Insurance ✗ | Commercial Insurance ✓ | Medicare Part D ✗ |

Eligible insured patients pay as low as $10 per month for JENTADUETO (maximum savings of $150/monthly Rx).

JENTADUETO® (linagliptin/metformin HCL)
BOEHRINGER INGELHEIM PHARMACEUTICALS, INC.

Boehringer Ingelheim Cares Foundation
1-800-556-8317 www.bipatientassistance.com

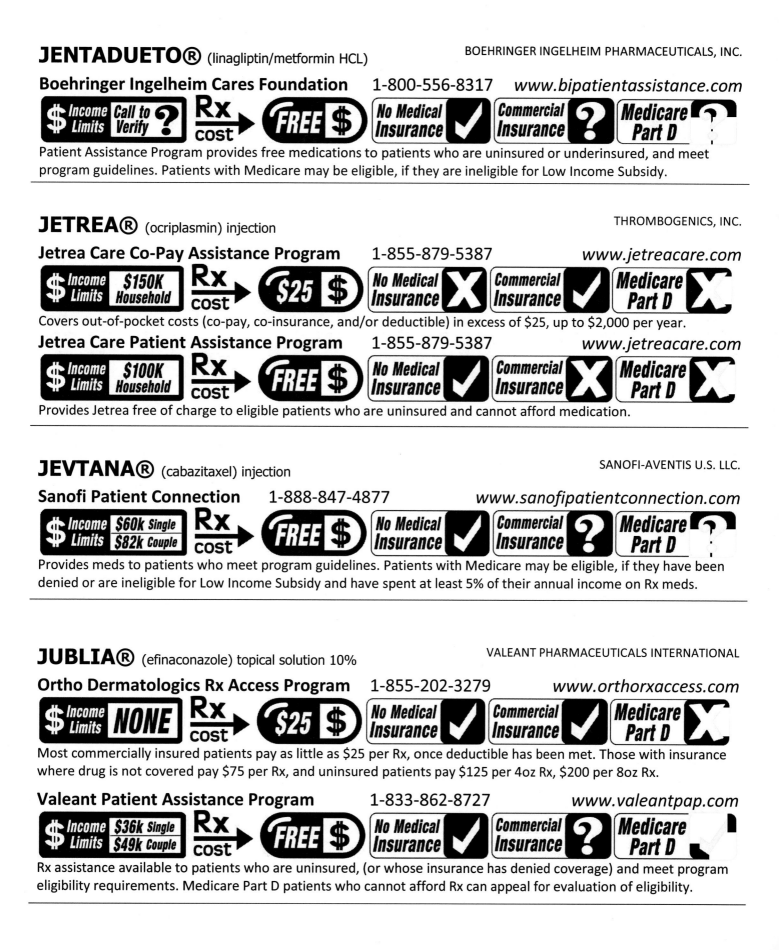

| $ Income Limits: Call to Verify ? | Rx cost → FREE $ | No Medical Insurance ✓ | Commercial Insurance ? | Medicare Part D ? |

Patient Assistance Program provides free medications to patients who are uninsured or underinsured, and meet program guidelines. Patients with Medicare may be eligible, if they are ineligible for Low Income Subsidy.

JETREA® (ocriplasmin) injection
THROMBOGENICS, INC.

Jetrea Care Co-Pay Assistance Program
1-855-879-5387 www.jetreacare.com

| $ Income Limits: $150K Household | Rx cost → $25 $ | No Medical Insurance X | Commercial Insurance ✓ | Medicare Part D X |

Covers out-of-pocket costs (co-pay, co-insurance, and/or deductible) in excess of $25, up to $2,000 per year.

Jetrea Care Patient Assistance Program
1-855-879-5387 www.jetreacare.com

| $ Income Limits: $100K Household | Rx cost → FREE $ | No Medical Insurance ✓ | Commercial Insurance X | Medicare Part D X |

Provides Jetrea free of charge to eligible patients who are uninsured and cannot afford medication.

JEVTANA® (cabazitaxel) injection
SANOFI-AVENTIS U.S. LLC.

Sanofi Patient Connection
1-888-847-4877 www.sanofipatientconnection.com

| $ Income Limits: $60k Single $82k Couple | Rx cost → FREE $ | No Medical Insurance ✓ | Commercial Insurance ? | Medicare Part D ? |

Provides meds to patients who meet program guidelines. Patients with Medicare may be eligible, if they have been denied or are ineligible for Low Income Subsidy and have spent at least 5% of their annual income on Rx meds.

JUBLIA® (efinaconazole) topical solution 10%
VALEANT PHARMACEUTICALS INTERNATIONAL

Ortho Dermatologics Rx Access Program
1-855-202-3279 www.orthorxaccess.com

| $ Income Limits: NONE | Rx cost → $25 $ | No Medical Insurance ✓ | Commercial Insurance ✓ | Medicare Part D X |

Most commercially insured patients pay as little as $25 per Rx, once deductible has been met. Those with insurance where drug is not covered pay $75 per Rx, and uninsured patients pay $125 per 4oz Rx, $200 per 8oz Rx.

Valeant Patient Assistance Program
1-833-862-8727 www.valeantpap.com

| $ Income Limits: $36k Single $49k Couple | Rx cost → FREE $ | No Medical Insurance ✓ | Commercial Insurance ? | Medicare Part D |

Rx assistance available to patients who are uninsured, (or whose insurance has denied coverage) and meet program eligibility requirements. Medicare Part D patients who cannot afford Rx can appeal for evaluation of eligibility.

JULUCA® (dolutegravir and rilpivirine)
ViiV HEALTHCARE

ViiVConnect Savings Card   1-844-588-3288   *www.viivconnect.com*

$ Income Limits **NONE** | **Rx cost** → | $0 CoPay $ | No Medical Insurance ✓ | Commercial Insurance ✓ | Medicare Part D ✗

Patients can pay as little as $0 copay, maximum savings $7500/year.

ViiV Healthcare Patient Assistance Program   1-844-588-3288   *www.viivconnect.com*

$ Income Limits **$60k Single / $82k Couple** | **Rx cost** → | FREE $ | No Medical Insurance ✓ | Commercial Insurance ? | Medicare Part D

Gives meds to patients who are uninsured, lack coverage, or on Medicare and have spent $600 on Rx meds this year.

KADCYLA® (ado-trastuzumab emtansine)
GENENTECH, INC.

Co-pay Card Assistance Program   1-855-692-6729   *www.copayassistancenow.com*

$ Income Limits **NONE** | **Rx cost** → | $5 Per Month $ | No Medical Insurance ✗ | Commercial Insurance ✓ | Medicare Part D ✗

Program provides up to $25,000/year in co-pay assistance. Patients pay only $5/month for their prescribed meds.

Genentech Access Solutions   1-866-422-2377   *www.genentech-access.com*

$ Income Limits **$100K Household** | **Rx cost** → | FREE $ | No Medical Insurance ✓ | Commercial Insurance ? | Medicare Part D ?

Program provides medications to patients who are uninsured or have been denied coverage by their insurance company. Patients who have insurance, but pay too much out of pocket per year, may also qualify for assistance.

KALBITOR® (ecallantide)
SHIRE

OnePath Patient Assistance   1-866-888-0660   *www.kalbitor.com*

$ Income Limits **Call to Verify** ? | **Rx cost** → | FREE $ | No Medical Insurance ✓ | Commercial Insurance ? | Medicare Part D ✗

Program helps cover the cost of insurance co-pays for KALBITOR, up to the program maximum, for eligible patients.

KALETRA® TABLETS or ORAL SOLUTION (lopinavir/ritonavir)
AbbVie, INC.

KALETRA® Savings Card   1-800-441-4987   *www.kaletra.com*

$ Income Limits **NONE** | **Rx cost** → | Discount Varies $ | No Medical Insurance ✗ | Commercial Insurance ✓ | Medicare Part D ✗

Eligible patients with commercial insurance can save up to $400 per month ($4,800 year maximum) .

AbbVie Patient Assistance Foundation   1-800-222-6885   *www.abbviepaf.org*

$ Income Limits **$60k Single / $82k Couple** | **Rx cost** → | FREE $ | No Medical Insurance ✓ | Commercial Insurance ✓ | Medicare Part D

Rx assistance available to patients who are uninsured and meet program eligibility requirements. Patients with Commercial Insurance or Medicare Part D, who are struggling to pay for their medications, are encouraged to apply.

KANUMA® (sebelipase alfa)

ALEXION PHARMACEUTICALS, INC.

Alexion Commercial Co-pay Program

1-888-765-4747

www.kanuma.com

| Income Limits: Call to Verify ? | Rx cost → | $5 Per Month $ | No Medical Insurance ✗ | Commercial Insurance ✓ | Medicare Part D ✗ |

Program can limit out-of-pocket expenses to $5/month for those with commercial insurance.

KALYDECO® (ivacaftor)

VERTEX PHARMACEUTICALS

Vertex Guidance & Patient Support

1-877-752-5933

www.kalydeco.com

| Income Limits: Call to Verify ? | Rx cost → | $15 $ | No Medical Insurance ✓ | Commercial Insurance ✓ | Medicare Part D ? |

Commercially insured patients can pay as little as $15 copay per prescription fill, a patient assistance program is also available for those who qualify. Call for eligibility guidelines.

KAZANO® (alogliptin and metformin HCL)

TAKEDA PHARMACEUTICALS AMERICA

Instant Savings Card

1-855-510-4545

www.nesinafamily.com

| Income Limits: NONE | Rx cost → | $35 $ | No Medical Insurance ✓ | Commercial Insurance ✓ | Medicare Part D ✗ |

Eligible commercially insured patients pay as little as $35 copay per Rx, maximum benefit for both insured and cash paying patients is $100 for a 30-day Rx and $300 for 90-day Rx.

Takeda Patient Assistance Program

1-800-830-9159

www.takedahelpathand.com

| Income Limits: $60k Single $82k Couple | Rx cost → | FREE $ | No Medical Insurance ✓ | Commercial Insurance ? | Medicare Part D ? |

Provides Kazano at no cost to eligible patients who do not have insurance or not enough coverage to obtain meds.

KEPIVANCE® (palifermin)

SOBI, INC.

Kepivance Patient Assistance Program

1-866-547-0644

www.sobi.com

| Income Limits: Call to Verify ? | Rx cost → | FREE $ | No Medical Insurance ✓ | Commercial Insurance ? | Medicare Part D ? |

Program provides meds to qualified patients who are uninsured or underinsured and cannot afford treatment.

ketorolac tromethamine ophthalmic solution → ACUVAIL™ 0.45%

KEVZARA® (sarilumab)

SANOFI AND REGENERON PHARMACEUTICALS, INC.

KevzaraConnect CoPay Card

1-844-218-0444

www.kevzara.com

| Income Limits: NONE | Rx cost → | $0 CoPay $ | No Medical Insurance ✗ | Commercial Insurance ✓ | Medicare Part D ✗ |

Commercially insured patients pay as little as $0 CoPay per month for Kevzara, $15,000 maximum savings per year.

KEVZARA® (sarilumab)

SANOFI AND REGENERON PHARMACEUTICALS, INC.

KevzaraConnect Patient Assistance 1-844-538-9272 *www.kevzara.com*

$ Income Limits | Call to Verify ? | **Rx** cost → | FREE $ | No Medical Insurance ✓ | Commercial Insurance ✗ | Medicare Part D ✗

Program provides Kevzara to patients who meet program guidelines.

KEYTRUDA® (pembrolizumab) Injection

MERCK & COMPANY, INC.

Merck Patient Assistance Program 1-800-727-5400 *www.merckhelps.com*

$ Income Limits | $48k Single $65k Couple | **Rx** cost → | FREE $ | No Medical Insurance ✓ | Commercial Insurance ? | Medicare Part D ?

Program is for patients who do not have Rx insurance coverage and cannot afford to pay for their medicine.

KINERET® (anakinra)

SOBI, INC.

Co-Pay Savings Program 1-866-547-0644 *www.kineretrx.com*

$ Income Limits | NONE | **Rx** cost → | $25 $ | No Medical Insurance ✗ | Commercial Insurance ✓ | Medicare Part D ✗

Eligible insured patients pay as little as $25 copay for each Kineret shipment, max savings $10,000 per year.

Kineret Patient Assistance Program 1-866-547-0644 *www.kineretrx.com*

$ Income Limits | Call to Verify ? | **Rx** cost → | FREE $ | No Medical Insurance ✓ | Commercial Insurance ? | Medicare Part D ?

Program provides meds to qualified patients who are uninsured or underinsured and cannot afford treatment.

KISQALI® (ribociclib)

NOVARTIS PHARMACEUTICALS

Universal Co-Pay Card 1-877-577-7756 *www.copay.novartisoncology.com*

$ Income Limits | NONE | **Rx** cost → | $25 $ | No Medical Insurance ✗ | Commercial Insurance ✓ | Medicare Part D ✗

Patients pay the first $25, the program pays the remaining co-pay or coinsurance to max benefit of $15,000/year.

Novartis Patient Assistance Foundation 1-800-277-2254 *www.pap.novartis.com*

$ Income Limits | $75k Single $100k Couple | **Rx** cost → | FREE $ | No Medical Insurance ✓ | Commercial Insurance ? | Medicare Part D ?

Program assists those without insurance, or with limited/inadequate Rx coverage to receive prescribed medications.

TIP: When in doubt... call the program and explain your situation. You may qualify for assistance.

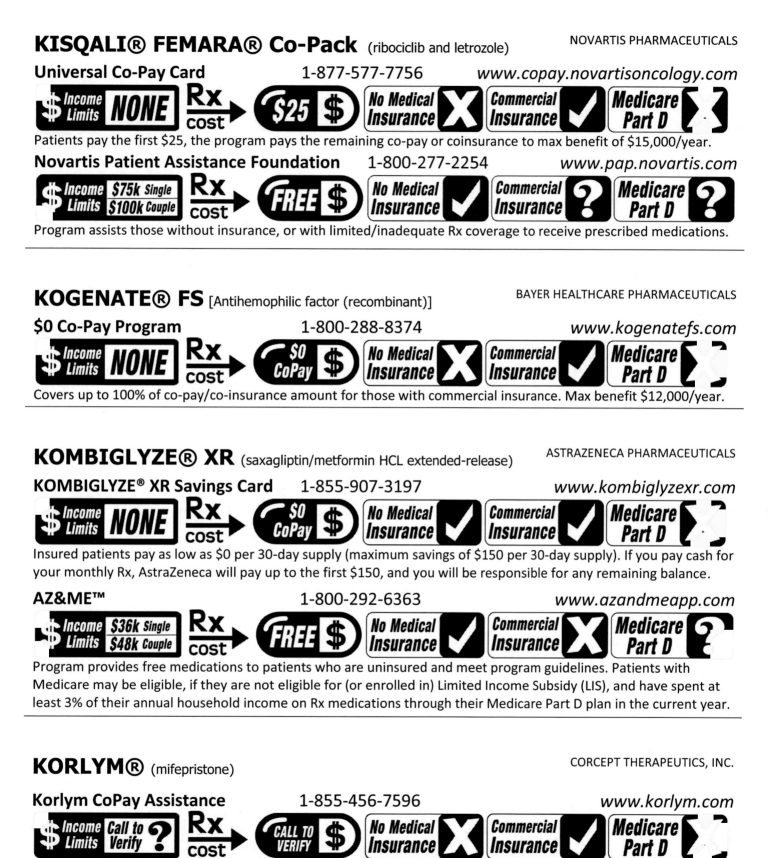

KISQALI® FEMARA® Co-Pack (ribociclib and letrozole)   NOVARTIS PHARMACEUTICALS

Universal Co-Pay Card   1-877-577-7756   *www.copay.novartisoncology.com*

Income Limits: **NONE** — Rx cost → **$25** — No Medical Insurance: X — Commercial Insurance: ✓ — Medicare Part D: X

Patients pay the first $25, the program pays the remaining co-pay or coinsurance to max benefit of $15,000/year.

Novartis Patient Assistance Foundation   1-800-277-2254   *www.pap.novartis.com*

Income Limits: **$75k Single / $100k Couple** — Rx cost → **FREE** — No Medical Insurance: ✓ — Commercial Insurance: ? — Medicare Part D: ?

Program assists those without insurance, or with limited/inadequate Rx coverage to receive prescribed medications.

KOGENATE® FS [Antihemophilic factor (recombinant)]   BAYER HEALTHCARE PHARMACEUTICALS

$0 Co-Pay Program   1-800-288-8374   *www.kogenatefs.com*

Income Limits: **NONE** — Rx cost → **$0 CoPay** — No Medical Insurance: X — Commercial Insurance: ✓ — Medicare Part D: X

Covers up to 100% of co-pay/co-insurance amount for those with commercial insurance. Max benefit $12,000/year.

KOMBIGLYZE® XR (saxagliptin/metformin HCL extended-release)   ASTRAZENECA PHARMACEUTICALS

KOMBIGLYZE® XR Savings Card   1-855-907-3197   *www.kombiglyzexr.com*

Income Limits: **NONE** — Rx cost → **$0 CoPay** — No Medical Insurance: ✓ — Commercial Insurance: ✓ — Medicare Part D: X

Insured patients pay as low as $0 per 30-day supply (maximum savings of $150 per 30-day supply). If you pay cash for your monthly Rx, AstraZeneca will pay up to the first $150, and you will be responsible for any remaining balance.

AZ&ME™   1-800-292-6363   *www.azandmeapp.com*

Income Limits: **$36k Single / $48k Couple** — Rx cost → **FREE** — No Medical Insurance: ✓ — Commercial Insurance: X — Medicare Part D: ?

Program provides free medications to patients who are uninsured and meet program guidelines. Patients with Medicare may be eligible, if they are not eligible for (or enrolled in) Limited Income Subsidy (LIS), and have spent at least 3% of their annual household income on Rx medications through their Medicare Part D plan in the current year.

KORLYM® (mifepristone)   CORCEPT THERAPEUTICS, INC.

Korlym CoPay Assistance   1-855-456-7596   *www.korlym.com*

Income Limits: **Call to Verify** ? — Rx cost → **CALL TO VERIFY** — No Medical Insurance: X — Commercial Insurance: ✓ — Medicare Part D: X

Provides co-pay assistance for eligible patients with valid Korlym Rx.

KORLYM® (mifepristone)

CORCEPT THERAPEUTICS, INC.

Korlym Patient Assistance   1-855-456-7596   www.korlym.com

$-Income Limits | Call to Verify ? | **Rx** cost → | FREE $ | No Medical Insurance ✓ | Commercial Insurance ? | Medicare Part D ✗

Rx assistance available to patients who are uninsured or underinsured, and meet program eligibility requirements.

KOVALTRY® [Antihemophilic factor (recombinant)]

BAYER HEALTHCARE PHARMACEUTICALS

$0 Co-Pay Program   1-800-288-8374   www.kovaltry-us.com

$-Income Limits | NONE | **Rx** cost → | $0 CoPay $ | No Medical Insurance ✗ | Commercial Insurance ✓ | Medicare Part D ✗

Covers up to 100% of co-pay/co-insurance amount for those with commercial insurance. Max benefit $12,000/year.

KRYSTEXXA® (pegloticase)

HORIZON PHARMA USA, INC.

Co-Pay Reduction Program   1-888-579-7839   www.krystexxa.com

$-Income Limits | NONE | **Rx** cost → | $0 CoPay $ | No Medical Insurance ✗ | Commercial Insurance ✓ | Medicare Part D ✗

Eligible insured patients pay as low as $0/month with a maximum Rx savings of $15,000 per year.

Patient Assistance Program   1-888-579-7839   www.krystexxa.com

$-Income Limits | $48k Single $65k Couple | **Rx** cost → | FREE $ | No Medical Insurance ✓ | Commercial Insurance ? | Medicare Part D ?

Program can help eligible patients who lack insurance coverage for KRYSTEXXA to get their Rx meds at no cost.

KUVAN® (sapropterin dihydrochloride)

BIOMARIN PHARMACEUTICALS, INC.

BioMarin RareConnections™   1-877-695-8826   www.kuvan.com

$-Income Limits | Call to Verify ? | **Rx** cost → | CALL TO VERIFY $ | No Medical Insurance ✓ | Commercial Insurance ✓ | Medicare Part D ✗

Program helps those who cannot afford their insurance co-payments or require additional financial assistance. Options may be available through the National Organization for Rare Disorders (NORD) or BioMarin. The BioMarin Patient Assistance Program provides KUVAN at no charge to eligible patients without insurance.

KYLEENA® (levonorgestrel-releasing intrauterine system)

BAYER HEALTHCARE PHARMACEUTICALS

ARCH™ Patient Assistance   1-877-393-9071   www.archpatientassistance.com

$-Income Limits | Call to Verify ? | **Rx** cost → | FREE $ | No Medical Insurance ✓ | Commercial Insurance ? | Medicare Part D ✗

Program provides Bayer IUDs (Kyleena, Mirena, and Skyla) at no cost to women in the United States who do not have private health insurance or Medicaid coverage for the devices. Patients may incur costs for insertion/removal of IUD.

KYPROLIS® (carfilzomib)

AMGEN, INC.

KYPROLIS FIRST STEP™ Program   1-888-657-8371   *www.amgenfirststep.com*

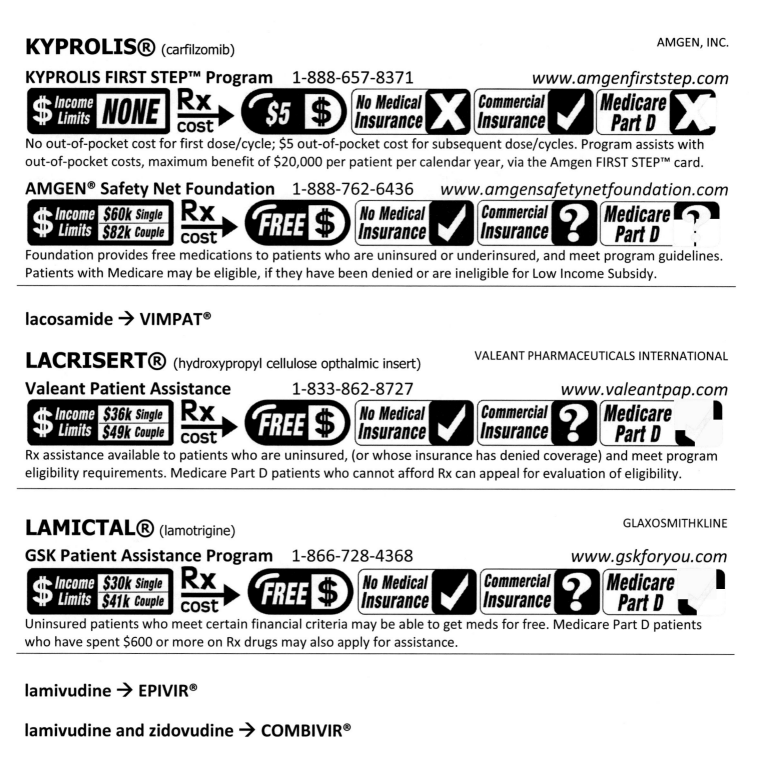

No out-of-pocket cost for first dose/cycle; $5 out-of-pocket cost for subsequent dose/cycles. Program assists with out-of-pocket costs, maximum benefit of $20,000 per patient per calendar year, via the Amgen FIRST STEP™ card.

AMGEN® Safety Net Foundation   1-888-762-6436   *www.amgensafetynetfoundation.com*

Foundation provides free medications to patients who are uninsured or underinsured, and meet program guidelines. Patients with Medicare may be eligible, if they have been denied or are ineligible for Low Income Subsidy.

---

lacosamide → VIMPAT®

LACRISERT® (hydroxypropyl cellulose opthalmic insert)

VALEANT PHARMACEUTICALS INTERNATIONAL

Valeant Patient Assistance   1-833-862-8727   *www.valeantpap.com*

Rx assistance available to patients who are uninsured, (or whose insurance has denied coverage) and meet program eligibility requirements. Medicare Part D patients who cannot afford Rx can appeal for evaluation of eligibility.

LAMICTAL® (lamotrigine)

GLAXOSMITHKLINE

GSK Patient Assistance Program   1-866-728-4368   *www.gskforyou.com*

Uninsured patients who meet certain financial criteria may be able to get meds for free. Medicare Part D patients who have spent $600 or more on Rx drugs may also apply for assistance.

---

lamivudine → EPIVIR®

lamivudine and zidovudine → COMBIVIR®

lamotrigine → LAMICTAL®

lanreotide → SOMATULINE® DEPOT

lansoprazole orally disintegrating tablet → PREVACID SOLUTAB®

lanthanum carbonate → FOSRENOL®

LANTUS®/Lantus® SoloStar® Pen (insulin glargine)

SANOFI-AVENTIS U.S. LLC.

Valyou Savings Program   1-866-390-5622   www.lantus.com

| $ Income Limits **NONE** | Rx cost → | Discount Varies $ | No Medical Insurance ✓ | Commercial Insurance ✗ | Medicare Part D ✗ |

Cash paying patients pay $99 per 10ml vial or $149 for 5-pack of pens. Maximum 10 vials or 10 5-packs per Rx.

$0 Copay Card   1-866-390-5622   www.lantus.com

| $ Income Limits **NONE** | Rx cost → | $0 CoPay $ | No Medical Insurance ✗ | Commercial Insurance ✓ | Medicare Part D ✗ |

Eligible patients pay $0 co-pay per Rx, maximum savings $500 per Rx.

Sanofi Patient Connection   1-888-847-4877   www.sanofipatientconnection.com

| $ Income Limits $30k Single / $41k Couple | Rx cost → | FREE $ | No Medical Insurance ✓ | Commercial Insurance ? | Medicare Part D ? |

Provides meds to patients who meet program guidelines. Patients with Medicare may be eligible, if they have been denied or are ineligible for Low Income Subsidy and have spent at least 5% of their annual income on Rx meds.

---

lapatinib → TYKERB®

laronidase → ALDURAZYME®

LARTRUVO® (olaratumab)

LILLY USA, LLC

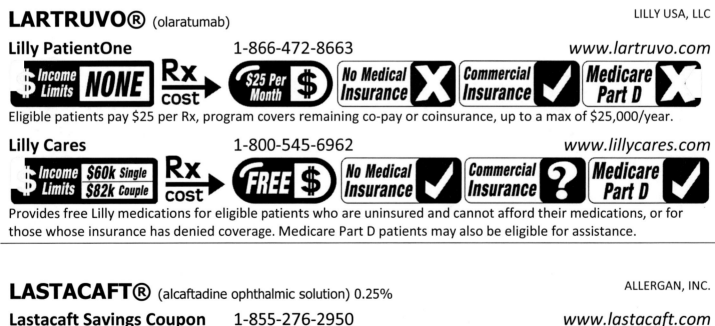

Lilly PatientOne   1-866-472-8663   www.lartruvo.com

| $ Income Limits **NONE** | Rx cost → | $25 Per Month $ | No Medical Insurance ✗ | Commercial Insurance ✓ | Medicare Part D ✗ |

Eligible patients pay $25 per Rx, program covers remaining co-pay or coinsurance, up to a max of $25,000/year.

Lilly Cares   1-800-545-6962   www.lillycares.com

| $ Income Limits $60k Single / $82k Couple | Rx cost → | FREE $ | No Medical Insurance ✓ | Commercial Insurance ? | Medicare Part D ✓ |

Provides free Lilly medications for eligible patients who are uninsured and cannot afford their medications, or for those whose insurance has denied coverage. Medicare Part D patients may also be eligible for assistance.

LASTACAFT® (alcaftadine ophthalmic solution) 0.25%

ALLERGAN, INC.

Lastacaft Savings Coupon   1-855-276-2950   www.lastacaft.com

| $ Income Limits **NONE** | Rx cost → | $30 OFF | No Medical Insurance ✗ | Commercial Insurance ✓ | Medicare Part D ✗ |

Commercially insured patients save up to $30 on their first Rx, and up to $20 on their second Rx.

latanoprost → XALATAN®

latanoprostene bunod ophthalmic solution 0.024%→ VYZULTA™

LATUDA® (lurasidone HCL) tablets

SUNOVION PHARMACEUTICALS, INC.

LATUDA Copay Savings Card   1-855-552-8832   *www.latuda.com*

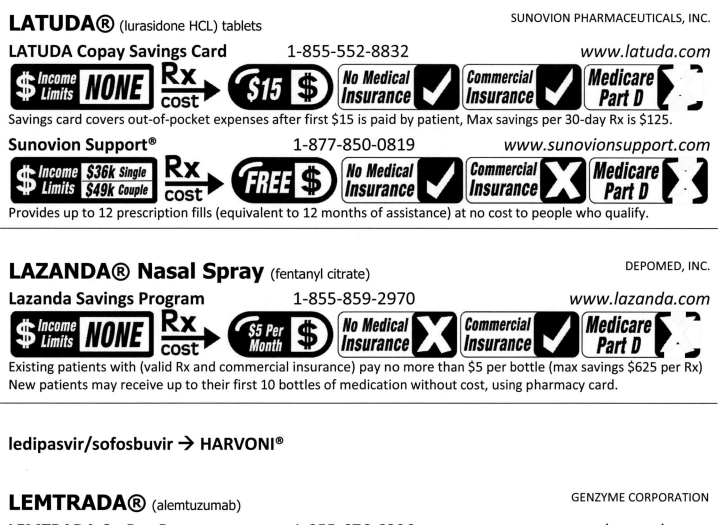

Savings card covers out-of-pocket expenses after first $15 is paid by patient, Max savings per 30-day Rx is $125.

Sunovion Support®   1-877-850-0819   *www.sunovionsupport.com*

Provides up to 12 prescription fills (equivalent to 12 months of assistance) at no cost to people who qualify.

LAZANDA® Nasal Spray (fentanyl citrate)

DEPOMED, INC.

Lazanda Savings Program   1-855-859-2970   *www.lazanda.com*

Existing patients with (valid Rx and commercial insurance) pay no more than $5 per bottle (max savings $625 per Rx)
New patients may receive up to their first 10 bottles of medication without cost, using pharmacy card.

ledipasvir/sofosbuvir → HARVONI®

LEMTRADA® (alemtuzumab)

GENZYME CORPORATION

LEMTRADA Co-Pay Program   1-855-676-6326   *www.lemtrada.com*

Covers up to 100% of your eligible out-of-pocket Lemtrada costs and up to $100/day for infusion related expenses.

Charitable Access Program   1-855-676-6326   *www.lemtrada.com*

Program provides medications to patients who are uninsured or have inadequate insurance coverage for Lemtrada

lenvatinib → LENVIMA®

lenalidomide → REVLIMID®

LENVIMA® (lenvatinib)

EISAI, INC.

$0 Co-Pay Program   1-866-613-4724   *www.lenvima.com*

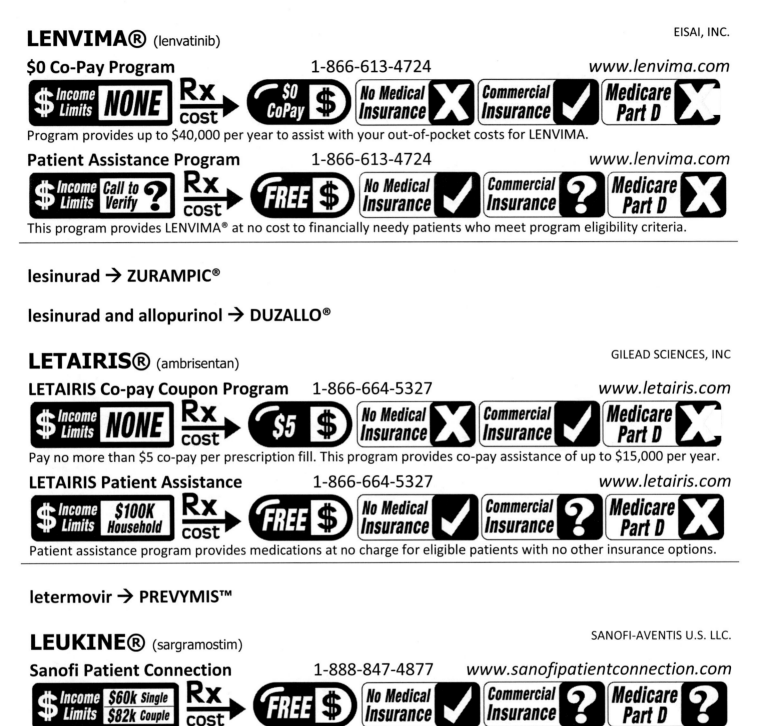

Program provides up to $40,000 per year to assist with your out-of-pocket costs for LENVIMA.

Patient Assistance Program   1-866-613-4724   *www.lenvima.com*

This program provides LENVIMA® at no cost to financially needy patients who meet program eligibility criteria.

---

lesinurad → ZURAMPIC®

lesinurad and allopurinol → DUZALLO®

LETAIRIS® (ambrisentan)

GILEAD SCIENCES, INC

LETAIRIS Co-pay Coupon Program   1-866-664-5327   *www.letairis.com*

Pay no more than $5 co-pay per prescription fill. This program provides co-pay assistance of up to $15,000 per year.

LETAIRIS Patient Assistance   1-866-664-5327   *www.letairis.com*

Patient assistance program provides medications at no charge for eligible patients with no other insurance options.

---

letermovir → PREVYMIS™

LEUKINE® (sargramostim)

SANOFI-AVENTIS U.S. LLC.

Sanofi Patient Connection   1-888-847-4877   *www.sanofipatientconnection.com*

Provides meds to patients who meet program guidelines. Patients with Medicare may be eligible, if they have been denied or are ineligible for Low Income Subsidy and have spent at least 5% of their annual income on Rx meds.

---

leuprolide acetate → ELIGARD®

leuprolide acetate → LUPRON DEPOT®

leuprolide acetate/norethindrone acetate tablets → LUPANETA PACK®

LEVEMIR® (insulin detemir [rDNA origin] injection)

NOVO NORDISK, INC.

Novo Nordisk Savings Card   1-877-304-6855   *www.novocare.com*

Pay as little as $25 per 30-day, $50 per 60-day, or $75 per 90-day supply for up to 24 months from the date of Savings Card activation, subject to a max savings of $100 per 30-day, $200 per 60-day, or $300 per 90-day supply.

Patient Access Program   1-866-310-7549   *www.novocare.com*

For patients who are uninsured. Also for Medicare patients who have spent more than $1000 this year on Rx meds.

---

levoleucovorin → FUSILEV®

levomilnacipran → FETZIMA®

levonorgestrel → LILETTA®

levonorgestrel-releasing intrauterine system → KYLEENA®

levonorgestrel-releasing intrauterine system → MIRENA®

levonorgestrel-releasing intrauterine system → SKYLA®

levothyroxine → LEVOXYL®

levothyroxine sodium → SYNTHROID®

levothyroxine sodium → TIROSINT®

LEVOXYL® (levothyroxine)

PFIZER, INC

Pfizer Savings Program   1-866-706-2400   *www.pfizerrxpathways.com*

Program helps uninsured patients receive discounted Pfizer medications through their local retail pharmacy.

LEXIVA® (fosamprenavir calcium)

ViiV HEALTHCARE

ViiVConnect Savings Card   1-844-588-3288   *www.viivconnect.com*

Patients can pay as little as $0 copay, maximum savings $4500/year.

LEXIVA® (fosamprenavir calcium)

ViiV HEALTHCARE

ViiV Healthcare Patient Assistance　　1-844-588-3288　　*www.viivconnect.com*

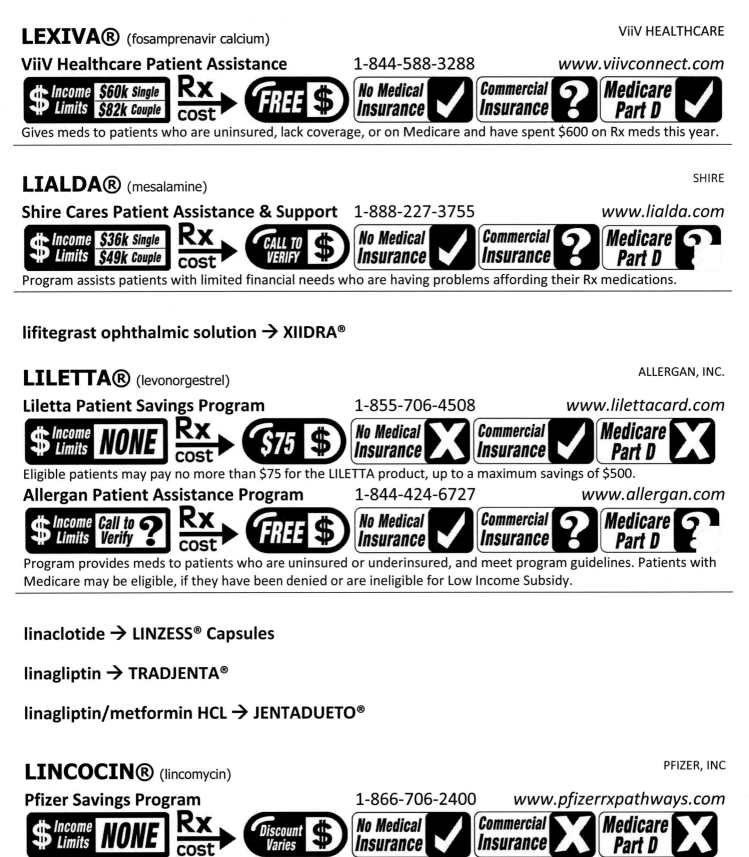

Gives meds to patients who are uninsured, lack coverage, or on Medicare and have spent $600 on Rx meds this year.

LIALDA® (mesalamine)

SHIRE

Shire Cares Patient Assistance & Support　1-888-227-3755　　*www.lialda.com*

Program assists patients with limited financial needs who are having problems affording their Rx medications.

lifitegrast ophthalmic solution → XIIDRA®

LILETTA® (levonorgestrel)

ALLERGAN, INC.

Liletta Patient Savings Program　　1-855-706-4508　　*www.lilettacard.com*

Eligible patients may pay no more than $75 for the LILETTA product, up to a maximum savings of $500.

Allergan Patient Assistance Program　　1-844-424-6727　　*www.allergan.com*

Program provides meds to patients who are uninsured or underinsured, and meet program guidelines. Patients with Medicare may be eligible, if they have been denied or are ineligible for Low Income Subsidy.

linaclotide → LINZESS® Capsules

linagliptin → TRADJENTA®

linagliptin/metformin HCL → JENTADUETO®

LINCOCIN® (lincomycin)

PFIZER, INC

Pfizer Savings Program　　1-866-706-2400　　*www.pfizerrxpathways.com*

Program helps uninsured patients receive discounted Pfizer medications through their local retail pharmacy.

LINCOCIN® (lincomycin)

PFIZER, INC

Pfizer Patient Assistance Program   1-844-989-7284   *www.pfizerrxpathways.com*

| $ Income Limits | $48k Single / $65k Couple | Rx cost → | FREE $ | No Medical Insurance ✓ | Commercial Insurance ? | Medicare Part D ✗ |

Assists eligible patients who are uninsured (or have inadequate drug coverage) and cannot afford their medications.

lincomycin → LINCOCIN®

linezolid → ZYVOX®

LINZESS® Capsules (linaclotide)

ALLERGAN, INC.

LINZESS Savings Card   1-855-859-5614   *www.linzess.com*

| $ Income Limits | NONE | Rx cost → | $30 $ | No Medical Insurance ✗ | Commercial Insurance ✓ | Medicare Part D ✗ |

Most eligible patients may pay as little as $30 per 30, 60, or 90-day supply of Linzess using the savings card.

Allergan Patient Assistance   1-844-424-6727   *www.allergan.com*

| $ Income Limits | Call to Verify ? | Rx cost → | FREE $ | No Medical Insurance ✓ | Commercial Insurance ? | Medicare Part D ? |

Program provides meds to patients who are uninsured or underinsured, and meet program guidelines. Patients with Medicare may be eligible, if they have been denied or are ineligible for Low Income Subsidy.

LIORESAL® (baclofen injectable; intrathecal)

SAOL THERAPEUTICS, INC.

Lioresal Patient Assistance Program   1-877-222-7715   *www.lioresal.com*

| $ Income Limits | $48k Single / $65k Couple | Rx cost → | FREE $ | No Medical Insurance ✓ | Commercial Insurance ? | Medicare Part D ? |

Program provides Lioresal to qualified patients who are uninsured, or whose insurance does not cover treatment.

liothyronine sodium → CYTOMEL®

LIPITOR® (atorvastatin calcium)

PFIZER, INC

Pfizer Savings Program   1-866-706-2400   *www.pfizerrxpathways.com*

| $ Income Limits | NONE | Rx cost → | Discount Varies $ | No Medical Insurance ✓ | Commercial Insurance ✗ | Medicare Part D ✗ |

Program helps uninsured patients receive discounted Pfizer medications through their local retail pharmacy.

liraglutide → SAXENDA®

liraglutide → VICTOZA®

lisdexamfetamine dimesylate → VYVANSE®

LIVALO® (pitavastatin)   KOWA PHARMACEUTICALS AMERICA, INC.

LIVALO Savings Program   1-844-567-9504   www.livalorx.com

Save up to $75 on Rx cost and/or co-pay on each 30-day supply. Most insured patients pay $18/month.

LIVALO® Patient Assistance   1-877-438-9759   www.livalorx.org

Provides LIVALO free to those who are uninsured, and Medicare Part D patients, if Rx is not covered under your plan.

lixisenatide injection → ADLYXIN™

LOCOID® (hydrocortisone butyrate) lotion 0.1%   VALEANT PHARMACEUTICALS INTERNATIONAL

Valeant Patient Assistance   1-833-862-8727   *www.valeantpap.com*

Rx assistance available to patients who are uninsured, (or whose insurance has denied coverage) and meet program eligibility requirements. Medicare Part D patients who cannot afford Rx can appeal for evaluation of eligibility.

lodoxamide tromethamine solution → ALOMIDE®

LOMOTIL® (diphenoxylate HCL / atropine)   PFIZER, INC

Pfizer Savings Program   1-866-706-2400   *www.pfizerrxpathways.com*

Program helps uninsured patients receive discounted Pfizer medications through their local retail pharmacy.

LONSURF® (trifluridine and tipiracil)   TAIHO ONCOLOGY, INC

Taiho Oncology Patient Support   1-888-454-8860   *www.taihopatientsupport.com*

Offers both a copay assistance program for insured patients, and a patient assistance program for those uninsured.

LOPID® (gemfibrozil)

PFIZER, INC

Pfizer Savings Program   1-866-706-2400   *www.pfizerrxpathways.com*

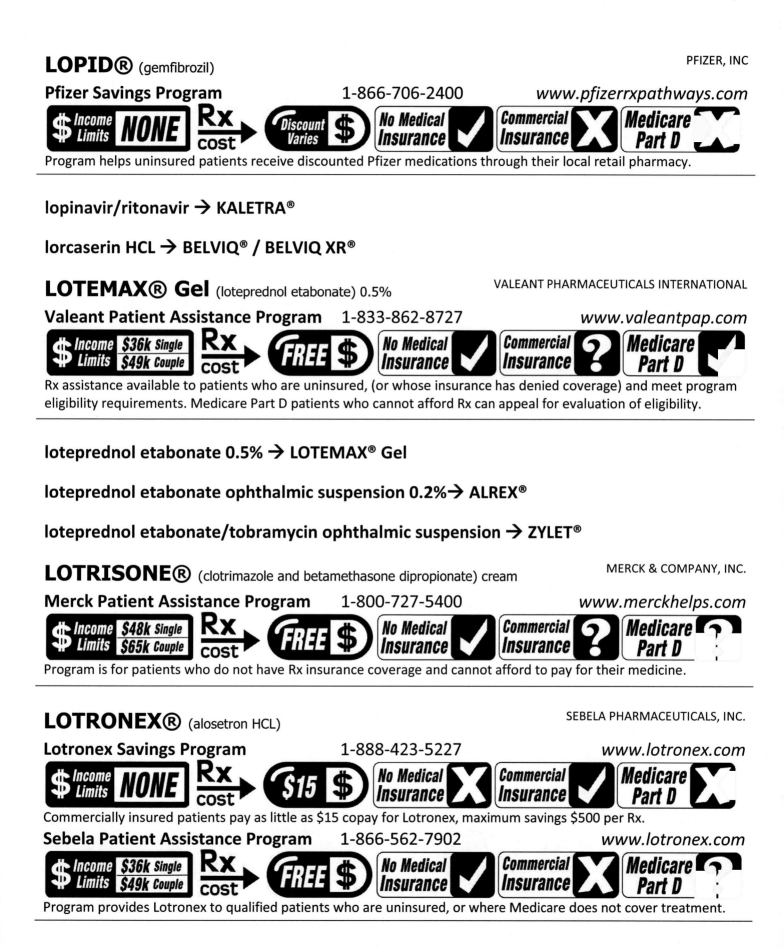

Program helps uninsured patients receive discounted Pfizer medications through their local retail pharmacy.

---

lopinavir/ritonavir → KALETRA®

lorcaserin HCL → BELVIQ® / BELVIQ XR®

LOTEMAX® Gel (loteprednol etabonate) 0.5%

VALEANT PHARMACEUTICALS INTERNATIONAL

Valeant Patient Assistance Program   1-833-862-8727   *www.valeantpap.com*

Rx assistance available to patients who are uninsured, (or whose insurance has denied coverage) and meet program eligibility requirements. Medicare Part D patients who cannot afford Rx can appeal for evaluation of eligibility.

---

loteprednol etabonate 0.5% → LOTEMAX® Gel

loteprednol etabonate ophthalmic suspension 0.2%→ ALREX®

loteprednol etabonate/tobramycin ophthalmic suspension → ZYLET®

LOTRISONE® (clotrimazole and betamethasone dipropionate) cream

MERCK & COMPANY, INC.

Merck Patient Assistance Program   1-800-727-5400   *www.merckhelps.com*

Program is for patients who do not have Rx insurance coverage and cannot afford to pay for their medicine.

LOTRONEX® (alosetron HCL)

SEBELA PHARMACEUTICALS, INC.

Lotronex Savings Program   1-888-423-5227   *www.lotronex.com*

Commercially insured patients pay as little as $15 copay for Lotronex, maximum savings $500 per Rx.

Sebela Patient Assistance Program   1-866-562-7902   *www.lotronex.com*

Program provides Lotronex to qualified patients who are uninsured, or where Medicare does not cover treatment.

LOVENOX® (enoxaparin sodium)

Sanofi Patient Connection   1-888-847-4877   *www.sanofipatientconnection.com*

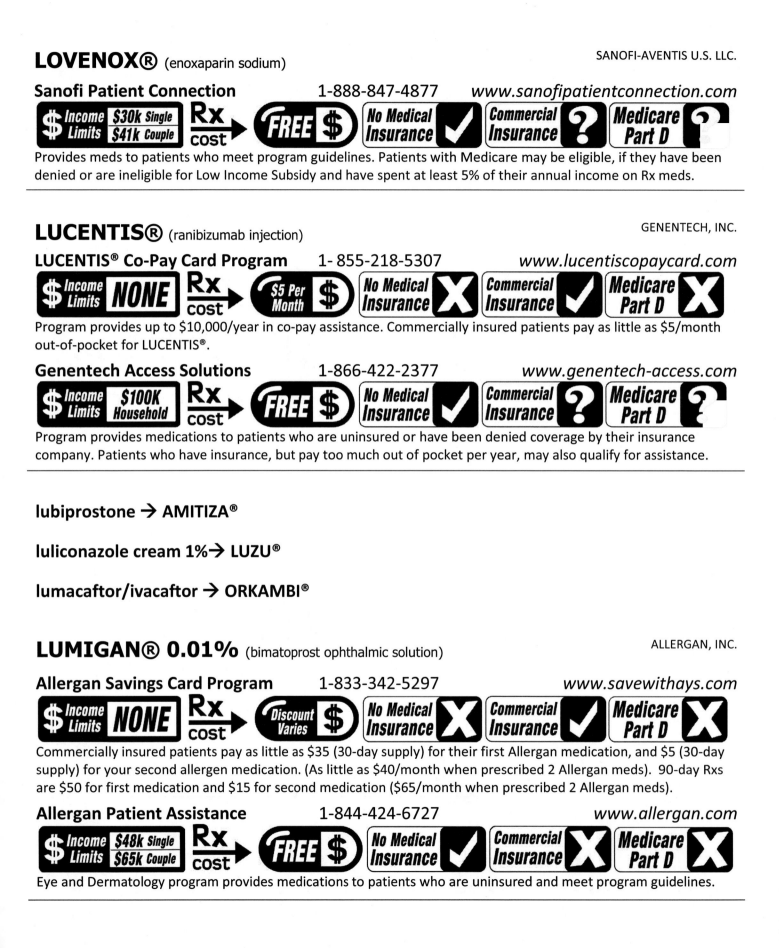

Income Limits **$30k Single $41k Couple** | Rx cost → | **FREE $** | No Medical Insurance ✓ | Commercial Insurance ? | Medicare Part D ?

Provides meds to patients who meet program guidelines. Patients with Medicare may be eligible, if they have been denied or are ineligible for Low Income Subsidy and have spent at least 5% of their annual income on Rx meds.

LUCENTIS® (ranibizumab injection)

GENENTECH, INC.

LUCENTIS® Co-Pay Card Program   1- 855-218-5307   *www.lucentiscopaycard.com*

Income Limits **NONE** | Rx cost → | **$5 Per Month $** | No Medical Insurance ✗ | Commercial Insurance ✓ | Medicare Part D ✗

Program provides up to $10,000/year in co-pay assistance. Commercially insured patients pay as little as $5/month out-of-pocket for LUCENTIS®.

Genentech Access Solutions   1-866-422-2377   *www.genentech-access.com*

Income Limits **$100K Household** | Rx cost → | **FREE $** | No Medical Insurance ✓ | Commercial Insurance ? | Medicare Part D ?

Program provides medications to patients who are uninsured or have been denied coverage by their insurance company. Patients who have insurance, but pay too much out of pocket per year, may also qualify for assistance.

lubiprostone → AMITIZA®

luliconazole cream 1%→ LUZU®

lumacaftor/ivacaftor → ORKAMBI®

LUMIGAN® 0.01% (bimatoprost ophthalmic solution)

ALLERGAN, INC.

Allergan Savings Card Program   1-833-342-5297   *www.savewithays.com*

Income Limits **NONE** | Rx cost → | **Discount Varies $** | No Medical Insurance ✗ | Commercial Insurance ✓ | Medicare Part D ✗

Commercially insured patients pay as little as $35 (30-day supply) for their first Allergan medication, and $5 (30-day supply) for your second allergen medication. (As little as $40/month when prescribed 2 Allergan meds). 90-day Rxs are $50 for first medication and $15 for second medication ($65/month when prescribed 2 Allergan meds).

Allergan Patient Assistance   1-844-424-6727   *www.allergan.com*

Income Limits **$48k Single $65k Couple** | Rx cost → | **FREE $** | No Medical Insurance ✓ | Commercial Insurance ✗ | Medicare Part D ✗

Eye and Dermatology program provides medications to patients who are uninsured and meet program guidelines.

LUMIZYME® (alglucosidase alfa)

GENZYME CORPORATION

Sanofi Genzyme Co-Pay Assistance Program   1-800-745-4447   *www.lumizyme.com*

Covers 100% of your eligible out-of-pocket Lumizyme drug and infusion-related costs up to the program maximum.

Charitable Access Program   1-800-745-4447   *www.lumizyme.com*

Program provides medications to patients who are uninsured or have inadequate insurance coverage for Lumizyme

LUPANETA PACK®

AbbVie, INC.

(leuprolide acetate for depot suspension and norethindrone acetate tablets)

Lupaneta Pack Savings Card   1-855-587-7663   *www.lupanetapack.com*

Eligible insured patients can pay as little as $10 per dose, max savings $150 for 1-month Rx, $250 for 3-month Rx.

AbbVie Patient Assistance Foundation   1-800-222-6885   *www.abbviepaf.org*

Rx assistance available to patients who are uninsured and meet program eligibility requirements. Patients with Commercial Insurance or Medicare Part D, who are struggling to pay for their medications, are encouraged to apply.

LUPRON DEPOT® (leuprolide acetate)

AbbVie, INC

Lupron Depot Savings Card   1-855-587-7663   *www.luprongyn.com*

Eligible patients can pay as little as $10 per dose, max savings $150 /1-month Rx, $250/3-month Rx.

Lupron Depot-Ped Savings Card   1-877-832-9755   *www.lupronped.com*

Eligible patients can pay as little as $10 per dose, max savings $150 /1-month Rx, $1000/3-month Rx, $2000/year.

AbbVie Patient Assistance Foundation   1-800-222-6885   *www.abbviepaf.org*

Rx assistance available to patients who are uninsured and meet program eligibility requirements. Patients with Commercial Insurance or Medicare Part D, who are struggling to pay for their medications, are encouraged to apply.

lurasidone HCL → LATUDA®

LUZU® (luliconazole) cream 1%
VALEANT PHARMACEUTICALS INTERNATIONAL

Ortho Dermatologics Rx Access   1-855-202-3279   *www.orthorxaccess.com*

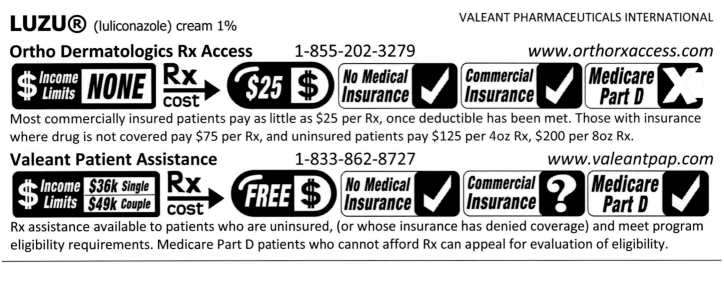

Most commercially insured patients pay as little as $25 per Rx, once deductible has been met. Those with insurance where drug is not covered pay $75 per Rx, and uninsured patients pay $125 per 4oz Rx, $200 per 8oz Rx.

Valeant Patient Assistance   1-833-862-8727   *www.valeantpap.com*

Rx assistance available to patients who are uninsured, (or whose insurance has denied coverage) and meet program eligibility requirements. Medicare Part D patients who cannot afford Rx can appeal for evaluation of eligibility.

---

lymphocyte immune globulin/anti-thymocyte globulin → ATGAM®

LYNPARZA® Tablets (olaparib)
ASTRAZENECA PHARMACEUTICALS

AZ&ME™   1-800-292-6363   *www.azandmeapp.com*

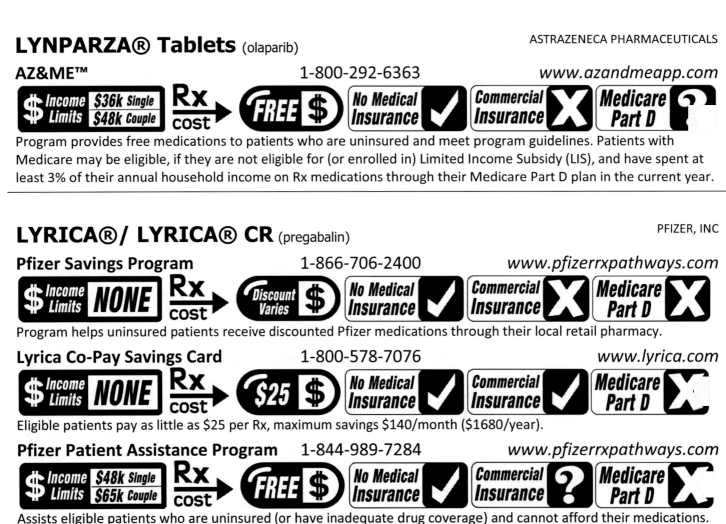

Program provides free medications to patients who are uninsured and meet program guidelines. Patients with Medicare may be eligible, if they are not eligible for (or enrolled in) Limited Income Subsidy (LIS), and have spent at least 3% of their annual household income on Rx medications through their Medicare Part D plan in the current year.

LYRICA®/ LYRICA® CR (pregabalin)
PFIZER, INC

Pfizer Savings Program   1-866-706-2400   *www.pfizerrxpathways.com*

Program helps uninsured patients receive discounted Pfizer medications through their local retail pharmacy.

Lyrica Co-Pay Savings Card   1-800-578-7076   *www.lyrica.com*

Eligible patients pay as little as $25 per Rx, maximum savings $140/month ($1680/year).

Pfizer Patient Assistance Program   1-844-989-7284   *www.pfizerrxpathways.com*

Assists eligible patients who are uninsured (or have inadequate drug coverage) and cannot afford their medications.

LYSODREN® (mitotane)

BRISTOL-MYERS SQUIBB

Access Support Program for Oncology   1-800-861-0048   *www.bmsaccesssupport.com*

Program provides free medications to eligible patients who are uninsured, had coverage denied by insurer, or Medicare patients who not eligible for the Low Income Subsidy and have significant financial and medical need.

---

macitentan → OPSUMIT® TABLETS

MACUGEN® (pegaptanb sodium injection)

VALEANT PHARMACEUTICALS INTERNATIONAL

Valeant Patient Assistance Program   1-833-862-8727   *www.valeantpap.com*

Rx assistance available to patients who are uninsured, (or whose insurance has denied coverage) and meet program eligibility requirements. Medicare Part D patients who cannot afford Rx can appeal for evaluation of eligibility.

MAKENA® Injection (hydroxyprogesterone caproate)

AMAG PHARMACEUTICALS

Makena Co-Pay Assistance Program   1-800-847-3418   *www.makenahcp.com*

Program helps lower out-of-pocket costs associated with copays, coinsurance, and deductibles for commercially insured patients.

Makena Patient Assistance Program   1-800-847-3418   *www.makenahcp.com*

Program offers a free course of therapyhelps to uninsured/underinsured patients.

MALARONE® (atovaquone and proguanil hydrochloride)

GLAXOSMITHKLINE

GSK Patient Assistance Program   1-866-728-4368   *www.gskforyou.com*

Uninsured patients who meet certain financial criteria may be able to get meds for free. Medicare Part D patients who have spent $600 or more on Rx drugs may also apply for assistance.

---

maraviroc → SELZENTRY®

MARPLAN® (isocarboxazid)
VALIDUS PHARMACEUTICALS

Discount Card   1-866-297-6945   *www.marplan.com*

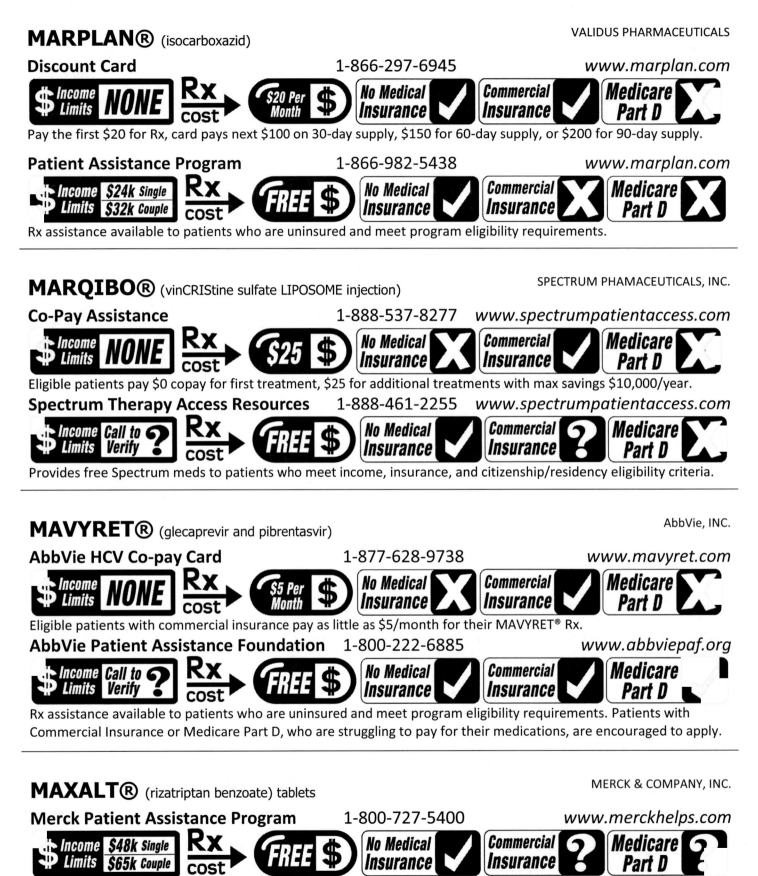

$ Income Limits **NONE** | **Rx** cost → | $20 Per Month $ | No Medical Insurance ✓ | Commercial Insurance ✓ | Medicare Part D ✗

Pay the first $20 for Rx, card pays next $100 on 30-day supply, $150 for 60-day supply, or $200 for 90-day supply.

Patient Assistance Program   1-866-982-5438   *www.marplan.com*

$ Income Limits $24k Single $32k Couple | **Rx** cost → | FREE $ | No Medical Insurance ✓ | Commercial Insurance ✗ | Medicare Part D ✗

Rx assistance available to patients who are uninsured and meet program eligibility requirements.

MARQIBO® (vinCRIStine sulfate LIPOSOME injection)
SPECTRUM PHAMACEUTICALS, INC.

Co-Pay Assistance   1-888-537-8277   *www.spectrumpatientaccess.com*

$ Income Limits **NONE** | **Rx** cost → | $25 $ | No Medical Insurance ✗ | Commercial Insurance ✓ | Medicare Part D ✗

Eligible patients pay $0 copay for first treatment, $25 for additional treatments with max savings $10,000/year.

Spectrum Therapy Access Resources   1-888-461-2255   *www.spectrumpatientaccess.com*

$ Income Limits Call to Verify ? | **Rx** cost → | FREE $ | No Medical Insurance ✓ | Commercial Insurance ? | Medicare Part D ✗

Provides free Spectrum meds to patients who meet income, insurance, and citizenship/residency eligibility criteria.

MAVYRET® (glecaprevir and pibrentasvir)
AbbVie, INC.

AbbVie HCV Co-pay Card   1-877-628-9738   *www.mavyret.com*

$ Income Limits **NONE** | **Rx** cost → | $5 Per Month $ | No Medical Insurance ✗ | Commercial Insurance ✓ | Medicare Part D ✗

Eligible patients with commercial insurance pay as little as $5/month for their MAVYRET® Rx.

AbbVie Patient Assistance Foundation   1-800-222-6885   *www.abbviepaf.org*

$ Income Limits Call to Verify ? | **Rx** cost → | FREE $ | No Medical Insurance ✓ | Commercial Insurance ✓ | Medicare Part D ✓

Rx assistance available to patients who are uninsured and meet program eligibility requirements. Patients with Commercial Insurance or Medicare Part D, who are struggling to pay for their medications, are encouraged to apply.

MAXALT® (rizatriptan benzoate) tablets
MERCK & COMPANY, INC.

Merck Patient Assistance Program   1-800-727-5400   *www.merckhelps.com*

$ Income Limits $48k Single $65k Couple | **Rx** cost → | FREE $ | No Medical Insurance ✓ | Commercial Insurance ? | Medicare Part D ?

Program is for patients who do not have Rx insurance coverage and cannot afford to pay for their medicine.

MAXIDEX® (dexamethasone suspension)

NOVARTIS PHARMACEUTICALS

Novartis Patient Assistance Foundation   1-800-277-2254   *www.pap.novartis.com*

$ Income Limits $75k Single / $100k Couple | Rx cost → | FREE $ | No Medical Insurance ✓ | Commercial Insurance ? | Medicare Part D ?

Program assists those without insurance, or with limited/inadequate Rx coverage to receive prescribed medications.

mebendazole → EMVERM®

mechlorethamine injectable → MUSTARGEN®

MEDROL® (methylprednisolone)

PFIZER, INC

Pfizer Savings Program   1-866-706-2400   *www.pfizerrxpathways.com*

$ Income Limits NONE | Rx cost → | Discount Varies $ | No Medical Insurance ✓ | Commercial Insurance ✗ | Medicare Part D ✗

Program helps uninsured patients receive discounted Pfizer medications through their local retail pharmacy.

medroxyprogesterone acetate → DEPO-PROVERA®

medroxyprogesterone acetate → PROVERA®

medroxyprogesterone acetate/conjugated estrogens → PREMPHASE®

medroxyprogesterone acetate/conjugated estrogens → PREMPRO®

mecasermin → INCRELEX®

MEKINIST® (tramitinib)

NOVARTIS PHARMACEUTICALS

Universal Co-Pay Card   1-877-577-7756   *www.copay.novartisoncology.com*

$ Income Limits NONE | Rx cost → | $25 $ | No Medical Insurance ✗ | Commercial Insurance ✓ | Medicare Part D ✗

Patients pay the first $25, the program pays the remaining co-pay or coinsurance to max benefit of $15,000/year.

Novartis Patient Assistance Foundation   1-800-277-2254   *www.pap.novartis.com*

$ Income Limits $75k Single / $100k Couple | Rx cost → | FREE $ | No Medical Insurance ✓ | Commercial Insurance ? | Medicare Part D ?

Program assists those without insurance, or with limited/inadequate Rx coverage to receive prescribed medications.

melphalan for injection → EVOMELA®

memantine HCL → NAMENDA® Tablets/Oral Solution

memantine HCL and donepezil HCL → NAMZARIC® Capsules

MENEST® (esterified estrogens)
PFIZER, INC

Pfizer Savings Program   1-866-706-2400   *www.pfizerrxpathways.com*

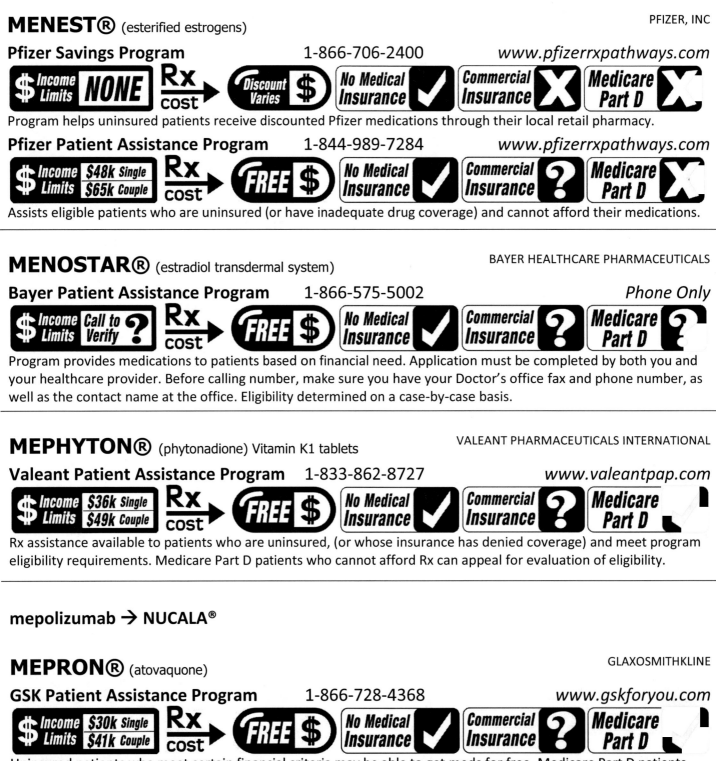

$ Income Limits **NONE** | **Rx** cost → | Discount Varies $ | No Medical Insurance ✔ | Commercial Insurance ✘ | Medicare Part D ✘

Program helps uninsured patients receive discounted Pfizer medications through their local retail pharmacy.

Pfizer Patient Assistance Program   1-844-989-7284   *www.pfizerrxpathways.com*

$ Income Limits **$48k Single / $65k Couple** | **Rx** cost → | FREE $ | No Medical Insurance ✔ | Commercial Insurance ? | Medicare Part D ✘

Assists eligible patients who are uninsured (or have inadequate drug coverage) and cannot afford their medications.

MENOSTAR® (estradiol transdermal system)
BAYER HEALTHCARE PHARMACEUTICALS

Bayer Patient Assistance Program   1-866-575-5002   *Phone Only*

$ Income Limits **Call to Verify ?** | **Rx** cost → | FREE $ | No Medical Insurance ✔ | Commercial Insurance ? | Medicare Part D ?

Program provides medications to patients based on financial need. Application must be completed by both you and your healthcare provider. Before calling number, make sure you have your Doctor's office fax and phone number, as well as the contact name at the office. Eligibility determined on a case-by-case basis.

MEPHYTON® (phytonadione) Vitamin K1 tablets
VALEANT PHARMACEUTICALS INTERNATIONAL

Valeant Patient Assistance Program   1-833-862-8727   *www.valeantpap.com*

$ Income Limits **$36k Single / $49k Couple** | **Rx** cost → | FREE $ | No Medical Insurance ✔ | Commercial Insurance ? | Medicare Part D

Rx assistance available to patients who are uninsured, (or whose insurance has denied coverage) and meet program eligibility requirements. Medicare Part D patients who cannot afford Rx can appeal for evaluation of eligibility.

mepolizumab → NUCALA®

MEPRON® (atovaquone)
GLAXOSMITHKLINE

GSK Patient Assistance Program   1-866-728-4368   *www.gskforyou.com*

$ Income Limits **$30k Single / $41k Couple** | **Rx** cost → | FREE $ | No Medical Insurance ✔ | Commercial Insurance ? | Medicare Part D

Uninsured patients who meet certain financial criteria may be able to get meds for free. Medicare Part D patients who have spent $600 or more on Rx drugs may also apply for assistance.

mesalamine → APRISO®

mesalamine → CANASA®

mesalamine → DELZICOL® DR Capsules

mesalamine → LIALDA®

mesalamine → PENTASA®

metaxalone → SKELAXIN®

methamphetamine hydrochloride → DESOXYN®

methotrexate → OTREXUP®

methoxsalen → OXSORALEN-ULTRA®

methsuximide capsules → CELONTIN®

methylnaltrexone bromide → RELISTOR®

methyphenidate HCL → CONCERTA®

methylphenidate HCl → QUILLICHEW ER™/ QUILLIVANT XR®

methylphenidate transdermal system → DAYTRANA®

methylprednisolone → MEDROL®

methylprednisolone acetate → DEPO-MEDROL®

methyltestosterone → ANDROID®

metronidazole → FLAGYL®

metronidazole cream 1%→ NORITATE®

metyrosine capsules → DEMSER®

midostaurin → RYDAPT®

mifepristone → KORLYM®

miglitol → GLYSET®

miglustat → ZAVESCA®

milnacipran HCl → SAVELLA® Tablets & Titration Pack

MINIVELLE® (estradiol transdermal system)   NOVEN THERAPEUTICS, LLC

Minivelle Savings Offer   1-855-497-8461   *www.minivelle.com*

$ Income Limits NONE | **Rx cost →** | **$15 $** | **No Medical Insurance ✓** | **Commercial Insurance ✓** | **Medicare Part D ✗**

Insured patients pay as little as $15 per Rx. Insured and uninsured patients receive $55 off Rx after first $15 is paid.

minocycline → ARESTIN®

minocycline HCl, USP → SOLODYN®

mirabegron → MYRBETRIQ®

MIRENA® (levonorgestrel-releasing intrauterine system)   BAYER HEALTHCARE PHARMACEUTICALS

ARCH™ Patient Assistance Program   1-877-393-9071   *www.archpatientassistance.com*

$ Income Limits Call to Verify ? | **Rx cost →** | **FREE $** | **No Medical Insurance ✓** | **Commercial Insurance ?** | **Medicare Part D ✗**

Program provides Bayer IUDs (Kyleena, Mirena, and Skyla) at no cost to women in the United States who do not have private health insurance or Medicaid coverage for the devices. Patients may incur costs for insertion/removal of IUD.

MIRVASO® (brimonidine)   GALDERMA LABORATORIES

CareConnect Patient Savings Card   1-855-280-0543   *www.mirvaso.com*

$ Income Limits NONE | **Rx cost →** | **$35 $** | **No Medical Insurance ✓** | **Commercial Insurance ✓** | **Medicare Part D ✗**

Insured patients pay as little a $35 for Rx, uninsured patients pay as little as $75.

misoprostol → CYTOTEC®

mitotane → LYSODREN®

mometasone furoate → ASMANEX® HFA / ASMANEX® TWISTHALER®

mometasone furoate → ELOCON®

mometasone furoate/formoterol fumarate dihydrate → DULERA®

mometasone furoate monohydrate → NASONEX®

MONOCLATE® [Antihemophilic Factor (Human) Factor VIII:C Pasteurized]

CSL BEHRING

CSL Behring Patient Assistance Program   1-844-727-2752   *www.cslbehring.com*

Provides meds to qualified patients who are uninsured or underinsured, and cannot afford their prescribed therapy.

MonoNine® (factor ix)

CSL BEHRING

CSL Behring Patient Assistance Program   1-844-727-2752   *www.cslbehring.com*

Provides meds to qualified patients who are uninsured or underinsured, and cannot afford their prescribed therapy.

montelukast sodium oral granules → SINGULAIR®

MONUROL® Powder (fosfomycin)

ALLERGAN, INC.

Allergan Patient Assistance Program   1-844-424-6727   *www.allergan.com*

Program provides meds to patients who are uninsured or underinsured, and meet program guidelines. Patients with Medicare may be eligible, if they have been denied or are ineligible for Low Income Subsidy.

morphine sulfate and naltrexone hydrochloride → EMBEDA®

MOVANTIK® (naloxegol oxalate)

ASTRAZENECA PHARMACEUTICALS

MOVANTIK Savings Card   1-844-327-1955   *www.movantik.com*

Insured patients pay as low as $0 per 30-day supply (maximum savings of $100 per 30-day supply). If you pay cash for your monthly Rx, AstraZeneca will pay up to the first $100, and you will be responsible for any remaining balance.

MOVANTIK® (naloxegol oxalate)

ASTRAZENECA PHARMACEUTICALS

AZ&ME™   1-800-292-6363   *www.azandmeapp.com*

Program provides free medications to patients who are uninsured and meet program guidelines. Patients with Medicare may be eligible, if they are not eligible for (or enrolled in) Limited Income Subsidy (LIS), and have spent at least 3% of their annual household income on Rx medications through their Medicare Part D plan in the current year.

---

moxifloxacin hydrochloride solution → VIGAMOX®

MOZOBIL® (plerixafor injection)

SANOFI-AVENTIS U.S. LLC.

Sanofi Patient Connection   1-888-847-4877   *www.sanofipatientconnection.com*

Provides meds to patients who meet program guidelines. Patients with Medicare may be eligible, if they have been denied or are ineligible for Low Income Subsidy and have spent at least 5% of their annual income on Rx meds.

---

mucadhesive → MUGARD® Oral Rinse

MUGARD® Oral Rinse (mucadhesive)

AMAG PHARMACEUTICALS

MuGard Patient Assistance   1-844-635-2624   *www.mugard.com*

For patients without commercial insurance coverage or insured patients whose insurance does not cover their Rx.

MULTAQ® (dronedarone)

SANOFI-AVENTIS U.S. LLC.

Multaq Savings Card   1-833-477-0227   *www.multaq.com*

Eligible insured patients pay as low as $0 co-pay per Rx, maximum savings $700 per Rx, $3000 maximum savings per year. Uninsured patients may receive up to $150 off each Rx.

Sanofi Patient Connection   1-888-847-4877   *www.sanofipatientconnection.com*

Provides meds to patients who meet program guidelines. Patients with Medicare may be eligible, if they have been denied or are ineligible for Low Income Subsidy and have spent at least 5% of their annual income on Rx meds.

MUSTARGEN® (mechlorethamine injectable)

RECORDATI RARE DISEASES, INC.

Patient Support Program   1-866-209-7604   *www.recordatirarediseases.com*

Offers both a copay assistance program for insured patients, and a patient assistance program for those uninsured.

MYCOBUTIN® (rifabutin)

PFIZER, INC

Pfizer Savings Program   1-866-706-2400   *www.pfizerrxpathways.com*

Program helps uninsured patients receive discounted Pfizer medications through their local retail pharmacy.

Pfizer Patient Assistance   1-844-989-7284   *www.pfizerrxpathways.com*

Assists eligible patients who are uninsured (or have inadequate drug coverage) and cannot afford their medications.

mycophenolic acid → MYFORTIC®

MYDAYIS® (mixed salts of a single-entity amphetamine product)

SHIRE

Mydayis Savings Card   1-844-492-9895   *www.mydayis.com*

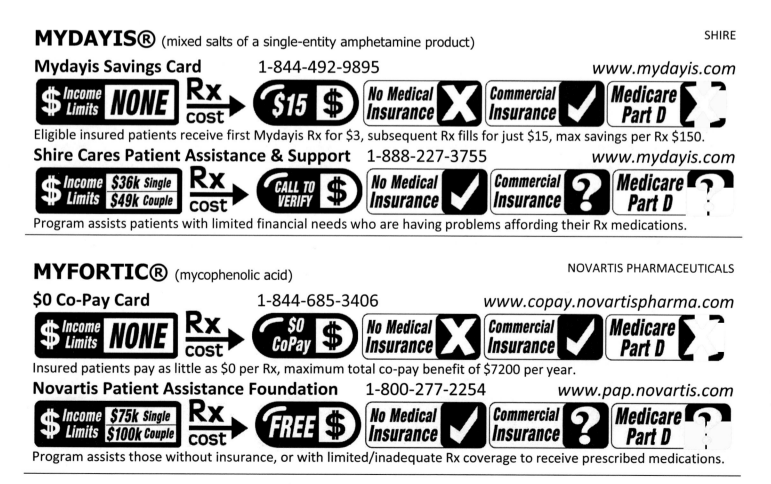

Eligible insured patients receive first Mydayis Rx for $3, subsequent Rx fills for just $15, max savings per Rx $150.

Shire Cares Patient Assistance & Support   1-888-227-3755   *www.mydayis.com*

Program assists patients with limited financial needs who are having problems affording their Rx medications.

MYFORTIC® (mycophenolic acid)

NOVARTIS PHARMACEUTICALS

$0 Co-Pay Card   1-844-685-3406   *www.copay.novartispharma.com*

Insured patients pay as little as $0 per Rx, maximum total co-pay benefit of $7200 per year.

Novartis Patient Assistance Foundation   1-800-277-2254   *www.pap.novartis.com*

Program assists those without insurance, or with limited/inadequate Rx coverage to receive prescribed medications.

MYLOTARG® (gemtuzumab ozogamicin)

PFIZER, INC

Pfizer Oncology together™ IV Co-Pay Program   1-877-744-5675   *www.mylotarg.com*

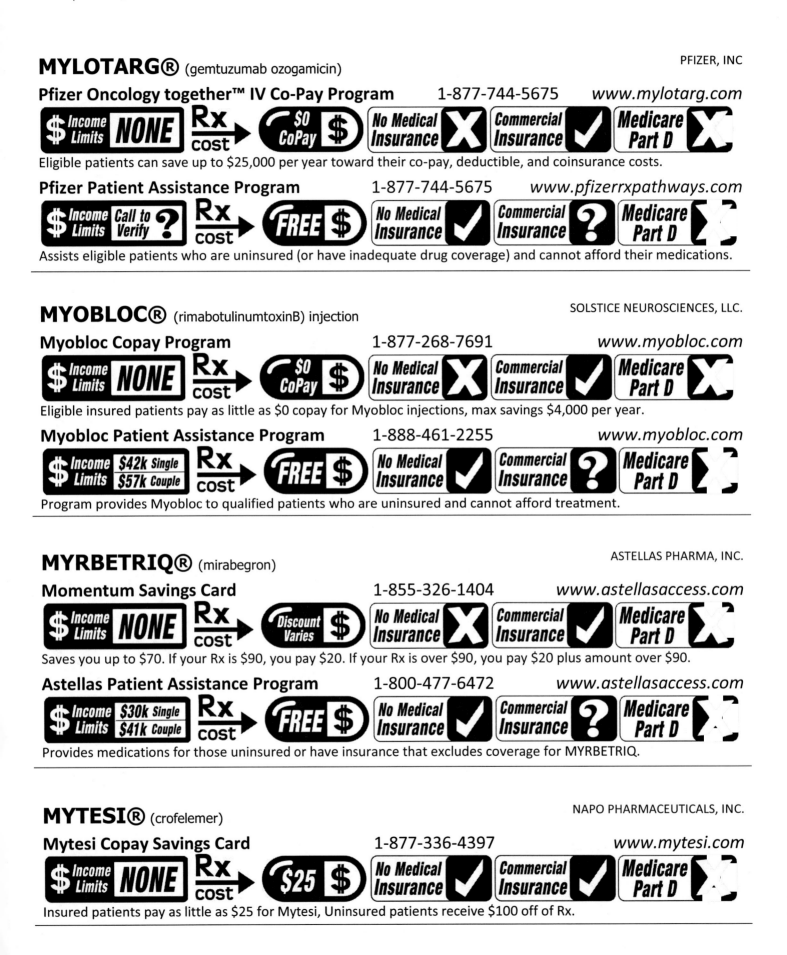

Eligible patients can save up to $25,000 per year toward their co-pay, deductible, and coinsurance costs.

Pfizer Patient Assistance Program   1-877-744-5675   *www.pfizerrxpathways.com*

Assists eligible patients who are uninsured (or have inadequate drug coverage) and cannot afford their medications.

MYOBLOC® (rimabotulinumtoxinB) injection

SOLSTICE NEUROSCIENCES, LLC.

Myobloc Copay Program   1-877-268-7691   *www.myobloc.com*

Eligible insured patients pay as little as $0 copay for Myobloc injections, max savings $4,000 per year.

Myobloc Patient Assistance Program   1-888-461-2255   *www.myobloc.com*

Program provides Myobloc to qualified patients who are uninsured and cannot afford treatment.

MYRBETRIQ® (mirabegron)

ASTELLAS PHARMA, INC.

Momentum Savings Card   1-855-326-1404   *www.astellasaccess.com*

Saves you up to $70. If your Rx is $90, you pay $20. If your Rx is over $90, you pay $20 plus amount over $90.

Astellas Patient Assistance Program   1-800-477-6472   *www.astellasaccess.com*

Provides medications for those uninsured or have insurance that excludes coverage for MYRBETRIQ.

MYTESI® (crofelemer)

NAPO PHARMACEUTICALS, INC.

Mytesi Copay Savings Card   1-877-336-4397   *www.mytesi.com*

Insured patients pay as little as $25 for Mytesi, Uninsured patients receive $100 off of Rx.

MYTESI® (crofelemer)

NAPO PHARMACEUTICALS, INC.

NapoCares Patient Assistance Program   1-888-527-6276   *www.mytesi.com*

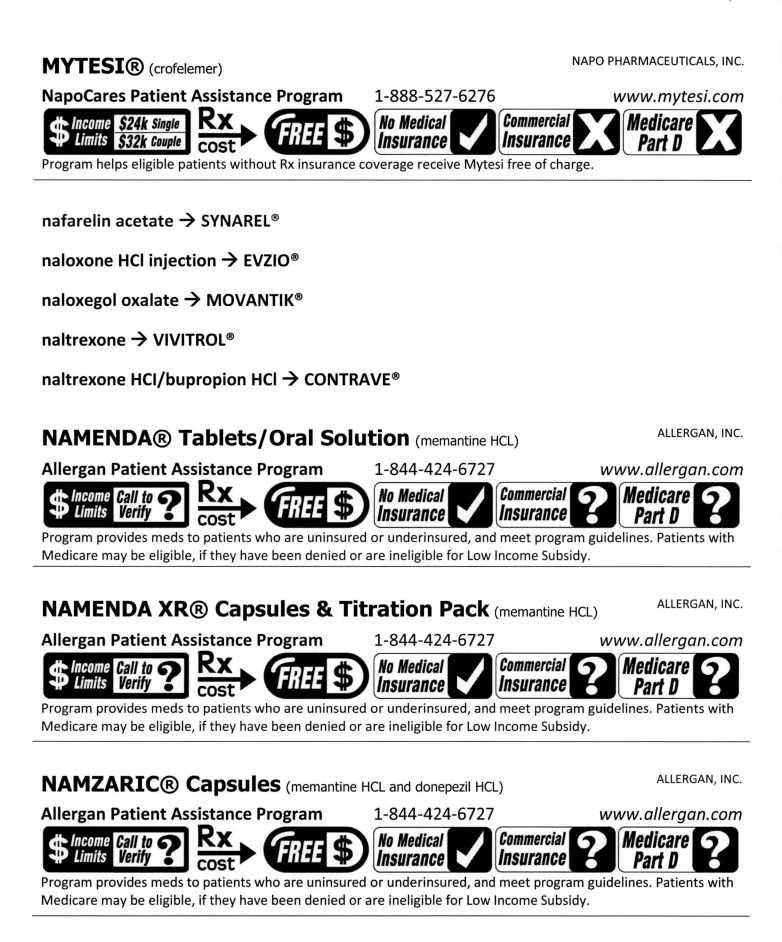

Program helps eligible patients without Rx insurance coverage receive Mytesi free of charge.

---

nafarelin acetate → SYNAREL®

naloxone HCl injection → EVZIO®

naloxegol oxalate → MOVANTIK®

naltrexone → VIVITROL®

naltrexone HCl/bupropion HCl → CONTRAVE®

NAMENDA® Tablets/Oral Solution (memantine HCL)

ALLERGAN, INC.

Allergan Patient Assistance Program   1-844-424-6727   *www.allergan.com*

Program provides meds to patients who are uninsured or underinsured, and meet program guidelines. Patients with Medicare may be eligible, if they have been denied or are ineligible for Low Income Subsidy.

NAMENDA XR® Capsules & Titration Pack (memantine HCL)

ALLERGAN, INC.

Allergan Patient Assistance Program   1-844-424-6727   *www.allergan.com*

Program provides meds to patients who are uninsured or underinsured, and meet program guidelines. Patients with Medicare may be eligible, if they have been denied or are ineligible for Low Income Subsidy.

NAMZARIC® Capsules (memantine HCL and donepezil HCL)

ALLERGAN, INC.

Allergan Patient Assistance Program   1-844-424-6727   *www.allergan.com*

Program provides meds to patients who are uninsured or underinsured, and meet program guidelines. Patients with Medicare may be eligible, if they have been denied or are ineligible for Low Income Subsidy.

naproxen/esomeprazole magnesium → VIMOVO®

NARDIL® (phenelzine sulfate)

PFIZER, INC

Pfizer Savings Program   1-866-706-2400   *www.pfizerrxpathways.com*

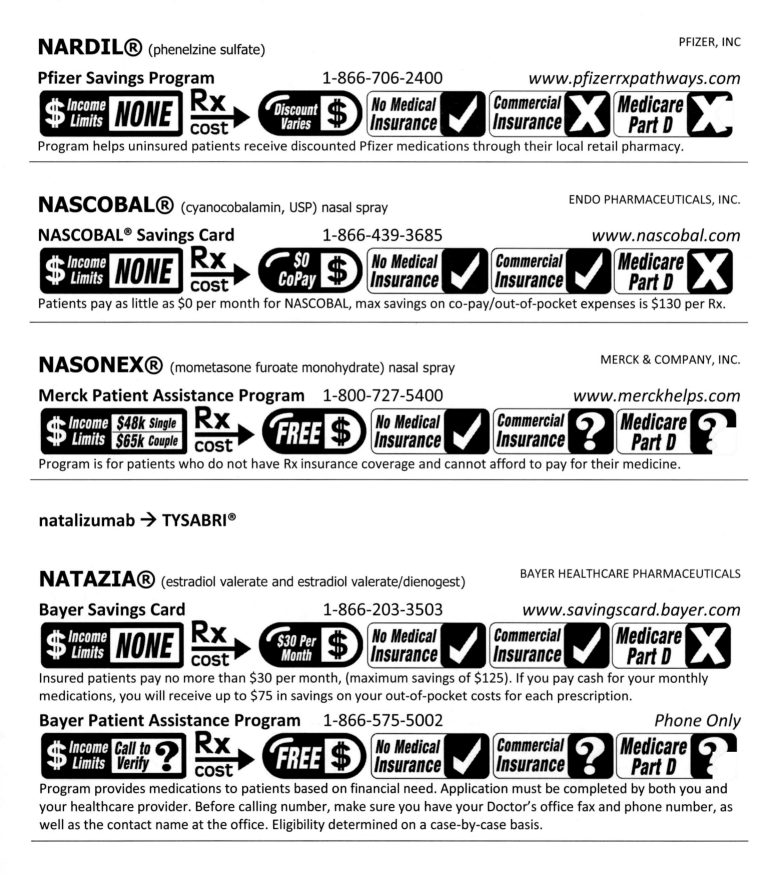

Program helps uninsured patients receive discounted Pfizer medications through their local retail pharmacy.

NASCOBAL® (cyanocobalamin, USP) nasal spray

ENDO PHARMACEUTICALS, INC.

NASCOBAL® Savings Card   1-866-439-3685   *www.nascobal.com*

Patients pay as little as $0 per month for NASCOBAL, max savings on co-pay/out-of-pocket expenses is $130 per Rx.

NASONEX® (mometasone furoate monohydrate) nasal spray

MERCK & COMPANY, INC.

Merck Patient Assistance Program   1-800-727-5400   *www.merckhelps.com*

Program is for patients who do not have Rx insurance coverage and cannot afford to pay for their medicine.

natalizumab → TYSABRI®

NATAZIA® (estradiol valerate and estradiol valerate/dienogest)

BAYER HEALTHCARE PHARMACEUTICALS

Bayer Savings Card   1-866-203-3503   *www.savingscard.bayer.com*

Insured patients pay no more than $30 per month, (maximum savings of $125). If you pay cash for your monthly medications, you will receive up to $75 in savings on your out-of-pocket costs for each prescription.

Bayer Patient Assistance Program   1-866-575-5002   *Phone Only*

Program provides medications to patients based on financial need. Application must be completed by both you and your healthcare provider. Before calling number, make sure you have your Doctor's office fax and phone number, as well as the contact name at the office. Eligibility determined on a case-by-case basis.

NATPARA® (parathyroid hormone)

SHIRE

OnePath Patient Assistance Program   1-866-888-0660   *www.natpara.com*

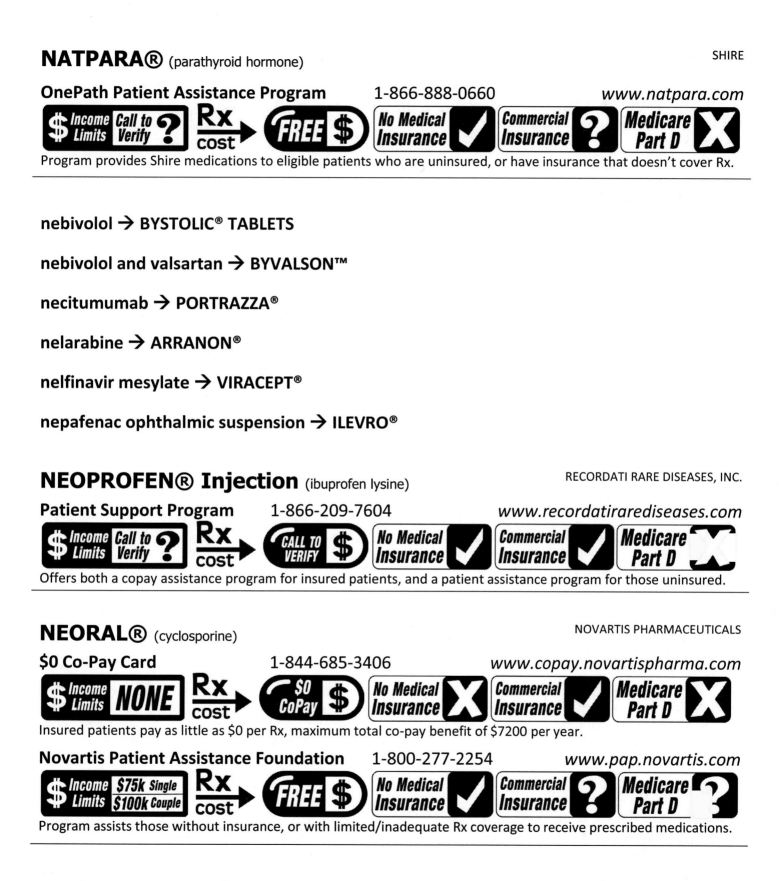

Program provides Shire medications to eligible patients who are uninsured, or have insurance that doesn't cover Rx.

---

nebivolol → **BYSTOLIC® TABLETS**

nebivolol and valsartan → **BYVALSON™**

necitumumab → **PORTRAZZA®**

nelarabine → **ARRANON®**

nelfinavir mesylate → **VIRACEPT®**

nepafenac ophthalmic suspension → **ILEVRO®**

NEOPROFEN® Injection (ibuprofen lysine)

RECORDATI RARE DISEASES, INC.

Patient Support Program   1-866-209-7604   *www.recordatirarediseases.com*

Offers both a copay assistance program for insured patients, and a patient assistance program for those uninsured.

NEORAL® (cyclosporine)

NOVARTIS PHARMACEUTICALS

$0 Co-Pay Card   1-844-685-3406   *www.copay.novartispharma.com*

Insured patients pay as little as $0 per Rx, maximum total co-pay benefit of $7200 per year.

Novartis Patient Assistance Foundation   1-800-277-2254   *www.pap.novartis.com*

Program assists those without insurance, or with limited/inadequate Rx coverage to receive prescribed medications.

nepafenac suspension → **NEVANAC**

NESINA® (alogliptin)

TAKEDA PHARMACEUTICALS AMERICA

Instant Savings Card   1-855-510-4545   *www.nesinafamily.com*

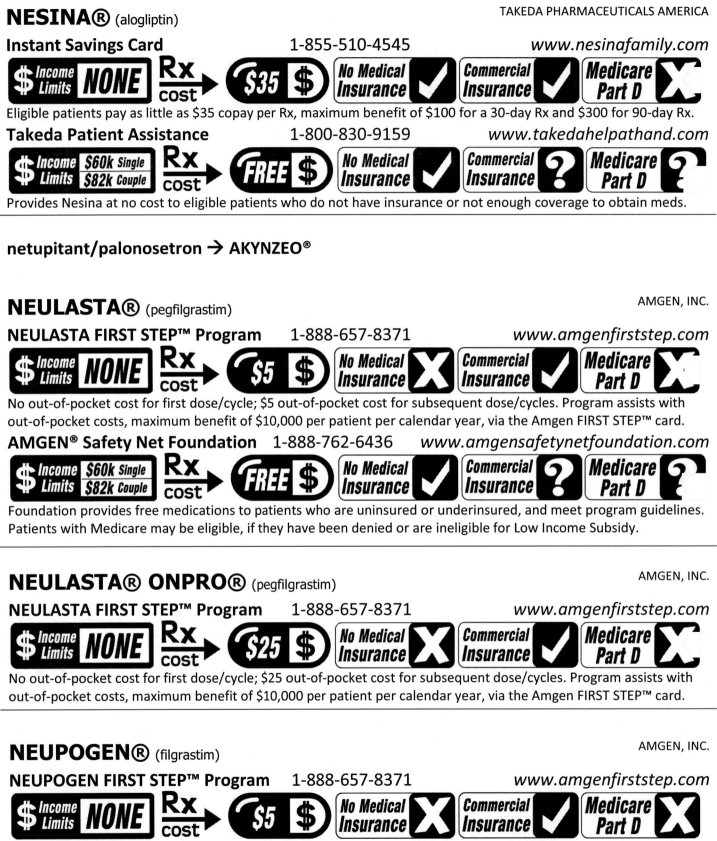

$ Income Limits NONE | **Rx cost** → **$35 $** | **No Medical Insurance ✓** | **Commercial Insurance ✓** | **Medicare Part D ✗**

Eligible patients pay as little as $35 copay per Rx, maximum benefit of $100 for a 30-day Rx and $300 for 90-day Rx.

Takeda Patient Assistance   1-800-830-9159   *www.takedahelpathand.com*

$ Income Limits $60k Single $82k Couple | **Rx cost** → **FREE $** | **No Medical Insurance ✓** | **Commercial Insurance ?** | **Medicare Part D ?**

Provides Nesina at no cost to eligible patients who do not have insurance or not enough coverage to obtain meds.

---

netupitant/palonosetron → AKYNZEO®

NEULASTA® (pegfilgrastim)

AMGEN, INC.

NEULASTA FIRST STEP™ Program   1-888-657-8371   *www.amgenfirststep.com*

$ Income Limits NONE | **Rx cost** → **$5 $** | **No Medical Insurance ✗** | **Commercial Insurance ✓** | **Medicare Part D ✗**

No out-of-pocket cost for first dose/cycle; $5 out-of-pocket cost for subsequent dose/cycles. Program assists with out-of-pocket costs, maximum benefit of $10,000 per patient per calendar year, via the Amgen FIRST STEP™ card.

AMGEN® Safety Net Foundation   1-888-762-6436   *www.amgensafetynetfoundation.com*

$ Income Limits $60k Single $82k Couple | **Rx cost** → **FREE $** | **No Medical Insurance ✓** | **Commercial Insurance ?** | **Medicare Part D ?**

Foundation provides free medications to patients who are uninsured or underinsured, and meet program guidelines. Patients with Medicare may be eligible, if they have been denied or are ineligible for Low Income Subsidy.

NEULASTA® ONPRO® (pegfilgrastim)

AMGEN, INC.

NEULASTA FIRST STEP™ Program   1-888-657-8371   *www.amgenfirststep.com*

$ Income Limits NONE | **Rx cost** → **$25 $** | **No Medical Insurance ✗** | **Commercial Insurance ✓** | **Medicare Part D ✗**

No out-of-pocket cost for first dose/cycle; $25 out-of-pocket cost for subsequent dose/cycles. Program assists with out-of-pocket costs, maximum benefit of $10,000 per patient per calendar year, via the Amgen FIRST STEP™ card.

NEUPOGEN® (filgrastim)

AMGEN, INC.

NEUPOGEN FIRST STEP™ Program   1-888-657-8371   *www.amgenfirststep.com*

$ Income Limits NONE | **Rx cost** → **$5 $** | **No Medical Insurance ✗** | **Commercial Insurance ✓** | **Medicare Part D ✗**

No out-of-pocket cost for first dose/cycle; $5 out-of-pocket cost for subsequent dose/cycles. Program assists with out-of-pocket costs, maximum benefit of $10,000 per patient per calendar year, via the Amgen FIRST STEP™ card.

NEUPOGEN® (filgrastim)

AMGEN, INC.

AMGEN® Safety Net Foundation   1-888-762-6436   *www.amgensafetynetfoundation.com*

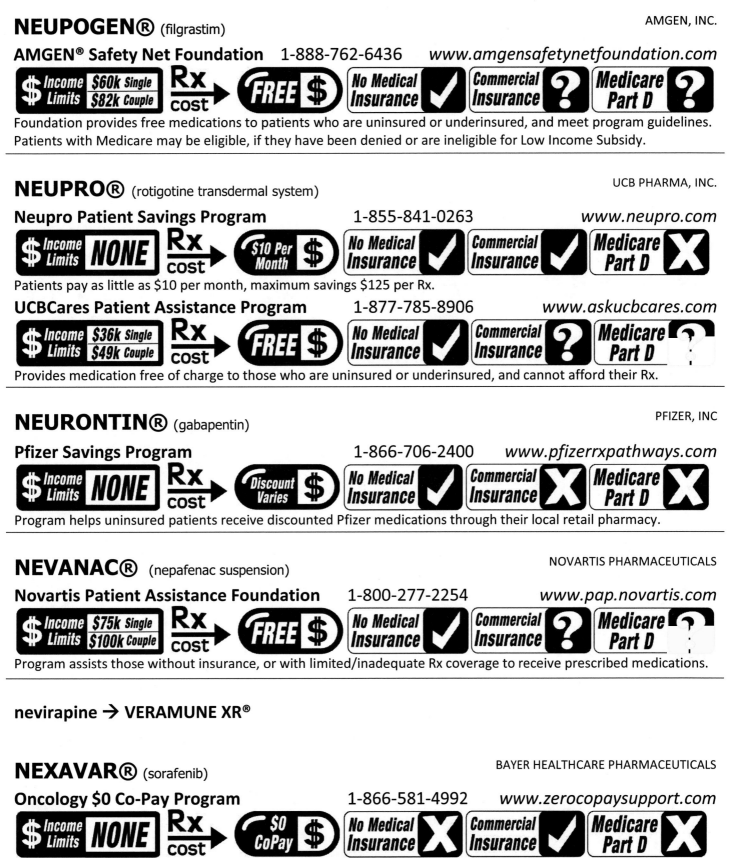

Foundation provides free medications to patients who are uninsured or underinsured, and meet program guidelines. Patients with Medicare may be eligible, if they have been denied or are ineligible for Low Income Subsidy.

NEUPRO® (rotigotine transdermal system)

UCB PHARMA, INC.

Neupro Patient Savings Program   1-855-841-0263   *www.neupro.com*

Patients pay as little as $10 per month, maximum savings $125 per Rx.

UCBCares Patient Assistance Program   1-877-785-8906   *www.askucbcares.com*

Provides medication free of charge to those who are uninsured or underinsured, and cannot afford their Rx.

NEURONTIN® (gabapentin)

PFIZER, INC

Pfizer Savings Program   1-866-706-2400   *www.pfizerrxpathways.com*

Program helps uninsured patients receive discounted Pfizer medications through their local retail pharmacy.

NEVANAC® (nepafenac suspension)

NOVARTIS PHARMACEUTICALS

Novartis Patient Assistance Foundation   1-800-277-2254   *www.pap.novartis.com*

Program assists those without insurance, or with limited/inadequate Rx coverage to receive prescribed medications.

nevirapine → VERAMUNE XR®

NEXAVAR® (sorafenib)

BAYER HEALTHCARE PHARMACEUTICALS

Oncology $0 Co-Pay Program   1-866-581-4992   *www.zerocopaysupport.com*

Program covers up to 100% of co-pay/co-insurance for those with commercial insurance. Up to $25,000/year.

NEXAVAR® (sorafenib)

BAYER HEALTHCARE PHARMACEUTICALS

Patient Assistance Program (PAP)   1-866-639-2827   *www.nexavar-us.com*

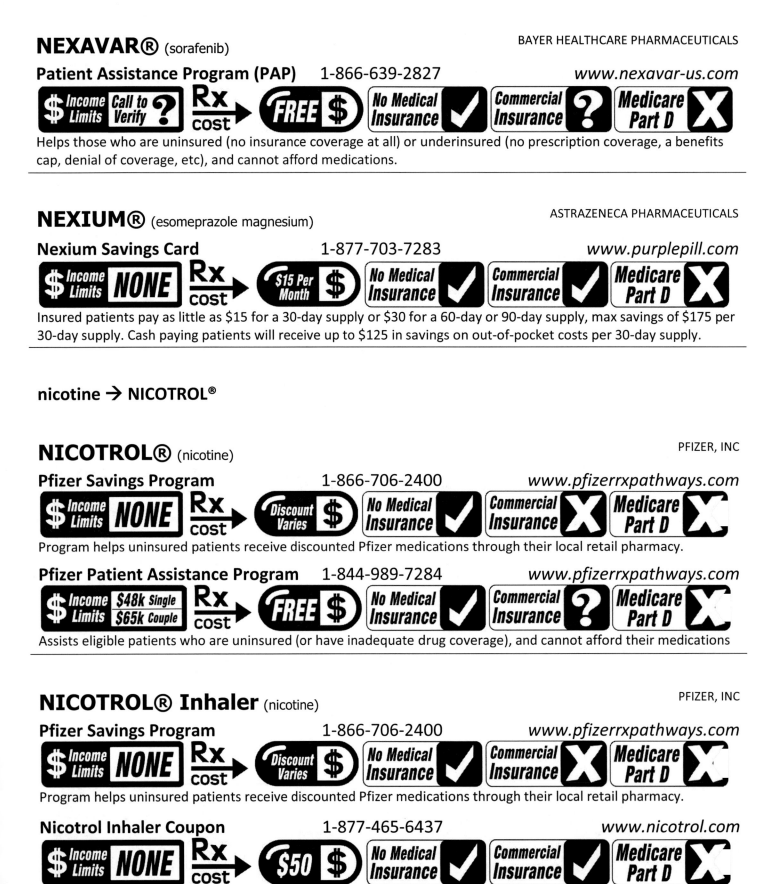

Helps those who are uninsured (no insurance coverage at all) or underinsured (no prescription coverage, a benefits cap, denial of coverage, etc), and cannot afford medications.

NEXIUM® (esomeprazole magnesium)

ASTRAZENECA PHARMACEUTICALS

Nexium Savings Card   1-877-703-7283   *www.purplepill.com*

Insured patients pay as little as $15 for a 30-day supply or $30 for a 60-day or 90-day supply, max savings of $175 per 30-day supply. Cash paying patients will receive up to $125 in savings on out-of-pocket costs per 30-day supply.

---

nicotine → NICOTROL®

NICOTROL® (nicotine)

PFIZER, INC

Pfizer Savings Program   1-866-706-2400   *www.pfizerrxpathways.com*

Program helps uninsured patients receive discounted Pfizer medications through their local retail pharmacy.

Pfizer Patient Assistance Program   1-844-989-7284   *www.pfizerrxpathways.com*

Assists eligible patients who are uninsured (or have inadequate drug coverage), and cannot afford their medications

---

NICOTROL® Inhaler (nicotine)

PFIZER, INC

Pfizer Savings Program   1-866-706-2400   *www.pfizerrxpathways.com*

Program helps uninsured patients receive discounted Pfizer medications through their local retail pharmacy.

Nicotrol Inhaler Coupon   1-877-465-6437   *www.nicotrol.com*

Eligible patients can pay as little as $50 for Rx, maximum savings $100 per Rx.

NICOTROL® Inhaler (nicotine)

PFIZER, INC

Pfizer Patient Assistance Program   1-844-989-7284   *www.pfizerrxpathways.com*

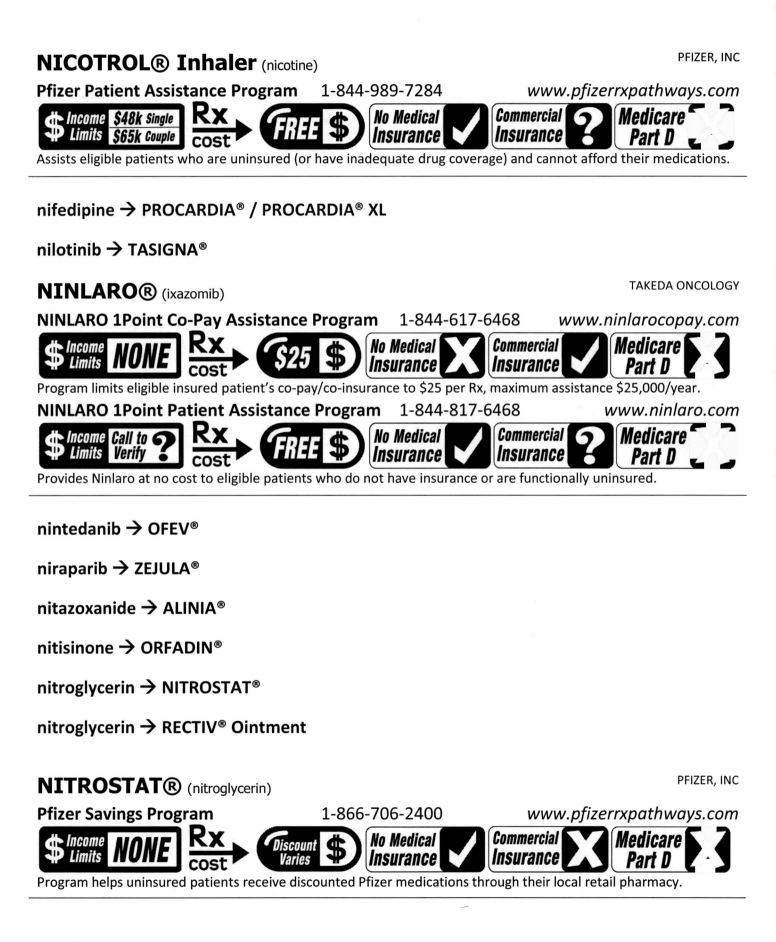

| $ Income Limits | $48k Single $65k Couple | Rx cost → | FREE $ | No Medical Insurance ✓ | Commercial Insurance ? | Medicare Part D ✗ |

Assists eligible patients who are uninsured (or have inadequate drug coverage) and cannot afford their medications.

---

nifedipine → PROCARDIA® / PROCARDIA® XL

nilotinib → TASIGNA®

NINLARO® (ixazomib)

TAKEDA ONCOLOGY

NINLARO 1Point Co-Pay Assistance Program   1-844-617-6468   *www.ninlarocopay.com*

| $ Income Limits | NONE | Rx cost → | $25 $ | No Medical Insurance ✗ | Commercial Insurance ✓ | Medicare Part D ✗ |

Program limits eligible insured patient's co-pay/co-insurance to $25 per Rx, maximum assistance $25,000/year.

NINLARO 1Point Patient Assistance Program   1-844-817-6468   *www.ninlaro.com*

| $ Income Limits | Call to Verify ? | Rx cost → | FREE $ | No Medical Insurance ✓ | Commercial Insurance ? | Medicare Part D ✗ |

Provides Ninlaro at no cost to eligible patients who do not have insurance or are functionally uninsured.

---

nintedanib → OFEV®

niraparib → ZEJULA®

nitazoxanide → ALINIA®

nitisinone → ORFADIN®

nitroglycerin → NITROSTAT®

nitroglycerin → RECTIV® Ointment

NITROSTAT® (nitroglycerin)

PFIZER, INC

Pfizer Savings Program   1-866-706-2400   *www.pfizerrxpathways.com*

| $ Income Limits | NONE | Rx cost → | Discount Varies $ | No Medical Insurance ✓ | Commercial Insurance ✗ | Medicare Part D ✗ |

Program helps uninsured patients receive discounted Pfizer medications through their local retail pharmacy.

NITROSTAT® (nitroglycerin)
PFIZER, INC

Pfizer Patient Assistance Program　　1-844-989-7284　　*www.pfizerrxpathways.com*

$ Income Limits $48k Single $65k Couple　**Rx cost** → **FREE $**　**No Medical Insurance** ✓　**Commercial Insurance** ?　**Medicare Part D** ✗

Assists eligible patients who are uninsured (or have inadequate drug coverage), and cannot afford their medications

---

nivolumab → OPDIVO®

NORDITROPIN® (somatropin) injection
NOVO NORDISK, INC.

NordiSure™ Co-pay Assistance Program　　1-888-668-6444　　*www.norditropin.com*

$ Income Limits NONE　**Rx cost** → **$0 CoPay $**　**No Medical Insurance** ✗　**Commercial Insurance** ✓　**Medicare Part D** ✗

Insured patients receive up to $250/month towards co-pay/co-insurance, to a maximum of $3,000 per year.

NordiSure™ Coinsurance Program　　1-888-668-6444　　*www.norditropin.com*

$ Income Limits Call to Verify ?　**Rx cost** → **$75 $**　**No Medical Insurance** ✗　**Commercial Insurance** ✓　**Medicare Part D** ✗

Up to $4000/year in assistance for insured patients with a co-pay greater than $1,500, after they pay first $75 per Rx

Patient Access Program　　1-888-668-6444　　*www.norditropin.com*

$ Income Limits Call to Verify ?　**Rx cost** → **FREE $**　**No Medical Insurance** ✓　**Commercial Insurance** ?　**Medicare Part D** ✗

Provides free medication to those who are uninsured/underinsured, and can demonstrate a true financial need.

NORITATE® (metronidazole) cream 1%
VALEANT PHARMACEUTICALS INTERNATIONAL

Ortho Dermatologics Rx Access Program　　1-855-202-3279　　*www.orthorxaccess.com*

$ Income Limits NONE　**Rx cost** → **$40 $**　**No Medical Insurance** ✓　**Commercial Insurance** ✓　**Medicare Part D** ✗

Most commercially insured patients pay as little as $40 per Rx, once deductible has been met. Those with insurance where drug is not covered pay $75 per Rx, and uninsured patients pay just $100 per Rx.

Valeant Patient Assistance Program　　1-833-862-8727　　*www.valeantpap.com*

$ Income Limits $36k Single $49k Couple　**Rx cost** → **FREE $**　**No Medical Insurance** ✓　**Commercial Insurance** ?　**Medicare Part D** ✓

Rx assistance available to patients who are uninsured, (or whose insurance has denied coverage) and meet program eligibility requirements. Medicare Part D patients who cannot afford Rx can appeal for evaluation of eligibility.

💡 **TIP:** When in doubt... call the program and explain your situation. You may qualify for assistance.

NORPACE® / NORPACE® CR (disopyramide phosphate)

PFIZER, INC

Pfizer Savings Program 1-866-706-2400 *www.pfizerrxpathways.com*

$ Income Limits NONE | **Rx cost** → | **Discount Varies $** | **No Medical Insurance** ✓ | **Commercial Insurance** ✗ | **Medicare Part D** ›

Program helps uninsured patients receive discounted Pfizer medications through their local retail pharmacy.

Pfizer Patient Assistance 1-844-989-7284 *www.pfizerrxpathways.com*

$ Income Limits $48k Single / $65k Couple | **Rx cost** → | **FREE $** | **No Medical Insurance** ✓ | **Commercial Insurance ?** | **Medicare Part D**

Assists eligible patients who are uninsured (or have inadequate drug coverage), and cannot afford their medications

NORTHERA® (droxidopa)

LUNDBECK, INC.

Northera Copay Assistance 1-844-601-0101 *www.northera.com*

$ Income Limits NONE | **Rx cost** → | **$10 Per Month $** | **No Medical Insurance** ✗ | **Commercial Insurance** ✓ | **Medicare Part D** ›

Eligible commercially insured patients pay as little as $10 per 30 day Rx.

nortriptyline HCl → PAMELOR™

NORVASC® (amlodipine besylate)

LUNDBECK, INC.

Pfizer Savings Program 1-866-706-2400 *www.pfizerrxpathways.com*

$ Income Limits NONE | **Rx cost** → | **Discount Varies $** | **No Medical Insurance** ✓ | **Commercial Insurance** ✗ | **Medicare Part D** ›

Program helps uninsured patients receive discounted Pfizer medications through their local retail pharmacy

NORVIR® TABLETS (ritonavir)

AbbVie, INC.

Norvir Savings Card 1-800-364-4767 *www.norvir.com*

$ Income Limits NONE | **Rx cost** → | **$100 SAVINGS $** | **No Medical Insurance** ✗ | **Commercial Insurance** ✓ | **Medicare Part D** ›

Eligible patients with commercial insurance save up to $100/month, $1200/year on their Norvir Rx.

AbbVie Patient Assistance Foundation 1-800-222-6885 *www.abbviepaf.org*

$ Income Limits Call to Verify ? | **Rx cost** → | **FREE $** | **No Medical Insurance** ✓ | **Commercial Insurance** ✓ | **Medicare Part D**

Rx assistance available to patients who are uninsured and meet program eligibility requirements. Patients with Commercial Insurance or Medicare Part D, who are struggling to pay for their medications, are encouraged to apply.

NOVOEIGHT® Vial (antihemophilic factor [recombinant] vial)

NOVO NORDISK, INC.

Co-Pay Assistance Program   1-844-668-6732   *www.novoeight.com*

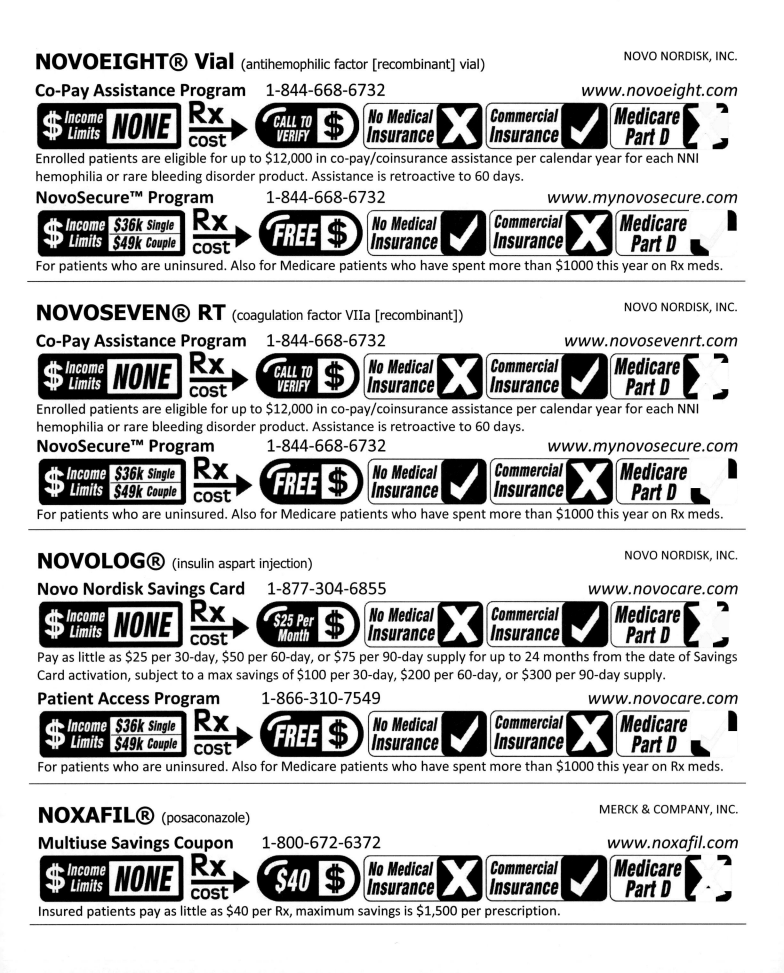

$ Income Limits | **NONE** | Rx cost → | **CALL TO VERIFY $** | **No Medical Insurance ✗** | **Commercial Insurance ✓** | **Medicare Part D**

Enrolled patients are eligible for up to $12,000 in co-pay/coinsurance assistance per calendar year for each NNI hemophilia or rare bleeding disorder product. Assistance is retroactive to 60 days.

NovoSecure™ Program   1-844-668-6732   *www.mynovosecure.com*

$ Income Limits | **$36k Single $49k Couple** | Rx cost → | **FREE $** | **No Medical Insurance ✓** | **Commercial Insurance ✗** | **Medicare Part D ✓**

For patients who are uninsured. Also for Medicare patients who have spent more than $1000 this year on Rx meds.

NOVOSEVEN® RT (coagulation factor VIIa [recombinant])

NOVO NORDISK, INC.

Co-Pay Assistance Program   1-844-668-6732   *www.novosevenrt.com*

$ Income Limits | **NONE** | Rx cost → | **CALL TO VERIFY $** | **No Medical Insurance ✗** | **Commercial Insurance ✓** | **Medicare Part D**

Enrolled patients are eligible for up to $12,000 in co-pay/coinsurance assistance per calendar year for each NNI hemophilia or rare bleeding disorder product. Assistance is retroactive to 60 days.

NovoSecure™ Program   1-844-668-6732   *www.mynovosecure.com*

$ Income Limits | **$36k Single $49k Couple** | Rx cost → | **FREE $** | **No Medical Insurance ✓** | **Commercial Insurance ✗** | **Medicare Part D ✓**

For patients who are uninsured. Also for Medicare patients who have spent more than $1000 this year on Rx meds.

NOVOLOG® (insulin aspart injection)

NOVO NORDISK, INC.

Novo Nordisk Savings Card   1-877-304-6855   *www.novocare.com*

$ Income Limits | **NONE** | Rx cost → | **$25 Per Month $** | **No Medical Insurance ✗** | **Commercial Insurance ✓** | **Medicare Part D**

Pay as little as $25 per 30-day, $50 per 60-day, or $75 per 90-day supply for up to 24 months from the date of Savings Card activation, subject to a max savings of $100 per 30-day, $200 per 60-day, or $300 per 90-day supply.

Patient Access Program   1-866-310-7549   *www.novocare.com*

$ Income Limits | **$36k Single $49k Couple** | Rx cost → | **FREE $** | **No Medical Insurance ✓** | **Commercial Insurance ✗** | **Medicare Part D**

For patients who are uninsured. Also for Medicare patients who have spent more than $1000 this year on Rx meds.

NOXAFIL® (posaconazole)

MERCK & COMPANY, INC.

Multiuse Savings Coupon   1-800-672-6372   *www.noxafil.com*

$ Income Limits | **NONE** | Rx cost → | **$40 $** | **No Medical Insurance ✗** | **Commercial Insurance ✓** | **Medicare Part D**

Insured patients pay as little as $40 per Rx, maximum savings is $1,500 per prescription.

NOXAFIL® (posaconazole)

MERCK & COMPANY, INC.

Merck Patient Assistance   1-800-727-5400   *www.merckhelps.com*

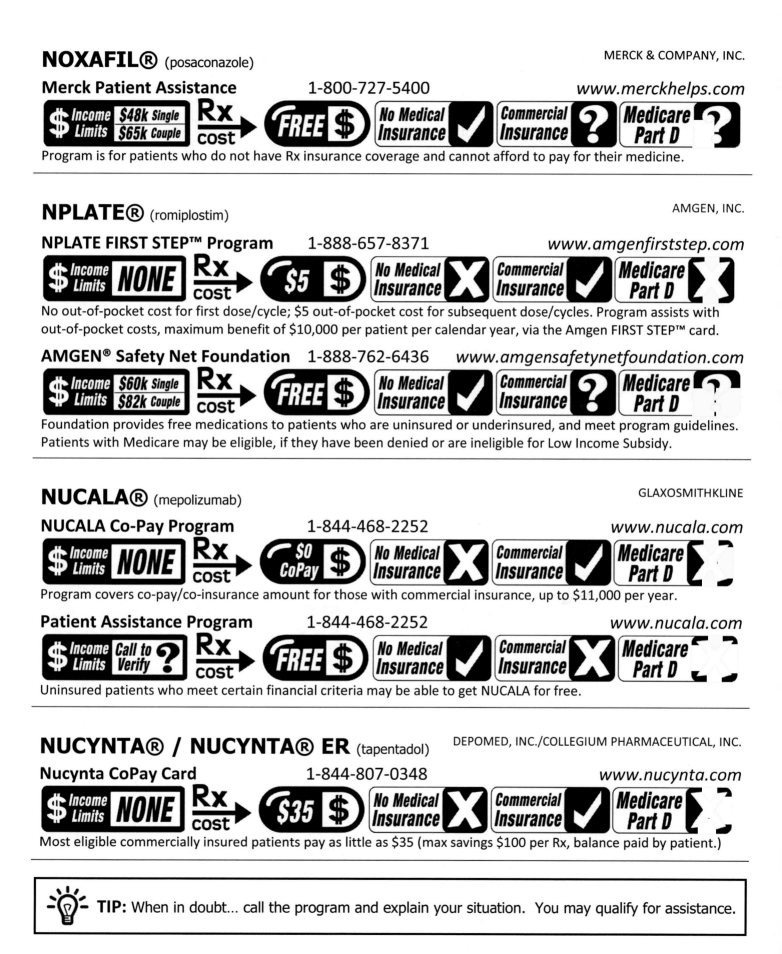

| $ Income Limits $48k Single / $65k Couple | Rx cost → | FREE $ | No Medical Insurance ✓ | Commercial Insurance ? | Medicare Part D ? |

Program is for patients who do not have Rx insurance coverage and cannot afford to pay for their medicine.

NPLATE® (romiplostim)

AMGEN, INC.

NPLATE FIRST STEP™ Program   1-888-657-8371   *www.amgenfirststep.com*

| $ Income Limits NONE | Rx cost → | $5 $ | No Medical Insurance ✗ | Commercial Insurance ✓ | Medicare Part D ✗ |

No out-of-pocket cost for first dose/cycle; $5 out-of-pocket cost for subsequent dose/cycles. Program assists with out-of-pocket costs, maximum benefit of $10,000 per patient per calendar year, via the Amgen FIRST STEP™ card.

AMGEN® Safety Net Foundation   1-888-762-6436   *www.amgensafetynetfoundation.com*

| $ Income Limits $60k Single / $82k Couple | Rx cost → | FREE $ | No Medical Insurance ✓ | Commercial Insurance ? | Medicare Part D ? |

Foundation provides free medications to patients who are uninsured or underinsured, and meet program guidelines. Patients with Medicare may be eligible, if they have been denied or are ineligible for Low Income Subsidy.

NUCALA® (mepolizumab)

GLAXOSMITHKLINE

NUCALA Co-Pay Program   1-844-468-2252   *www.nucala.com*

| $ Income Limits NONE | Rx cost → | $0 CoPay $ | No Medical Insurance ✗ | Commercial Insurance ✓ | Medicare Part D ✗ |

Program covers co-pay/co-insurance amount for those with commercial insurance, up to $11,000 per year.

Patient Assistance Program   1-844-468-2252   *www.nucala.com*

| $ Income Limits Call to Verify ? | Rx cost → | FREE $ | No Medical Insurance ✓ | Commercial Insurance ✗ | Medicare Part D |

Uninsured patients who meet certain financial criteria may be able to get NUCALA for free.

NUCYNTA® / NUCYNTA® ER (tapentadol)

DEPOMED, INC./COLLEGIUM PHARMACEUTICAL, INC.

Nucynta CoPay Card   1-844-807-0348   *www.nucynta.com*

| $ Income Limits NONE | Rx cost → | $35 $ | No Medical Insurance ✗ | Commercial Insurance ✓ | Medicare Part D |

Most eligible commercially insured patients pay as little as $35 (max savings $100 per Rx, balance paid by patient.)

TIP: When in doubt... call the program and explain your situation. You may qualify for assistance.

NUEDEXTA® (dextromethorphan HBr and quinidine sulfate)

AVANIR PHARMACEUTICALS, INC.

NUEDEXTA Co-Pay Savings Card   1-855-468-3339   www.nuedexta.com

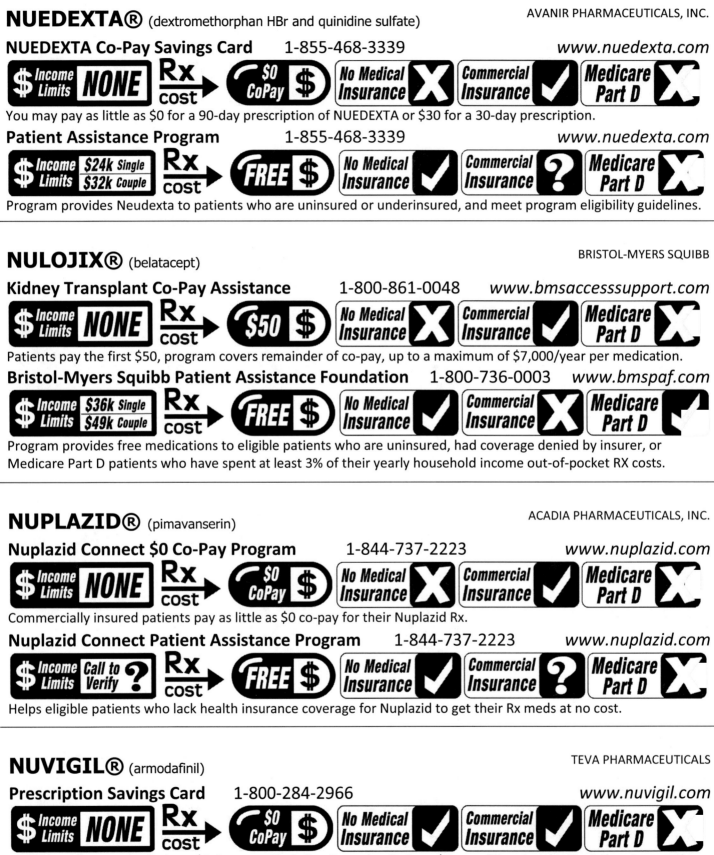

You may pay as little as $0 for a 90-day prescription of NUEDEXTA or $30 for a 30-day prescription.

Patient Assistance Program   1-855-468-3339   www.nuedexta.com

Program provides Neudexta to patients who are uninsured or underinsured, and meet program eligibility guidelines.

NULOJIX® (belatacept)

BRISTOL-MYERS SQUIBB

Kidney Transplant Co-Pay Assistance   1-800-861-0048   www.bmsaccesssupport.com

Patients pay the first $50, program covers remainder of co-pay, up to a maximum of $7,000/year per medication.

Bristol-Myers Squibb Patient Assistance Foundation   1-800-736-0003   www.bmspaf.com

Program provides free medications to eligible patients who are uninsured, had coverage denied by insurer, or Medicare Part D patients who have spent at least 3% of their yearly household income out-of-pocket RX costs.

NUPLAZID® (pimavanserin)

ACADIA PHARMACEUTICALS, INC.

Nuplazid Connect $0 Co-Pay Program   1-844-737-2223   www.nuplazid.com

Commercially insured patients pay as little as $0 co-pay for their Nuplazid Rx.

Nuplazid Connect Patient Assistance Program   1-844-737-2223   www.nuplazid.com

Helps eligible patients who lack health insurance coverage for Nuplazid to get their Rx meds at no cost.

NUVIGIL® (armodafinil)

TEVA PHARMACEUTICALS

Prescription Savings Card   1-800-284-2966   www.nuvigil.com

Eligible patients pay as little as $0 Copay on their first Rx and as little as $5 on refills using the Nuvigil savings card.

NUVIGIL® (armodafinil)

TEVA PHARMACEUTICALS

Teva Cares Foundation Patient Assistance Program   1-877-237-4881   *www.tevacares.org*

Provides Teva meds at no cost. If you don't qualify for Teva Cares, call 1-888-838-2872 for other assistance options.

obinutuzumab → GAZYVA®

ocrelizumab → OCREVUS®

OCREVUS® (ocrelizumab)

GENENTECH, INC.

OCREVUS Co-pay Program   1-844-672-6729   *www.ocrevuscopay.com*

Program provides up to $20,000/year in drug co-pay assistance, and/or up to $500 per day for infusion co-pay costs. Patients pay as little as $5 for their prescribed Rx meds and/or infusions.

Genentech Access Solutions   1-866-422-2377   *www.genentech-access.com*

Program provides medications to patients who are uninsured or have been denied coverage by their insurance company. Patients who have insurance, but pay too much out of pocket per year, may also qualify for assistance.

ocriplasmin → JETREA®

octreotide acetate → SANDOSTATIN® LAR Depot

ODEFSEY® (emtricitabine/rilpivirine/tenofovir alafenamide)

GILEAD SCIENCES, INC

Co-Pay Assistance Card Program   1-800-226-2056   *www.odefsey.com*

Program helps pay for the cost of prescription co-pays up to $6000 per product per year.

Gilead Advancing Access   1-800-226-2056   *www.gileadadvancingaccess.com*

Patient assistance program provides medications at no charge for eligible patients with no other insurance options.

ofatumumab → ARZERRA®

OFEV® (nintedanib)

BOEHRINGER INGELHEIM PHARMACEUTICALS, INC.

OFEV Commercial Copay Program   1-866-673-6366   *www.ofev.com*

| $ Income Limits **NONE** | **Rx** cost → | $0 CoPay $ | No Medical Insurance ✗ | Commercial Insurance ✓ | Medicare Part D ✗ |

Eligible insured patients pay as low as $0 per month for OFEV (maximum savings of $10,000).

Boehringer Ingelheim Cares Foundation   1-800-556-8317   *www.bipatientassistance.com*

| $ Income Limits Call to Verify ? | **Rx** cost → | FREE $ | No Medical Insurance ✓ | Commercial Insurance ? | Medicare Part D ? |

Patient Assistance Program provides free medications to patients who are uninsured or underinsured, and meet program guidelines. Patients with Medicare may be eligible, if they are ineligible for Low Income Subsidy.

---

olanzapine → ZYPREXA®

olanzapine and fluoxetine → SYMBYAX®

olaparib → LYNPARZA® Tablets

olaratumab → LARTRUVO®

olmesartan medoxomil → BENICAR®

olmesartan medoxomil/amlodipine/hydrocholorothiazide → TRIBENZOR®

olmesartan medoxomil /hydrocholorothiazide → BENICAR HCT®

olodaterol → STRIVERDI® RESPIMAT®

olopatadine hydrochloride ophthalmic solution → PATADAY®

olopatadine hydrochloride ophthalmic solution → PAZEO®

OLUMIANT® (baricitinib)

LILLY USA, LLC

Olumiant Savings Card   1-844-658-6426   *www.olumiant.com*

| $ Income Limits **NONE** | **Rx** cost → | $5 Per Month $ | Commercial Insurance ✗ | Commercial Insurance ✓ | Medicare Part D ✗ |

Eligible patients pay $5/month if your plan covers Olumiant, $25/month if not covered, max savings $12,000/year.

OLUMIANT® (baricitinib)

LILLY USA, LLC

Lilly Cares　　　　　1-800-545-6962　　　*www.lillycares.com*

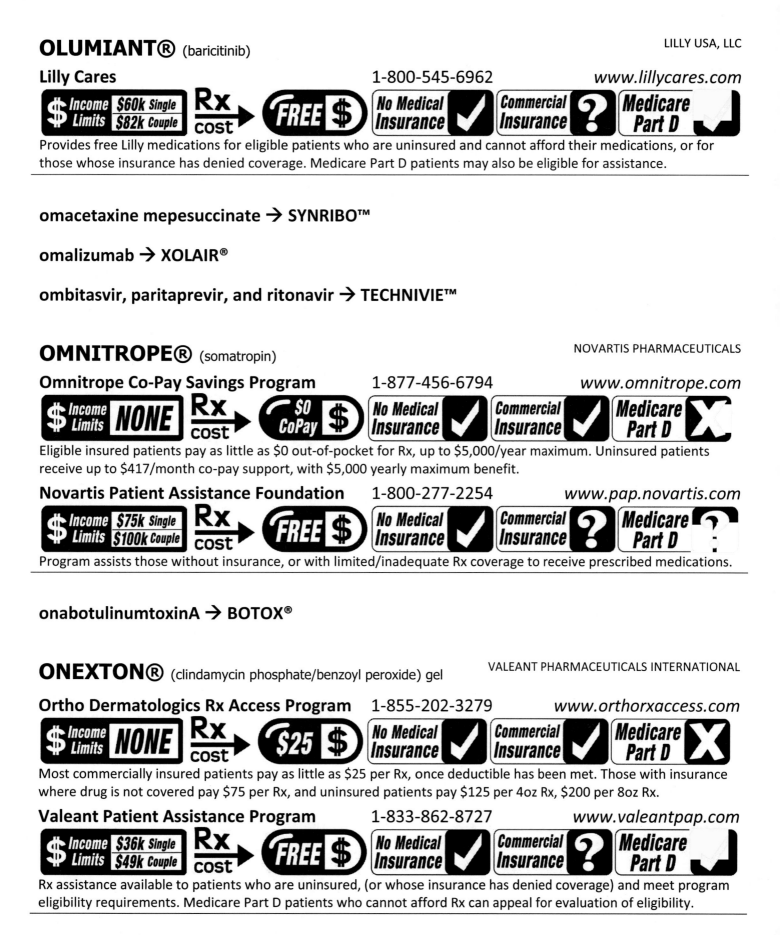

Provides free Lilly medications for eligible patients who are uninsured and cannot afford their medications, or for those whose insurance has denied coverage. Medicare Part D patients may also be eligible for assistance.

---

omacetaxine mepesuccinate → SYNRIBO™

omalizumab → XOLAIR®

ombitasvir, paritaprevir, and ritonavir → TECHNIVIE™

OMNITROPE® (somatropin)

NOVARTIS PHARMACEUTICALS

Omnitrope Co-Pay Savings Program　　1-877-456-6794　　*www.omnitrope.com*

Eligible insured patients pay as little as $0 out-of-pocket for Rx, up to $5,000/year maximum. Uninsured patients receive up to $417/month co-pay support, with $5,000 yearly maximum benefit.

Novartis Patient Assistance Foundation　1-800-277-2254　　*www.pap.novartis.com*

Program assists those without insurance, or with limited/inadequate Rx coverage to receive prescribed medications.

---

onabotulinumtoxinA → BOTOX®

ONEXTON® (clindamycin phosphate/benzoyl peroxide) gel

VALEANT PHARMACEUTICALS INTERNATIONAL

Ortho Dermatologics Rx Access Program　1-855-202-3279　　*www.orthorxaccess.com*

Most commercially insured patients pay as little as $25 per Rx, once deductible has been met. Those with insurance where drug is not covered pay $75 per Rx, and uninsured patients pay $125 per 4oz Rx, $200 per 8oz Rx.

Valeant Patient Assistance Program　　1-833-862-8727　　*www.valeantpap.com*

Rx assistance available to patients who are uninsured, (or whose insurance has denied coverage) and meet program eligibility requirements. Medicare Part D patients who cannot afford Rx can appeal for evaluation of eligibility.

ONFI® (clobazam)

ONFI Savings Card   1-855-345-6634   *www.onfi.com*

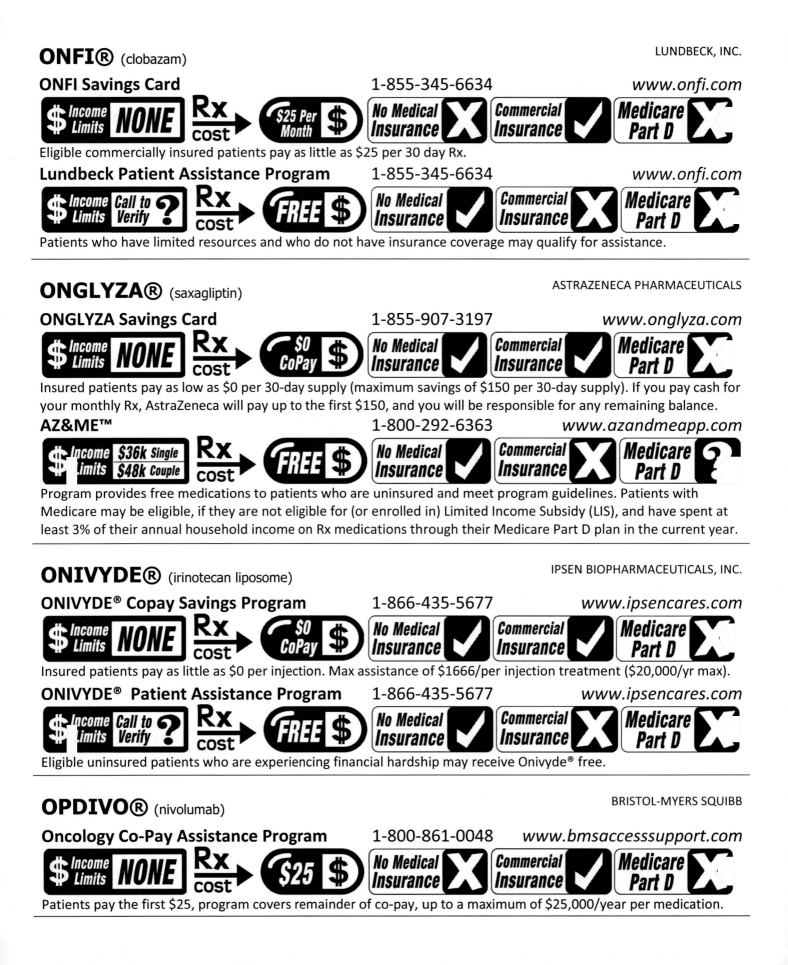

$ Income Limits **NONE** | Rx cost → | **$25 Per Month** $ | No Medical Insurance **X** | Commercial Insurance **✓** | Medicare Part D **X**

Eligible commercially insured patients pay as little as $25 per 30 day Rx.

Lundbeck Patient Assistance Program   1-855-345-6634   *www.onfi.com*

$ Income Limits Call to Verify **?** | Rx cost → | **FREE** $ | No Medical Insurance **✓** | Commercial Insurance **X** | Medicare Part D **X**

Patients who have limited resources and who do not have insurance coverage may qualify for assistance.

ONGLYZA® (saxagliptin)

ONGLYZA Savings Card   1-855-907-3197   *www.onglyza.com*

$ Income Limits **NONE** | Rx cost → | **$0 CoPay** $ | No Medical Insurance **✓** | Commercial Insurance **✓** | Medicare Part D **X**

Insured patients pay as low as $0 per 30-day supply (maximum savings of $150 per 30-day supply). If you pay cash for your monthly Rx, AstraZeneca will pay up to the first $150, and you will be responsible for any remaining balance.

AZ&ME™   1-800-292-6363   *www.azandmeapp.com*

$ Income Limits **$36k Single $48k Couple** | Rx cost → | **FREE** $ | No Medical Insurance **✓** | Commercial Insurance **X** | Medicare Part D **?**

Program provides free medications to patients who are uninsured and meet program guidelines. Patients with Medicare may be eligible, if they are not eligible for (or enrolled in) Limited Income Subsidy (LIS), and have spent at least 3% of their annual household income on Rx medications through their Medicare Part D plan in the current year.

ONIVYDE® (irinotecan liposome)

ONIVYDE® Copay Savings Program   1-866-435-5677   *www.ipsencares.com*

$ Income Limits **NONE** | Rx cost → | **$0 CoPay** $ | No Medical Insurance **✓** | Commercial Insurance **✓** | Medicare Part D **X**

Insured patients pay as little as $0 per injection. Max assistance of $1666/per injection treatment ($20,000/yr max).

ONIVYDE® Patient Assistance Program   1-866-435-5677   *www.ipsencares.com*

$ Income Limits Call to Verify **?** | Rx cost → | **FREE** $ | No Medical Insurance **✓** | Commercial Insurance **X** | Medicare Part D **X**

Eligible uninsured patients who are experiencing financial hardship may receive Onivyde® free.

OPDIVO® (nivolumab)

Oncology Co-Pay Assistance Program   1-800-861-0048   *www.bmsaccesssupport.com*

$ Income Limits **NONE** | Rx cost → | **$25** $ | No Medical Insurance **X** | Commercial Insurance **✓** | Medicare Part D **X**

Patients pay the first $25, program covers remainder of co-pay, up to a maximum of $25,000/year per medication.

OPDIVO® (nivolumab)

Bristol-Myers Squibb Patient Assistance Foundation   1-800-736-0003   www.bmspaf.com

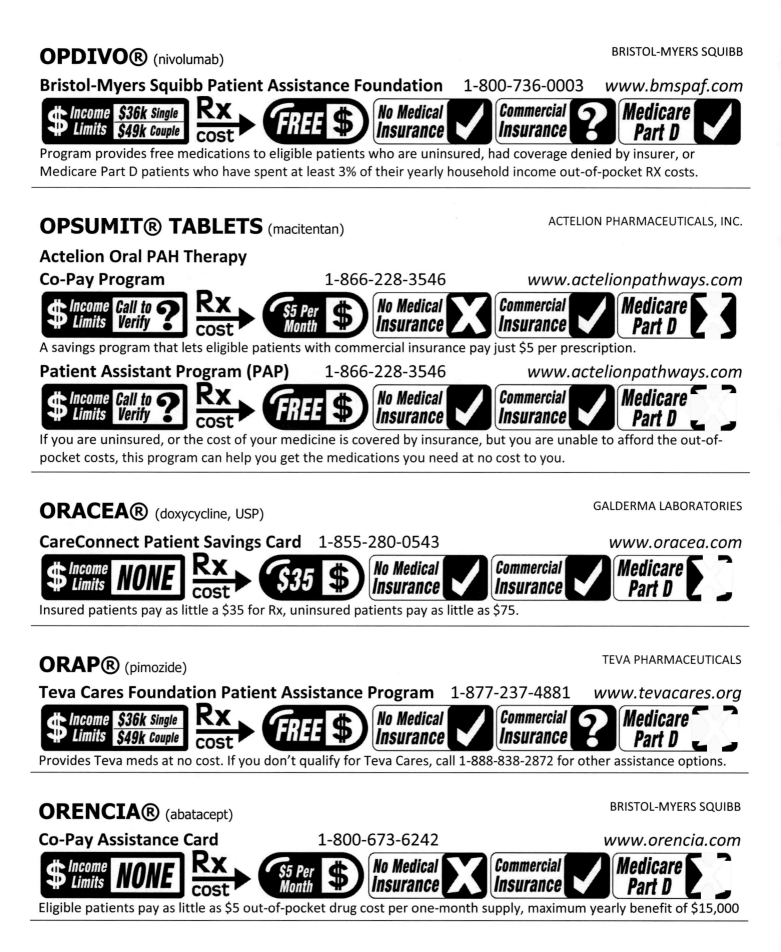

Program provides free medications to eligible patients who are uninsured, had coverage denied by insurer, or Medicare Part D patients who have spent at least 3% of their yearly household income out-of-pocket RX costs.

OPSUMIT® TABLETS (macitentan)
ACTELION PHARMACEUTICALS, INC.

Actelion Oral PAH Therapy

Co-Pay Program   1-866-228-3546   www.actelionpathways.com

A savings program that lets eligible patients with commercial insurance pay just $5 per prescription.

Patient Assistant Program (PAP)   1-866-228-3546   www.actelionpathways.com

If you are uninsured, or the cost of your medicine is covered by insurance, but you are unable to afford the out-of-pocket costs, this program can help you get the medications you need at no cost to you.

ORACEA® (doxycycline, USP)
GALDERMA LABORATORIES

CareConnect Patient Savings Card   1-855-280-0543   www.oracea.com

Insured patients pay as little a $35 for Rx, uninsured patients pay as little as $75.

ORAP® (pimozide)
TEVA PHARMACEUTICALS

Teva Cares Foundation Patient Assistance Program   1-877-237-4881   www.tevacares.org

Provides Teva meds at no cost. If you don't qualify for Teva Cares, call 1-888-838-2872 for other assistance options.

ORENCIA® (abatacept)
BRISTOL-MYERS SQUIBB

Co-Pay Assistance Card   1-800-673-6242   www.orencia.com

Eligible patients pay as little as $5 out-of-pocket drug cost per one-month supply, maximum yearly benefit of $15,000

ORENCIA® (abatacept)

BRISTOL-MYERS SQUIBB

Bristol-Myers Squibb Patient Assistance Foundation   1-800-736-0003   *www.bmspaf.com*

$ Income Limits $36k Single / $49k Couple | **Rx cost** → | **FREE $** | **No Medical Insurance** ✓ | **Commercial Insurance** ? | **Medicare Part D** ◤

Program provides free medications to eligible patients who are uninsured, had Rx coverage denied by insurer, or Medicare Part D patients who have spent at least 3% of their yearly household income out-of-pocket RX costs.

ORENITRAM® (treprostinil)

UNITED THERAPEUTICS CORPORATION

Orenitram Co-Pay Assistance Card   1-877-864-8437   *www.utcopay.com*

$ Income Limits NONE | **Rx cost** → | **$10 Per Month $** | **No Medical Insurance** X | **Commercial Insurance** ✓ | **Medicare Part D** X

Commercially Insured patients pay as little as $10 per month for Rx, maximum savings $5000 per year.

ASSIST Patient Assistance Program   1-877-864-8437   *www.orenitram.com*

$ Income Limits Call to Verify ? | **Rx cost** → | **FREE $** | **No Medical Insurance** ✓ | **Commercial Insurance** X | **Medicare Part D** X

Provides medication free of charge to qualified individuals who are uninsured and cannot afford their Rx.

ORFADIN® (nitisinone)

SOBI, INC.

Orfadin4U   1-877-473-3179   *www.orfadin.com*

$ Income Limits NONE | **Rx cost** → | **$0 CoPay $** | **No Medical Insurance** X | **Commercial Insurance** ✓ | **Medicare Part D** X

Eligible insured patients pay as little as $0 copay for Orfadin, max savings $10,000 per year.

SOBI Patient Assistance Program   1-877-473-3179   *www.orfadin.com*

$ Income Limits Call to Verify ? | **Rx cost** → | **FREE $** | **No Medical Insurance** ✓ | **Commercial Insurance** ? | **Medicare Part D** ?

Program provides meds to qualified patients who are uninsured or underinsured and cannot afford treatment.

ORKAMBI® (lumacaftor/ivacaftor)

VERTEX PHARMACEUTICALS

Vertex Guidance & Patient Support   1-877-752-5933   *www.orkambi.com*

$ Income Limits Call to Verify ? | **Rx cost** → | **$15 $** | **No Medical Insurance** ✓ | **Commercial Insurance** ✓ | **Medicare Part D** ?

Insured patients can pay as little as $15 copay per Rx, patient assistance program available for those who qualify.

💡 **TIP:** When in doubt... call the program and explain your situation. You may qualify for assistance.

OSENI® (alogliptin and pioglitazone)
TAKEDA PHARMACEUTICALS AMERICA

Instant Savings Card 1-855-510-4545 *www.nesinafamily.com*

Eligible patients pay as little as $35 copay per Rx, maximum benefit of $100 for a 30-day Rx and $300 for 90-day Rx.

Takeda Patient Assistance Program 1-800-830-9159 *www.takedahelpathand.com*

Provides Oseni at no cost to eligible patients who do not have insurance or not enough coverage to obtain meds.

osimertinib → TAGRISSO® Tablets

OTEZLA® (enasidenib)
CELGENE CORPORATION

OTEZLA SupportPlus 1-844-468-3952 *www.otezla.com*

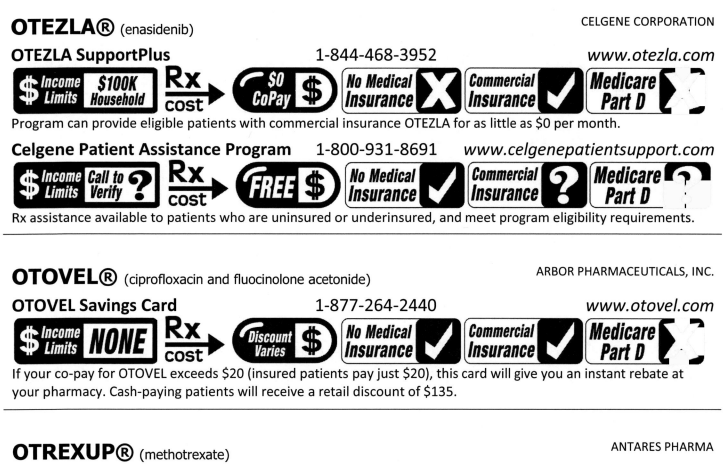

Program can provide eligible patients with commercial insurance OTEZLA for as little as $0 per month.

Celgene Patient Assistance Program 1-800-931-8691 *www.celgenepatientsupport.com*

Rx assistance available to patients who are uninsured or underinsured, and meet program eligibility requirements.

OTOVEL® (ciprofloxacin and fluocinolone acetonide)
ARBOR PHARMACEUTICALS, INC.

OTOVEL Savings Card 1-877-264-2440 *www.otovel.com*

If your co-pay for OTOVEL exceeds $20 (insured patients pay just $20), this card will give you an instant rebate at your pharmacy. Cash-paying patients will receive a retail discount of $135.

OTREXUP® (methotrexate)
ANTARES PHARMA

Otrexup Co-pay Assistance Program 1-855-202-5711 *www.otrexup.com*

Program provides up to $250 of co-pay assistance per Rx filled, up to 13 times per year. Eligible patients pay as low as $0 out-of-pocket for their prescribed meds.

OTREXUP® (methotrexate)

ANTARES PHARMA

Otrexup TotalCare Support Program   1-855-687-3987   *www.otrexup.com*

The Patient Assistance program works with doctors to help eligible Otrexup patients afford their medication.

oxaprozin → DAYPRO®

oxcarbazepine → OXTELLAR XR®

oxcarbazepine → TRILEPTAL®

OXSORALEN-ULTRA® (methoxsalen) capsules

VALEANT PHARMACEUTICALS INTERNATIONAL

Valeant Patient Assistance Program   1-833-862-8727   *www.valeantpap.com*

Rx assistance available to patients who are uninsured, (or whose insurance has denied coverage) and meet program eligibility requirements. Medicare Part D patients who cannot afford Rx can appeal for evaluation of eligibility.

OXTELLAR XR® (oxcarbazepine)

SUPERNUS PHARMACEUTICALS INC.

$0 Co-pay Program   1-866-398-0833   *www.oxtellarxr.com*

Savings card covers up to $250 of out-of-pocket expenses for each 30-day Rx. Commercially insured patients can pay as little as $0 out-of-pocket.

Supernus Patient Assistance Program   1-866-398-0833   *www.oxtellarxr.com*

Provides Oxtellar XR at no cost to eligible uninsured patients with financial need, who qualify for program.

oxybutynin chloride 10% gel → GELNIQUE®

oxycodone → OXYCONTIN®

oxycodone hydrochloride → ROXICODONE™

oxycodone HCl/acetaminophen → PRIMLEV®

OXYCONTIN® (oxycodone)

PURDUE PHARMA, L.P.

OxyContin Savings Card　　　1-855-227-0303　　　*www.oxycontin.com*

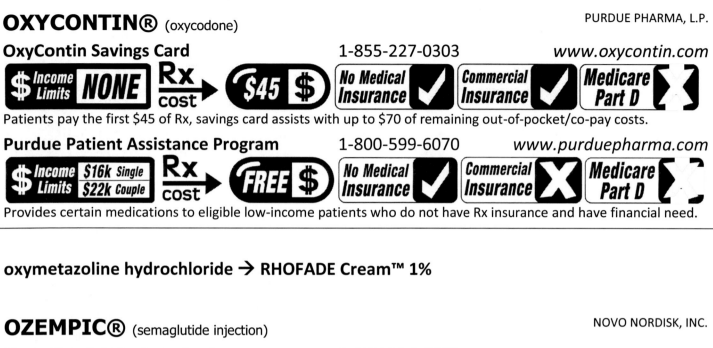

Patients pay the first $45 of Rx, savings card assists with up to $70 of remaining out-of-pocket/co-pay costs.

Purdue Patient Assistance Program　　　1-800-599-6070　　　*www.purduepharma.com*

Provides certain medications to eligible low-income patients who do not have Rx insurance and have financial need.

---

oxymetazoline hydrochloride → RHOFADE Cream™ 1%

OZEMPIC® (semaglutide injection)

NOVO NORDISK, INC.

Novo Nordisk Savings Card　　　1-877-304-6855　　　*www.novocare.com*

Pay as little as $25 per 30-day, $50 per 60-day, or $75 per 90-day supply for up to 24 months from the date of Savings Card activation, subject to a max savings of $100 per 30-day, $200 per 60-day, or $300 per 90-day supply.

Patient Access Program　　　1-866-310-7549　　　*www.novocare.com*

For patients who are uninsured. Also for Medicare patients who have spent more than $1000 this year on Rx meds.

OZURDEX® (dexamethasone)

ALLERGAN, INC.

Ozurdex Patient Assistance Program　　　1-866-698-7339　　　*www.ozurdex.com*

Program provides Ozurdex to patients who are uninsured or underinsured, and meet program eligibility guidelines.

---

paclitaxel → ABRAXANE®

palbociclib → IBRANCE®

palifermin → KEPIVANCE®

paliperidone palmitate → INVEGA® SUSTENNA/TRINZA

palivizumab → SYNAGIS®

PAMELOR™ (nortriptyline HCL)

MALLINCKRODT PHARMACEUTICALS

Mallinckrodt Patient Assistance Program   1-800-259-7765   *www.mallinckrodt.com*

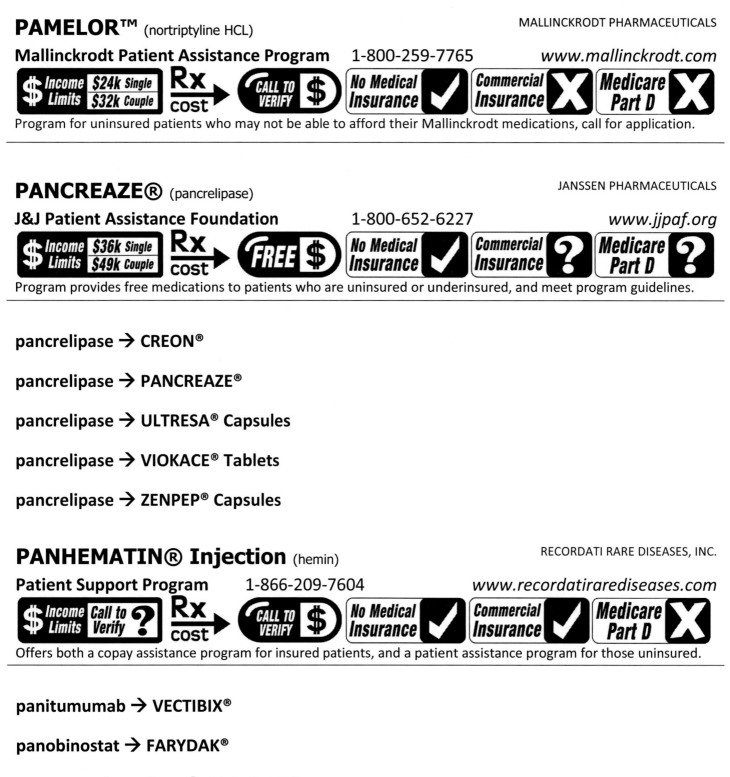

Program for uninsured patients who may not be able to afford their Mallinckrodt medications, call for application.

PANCREAZE® (pancrelipase)

JANSSEN PHARMACEUTICALS

J&J Patient Assistance Foundation   1-800-652-6227   *www.jjpaf.org*

Program provides free medications to patients who are uninsured or underinsured, and meet program guidelines.

pancrelipase → CREON®

pancrelipase → PANCREAZE®

pancrelipase → ULTRESA® Capsules

pancrelipase → VIOKACE® Tablets

pancrelipase → ZENPEP® Capsules

PANHEMATIN® Injection (hemin)

RECORDATI RARE DISEASES, INC.

Patient Support Program   1-866-209-7604   *www.recordatirarediseases.com*

Offers both a copay assistance program for insured patients, and a patient assistance program for those uninsured.

panitumumab → VECTIBIX®

panobinostat → FARYDAK®

pantoprazole sodium → PROTONIX®

paroxetine → BRISDELLE®

PARSABIV® (etelcalcetide)
AMGEN, INC.

AMGEN® Safety Net Foundation   1-888-762-6436   *www.amgensafetynetfoundation.com*

$ Income Limits $60k Single / $82k Couple | **Rx cost** → FREE $ | **No Medical Insurance** ✓ | **Commercial Insurance** ? | **Medicare Part D** ?

Foundation provides free medications to patients who are uninsured or underinsured, and meet program guidelines. Patients with Medicare may be eligible, if they have been denied or are ineligible for Low Income Subsidy.

---

pasireotide injection → SIGNIFOR®

PATADAY® (olopatadine hydrochloride ophthalmic solution)
NOVARTIS PHARMACEUTICALS

Novartis Patient Assistance Foundation   1-800-277-2254   *www.pap.novartis.com*

$ Income Limits $75k Single / $100k Couple | **Rx cost** → FREE $ | **No Medical Insurance** ✓ | **Commercial Insurance** ? | **Medicare Part D** ?

Program assists those without insurance, or with limited/inadequate Rx coverage to receive prescribed medications.

---

patiromer → VELTASSA®

PAZEO® (olopatadine hydrochloride ophthalmic solution)
NOVARTIS PHARMACEUTICALS

Co-Pay Savings Card   1-844-685-3406   *www.copay.novartispharma.com*

$ Income Limits NONE | **Rx cost** → $10 $ | **No Medical Insurance** ✗ | **Commercial Insurance** ✓ | **Medicare Part D** ✗

Commercially insured patients can pay as little as $10 per Rx, maximum total co-pay benefit of $125 per bottle.

Novartis Patient Assistance Foundation   1-800-277-2254   *www.pap.novartis.com*

$ Income Limits $75k Single / $100k Couple | **Rx cost** → FREE $ | **No Medical Insurance** ✓ | **Commercial Insurance** ? | **Medicare Part D** ?

Program assists those without insurance, or with limited/inadequate Rx coverage to receive prescribed medications.

---

pazopanib → VOTRIENT®

PCE® Tablets (erythromycin)
ARBOR PHARMACEUTICALS, INC.

Patient Assistance Program   1-844-884-8700   *www.arborpharma.com*

$ Income Limits $24k Single / $32k Couple | **Rx cost** → FREE $ | **No Medical Insurance** ✓ | **Commercial Insurance** ? | **Medicare Part D** ?

Program provides free medications to patients who are uninsured or underinsured, and meet program guidelines. Patients with Medicare may be eligible, if they have been denied or are ineligible for Low Income Subsidy.

PEGANONE® Tablets (ethotoin)

RECORDATI RARE DISEASES, INC.

Patient Support Program 1-866-209-7604 *www.recordatirarediseases.com*

Offers both a copay assistance program for insured patients, and a patient assistance program for those uninsured.

---

pegaptanb sodium injection → MACUGEN®

pegfilgrastim → NEULASTA®

peginterferon beta-1a → PLEGRITY®

pegloticase → KRYSTEXXA®

pegvisomant → SOMAVERT®

pembrolizumab → KEYTRUDA®

pemetrexed for injection → ALIMTA®

penicillamine → CUPRIMINE®

PENNSAID® 2% (diclofenac sodium solution; topical)

HORIZON PHARMA USA, INC.

PENNSAID 2% Co-Pay Card 1-844-865-8694 *www.pennsaid.com*

Eligible insured patients pay as low as $0/month with a maximum Rx savings of $1,200 per bottle.

Horizon Pharma Patient Assistance Program 1-888-958-5502 *www.pennsaid.com*

Helps eligible patients who lack health insurance coverage for PENNSAID 2% to get their Rx meds at no cost.

PENTASA® (mesalamine)

SHIRE

Shire Cares Patient Assistance & Support 1-888-227-3755 *www.pentasa.com*

Program assists patients with limited financial needs who are having problems affording their Rx medications.

pentosan polysulfate sodium → ELMIRON®

perampanel → FYCOMPA®

PERFOROMIST® (formoterol fumarate)   MYLAN

PERFOROMIST® Savings Card   1-800-395-3376   *www.perforomist.com*

Income Limits: NONE	Rx cost →	$0 CoPay	No Medical Insurance ✗	Commercial Insurance ✓	Medicare Part D ✗

Pay as little as $0 after you save up to $350 for 90 day Rx, or Pay $25 after you save $50 on 30 or 60 day Rx.

PERJETA® (pertuzumab)   GENENTECH, INC.

Co-pay Card Assistance Program   1-855-692-6729   *www.copayassistancenow.com*

Income Limits: NONE	Rx cost →	$5 Per Month	No Medical Insurance ✗	Commercial Insurance ✓	Medicare Part D ✗

Program provides up to $25,000/year in co-pay assistance. Patients pay only $5/month for their prescribed meds.

Genentech Access Solutions   1-866-422-2377   *www.genentech-access.com*

Income Limits: $100K Household	Rx cost →	FREE	No Medical Insurance ✓	Commercial Insurance ?	Medicare Part D ?

Program provides medications to patients who are uninsured or have been denied coverage by their insurance company. Patients who have insurance, but pay too much out of pocket per year, may also qualify for assistance.

pertuzumab → PERJETA®

PERTZYE® (amylase/lipase/pancrelipase/protease)   CHIESI USA, INC.

Chiesi CAREDIRECT®   1-888-865-1222   *www.pertzye.com*

Income Limits: $48k Single $65k Couple	Rx cost →	FREE	No Medical Insurance ✓	Commercial Insurance ?	Medicare Part D ✗

Rx assistance available to patients who are uninsured or underinsured, and meet program eligibility requirements.

PFIZERPEN® (penicillin G potassium)   PFIZER, INC

Pfizer Savings Program   1-866-706-2400   *www.pfizerrxpathways.com*

Income Limits: NONE	Rx cost →	Discount Varies	No Medical Insurance ✓	Commercial Insurance ✗	Medicare Part D ✗

Program helps uninsured patients receive discounted Pfizer medications through their local retail pharmacy.

phenelzine sulfate → NARDIL®

phenytoin sodium → DILANTIN®

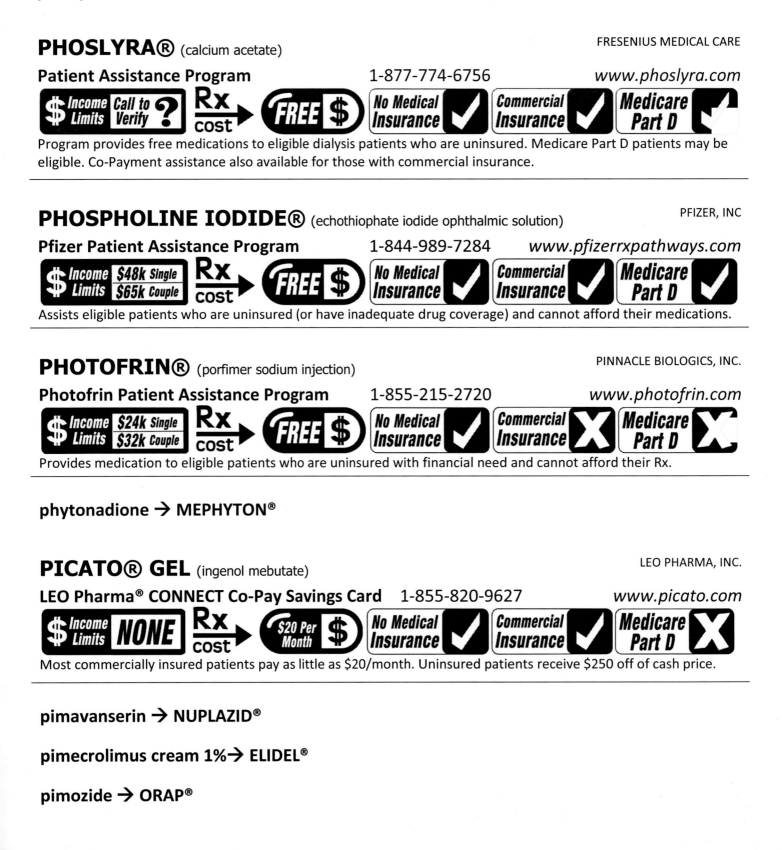

PHOSLYRA® (calcium acetate)   FRESENIUS MEDICAL CARE

Patient Assistance Program   1-877-774-6756   *www.phoslyra.com*

| $ Income Limits | Call to Verify ? | Rx cost → | FREE $ | No Medical Insurance ✓ | Commercial Insurance ✓ | Medicare Part D ✓ |

Program provides free medications to eligible dialysis patients who are uninsured. Medicare Part D patients may be eligible. Co-Payment assistance also available for those with commercial insurance.

PHOSPHOLINE IODIDE® (echothiophate iodide ophthalmic solution)   PFIZER, INC

Pfizer Patient Assistance Program   1-844-989-7284   *www.pfizerrxpathways.com*

| $ Income Limits | $48k Single $65k Couple | Rx cost → | FREE $ | No Medical Insurance ✓ | Commercial Insurance ✓ | Medicare Part D ✓ |

Assists eligible patients who are uninsured (or have inadequate drug coverage) and cannot afford their medications.

PHOTOFRIN® (porfimer sodium injection)   PINNACLE BIOLOGICS, INC.

Photofrin Patient Assistance Program   1-855-215-2720   *www.photofrin.com*

| $ Income Limits | $24k Single $32k Couple | Rx cost → | FREE $ | No Medical Insurance ✓ | Commercial Insurance X | Medicare Part D X |

Provides medication to eligible patients who are uninsured with financial need and cannot afford their Rx.

phytonadione → MEPHYTON®

PICATO® GEL (ingenol mebutate)   LEO PHARMA, INC.

LEO Pharma® CONNECT Co-Pay Savings Card   1-855-820-9627   *www.picato.com*

| $ Income Limits | NONE | Rx cost → | $20 Per Month $ | No Medical Insurance ✓ | Commercial Insurance ✓ | Medicare Part D X |

Most commercially insured patients pay as little as $20/month. Uninsured patients receive $250 off of cash price.

pimavanserin → NUPLAZID®

pimecrolimus cream 1% → ELIDEL®

pimozide → ORAP®

pirfenidone → ESBRIET®

piroxicam → FELDENE®

pitavastatin → LIVALO®

PLEGRITY® (peginterferon beta-1a) — BIOGEN

$0 CoPay Program　　　1-800-456-2255　　　*www.plegrity.com*

Commercially insured patients can pay as little as $0 out-of-pocket for each needed injection. If you pay cash for your injections, you may also qualify for some assistance. Call for details.

Above MS™ Free Drug Program　　　1-800-456-2255　　　*www.plegrity.com*

Rx assistance available to patients who are uninsured or underinsured, and meet program eligibility requirements.

plerixafor injection → MOZOBIL®

pomalidomide → POMALYST®

POMALYST® (pomalidomide) — CELGENE CORPORATION

Celgene Co-Pay Assistance Program　　　1-800-931-8691　　　*www.celgenepatientsupport.com*

Program can provide up to $10,000/year in Deductible/Co-Pay Assistance if you are commercially insured, making your Rx cost $25/month or less.

Celgene Patient Assistance Program　　　1-800-931-8691　　　*www.celgenepatientsupport.com*

Rx assistance available to patients who are uninsured or underinsured, and meet program eligibility requirements.

ponatinib → ICLUSIG®

porfimer sodium injection → PHOTOFRIN®

> **TIP:** When in doubt... call the program and explain your situation. You may qualify for assistance.

PORTRAZZA® (necitumumab)

LILLY USA, LLC

Lilly PatientOne   1-866-472-8663   *www.lillypatientone.com*

Eligible patients pay $25 per Rx, program covers remaining co-pay or coinsurance, up to a max of $25,000/year.

Lilly Cares   1-800-545-6962   *www.lillycares.com*

Provides free Lilly medications for eligible patients who are uninsured and cannot afford their medications, or for those whose insurance has denied coverage. Medicare Part D patients may also be eligible for assistance.

---

posaconazole → **NOXAFIL®**

PRADAXA® (dabigatran etexilate)

BOEHRINGER INGELHEIM PHARMACEUTICALS, INC.

PRADAXA Savings Card   1-877-481-5332   *www.pradaxa.com*

Eligible insured patients pay as low as $0 per month for PRADAXA (maximum savings of $2,400). Government insured (Medicare) and uninsured (cash-paying) patients may receive a one-time, Free 30-day supply of PRADAXA.

Boehringer Ingelheim Cares Foundation   1-800-556-8317   *www.bipatientassistance.com*

Patient Assistance Program provides free medications to patients who are uninsured or underinsured, and meet program guidelines. Patients with Medicare may be eligible, if they are ineligible for Low Income Subsidy.

---

pralatrexate injection → **FOLOTYN®**

PRALUENT® (alirocumab)

SANOFI-AVENTIS U.S. LLC.

MyPraluent Copay Card   1-844-240-3655   *www.praluent.com*

Eligible insured patients pay as little as $0 out-of-pocket for Praluent, maximum benefit of $5,500/year.

PASS Program   1-844-855-7277   *www.praluent.com*

Provides meds to patients who are uninsured, underinsured, or on Medicare and meet program guidelines.

pramlintide acetate injection → SymlinPen®

praziquantel → BILTRICIDE®

PRED FORTE® 1.0% (prednisolone acetate ophthalmic suspension)

ALLERGAN, INC.

Allergan Patient Assistance Program   1-844-424-6727   *www.allergan.com*

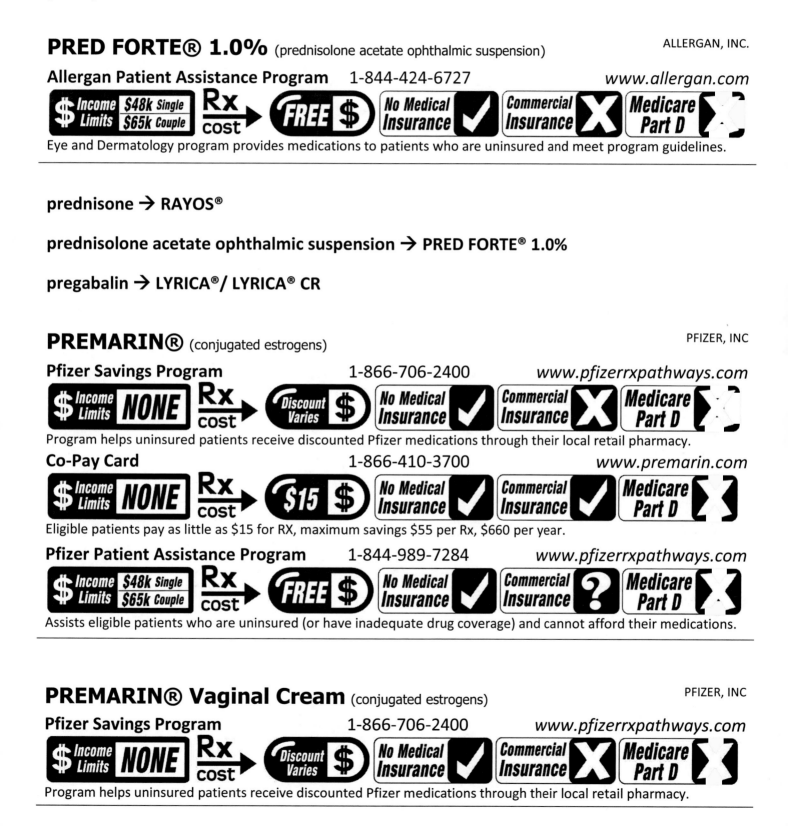

| $ Income Limits $48k Single / $65k Couple | Rx cost → | FREE $ | No Medical Insurance ✔ | Commercial Insurance ✗ | Medicare Part D 〉 |

Eye and Dermatology program provides medications to patients who are uninsured and meet program guidelines.

prednisone → RAYOS®

prednisolone acetate ophthalmic suspension → PRED FORTE® 1.0%

pregabalin → LYRICA®/ LYRICA® CR

PREMARIN® (conjugated estrogens)

PFIZER, INC

Pfizer Savings Program   1-866-706-2400   *www.pfizerrxpathways.com*

| $ Income Limits NONE | Rx cost → | Discount Varies $ | No Medical Insurance ✔ | Commercial Insurance ✗ | Medicare Part D 〉 |

Program helps uninsured patients receive discounted Pfizer medications through their local retail pharmacy.

Co-Pay Card   1-866-410-3700   *www.premarin.com*

| $ Income Limits NONE | Rx cost → | $15 $ | No Medical Insurance ✔ | Commercial Insurance ✔ | Medicare Part D 〉 |

Eligible patients pay as little as $15 for RX, maximum savings $55 per Rx, $660 per year.

Pfizer Patient Assistance Program   1-844-989-7284   *www.pfizerrxpathways.com*

| $ Income Limits $48k Single / $65k Couple | Rx cost → | FREE $ | No Medical Insurance ✔ | Commercial Insurance ? | Medicare Part D 〉 |

Assists eligible patients who are uninsured (or have inadequate drug coverage) and cannot afford their medications.

PREMARIN® Vaginal Cream (conjugated estrogens)

PFIZER, INC

Pfizer Savings Program   1-866-706-2400   *www.pfizerrxpathways.com*

| $ Income Limits NONE | Rx cost → | Discount Varies $ | No Medical Insurance ✔ | Commercial Insurance ✗ | Medicare Part D 〉 |

Program helps uninsured patients receive discounted Pfizer medications through their local retail pharmacy.

PREMARIN® Vaginal Cream (conjugated estrogens)
PFIZER, INC

Co-Pay Card   1-866-879-4600   *www.premarinvaginalcream.com*

$ Income Limits **NONE** | Rx cost → | **$15** $ | **No Medical Insurance** ✓ | **Commercial Insurance** ✓ | **Medicare Part D** ✗

Eligible patients pay as little as $15 for RX, maximum savings $150 per Rx, $300 per year.

Pfizer Patient Assistance Program   1-844-989-7284   *www.pfizerrxpathways.com*

$ Income Limits **$48k Single $65k Couple** | Rx cost → | **FREE** $ | **No Medical Insurance** ✓ | **Commercial Insurance** ? | **Medicare Part D** ✗

Assists eligible patients who are uninsured (or have inadequate drug coverage) and cannot afford their medications.

PREMPHASE® (conjugated estrogens/medroxyprogesterone acetate)
PFIZER, INC

Pfizer Savings Program   1-866-706-2400   *www.pfizerrxpathways.com*

$ Income Limits **NONE** | Rx cost → | **Discount Varies** $ | **No Medical Insurance** ✓ | **Commercial Insurance** ✗ | **Medicare Part D** ✗

Program helps uninsured patients receive discounted Pfizer medications through their local retail pharmacy.

Pfizer Patient Assistance Program   1-844-989-7284   *www.pfizerrxpathways.com*

$ Income Limits **$48k Single $65k Couple** | Rx cost → | **FREE** $ | **No Medical Insurance** ✓ | **Commercial Insurance** ? | **Medicare Part D** ✗

Assists eligible patients who are uninsured (or have inadequate drug coverage) and cannot afford their medications.

PREMPRO® (conjugated estrogens, medroxyprogesterone acetate)
PFIZER, INC

Pfizer Savings Program   1-866-706-2400   *www.pfizerrxpathways.com*

$ Income Limits **NONE** | Rx cost → | **Discount Varies** $ | **No Medical Insurance** ✓ | **Commercial Insurance** ✗ | **Medicare Part D** ✗

Program helps uninsured patients receive discounted Pfizer medications through their local retail pharmacy.

Pfizer Patient Assistance Program   1-844-989-7284   *www.pfizerrxpathways.com*

$ Income Limits **$48k Single $65k Couple** | Rx cost → | **FREE** $ | **No Medical Insurance** ✓ | **Commercial Insurance** ? | **Medicare Part D** ✗

Assists eligible patients who are uninsured (or have inadequate drug coverage) and cannot afford their medications.

PREVACID SOLUTAB® (lansoprazole orally disintegrating tablet)
TAKEDA PHARMACEUTICALS

Takeda Patient Assistance Program   1-800-830-9159   *www.takedahelpathand.com*

$ Income Limits **$60k Single $82k Couple** | Rx cost → | **FREE** $ | **No Medical Insurance** ✓ | **Commercial Insurance** ? | **Medicare Part D** ?

Provides medications at no cost to eligible patients who do not have insurance or not enough coverage to obtain Rx.

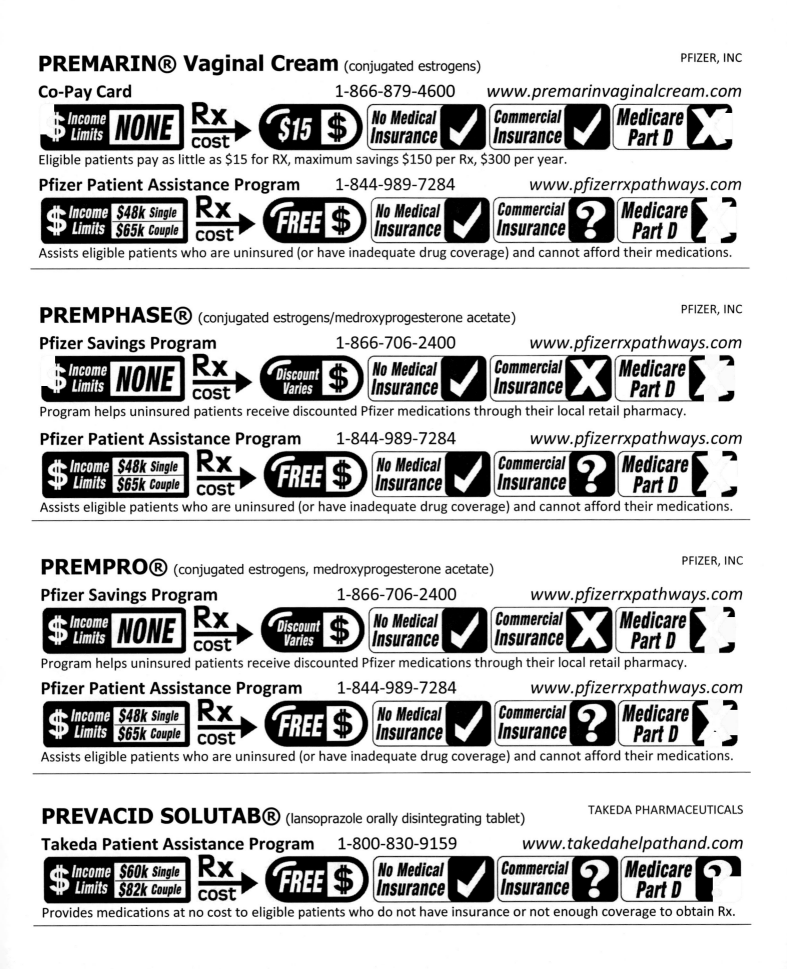

PREVYMIS™ (letermovir)

MERCK & COMPANY, INC.

Multiuse Savings Coupon　　　1-800-672-6372　　　*www.prevymis.com*

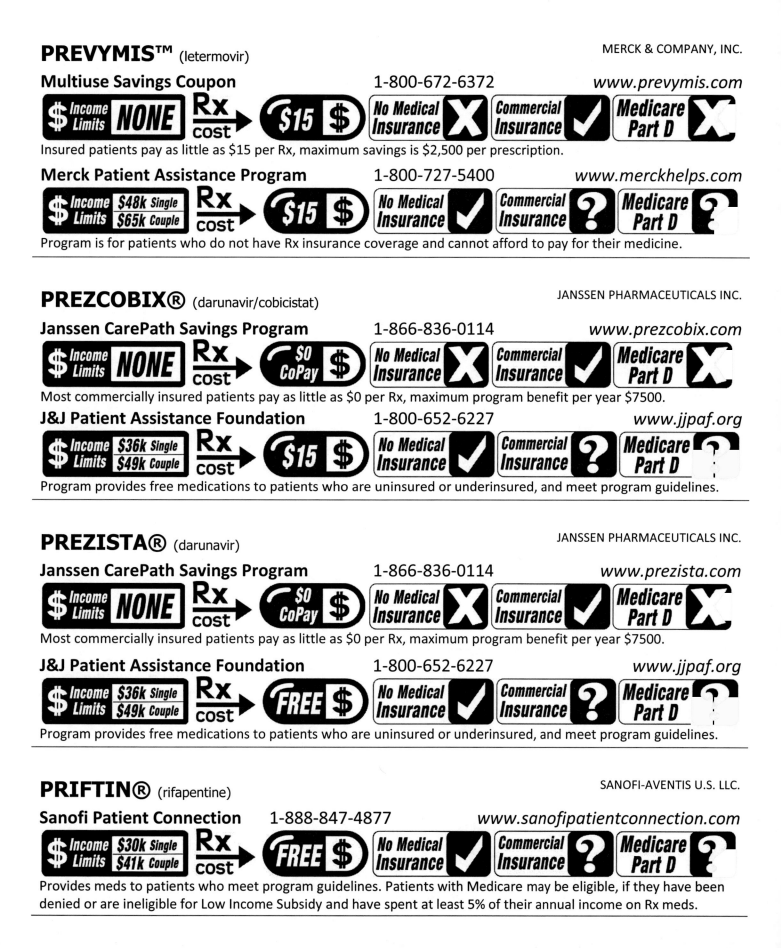

$ Income Limits **NONE** | **Rx cost** → **$15 $** | **No Medical Insurance** ✗ | **Commercial Insurance** ✓ | **Medicare Part D** ✗

Insured patients pay as little as $15 per Rx, maximum savings is $2,500 per prescription.

Merck Patient Assistance Program　　　1-800-727-5400　　　*www.merckhelps.com*

$ Income Limits **$48k Single / $65k Couple** | **Rx cost** → **$15 $** | **No Medical Insurance** ✓ | **Commercial Insurance** ? | **Medicare Part D** ?

Program is for patients who do not have Rx insurance coverage and cannot afford to pay for their medicine.

PREZCOBIX® (darunavir/cobicistat)

JANSSEN PHARMACEUTICALS INC.

Janssen CarePath Savings Program　　　1-866-836-0114　　　*www.prezcobix.com*

$ Income Limits **NONE** | **Rx cost** → **$0 CoPay $** | **No Medical Insurance** ✗ | **Commercial Insurance** ✓ | **Medicare Part D** ✗

Most commercially insured patients pay as little as $0 per Rx, maximum program benefit per year $7500.

J&J Patient Assistance Foundation　　　1-800-652-6227　　　*www.jjpaf.org*

$ Income Limits **$36k Single / $49k Couple** | **Rx cost** → **$15 $** | **No Medical Insurance** ✓ | **Commercial Insurance** ? | **Medicare Part D** ?

Program provides free medications to patients who are uninsured or underinsured, and meet program guidelines.

PREZISTA® (darunavir)

JANSSEN PHARMACEUTICALS INC.

Janssen CarePath Savings Program　　　1-866-836-0114　　　*www.prezista.com*

$ Income Limits **NONE** | **Rx cost** → **$0 CoPay $** | **No Medical Insurance** ✗ | **Commercial Insurance** ✓ | **Medicare Part D** ✗

Most commercially insured patients pay as little as $0 per Rx, maximum program benefit per year $7500.

J&J Patient Assistance Foundation　　　1-800-652-6227　　　*www.jjpaf.org*

$ Income Limits **$36k Single / $49k Couple** | **Rx cost** → **FREE $** | **No Medical Insurance** ✓ | **Commercial Insurance** ? | **Medicare Part D** ?

Program provides free medications to patients who are uninsured or underinsured, and meet program guidelines.

PRIFTIN® (rifapentine)

SANOFI-AVENTIS U.S. LLC.

Sanofi Patient Connection　　　1-888-847-4877　　　*www.sanofipatientconnection.com*

$ Income Limits **$30k Single / $41k Couple** | **Rx cost** → **FREE $** | **No Medical Insurance** ✓ | **Commercial Insurance** ? | **Medicare Part D** ?

Provides meds to patients who meet program guidelines. Patients with Medicare may be eligible, if they have been denied or are ineligible for Low Income Subsidy and have spent at least 5% of their annual income on Rx meds.

PRIMLEV® (oxycodone HCL/acetaminophen)

Co-Pay Assistance Card Program   1-844-205-3612   *www.primlev.com*

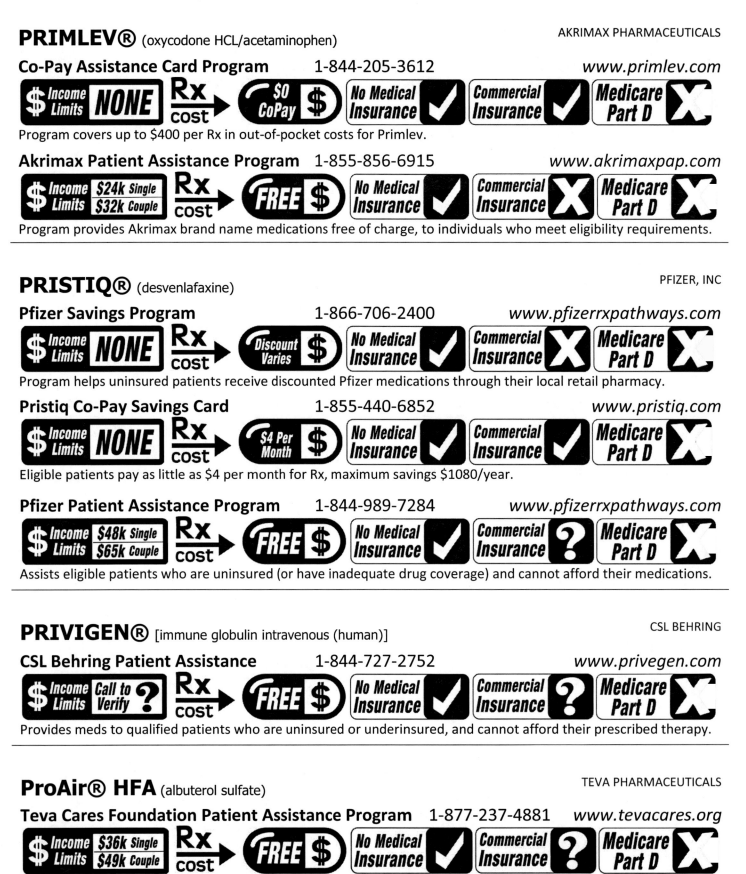

$ Income Limits NONE | **Rx cost** → | **$0 CoPay $** | **No Medical Insurance ✓** | **Commercial Insurance ✓** | **Medicare Part D ✗**

Program covers up to $400 per Rx in out-of-pocket costs for Primlev.

Akrimax Patient Assistance Program   1-855-856-6915   *www.akrimaxpap.com*

$ Income Limits $24k Single / $32k Couple | **Rx cost** → | **FREE $** | **No Medical Insurance ✓** | **Commercial Insurance ✗** | **Medicare Part D ✗**

Program provides Akrimax brand name medications free of charge, to individuals who meet eligibility requirements.

PRISTIQ® (desvenlafaxine)

Pfizer Savings Program   1-866-706-2400   *www.pfizerrxpathways.com*

$ Income Limits NONE | **Rx cost** → | **Discount Varies $** | **No Medical Insurance ✓** | **Commercial Insurance ✗** | **Medicare Part D ✗**

Program helps uninsured patients receive discounted Pfizer medications through their local retail pharmacy.

Pristiq Co-Pay Savings Card   1-855-440-6852   *www.pristiq.com*

$ Income Limits NONE | **Rx cost** → | **$4 Per Month $** | **No Medical Insurance ✓** | **Commercial Insurance ✓** | **Medicare Part D ✗**

Eligible patients pay as little as $4 per month for Rx, maximum savings $1080/year.

Pfizer Patient Assistance Program   1-844-989-7284   *www.pfizerrxpathways.com*

$ Income Limits $48k Single / $65k Couple | **Rx cost** → | **FREE $** | **No Medical Insurance ✓** | **Commercial Insurance ?** | **Medicare Part D ✗**

Assists eligible patients who are uninsured (or have inadequate drug coverage) and cannot afford their medications.

PRIVIGEN® [immune globulin intravenous (human)]

CSL Behring Patient Assistance   1-844-727-2752   *www.privegen.com*

$ Income Limits Call to Verify ? | **Rx cost** → | **FREE $** | **No Medical Insurance ✓** | **Commercial Insurance ?** | **Medicare Part D ✗**

Provides meds to qualified patients who are uninsured or underinsured, and cannot afford their prescribed therapy.

ProAir® HFA (albuterol sulfate)

Teva Cares Foundation Patient Assistance Program   1-877-237-4881   *www.tevacares.org*

$ Income Limits $36k Single / $49k Couple | **Rx cost** → | **FREE $** | **No Medical Insurance ✓** | **Commercial Insurance ?** | **Medicare Part D ✗**

Provides Teva meds at no cost. If you don't qualify for Teva Cares, call 1-888-838-2872 for other assistance options.

ProAir RespiClick® (albuterol sulfate) inhalation powder

Savings Card　　　　　1-800-284-2966　　　*www.proair.com*

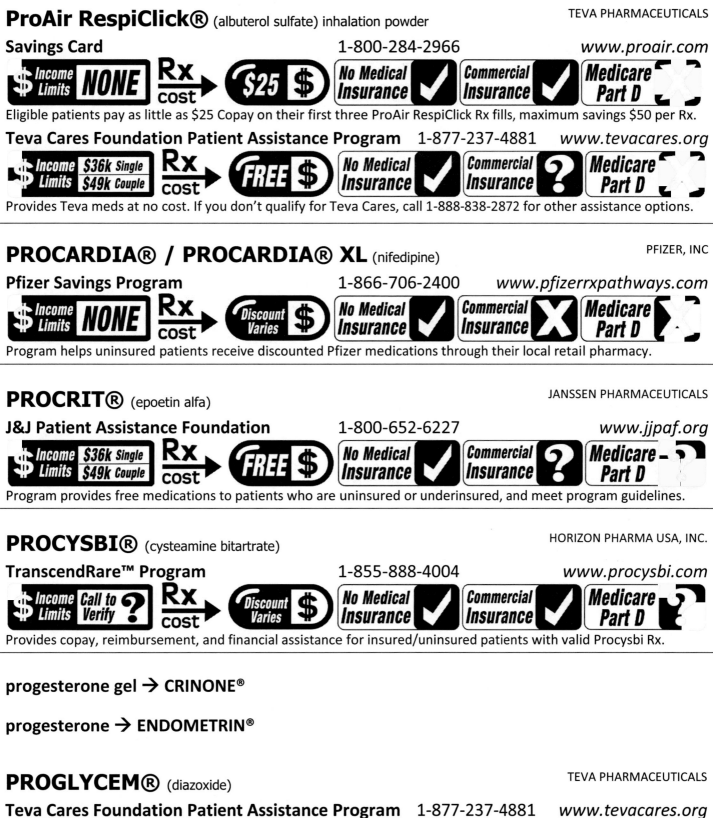

Income Limits **NONE** | **Rx** cost → **$25 $** | **No Medical Insurance** ✓ | **Commercial Insurance** ✓ | **Medicare Part D** ✗

Eligible patients pay as little as $25 Copay on their first three ProAir RespiClick Rx fills, maximum savings $50 per Rx.

Teva Cares Foundation Patient Assistance Program　1-877-237-4881　*www.tevacares.org*

Income Limits **$36k Single $49k Couple** | **Rx** cost → **FREE $** | **No Medical Insurance** ✓ | **Commercial Insurance ?** | **Medicare Part D** ✗

Provides Teva meds at no cost. If you don't qualify for Teva Cares, call 1-888-838-2872 for other assistance options.

PROCARDIA® / PROCARDIA® XL (nifedipine)

Pfizer Savings Program　　　1-866-706-2400　　*www.pfizerrxpathways.com*

Income Limits **NONE** | **Rx** cost → **Discount Varies $** | **No Medical Insurance** ✓ | **Commercial Insurance** ✗ | **Medicare Part D** ▶

Program helps uninsured patients receive discounted Pfizer medications through their local retail pharmacy.

PROCRIT® (epoetin alfa)

J&J Patient Assistance Foundation　　1-800-652-6227　　　*www.jjpaf.org*

Income Limits **$36k Single $49k Couple** | **Rx** cost → **FREE $** | **No Medical Insurance** ✓ | **Commercial Insurance ?** | **Medicare Part D** ?

Program provides free medications to patients who are uninsured or underinsured, and meet program guidelines.

PROCYSBI® (cysteamine bitartrate)

TranscendRare™ Program　　　1-855-888-4004　　　*www.procysbi.com*

Income Limits **Call to Verify ?** | **Rx** cost → **Discount Varies $** | **No Medical Insurance** ✓ | **Commercial Insurance** ✓ | **Medicare Part D** ?

Provides copay, reimbursement, and financial assistance for insured/uninsured patients with valid Procysbi Rx.

progesterone gel → CRINONE®

progesterone → ENDOMETRIN®

PROGLYCEM® (diazoxide)

Teva Cares Foundation Patient Assistance Program　1-877-237-4881　*www.tevacares.org*

Income Limits **$36k Single $49k Couple** | **Rx** cost → **FREE $** | **No Medical Insurance** ✓ | **Commercial Insurance ?** | **Medicare Part D**

Provides Teva meds at no cost. If you don't qualify for Teva Cares, call 1-888-838-2872 for other assistance options.

PROGRAF® (tacrolimus)
ASTELLAS PHARMA, INC.

PROGRAF Co-Pay Card   1-866-790-7659   *www.astellasaccess.com*

| $ Income Limits **NONE** | Rx cost → | $0 CoPay $ | No Medical Insurance **X** | Commercial Insurance **✓** | Medicare Part D **X** |

Provides up to $3000/year in co-pay assistance. Eligible patients pay as low as $0 out-of-pocket for prescribed meds.

PROGRAF Support Solutions®   1-800-477-6472   *www.astellasaccess.com*

| $ Income Limits **$125K Household** | Rx cost → | FREE $ | No Medical Insurance **✓** | Commercial Insurance **?** | Medicare Part D **?** |

Provides medications for those uninsured or have insurance that excludes coverage for PROGRAF.

PROLASTIN-C® [alpha1-proteinase inhibitor (human)]
GRIFOLS

Patient Assistance Program (PAP)   1-800-305-7881   *www.prolastin.com*

| $ Income Limits **Call to Verify ?** | Rx cost → | FREE $ | No Medical Insurance **✓** | Commercial Insurance **?** | Medicare Part D **X** |

Assists eligible uninsured/underinsured patients to receive treatment.

PROLENSA® (bromfenac sodium solution) 0.07%
VALEANT PHARMACEUTICALS INTERNATIONAL

Valeant Patient Assistance Program   1-833-862-8727   *www.valeantpap.com*

| $ Income Limits **$36k Single / $49k Couple** | Rx cost → | FREE $ | No Medical Insurance **✓** | Commercial Insurance **?** | Medicare Part D |

Rx assistance available to patients who are uninsured, (or whose insurance has denied coverage) and meet program eligibility requirements. Medicare Part D patients who cannot afford Rx can appeal for evaluation of eligibility.

PROLIA® (denosumab)
AMGEN, INC.

NPLATE FIRST STEP™ Program   1-888-657-8371   *www.amgenfirststep.com*

| $ Income Limits **NONE** | Rx cost → | $25 $ | No Medical Insurance **X** | Commercial Insurance **✓** | Medicare Part D **X** |

No out-of-pocket cost for first dose/cycle; $25 out-of-pocket cost for subsequent dose/cycles. Program assists with out-of-pocket costs, maximum benefit of $1,500 per patient per calendar year, via the Amgen FIRST STEP™ card.

AMGEN® Safety Net Foundation   1-888-762-6436   *www.amgensafetynetfoundation.com*

| $ Income Limits **$60k Single / $82k Couple** | Rx cost → | FREE $ | No Medical Insurance **✓** | Commercial Insurance **?** | Medicare Part D **?** |

Foundation provides free medications to patients who are uninsured or underinsured, and meet program guidelines. Patients with Medicare may be eligible, if they have been denied or are ineligible for Low Income Subsidy.

💡 **TIP:** Income limits are higher for households with three or more people. Call programs for details.

PROMACTA® (eltrombopag)

NOVARTIS PHARMACEUTICALS

Universal Co-Pay Card   1-877-577-7756   *www.copay.novartisoncology.com*

Income Limits **NONE** | Rx cost → | **$25** $ | No Medical Insurance ✗ | Commercial Insurance ✓ | Medicare Part D ✗

Patients pay the first $25, the program pays the remaining co-pay or coinsurance to max benefit of $15,000/year.

Novartis Patient Assistance Foundation   1-800-277-2254   *www.pap.novartis.com*

Income Limits **$75k Single $100k Couple** | Rx cost → | **FREE** $ | No Medical Insurance ✓ | Commercial Insurance ? | Medicare Part D ?

Program assists those without insurance, or with limited/inadequate Rx coverage to receive prescribed medications.

---

propafenone hydrochloride → RYTHMOL® SR

propranolol hydrochloride → INNOPRAN® XL

PROTONIX® (pantoprazole sodium)

PFIZER, INC

Pfizer Savings Program   1-866-706-2400   *www.pfizerrxpathways.com*

Income Limits **NONE** | Rx cost → | **Discount Varies** $ | No Medical Insurance ✓ | Commercial Insurance ✗ | Medicare Part D ✗

Program helps uninsured patients receive discounted Pfizer medications through their local retail pharmacy.

Protonix Savings Card   1-855-807-7901   *www.protonix.com*

Income Limits **NONE** | Rx cost → | **$4 Per Month** $ | No Medical Insurance ✓ | Commercial Insurance ✓ | Medicare Part D ✗

Eligible patients pay as little as $4 per month for Rx, maximum savings $79 per Rx, $840/year.

PROVENGE® (sipuleucel-t)

DENDREON CORPORATION

PROvide Commercial Co-pay Program   1-877-336-3736   *www.provenge.com*

Income Limits **NONE** | Rx cost → | **Discount Varies** $ | No Medical Insurance ✗ | Commercial Insurance ✓ | Medicare Part D ✗

Flexible coverage of up to $6,000 (over 3 PROVENGE treatments) for co-pays, co-insurance, and deductible costs.

Uninsured Patient Assistance Program   1-877-336-3736   *www.provenge.com*

Income Limits **$150K Household** | Rx cost → | **FREE** $ | No Medical Insurance ✓ | Commercial Insurance ? | Medicare Part D ✗

Provides PROVENGE to eligible uninsured patients and insured patients who have received final payer claim denial.

TIP: When in doubt... call the program and explain your situation. You may qualify for assistance.

PROVENTIL® HFA (albuterol sulfate) Inhalation Aerosol

MERCK & COMPANY, INC.

Multiuse Savings Coupon

1-800-672-6372 — *www.proventilhfa.com*

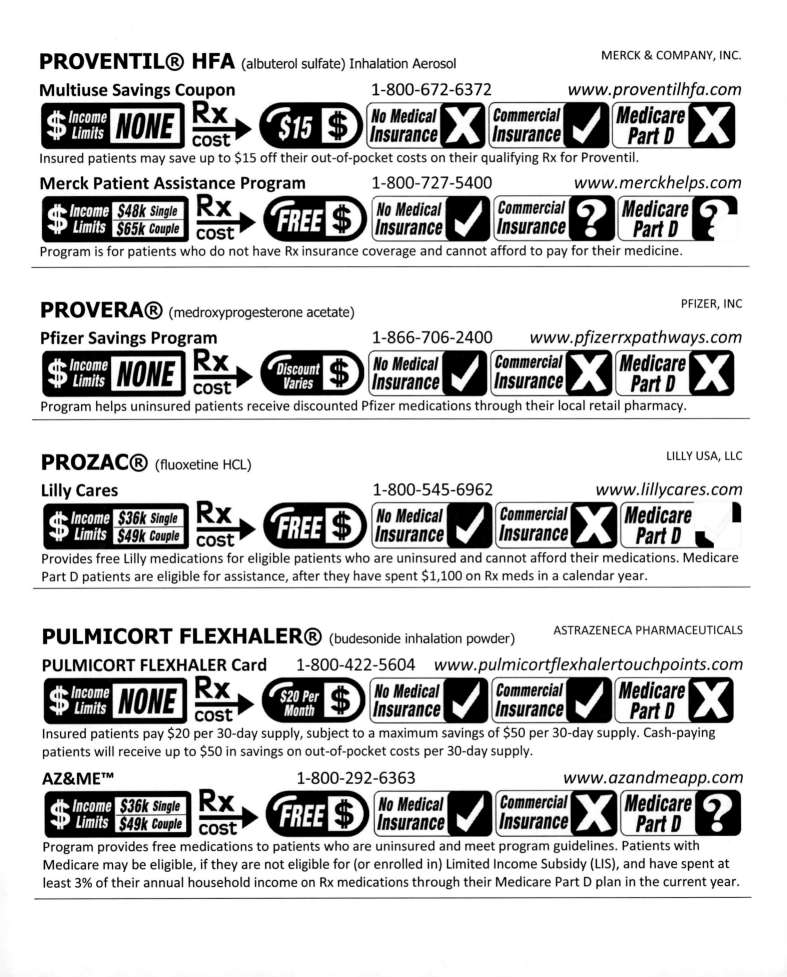

$ Income Limits NONE — **Rx cost** → **$15 $** — **No Medical Insurance** ✗ — **Commercial Insurance** ✓ — **Medicare Part D** ✗

Insured patients may save up to $15 off their out-of-pocket costs on their qualifying Rx for Proventil.

Merck Patient Assistance Program

1-800-727-5400 — *www.merckhelps.com*

$ Income Limits $48k Single $65k Couple — **Rx cost** → **FREE $** — **No Medical Insurance** ✓ — **Commercial Insurance** ? — **Medicare Part D** ?

Program is for patients who do not have Rx insurance coverage and cannot afford to pay for their medicine.

PROVERA® (medroxyprogesterone acetate)

PFIZER, INC

Pfizer Savings Program

1-866-706-2400 — *www.pfizerrxpathways.com*

$ Income Limits NONE — **Rx cost** → **Discount Varies $** — **No Medical Insurance** ✓ — **Commercial Insurance** ✗ — **Medicare Part D** ✗

Program helps uninsured patients receive discounted Pfizer medications through their local retail pharmacy.

PROZAC® (fluoxetine HCL)

LILLY USA, LLC

Lilly Cares

1-800-545-6962 — *www.lillycares.com*

$ Income Limits $36k Single $49k Couple — **Rx cost** → **FREE $** — **No Medical Insurance** ✓ — **Commercial Insurance** ✗ — **Medicare Part D**

Provides free Lilly medications for eligible patients who are uninsured and cannot afford their medications. Medicare Part D patients are eligible for assistance, after they have spent $1,100 on Rx meds in a calendar year.

PULMICORT FLEXHALER® (budesonide inhalation powder)

ASTRAZENECA PHARMACEUTICALS

PULMICORT FLEXHALER Card

1-800-422-5604 — *www.pulmicortflexhalertouchpoints.com*

$ Income Limits NONE — **Rx cost** → **$20 Per Month $** — **No Medical Insurance** ✓ — **Commercial Insurance** ✓ — **Medicare Part D** ✗

Insured patients pay $20 per 30-day supply, subject to a maximum savings of $50 per 30-day supply. Cash-paying patients will receive up to $50 in savings on out-of-pocket costs per 30-day supply.

AZ&ME™

1-800-292-6363 — *www.azandmeapp.com*

$ Income Limits $36k Single $49k Couple — **Rx cost** → **FREE $** — **No Medical Insurance** ✓ — **Commercial Insurance** ✗ — **Medicare Part D** ?

Program provides free medications to patients who are uninsured and meet program guidelines. Patients with Medicare may be eligible, if they are not eligible for (or enrolled in) Limited Income Subsidy (LIS), and have spent at least 3% of their annual household income on Rx medications through their Medicare Part D plan in the current year.

PULMOZYME® (dornase alfa)
GENENTECH, INC.

PULMOZYME® Co-pay Card Program   1-877-794-8723   *www.pulmozymecopaycard.com*

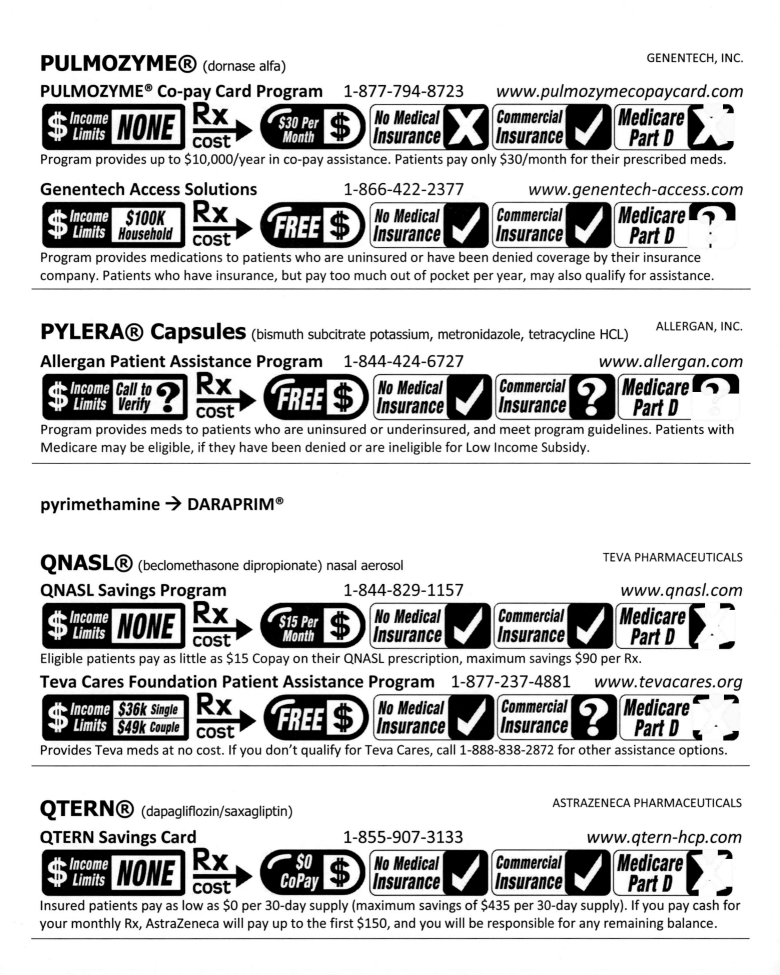

| $ Income Limits **NONE** | Rx cost → | $30 Per Month $ | No Medical Insurance ✗ | Commercial Insurance ✓ | Medicare Part D ✗ |

Program provides up to $10,000/year in co-pay assistance. Patients pay only $30/month for their prescribed meds.

Genentech Access Solutions   1-866-422-2377   *www.genentech-access.com*

| $ Income Limits **$100K Household** | Rx cost → | FREE $ | No Medical Insurance ✓ | Commercial Insurance ✓ | Medicare Part D ? |

Program provides medications to patients who are uninsured or have been denied coverage by their insurance company. Patients who have insurance, but pay too much out of pocket per year, may also qualify for assistance.

PYLERA® Capsules (bismuth subcitrate potassium, metronidazole, tetracycline HCL)
ALLERGAN, INC.

Allergan Patient Assistance Program   1-844-424-6727   *www.allergan.com*

| $ Income Limits **Call to Verify** ? | Rx cost → | FREE $ | No Medical Insurance ✓ | Commercial Insurance ? | Medicare Part D ? |

Program provides meds to patients who are uninsured or underinsured, and meet program guidelines. Patients with Medicare may be eligible, if they have been denied or are ineligible for Low Income Subsidy.

pyrimethamine → DARAPRIM®

QNASL® (beclomethasone dipropionate) nasal aerosol
TEVA PHARMACEUTICALS

QNASL Savings Program   1-844-829-1157   *www.qnasl.com*

| $ Income Limits **NONE** | Rx cost → | $15 Per Month $ | No Medical Insurance ✓ | Commercial Insurance ✓ | Medicare Part D ✗ |

Eligible patients pay as little as $15 Copay on their QNASL prescription, maximum savings $90 per Rx.

Teva Cares Foundation Patient Assistance Program   1-877-237-4881   *www.tevacares.org*

| $ Income Limits **$36k Single $49k Couple** | Rx cost → | FREE $ | No Medical Insurance ✓ | Commercial Insurance ? | Medicare Part D ✗ |

Provides Teva meds at no cost. If you don't qualify for Teva Cares, call 1-888-838-2872 for other assistance options.

QTERN® (dapagliflozin/saxagliptin)
ASTRAZENECA PHARMACEUTICALS

QTERN Savings Card   1-855-907-3133   *www.qtern-hcp.com*

| $ Income Limits **NONE** | Rx cost → | $0 CoPay $ | No Medical Insurance ✓ | Commercial Insurance ✓ | Medicare Part D ✗ |

Insured patients pay as low as $0 per 30-day supply (maximum savings of $435 per 30-day supply). If you pay cash for your monthly Rx, AstraZeneca will pay up to the first $150, and you will be responsible for any remaining balance.

QTERN® (dapagliflozin/saxagliptin)

AZ&ME™　　　　　1-800-292-6363　　　　*www.azandmeapp.com*

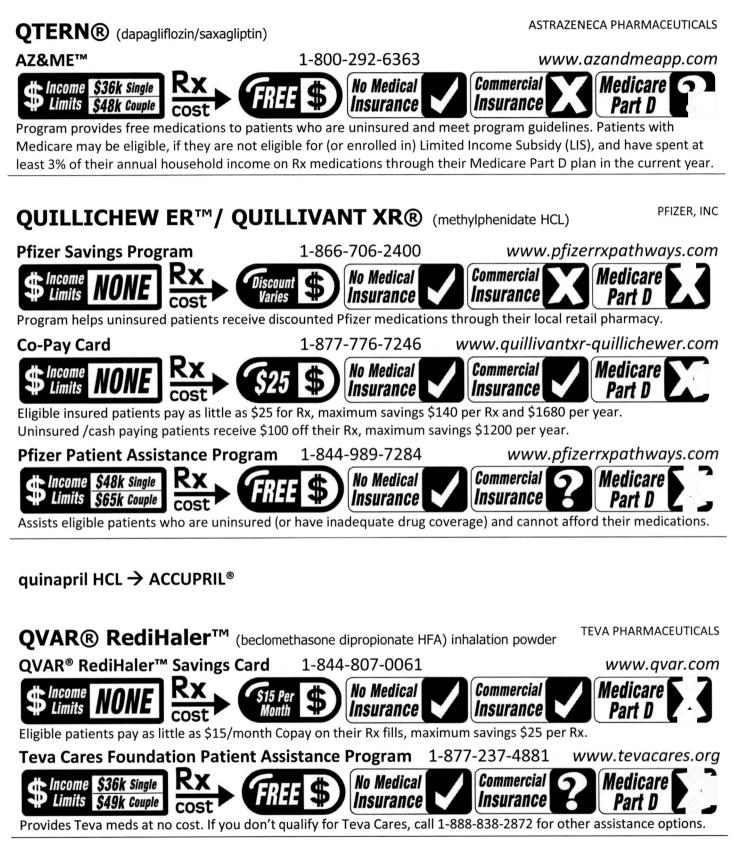

$ Income Limits $36k Single / $48k Couple — **Rx cost** → **FREE $** — **No Medical Insurance** ✔ — **Commercial Insurance** ✘ — **Medicare Part D** ?

Program provides free medications to patients who are uninsured and meet program guidelines. Patients with Medicare may be eligible, if they are not eligible for (or enrolled in) Limited Income Subsidy (LIS), and have spent at least 3% of their annual household income on Rx medications through their Medicare Part D plan in the current year.

QUILLICHEW ER™/ QUILLIVANT XR® (methylphenidate HCL)

Pfizer Savings Program　　　　1-866-706-2400　　　　*www.pfizerrxpathways.com*

$ Income Limits NONE — **Rx cost** → **Discount Varies $** — **No Medical Insurance** ✔ — **Commercial Insurance** ✘ — **Medicare Part D** ✘

Program helps uninsured patients receive discounted Pfizer medications through their local retail pharmacy.

Co-Pay Card　　　　1-877-776-7246　　　　*www.quillivantxr-quillichewer.com*

$ Income Limits NONE — **Rx cost** → **$25 $** — **No Medical Insurance** ✔ — **Commercial Insurance** ✔ — **Medicare Part D** ✘

Eligible insured patients pay as little as $25 for Rx, maximum savings $140 per Rx and $1680 per year.
Uninsured /cash paying patients receive $100 off their Rx, maximum savings $1200 per year.

Pfizer Patient Assistance Program　　　1-844-989-7284　　　*www.pfizerrxpathways.com*

$ Income Limits $48k Single / $65k Couple — **Rx cost** → **FREE $** — **No Medical Insurance** ✔ — **Commercial Insurance** ? — **Medicare Part D** ✘

Assists eligible patients who are uninsured (or have inadequate drug coverage) and cannot afford their medications.

---

quinapril HCL → ACCUPRIL®

QVAR® RediHaler™ (beclomethasone dipropionate HFA) inhalation powder

QVAR® RediHaler™ Savings Card　　　1-844-807-0061　　　*www.qvar.com*

$ Income Limits NONE — **Rx cost** → **$15 Per Month $** — **No Medical Insurance** ✔ — **Commercial Insurance** ✔ — **Medicare Part D** ✘

Eligible patients pay as little as $15/month Copay on their Rx fills, maximum savings $25 per Rx.

Teva Cares Foundation Patient Assistance Program　　1-877-237-4881　　*www.tevacares.org*

$ Income Limits $36k Single / $49k Couple — **Rx cost** → **FREE $** — **No Medical Insurance** ✔ — **Commercial Insurance** ? — **Medicare Part D** ✘

Provides Teva meds at no cost. If you don't qualify for Teva Cares, call 1-888-838-2872 for other assistance options.

---

raltegravir → ISENTRESS®/ ISENTRESS® HD

ramelteon → ROZEREM®

ramipril → ALTACE®

ramucirumab → CYRAMZA®

RANEXA® (ranolazine)

GILEAD SCIENCES, INC

RANEXA Co-pay Coupon Program   1-888-726-3925   *www.RanexaConnect.com*

Covers cost over $5, up to $70 per month. Use coupon maximum of 12 times a year for an annual benefit of $840.

Patient Assistance Program   1-888-726-3925   *www.RanexaConnect.com*

Patient assistance program provides medications at no charge for eligible patients with no other insurance options.

ranibizumab injection → LUCENTIS®

ranolazine → RANEXA®

RAPAFLO® Capsules (silodosin)

ALLERGAN, INC.

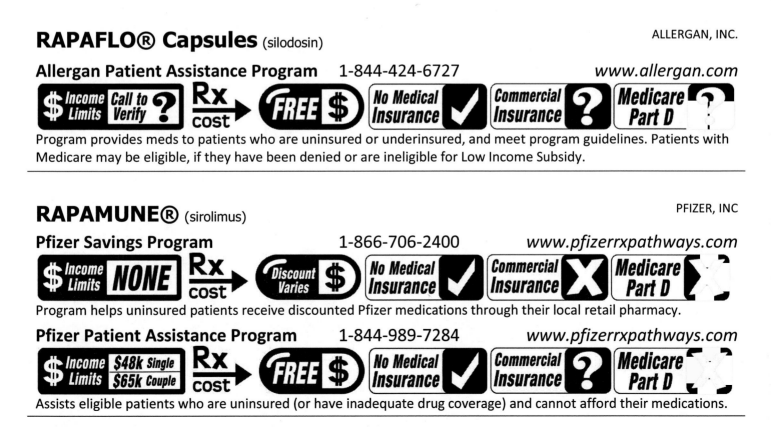

Allergan Patient Assistance Program   1-844-424-6727   *www.allergan.com*

Program provides meds to patients who are uninsured or underinsured, and meet program guidelines. Patients with Medicare may be eligible, if they have been denied or are ineligible for Low Income Subsidy.

RAPAMUNE® (sirolimus)

PFIZER, INC

Pfizer Savings Program   1-866-706-2400   *www.pfizerrxpathways.com*

Program helps uninsured patients receive discounted Pfizer medications through their local retail pharmacy.

Pfizer Patient Assistance Program   1-844-989-7284   *www.pfizerrxpathways.com*

Assists eligible patients who are uninsured (or have inadequate drug coverage) and cannot afford their medications.

RAVICTI® (glycerol phenylbutyrate)
HORIZON PHARMA USA, INC.

TranscendRare™ Program   1-833-830-7273   *www.ravicti.com*

Provides copay, reimbursement, and financial assistance for insured/uninsured patients with valid RAVICTI Rx.

RAYALDEE® (calcifediol)
OPKO RENAL/OPKO HEALTH, INC.

Rayaldee Co-Pay Assistance Program   1-844-414-6756   *www.rayaldee.com*

Insured patients pay as little as $5 per month, until yearly maximum assistance level is reached.

Rayaldee Patient Assistance Program   1-844-414-6756   *www.rayaldee.com*

Provides Rayaldee to patients who are uninsured (or lack adequate Rx coverage) and are financially distressed.

RAYOS® (prednisone)
HORIZON PHARMA USA, INC.

RAYOS Savings Program   1-855-226-4006   *www.rayosrx.com*

Eligible patients with commercial insurance can pay as low as $0/month out-of-pocket, with a maximum prescription savings of $800 per 30 pill supply.

Horizon Pharma Patient Assistance Program   1-888-958-5502   *www.rayosrx.com*

Helps eligible patients who lack health insurance coverage to get their Rx meds at no cost.

REBIF® (interferon beta-1a)
EMD SERONO, INC.

MS LifeLines Access Made Simple Program   1-877-447-3243   *www.rebif.com*

$0 co-pay for those who are eligible and have insurance or co-insurance. Or, you can get 1 year of REBIF® free if you're eligible and don't have insurance or are underinsured.

TIP: When in doubt... call the program and explain your situation. You may qualify for assistance.

REBINYN® (coagulation factor IX [recombinant] glycopegylated)
NOVO NORDISK, INC.

Co-Pay Assistance Program   1-844-668-6732   *www.rebinyn.com*

Enrolled patients are eligible for up to $12,000 in co-pay/coinsurance assistance per calendar year for each NNI hemophilia or rare bleeding disorder product. Assistance is retroactive to 60 days.

NovoSecure™ Program   1-844-668-6732   *www.mynovosecure.com*

For patients who are uninsured. Also for Medicare patients who have spent more than $1000 this year on Rx meds.

RECLAST® (zoledronic acid)
NOVARTIS PHARMACEUTICALS

Novartis Patient Assistance Foundation   1-800-277-2254   *www.pap.novartis.com*

Program assists those without insurance, or with limited/inadequate Rx coverage to receive prescribed medications.

RECOMBINATE® [Antihemophilic factor (recombinant)]
BAXALTA, INC / SHIRE

Shire's CoPay Assistance Program   1-888-229-8379   *www.hematologysupport.com*

Patients with commercial insurance may be eligible to receive up to $12,000 in CoPay support thru this program.

RECTIV® Ointment (nitroglycerin)
ALLERGAN, INC.

Allergan Patient Assistance Program   1-844-424-6727   *www.allergan.com*

Program provides meds to patients who are uninsured or underinsured, and meet program guidelines. Patients with Medicare may be eligible, if they have been denied or are ineligible for Low Income Subsidy.

---

regorafenib → STIVARGA®

RELENZA® (zanamivir)
GLAXOSMITHKLINE

GSK Patient Assistance Program   1-866-728-4368   *www.gskforyou.com*

Uninsured patients who meet certain financial criteria may be able to get meds for free. Medicare Part D patients who have spent $600 or more on Rx drugs may also apply for assistance.

RELISTOR® (methylnaltrexone bromide)

SALIX PHARMACEUTICALS

Savings Card Program
1-855-298-6939   www.relistor.com

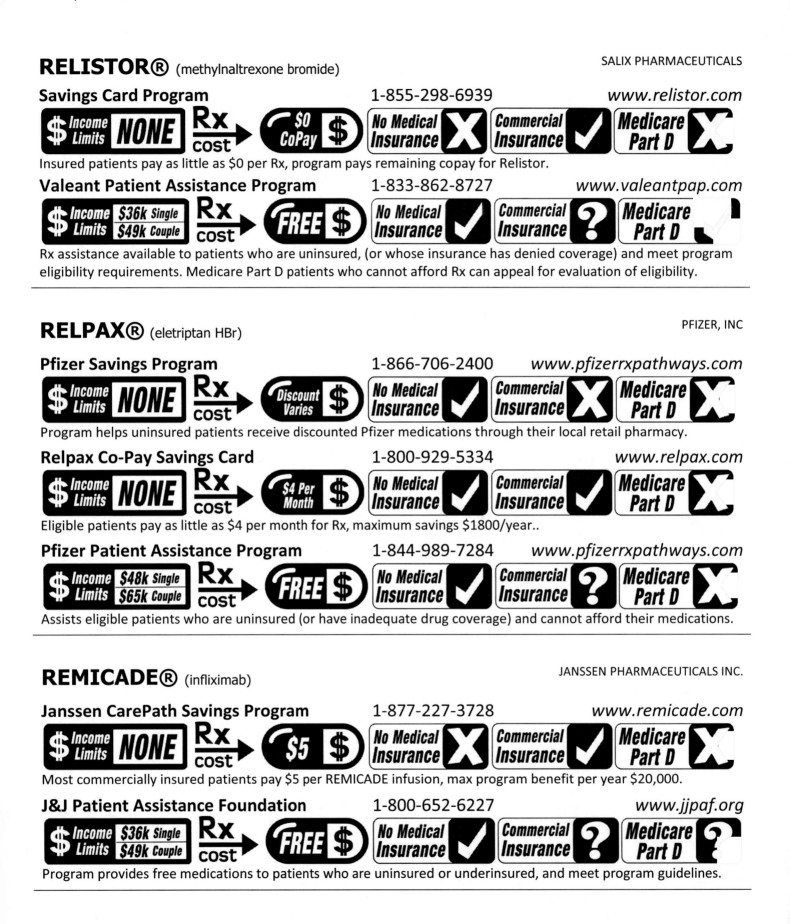

$ Income Limits NONE | **Rx cost →** | **$0 CoPay $** | **No Medical Insurance ✗** | **Commercial Insurance ✓** | **Medicare Part D ✗**

Insured patients pay as little as $0 per Rx, program pays remaining copay for Relistor.

Valeant Patient Assistance Program
1-833-862-8727   www.valeantpap.com

$ Income Limits $36k Single / $49k Couple | **Rx cost →** | **FREE $** | **No Medical Insurance ✓** | **Commercial Insurance ?** | **Medicare Part D ✓**

Rx assistance available to patients who are uninsured, (or whose insurance has denied coverage) and meet program eligibility requirements. Medicare Part D patients who cannot afford Rx can appeal for evaluation of eligibility.

RELPAX® (eletriptan HBr)

PFIZER, INC

Pfizer Savings Program
1-866-706-2400   www.pfizerrxpathways.com

$ Income Limits NONE | **Rx cost →** | **Discount Varies $** | **No Medical Insurance ✓** | **Commercial Insurance ✗** | **Medicare Part D ✗**

Program helps uninsured patients receive discounted Pfizer medications through their local retail pharmacy.

Relpax Co-Pay Savings Card
1-800-929-5334   www.relpax.com

$ Income Limits NONE | **Rx cost →** | **$4 Per Month $** | **No Medical Insurance ✓** | **Commercial Insurance ✓** | **Medicare Part D ✗**

Eligible patients pay as little as $4 per month for Rx, maximum savings $1800/year..

Pfizer Patient Assistance Program
1-844-989-7284   www.pfizerrxpathways.com

$ Income Limits $48k Single / $65k Couple | **Rx cost →** | **FREE $** | **No Medical Insurance ✓** | **Commercial Insurance ?** | **Medicare Part D ✗**

Assists eligible patients who are uninsured (or have inadequate drug coverage) and cannot afford their medications.

REMICADE® (infliximab)

JANSSEN PHARMACEUTICALS INC.

Janssen CarePath Savings Program
1-877-227-3728   www.remicade.com

$ Income Limits NONE | **Rx cost →** | **$5 $** | **No Medical Insurance ✗** | **Commercial Insurance ✓** | **Medicare Part D ✗**

Most commercially insured patients pay $5 per REMICADE infusion, max program benefit per year $20,000.

J&J Patient Assistance Foundation
1-800-652-6227   www.jjpaf.org

$ Income Limits $36k Single / $49k Couple | **Rx cost →** | **FREE $** | **No Medical Insurance ✓** | **Commercial Insurance ?** | **Medicare Part D ?**

Program provides free medications to patients who are uninsured or underinsured, and meet program guidelines.

REMODULIN® (treprostinil) injection

UNITED THERAPEUTICS CORPORATION

Remodulin Co-Pay Assistance   1-877-864-8437   www.utcopay.com

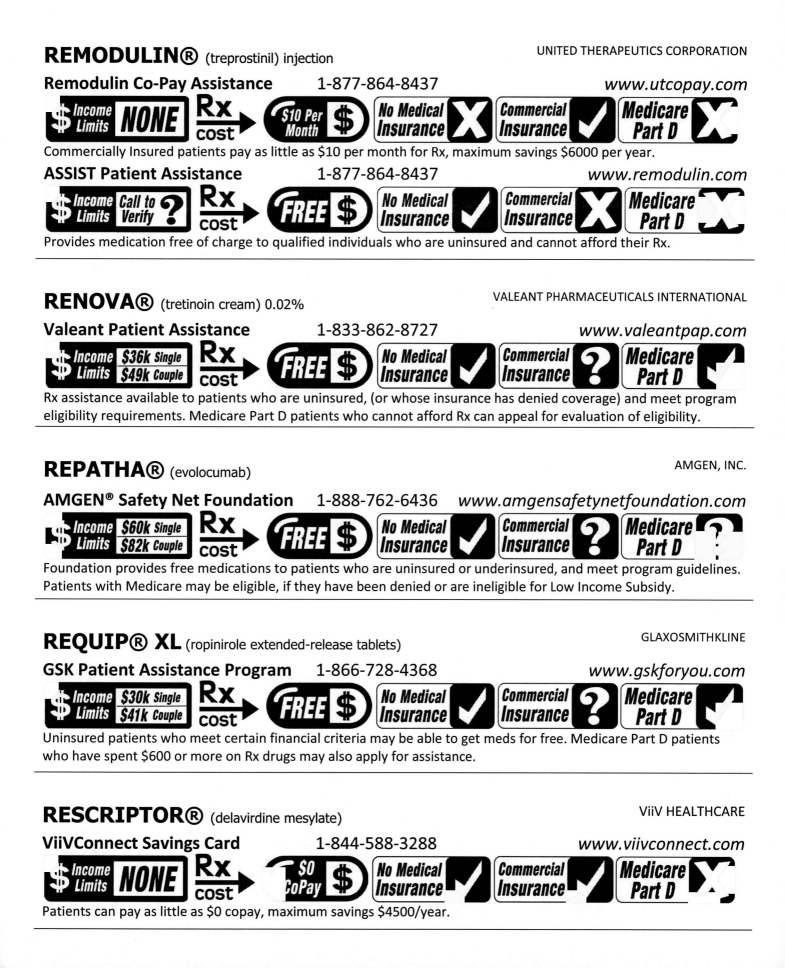

$ Income Limits **NONE** | Rx cost → | **$10 Per Month** $ | No Medical Insurance ✗ | Commercial Insurance ✓ | Medicare Part D ✗

Commercially Insured patients pay as little as $10 per month for Rx, maximum savings $6000 per year.

ASSIST Patient Assistance   1-877-864-8437   www.remodulin.com

$ Income Limits **Call to Verify** ? | Rx cost → | **FREE** $ | No Medical Insurance ✓ | Commercial Insurance ✗ | Medicare Part D ✗

Provides medication free of charge to qualified individuals who are uninsured and cannot afford their Rx.

RENOVA® (tretinoin cream) 0.02%

VALEANT PHARMACEUTICALS INTERNATIONAL

Valeant Patient Assistance   1-833-862-8727   www.valeantpap.com

$ Income Limits **$36k Single $49k Couple** | Rx cost → | **FREE** $ | No Medical Insurance ✓ | Commercial Insurance ? | Medicare Part D ✓

Rx assistance available to patients who are uninsured, (or whose insurance has denied coverage) and meet program eligibility requirements. Medicare Part D patients who cannot afford Rx can appeal for evaluation of eligibility.

REPATHA® (evolocumab)

AMGEN, INC.

AMGEN® Safety Net Foundation   1-888-762-6436   www.amgensafetynetfoundation.com

$ Income Limits **$60k Single $82k Couple** | Rx cost → | **FREE** $ | No Medical Insurance ✓ | Commercial Insurance ? | Medicare Part D ?

Foundation provides free medications to patients who are uninsured or underinsured, and meet program guidelines. Patients with Medicare may be eligible, if they have been denied or are ineligible for Low Income Subsidy.

REQUIP® XL (ropinirole extended-release tablets)

GLAXOSMITHKLINE

GSK Patient Assistance Program   1-866-728-4368   www.gskforyou.com

$ Income Limits **$30k Single $41k Couple** | Rx cost → | **FREE** $ | No Medical Insurance ✓ | Commercial Insurance ? | Medicare Part D ✓

Uninsured patients who meet certain financial criteria may be able to get meds for free. Medicare Part D patients who have spent $600 or more on Rx drugs may also apply for assistance.

RESCRIPTOR® (delavirdine mesylate)

ViiV HEALTHCARE

ViiVConnect Savings Card   1-844-588-3288   www.viivconnect.com

$ Income Limits **NONE** | Rx cost → | **$0 CoPay** $ | No Medical Insurance ✓ | Commercial Insurance ✓ | Medicare Part D ✗

Patients can pay as little as $0 copay, maximum savings $4500/year.

RESCRIPTOR® (delavirdine mesylate)

ViiV HEALTHCARE

ViiV Healthcare Patient Assistance   1-844-588-3288   *www.viivconnect.com*

$ Income Limits $60k Single $82k Couple | Rx cost → FREE $ | No Medical Insurance ✓ | Commercial Insurance ? | Medicare Part D ✓

Gives meds to patients who are uninsured, lack coverage, or on Medicare and have spent $600 on Rx meds this year.

RESTASIS® 0.05% (cyclosporine opthalmic emulsion)

ALLERGAN, INC.

My Tears, My Rewards® Savings Card   1-844-469-8327   *www.restasis.com*

$ Income Limits NONE | Rx cost → $5 $ | No Medical Insurance X | Commercial Insurance ✓ | Medicare Part D X

Eligible patients pay as little as $5 for 1 OR 3 bottles of RESTASIS MultiDose®, or $35 for a 30-day OR 90-day supply of RESTASIS® single-use vials.

Allergan Patient Assistance Program   1-844-424-6727   *www.allergan.com*

$ Income Limits $48k Single $65k Couple | Rx cost → FREE $ | No Medical Insurance ✓ | Commercial Insurance X | Medicare Part D X

Eye and Dermatology program provides medications to patients who are uninsured and meet program guidelines.

RETACRIT™ (epoetin alfa-epbx) for injection

PFIZER, INC

Pfizer Patient Assistance Program   1-844-722-6672   *www.pfizerencompass.com*

$ Income Limits Call to Verify ? | Rx cost → FREE $ | No Medical Insurance ✓ | Commercial Insurance ? | Medicare Part D X

Assists eligible patients who are uninsured (or have inadequate drug coverage) and cannot afford their medications.

RETIN-A MICRO® (tretinoin) Gel Microsphere

VALEANT PHARMACEUTICALS INTERNATIONAL

Ortho Dermatologics Rx Access Program   1-855-202-3279   *www.orthorxaccess.com*

$ Income Limits NONE | Rx cost → $25 $ | No Medical Insurance ✓ | Commercial Insurance ✓ | Medicare Part D X

Most commercially insured patients pay as little as $25 per Rx, once deductible has been met. Those with insurance where drug is not covered pay $75 per Rx, and uninsured patients pay $125 per 4oz Rx, $200 per 8oz Rx.

Valeant Patient Assistance Program   1-833-862-8727   *www.valeantpap.com*

$ Income Limits $36k Single $49k Couple | Rx cost → FREE $ | No Medical Insurance ✓ | Commercial Insurance ? | Medicare Part D ✓

Rx assistance available to patients who are uninsured, (or whose insurance has denied coverage) and meet program eligibility requirements. Medicare Part D patients who cannot afford Rx can appeal for evaluation of eligibility.

RETISERT® (fluocinolone acetonide intravitreal implant)   VALEANT PHARMACEUTICALS INTERNATIONAL

Valeant Patient Assistance Program   1-833-862-8727   *www.valeantpap.com*

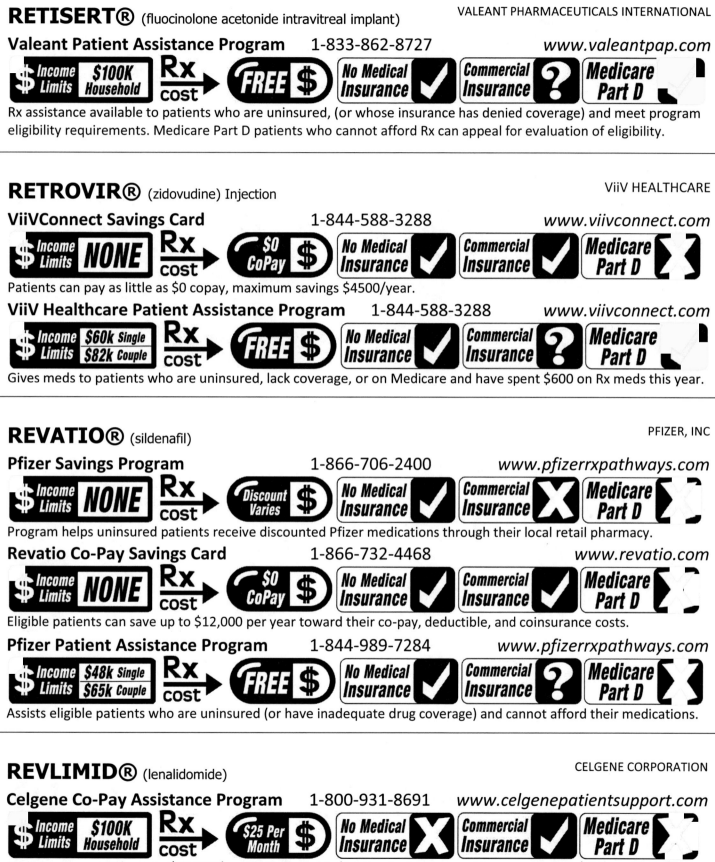

Rx assistance available to patients who are uninsured, (or whose insurance has denied coverage) and meet program eligibility requirements. Medicare Part D patients who cannot afford Rx can appeal for evaluation of eligibility.

RETROVIR® (zidovudine) Injection   ViiV HEALTHCARE

ViiVConnect Savings Card   1-844-588-3288   *www.viivconnect.com*

Patients can pay as little as $0 copay, maximum savings $4500/year.

ViiV Healthcare Patient Assistance Program   1-844-588-3288   *www.viivconnect.com*

Gives meds to patients who are uninsured, lack coverage, or on Medicare and have spent $600 on Rx meds this year.

REVATIO® (sildenafil)   PFIZER, INC

Pfizer Savings Program   1-866-706-2400   *www.pfizerrxpathways.com*

Program helps uninsured patients receive discounted Pfizer medications through their local retail pharmacy.

Revatio Co-Pay Savings Card   1-866-732-4468   *www.revatio.com*

Eligible patients can save up to $12,000 per year toward their co-pay, deductible, and coinsurance costs.

Pfizer Patient Assistance Program   1-844-989-7284   *www.pfizerrxpathways.com*

Assists eligible patients who are uninsured (or have inadequate drug coverage) and cannot afford their medications.

REVLIMID® (lenalidomide)   CELGENE CORPORATION

Celgene Co-Pay Assistance Program   1-800-931-8691   *www.celgenepatientsupport.com*

Program can provide up to $10,000/year in Deductible/Co-Pay Assistance, making your Rx cost $25/month or less.

REVLIMID® (lenalidomide)

CELGENE CORPORATION

Celgene Patient Assistance Program   1-800-931-8691   *www.celgenepatientsupport.com*

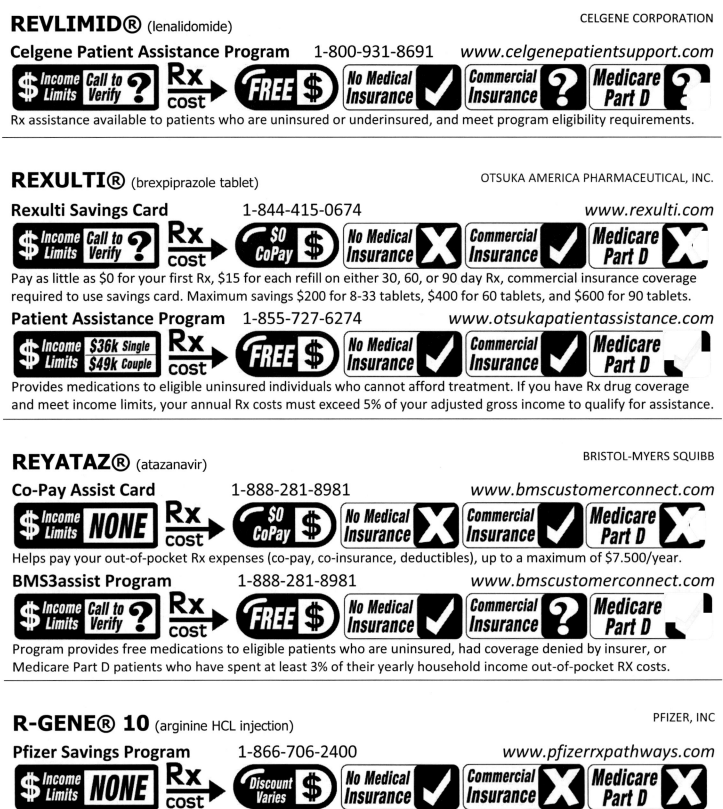

Rx assistance available to patients who are uninsured or underinsured, and meet program eligibility requirements.

REXULTI® (brexpiprazole tablet)

OTSUKA AMERICA PHARMACEUTICAL, INC.

Rexulti Savings Card   1-844-415-0674   *www.rexulti.com*

Pay as little as $0 for your first Rx, $15 for each refill on either 30, 60, or 90 day Rx, commercial insurance coverage required to use savings card. Maximum savings $200 for 8-33 tablets, $400 for 60 tablets, and $600 for 90 tablets.

Patient Assistance Program   1-855-727-6274   *www.otsukapatientassistance.com*

Provides medications to eligible uninsured individuals who cannot afford treatment. If you have Rx drug coverage and meet income limits, your annual Rx costs must exceed 5% of your adjusted gross income to qualify for assistance.

REYATAZ® (atazanavir)

BRISTOL-MYERS SQUIBB

Co-Pay Assist Card   1-888-281-8981   *www.bmscustomerconnect.com*

Helps pay your out-of-pocket Rx expenses (co-pay, co-insurance, deductibles), up to a maximum of $7.500/year.

BMS3assist Program   1-888-281-8981   *www.bmscustomerconnect.com*

Program provides free medications to eligible patients who are uninsured, had coverage denied by insurer, or Medicare Part D patients who have spent at least 3% of their yearly household income out-of-pocket RX costs.

R-GENE® 10 (arginine HCL injection)

PFIZER, INC

Pfizer Savings Program   1-866-706-2400   *www.pfizerrxpathways.com*

Program helps uninsured patients receive discounted Pfizer medications through their local retail pharmacy.

RHOFADE Cream™ 1% (oxymetazoline hydrochloride)

ALLERGAN, INC.

Allergan Patient Assistance Program   1-844-424-6727   *www.allergan.com*

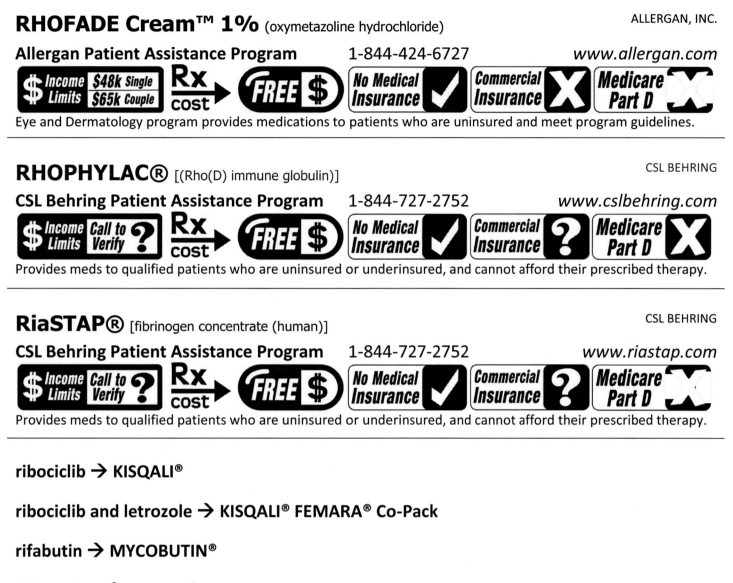

Eye and Dermatology program provides medications to patients who are uninsured and meet program guidelines.

RHOPHYLAC® [(Rho(D) immune globulin)]

CSL BEHRING

CSL Behring Patient Assistance Program   1-844-727-2752   *www.cslbehring.com*

Provides meds to qualified patients who are uninsured or underinsured, and cannot afford their prescribed therapy.

RiaSTAP® [fibrinogen concentrate (human)]

CSL BEHRING

CSL Behring Patient Assistance Program   1-844-727-2752   *www.riastap.com*

Provides meds to qualified patients who are uninsured or underinsured, and cannot afford their prescribed therapy.

ribociclib → KISQALI®

ribociclib and letrozole → KISQALI® FEMARA® Co-Pack

rifabutin → MYCOBUTIN®

rifapentine → PRIFTIN®

rifaximin → XIFAXAN®

rilpivirine → EDURANT®

rimabotulinumtoxinB injection → MYOBLOC®

riociguat → ADEMPAS®

RISPERDAL CONSTA® (rispiridone)

JANSSEN PHARMACEUTICALS

J&J Patient Assistance Foundation   1-800-652-6227   *www.jjpaf.org*

Program provides free medications to patients who are uninsured or underinsured, and meet program guidelines.

rispiridone → RISPERDAL CONSTA®

ritonavir → NORVIR® TABLETS

RITUXAN® (rituximab)
GENENTECH, INC.

Co-pay Card Assistance Program   1-855-692-6729   *www.copayassistancenow.com*

Program provides up to $25,000/year in co-pay assistance. Patients pay only $5/month for their prescribed meds.

Genentech Access Solutions   1-866-422-2377   *www.genentech-access.com*

Program provides medications to patients who are uninsured or have been denied coverage by their insurance company. Patients who have insurance, but pay too much out of pocket per year, may also qualify for assistance.

RITUXAN HYCELA™ (rituximab/hyaluronidase human)
GENENTECH, INC.

Co-pay Card Assistance Program   1-855-692-6729   *www.copayassistancenow.com*

Program provides up to $25,000/year in co-pay assistance. Patients pay only $5/month for their prescribed meds.

Genentech Access Solutions   1-866-422-2377   *www.genentech-access.com*

Program provides medications to patients who are uninsured or have been denied coverage by their insurance company. Patients who have insurance, but pay too much out of pocket per year, may also qualify for assistance.

rituximab → RITUXAN®

rituximab/hyaluronidase human → RITUXAN HYCELA™

rivaroxaban → XARELTO®

RIXUBIS® [Coagulation Factor IX (Recombinant)]
BAXALTA, INC / SHIRE

Shire's CoPay Assistance Program   1-888-229-8379   *www.hematologysupport.com*

Patients with commercial insurance may be eligible to receive up to $12,000 in CoPay support thru this program.

rizatriptan benzoate tablets → MAXALT®

roflumilast → DALIRESP®

rolapitant → VARUBI® Tablets/Injectable Emulsion

romidepsin → ISTODAX®

romiplostim → NPLATE®

ropinirole extended-release tablets → REQUIP® XL

rosiglitazone maleate → AVANDIA®

rotigotine transdermal system → NEUPRO®

ROXICODONE™ (oxycodone hydrochloride)
MALLINCKRODT PHARMACEUTICALS

Mallinckrodt Patient Assistance Program   1-800-259-7765   *www.mallinckrodt.com*

| $ Income Limits $24k Single / $32k Couple | Rx cost → | CALL TO VERIFY $ | No Medical Insurance ✓ | Commercial Insurance ✗ | Medicare Part D ✗ |

Program for uninsured patients who may not be able to afford their Mallinckrodt medications, call for application.

ROZEREM® (ramelteon)
TAKEDA PHARMACEUTICALS AMERICA

Takeda Patient Assistance Program   1-800-830-9159   *www.takedahelpathand.com*

| $ Income Limits $60k Single / $82k Couple | Rx cost → | FREE $ | No Medical Insurance ✓ | Commercial Insurance ? | Medicare Part D ? |

Provides Rozerm at no cost to eligible patients who do not have insurance or not enough coverage to obtain meds.

RUBRACA™ (rucaparib)
CLOVIS ONCOLOGY

$0 Co-Pay Program   1-877-779-7707   *www.rubracaconnections.com*

| $ Income Limits NONE | Rx cost → | $0 CoPay $ | No Medical Insurance ✗ | Commercial Insurance ✓ | Medicare Part D ✗ |

Provides up to $1,400/month in co-pay assistance. Eligible patients pay as low as $0 out-of-pocket for RUBRACA.

RUBRACA Connections   1-877-779-7707   *www.rubracaconnections.com*

| $ Income Limits Call to Verify ? | Rx cost → | FREE $ | No Medical Insurance ✓ | Commercial Insurance ? | Medicare Part D ✗ |

Rx assistance available to patients who are uninsured or underinsured, and meet program eligibility requirements.

rucaparib → RUBRACA™

rufinamide → BANZEL®

ruxolitinib → JAKAFI®

RYDAPT® (midostaurin)
NOVARTIS PHARMACEUTICALS

Universal Co-Pay Card   1-877-577-7756   *www.copay.novartisoncology.com*

Income Limits **NONE** | Rx cost → | $25 | No Medical Insurance ✗ | Commercial Insurance ✓ | Medicare Part D ✗

Patients pay the first $25, the program pays the remaining co-pay or coinsurance to max benefit of $15,000/year.

Novartis Patient Assistance Foundation   1-800-277-2254   *www.pap.novartis.com*

Income Limits $75k Single $100k Couple | Rx cost → | FREE | No Medical Insurance ✓ | Commercial Insurance ? | Medicare Part D ?

Program assists those without insurance, or with limited/inadequate Rx coverage to receive prescribed medications.

RYTARY® (carbidopa/levodopa)
IMPAX LABORATORIES, INC.

RYTARY Savings Card   1-844-467-2928   *www.rytary.com*

Income Limits **NONE** | Rx cost → | $25 | No Medical Insurance ? | Commercial Insurance ✓ | Medicare Part D ✗

Patient pays first $25 of prescription cost, remaining balance (Up to $100/max benefit) covered by savings card.

Impax Patient Assistance Program   1-877-764-9021   *www.rytary.com*

Income Limits Call to Verify ? | Rx cost → | FREE | No Medical Insurance ✓ | Commercial Insurance ? | Medicare Part D ✓

Provides free meds for qualified patients that do not have affordable coverage for the Rx. Medicare Part D patients must have spent at least 3% of annual household income out-of-pocket on prescription medicines to qualify.

RYTHMOL® SR (propafenone hydrochloride)
GLAXOSMITHKLINE

GSK Patient Assistance Program   1-866-728-4368   *www.gskforyou.com*

Income Limits $30k Single $41k Couple | Rx cost → | FREE | No Medical Insurance ✓ | Commercial Insurance ? | Medicare Part D ✓

Uninsured patients who meet certain financial criteria may be able to get meds for free. Medicare Part D patients who have spent $600 or more on Rx drugs may also apply for assistance.

sacrosidase oral solution → SUCRAID®

sacubitril/valsartan → ENTRESTO®

SAFYRAL®

BAYER HEALTHCARE PHARMACEUTICALS

(drospirenone/ethinyl estradiol/levomefolate calcium tablets and levomefolate calcium tablets)

Bayer Savings Card 1-866-203-3503 *www.savingscard.bayer.com*

| Income Limits | NONE | Rx cost → | $0 CoPay $ | No Medical Insurance ✓ | Commercial Insurance ✓ | Medicare Part D ✗ |

Insured patients pay as little as $0 per month, (maximum savings of $125). If you pay cash for your monthly medications, you will receive up to $100 in savings on your out-of-pocket costs for each prescription.

SAIZEN® (somatropin)

EMD SERONO, INC.

Self-Pay Support Program 1-800-582-7989 *www.saizen.com*

| Income Limits | NONE | Rx cost → | $23/mg $ | No Medical Insurance ✓ | Commercial Insurance ? | Medicare Part D ✗ |

Patients pay no more than $23 per milligram of Saizen®, offer may be used once every 21 days with valid Rx.

SAVINGS Co-Pay Program 1-800-582-7989 *www.saizen.com*

| Income Limits | NONE | Rx cost → | Discount Varies $ | No Medical Insurance ✗ | Commercial Insurance ✓ | Medicare Part D ✗ |

Insured patients save up to $200 per month on their Rx co-pays/co-insurance, up to a maximum of $2,400 per year.

Patient Assistance Program 1-800-582-7989 *www.saizen.com*

| Income Limits Call to Verify ? | Rx cost → | FREE $ | No Medical Insurance ✓ | Commercial Insurance ? | Medicare Part D ✗ |

This program provides medications at no cost to financially needy patients who meet program eligibility criteria.

salmeterol xinafoate inhalation powder → SEREVENT DISKUS®

SANCUSO® (granisetron transdermal system)

KYOWA KIRIN, INC.

Copay Assistance Program 1-866-261-8554 *www.sancuso.com*

| Income Limits | NONE | Rx cost → | $20 $ | No Medical Insurance ✓ | Commercial Insurance ✓ | Medicare Part D ✗ |

Eligible patients pay the first $20 for Sancuso patch, remaining out-of-pocket costs reduced by $300 per patch, by program. Maximum savings $1200 per month (4 patches).

Sancuso Patient Assistance Program 1-866-325-8231 *www.patientrxsolutions.com*

| Income Limits $36k Single $48k Couple | Rx cost → | FREE $ | No Medical Insurance ✓ | Commercial Insurance ✗ | Medicare Part D ✗ |

Provides Fareston to eligible patients who are uninsured or have been denied by Medicare, and have financial need.

SANDIMMUNE® (cyclosporine)

NOVARTIS PHARMACEUTICALS

$0 Co-Pay Card   1-844-685-3406   *www.copay.novartispharma.com*

$ Income Limits **NONE** | **Rx** cost → | $0 CoPay $ | No Medical Insurance **X** | Commercial Insurance ✔ | Medicare Part D **X**

Insured patients pay as little as $0 per Rx, maximum total co-pay benefit of $7200 per year.

Novartis Patient Assistance Foundation   1-800-277-2254   *www.pap.novartis.com*

$ Income Limits **$75k Single / $100k Couple** | **Rx** cost → | FREE $ | No Medical Insurance ✔ | Commercial Insurance **?** | Medicare Part D **?**

Program assists those without insurance, or with limited/inadequate Rx coverage to receive prescribed medications.

SANDOSTATIN® LAR Depot (octreotide acetate)

NOVARTIS PHARMACEUTICALS

Universal Co-Pay Card   1-877-577-7756   *www.copay.novartisoncology.com*

$ Income Limits **NONE** | **Rx** cost → | $25 $ | No Medical Insurance **X** | Commercial Insurance ✔ | Medicare Part D **X**

Patients pay the first $25, the program pays the remaining co-pay or coinsurance to max benefit of $15,000/year.

Novartis Patient Assistance Foundation   1-800-277-2254   *www.pap.novartis.com*

$ Income Limits **$75k Single / $100k Couple** | **Rx** cost → | FREE $ | No Medical Insurance ✔ | Commercial Insurance **?** | Medicare Part D **?**

Program assists those without insurance, or with limited/inadequate Rx coverage to receive prescribed medications.

SAPHRIS® (asenapine maleate)

ALLERGAN, INC.

Allergan Patient Assistance Program   1-844-424-6727   *www.allergan.com*

$ Income Limits **Call to Verify ?** | **Rx** cost → | FREE $ | No Medical Insurance ✔ | Commercial Insurance **?** | Medicare Part D **?**

Program provides meds to patients who are uninsured or underinsured, and meet program guidelines. Patients with Medicare may be eligible, if they have been denied or are ineligible for Low Income Subsidy.

sapropterin dihydrochloride → KUVAN®

sargramostim → LEUKINE®

sarilumab → KEVZARA®

💡 **TIP:** When in doubt... call the program and explain your situation. You may qualify for assistance.

SAVAYSA® (edoxaban)

DAIICHI SANKYO, INC.

SAVAYSA Savings Card   1-844-728-2972   www.savaysa.com

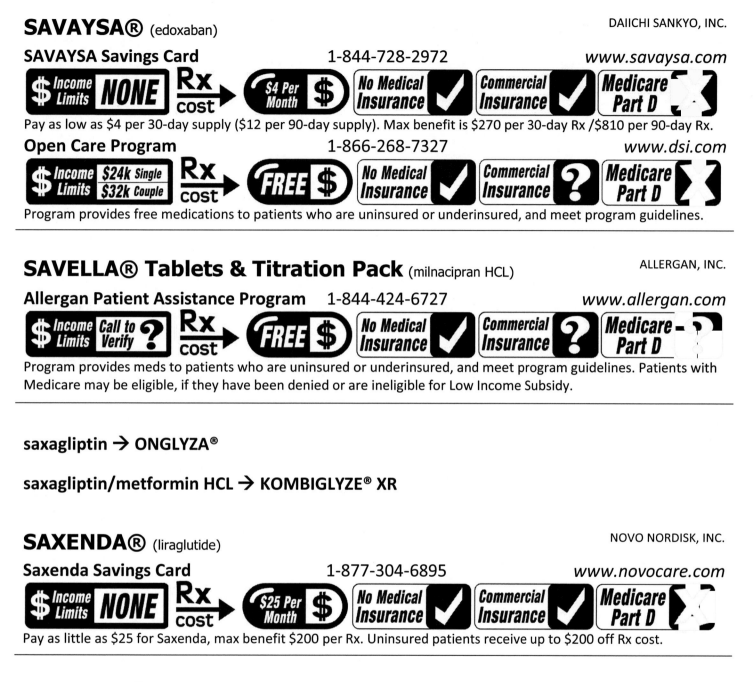

Pay as low as $4 per 30-day supply ($12 per 90-day supply). Max benefit is $270 per 30-day Rx /$810 per 90-day Rx.

Open Care Program   1-866-268-7327   www.dsi.com

Program provides free medications to patients who are uninsured or underinsured, and meet program guidelines.

SAVELLA® Tablets & Titration Pack (milnacipran HCL)

ALLERGAN, INC.

Allergan Patient Assistance Program   1-844-424-6727   www.allergan.com

Program provides meds to patients who are uninsured or underinsured, and meet program guidelines. Patients with Medicare may be eligible, if they have been denied or are ineligible for Low Income Subsidy.

saxagliptin → ONGLYZA®

saxagliptin/metformin HCL → KOMBIGLYZE® XR

SAXENDA® (liraglutide)

NOVO NORDISK, INC.

Saxenda Savings Card   1-877-304-6895   www.novocare.com

Pay as little as $25 for Saxenda, max benefit $200 per Rx. Uninsured patients receive up to $200 off Rx cost.

secukinumab → COSENTYX®

sebelipase alfa → KANUMA®

SEEBRI® NEOHALER® (glycopyrrolate)

SUNOVION PHARMACEUTICALS, INC.

SEEBRI NEOHALER Savings Card   1-844-276-8262   www.seebri.us

Insured patients pay as little as $10 for their Rx, max savings $250 per Rx fill for both insured & uninsured patients.

SEEBRI® NEOHALER® (glycopyrrolate)

SUNOVION PHARMACEUTICALS, INC.

Sunovion Support®   1-877-850-0819   *www.sunovionsupport.com*

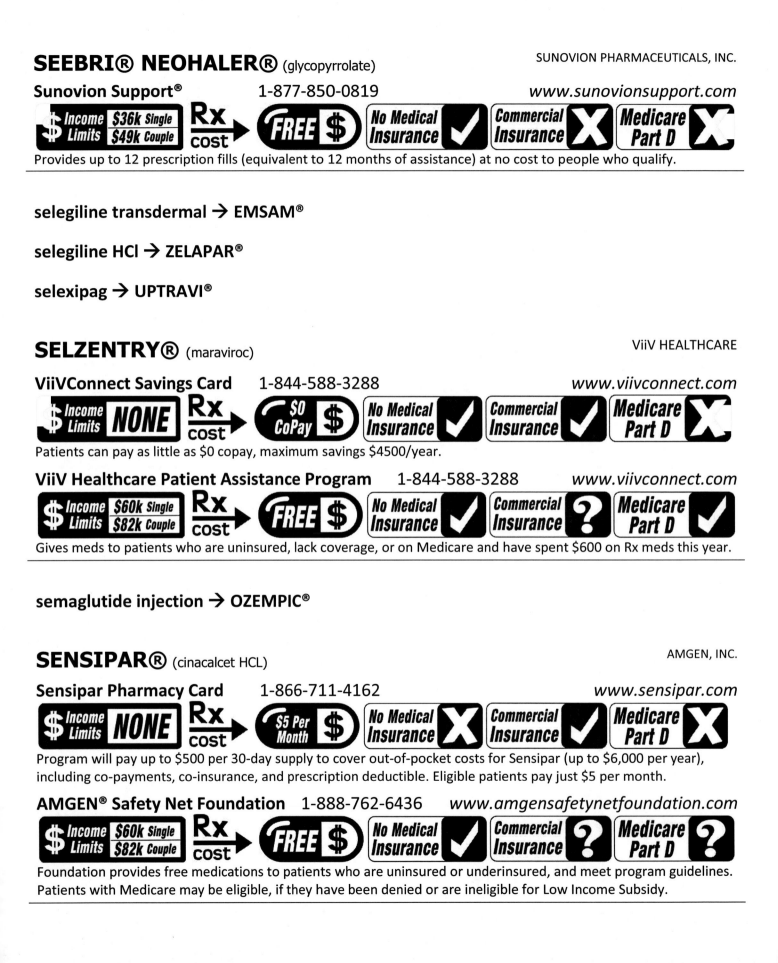

Income Limits $36k Single / $49k Couple | Rx cost → FREE $ | No Medical Insurance ✓ | Commercial Insurance ✗ | Medicare Part D ✗

Provides up to 12 prescription fills (equivalent to 12 months of assistance) at no cost to people who qualify.

selegiline transdermal → EMSAM®

selegiline HCl → ZELAPAR®

selexipag → UPTRAVI®

SELZENTRY® (maraviroc)

ViiV HEALTHCARE

ViiVConnect Savings Card   1-844-588-3288   *www.viivconnect.com*

Income Limits NONE | Rx cost → $0 CoPay $ | No Medical Insurance ✓ | Commercial Insurance ✓ | Medicare Part D ✗

Patients can pay as little as $0 copay, maximum savings $4500/year.

ViiV Healthcare Patient Assistance Program   1-844-588-3288   *www.viivconnect.com*

Income Limits $60k Single / $82k Couple | Rx cost → FREE $ | No Medical Insurance ✓ | Commercial Insurance ? | Medicare Part D ✓

Gives meds to patients who are uninsured, lack coverage, or on Medicare and have spent $600 on Rx meds this year.

semaglutide injection → OZEMPIC®

SENSIPAR® (cinacalcet HCL)

AMGEN, INC.

Sensipar Pharmacy Card   1-866-711-4162   *www.sensipar.com*

Income Limits NONE | Rx cost → $5 Per Month $ | No Medical Insurance ✗ | Commercial Insurance ✓ | Medicare Part D ✗

Program will pay up to $500 per 30-day supply to cover out-of-pocket costs for Sensipar (up to $6,000 per year), including co-payments, co-insurance, and prescription deductible. Eligible patients pay just $5 per month.

AMGEN® Safety Net Foundation   1-888-762-6436   *www.amgensafetynetfoundation.com*

Income Limits $60k Single / $82k Couple | Rx cost → FREE $ | No Medical Insurance ✓ | Commercial Insurance ? | Medicare Part D ?

Foundation provides free medications to patients who are uninsured or underinsured, and meet program guidelines. Patients with Medicare may be eligible, if they have been denied or are ineligible for Low Income Subsidy.

SEREVENT DISKUS® (salmeterol xinafoate inhalation powder)

GSK Patient Assistance   1-866-728-4368   *www.gskforyou.com*

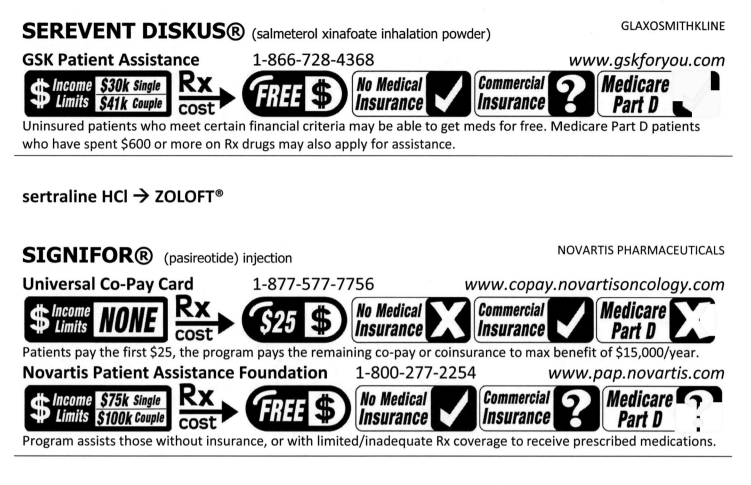

Uninsured patients who meet certain financial criteria may be able to get meds for free. Medicare Part D patients who have spent $600 or more on Rx drugs may also apply for assistance.

---

sertraline HCl → ZOLOFT®

SIGNIFOR® (pasireotide) injection
NOVARTIS PHARMACEUTICALS

Universal Co-Pay Card   1-877-577-7756   *www.copay.novartisoncology.com*

Patients pay the first $25, the program pays the remaining co-pay or coinsurance to max benefit of $15,000/year.

Novartis Patient Assistance Foundation   1-800-277-2254   *www.pap.novartis.com*

Program assists those without insurance, or with limited/inadequate Rx coverage to receive prescribed medications.

---

sildenafil → REVATIO®

sildenafil citrate tablets → VIAGRA®

SILENOR® (doxepin)
PERNIX THERAPUETICS

Co-Pay Savings Card   1-800-793-2145   *www.selenor.com*

Commercially insured patients pay as little as $25 for their Selenor Rx when using co-pay savings card.

SILIQ® (brodalumab)
VALEANT PHARMACEUTICALS INTERNATIONAL

Siliq Instant Savings Card   1-855-797-4547   *www.siliq.com*

Commercially insured patients pay as little as $5/month if Siliq is covered, $25/month if coverage delayed or denied.

SILIQ® (brodalumab)

Siliq Solutions Patient Assistance Program 1-855-797-4547 *www.siliq.com*

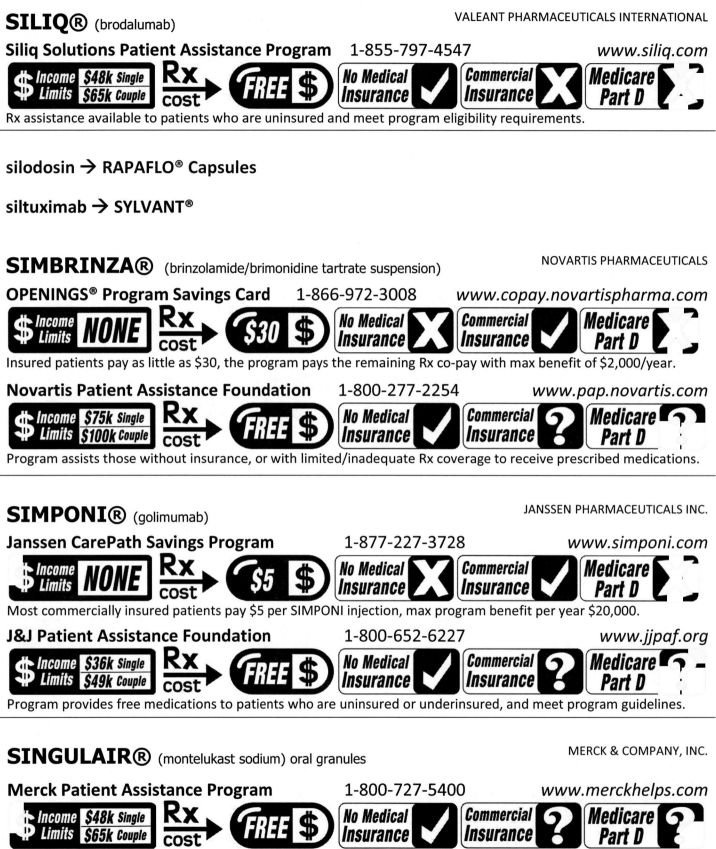

$ Income Limits $48k Single / $65k Couple | **Rx cost** → **FREE $** | **No Medical Insurance** ✓ | **Commercial Insurance** ✗ | **Medicare Part D**

Rx assistance available to patients who are uninsured and meet program eligibility requirements.

---

silodosin → RAPAFLO® Capsules

siltuximab → SYLVANT®

SIMBRINZA® (brinzolamide/brimonidine tartrate suspension)
NOVARTIS PHARMACEUTICALS

OPENINGS® Program Savings Card 1-866-972-3008 *www.copay.novartispharma.com*

$ Income Limits NONE | **Rx cost** → **$30 $** | **No Medical Insurance** ✗ | **Commercial Insurance** ✓ | **Medicare Part D**

Insured patients pay as little as $30, the program pays the remaining Rx co-pay with max benefit of $2,000/year.

Novartis Patient Assistance Foundation 1-800-277-2254 *www.pap.novartis.com*

$ Income Limits $75k Single / $100k Couple | **Rx cost** → **FREE $** | **No Medical Insurance** ✓ | **Commercial Insurance** ? | **Medicare Part D** ?

Program assists those without insurance, or with limited/inadequate Rx coverage to receive prescribed medications.

SIMPONI® (golimumab)
JANSSEN PHARMACEUTICALS INC.

Janssen CarePath Savings Program 1-877-227-3728 *www.simponi.com*

$ Income Limits NONE | **Rx cost** → **$5 $** | **No Medical Insurance** ✗ | **Commercial Insurance** ✓ | **Medicare Part D**

Most commercially insured patients pay $5 per SIMPONI injection, max program benefit per year $20,000.

J&J Patient Assistance Foundation 1-800-652-6227 *www.jjpaf.org*

$ Income Limits $36k Single / $49k Couple | **Rx cost** → **FREE $** | **No Medical Insurance** ✓ | **Commercial Insurance** ? | **Medicare Part D** ?

Program provides free medications to patients who are uninsured or underinsured, and meet program guidelines.

SINGULAIR® (montelukast sodium) oral granules
MERCK & COMPANY, INC.

Merck Patient Assistance Program 1-800-727-5400 *www.merckhelps.com*

$ Income Limits $48k Single / $65k Couple | **Rx cost** → **FREE $** | **No Medical Insurance** ✓ | **Commercial Insurance** ? | **Medicare Part D** ?

Program is for patients who do not have Rx insurance coverage and cannot afford to pay for their medicine.

sipuleucel-t → PROVENGE®

sirolimus → RAPAMUNE®

SIRTURO® (bedaquiline)
JOHNSON & JOHNSON PATIENT ASSISTANCE FOUNDATION, INC.

J&J Patient Assistance Foundation 1-800-652-6227 *www.jjpaf.org*

$ Income Limits $36k Single / $49k Couple | Rx cost → FREE $ | No Medical Insurance ✓ | Commercial Insurance ? | Medicare Part D ?

Program provides free medications to patients who are uninsured or underinsured, and meet program guidelines.

sitagliptin → JANUVIA®

sitagliptin and metformin HCL → JANUMET®/ JANUMET® XR

SIVEXTRO® (tedizolid phosphate)
MERCK & COMPANY, INC.

Multiuse Savings Coupon 1-800-672-6372 *www.sivextrocoupon.com*

$ Income Limits NONE | Rx cost → $15 $ | No Medical Insurance X | Commercial Insurance ✓ | Medicare Part D X

Insured patients pay as little as $15 per Rx, maximum savings is $1,500 per prescription.

Merck Patient Assistance Program 1-800-727-5400 *www.merckhelps.com*

$ Income Limits $48k Single / $65k Couple | Rx cost → FREE $ | No Medical Insurance ✓ | Commercial Insurance ? | Medicare Part D ?

Program is for patients who do not have Rx insurance coverage and cannot afford to pay for their medicine.

SKELAXIN® (metaxalone)
PFIZER, INC

Pfizer Savings Program 1-866-706-2400 *www.pfizerrxpathways.com*

$ Income Limits NONE | Rx cost → Discount Varies $ | No Medical Insurance ✓ | Commercial Insurance X | Medicare Part D X

Program helps uninsured patients receive discounted Pfizer medications through their local retail pharmacy.

Pfizer Patient Assistance Program 1-844-989-7284 *www.pfizerrxpathways.com*

$ Income Limits $48k Single / $65k Couple | Rx cost → FREE $ | No Medical Insurance ✓ | Commercial Insurance ? | Medicare Part D X

Assists eligible patients who are uninsured (or have inadequate drug coverage) and cannot afford their medications.

SKLICE® (ivermectin lotion)

ARBOR PHARMACEUTICALS, INC.

SKLICE Lotion Coupon   1-855-575-5423   *www.sklice.com*

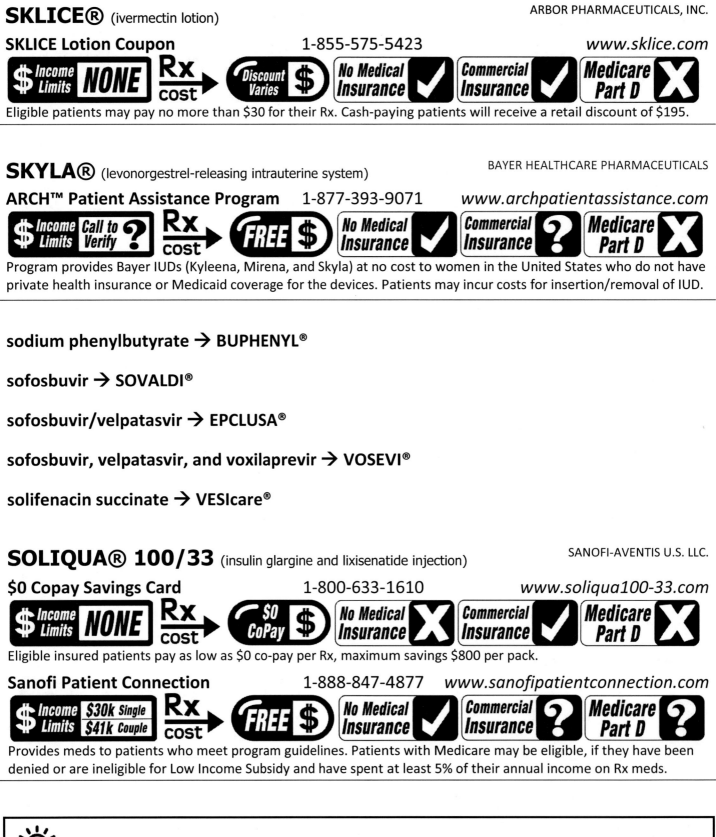

Eligible patients may pay no more than $30 for their Rx. Cash-paying patients will receive a retail discount of $195.

SKYLA® (levonorgestrel-releasing intrauterine system)

BAYER HEALTHCARE PHARMACEUTICALS

ARCH™ Patient Assistance Program   1-877-393-9071   *www.archpatientassistance.com*

Program provides Bayer IUDs (Kyleena, Mirena, and Skyla) at no cost to women in the United States who do not have private health insurance or Medicaid coverage for the devices. Patients may incur costs for insertion/removal of IUD.

sodium phenylbutyrate → **BUPHENYL®**

sofosbuvir → **SOVALDI®**

sofosbuvir/velpatasvir → **EPCLUSA®**

sofosbuvir, velpatasvir, and voxilaprevir → **VOSEVI®**

solifenacin succinate → **VESIcare®**

SOLIQUA® 100/33 (insulin glargine and lixisenatide injection)

SANOFI-AVENTIS U.S. LLC.

$0 Copay Savings Card   1-800-633-1610   *www.soliqua100-33.com*

Eligible insured patients pay as low as $0 co-pay per Rx, maximum savings $800 per pack.

Sanofi Patient Connection   1-888-847-4877   *www.sanofipatientconnection.com*

Provides meds to patients who meet program guidelines. Patients with Medicare may be eligible, if they have been denied or are ineligible for Low Income Subsidy and have spent at least 5% of their annual income on Rx meds.

TIP: Income limits are higher for households with three or more people. Call programs for details.

SOLIRIS® (eculizumab)   ALEXION PHARMACEUTICALS, INC.

OneSource™ Treatment Support   1-888-765-4747   *www.soliris.net*

Call for information regarding financial assistance, co-pay programs, and the Alexion Access Foundation.

SOLODYN® (minocycline HCL, USP) extended release tablets   VALEANT PHARMACEUTICALS INTERNATIONAL

Ortho Dermatologics Rx Access Program   1-855-202-3279   *www.orthorxaccess.com*

Most commercially insured patients pay as little as $25 per Rx, once deductible has been met. Those with insurance where drug is not covered pay $75 per Rx, and uninsured patients pay $125 per 4oz Rx, $200 per 8oz Rx.

Valeant Patient Assistance Program   1-833-862-8727   *www.valeantpap.com*

Rx assistance available to patients who are uninsured, (or whose insurance has denied coverage) and meet program eligibility requirements. Medicare Part D patients who cannot afford Rx can appeal for evaluation of eligibility.

---

somatropin → **GENOTROPIN®**

somatropin → **HUMATROPE®**

somatropin → **NORDITROPIN®**

somatropin → **OMNITROPE®**

somatropin → **SAIZEN®**

SOMATULINE® DEPOT (lanreotide)   IPSEN BIOPHARMACEUTICALS, INC.

SOMATULINE® Copay Savings Program   1-866-435-5677   *www.ipsencares.com*

Insured patients pay as little as $5 per injection. Max assistance of $1666/per injection treatment ($20,000/yr max).

ONIVYDE® Patient Assistance Program   1-866-435-5677   *www.ipsencares.com*

Eligible uninsured patients who are experiencing financial hardship may receive Somatuline® free.

SOMAVERT® (pegvisomant)

PFIZER, INC

Somavert CoPay/CoInsurance Program 1-800-645-1280 *www.somavert.com*

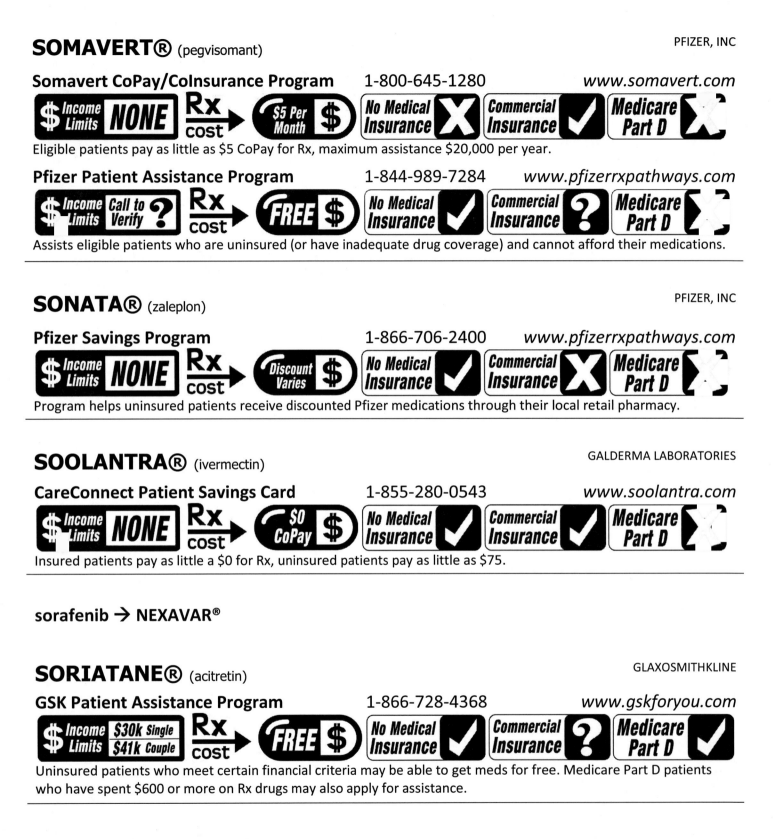

Income Limits NONE | **Rx cost → $5 Per Month $** | **No Medical Insurance X** | **Commercial Insurance ✓** | **Medicare Part D X**

Eligible patients pay as little as $5 CoPay for Rx, maximum assistance $20,000 per year.

Pfizer Patient Assistance Program 1-844-989-7284 *www.pfizerrxpathways.com*

Income Limits Call to Verify ? | **Rx cost → FREE $** | **No Medical Insurance ✓** | **Commercial Insurance ?** | **Medicare Part D X**

Assists eligible patients who are uninsured (or have inadequate drug coverage) and cannot afford their medications.

SONATA® (zaleplon)

PFIZER, INC

Pfizer Savings Program 1-866-706-2400 *www.pfizerrxpathways.com*

Income Limits NONE | **Rx cost → Discount Varies $** | **No Medical Insurance ✓** | **Commercial Insurance X** | **Medicare Part D X**

Program helps uninsured patients receive discounted Pfizer medications through their local retail pharmacy.

SOOLANTRA® (ivermectin)

GALDERMA LABORATORIES

CareConnect Patient Savings Card 1-855-280-0543 *www.soolantra.com*

Income Limits NONE | **Rx cost → $0 CoPay $** | **No Medical Insurance ✓** | **Commercial Insurance ✓** | **Medicare Part D X**

Insured patients pay as little a $0 for Rx, uninsured patients pay as little as $75.

sorafenib → NEXAVAR®

SORIATANE® (acitretin)

GLAXOSMITHKLINE

GSK Patient Assistance Program 1-866-728-4368 *www.gskforyou.com*

Income Limits $30k Single $41k Couple | **Rx cost → FREE $** | **No Medical Insurance ✓** | **Commercial Insurance ?** | **Medicare Part D ✓**

Uninsured patients who meet certain financial criteria may be able to get meds for free. Medicare Part D patients who have spent $600 or more on Rx drugs may also apply for assistance.

sotalol HCl → BETAPACE® / BETAPACE AF®

sotalol HCl → SOTYLIZE®

SOTYLIZE® (sotalol hydrochloride)　　　ARBOR PHARMACEUTICALS, INC.

SOTYLIZE Savings Card　　1-844-415-0675　　www.sotylize.com

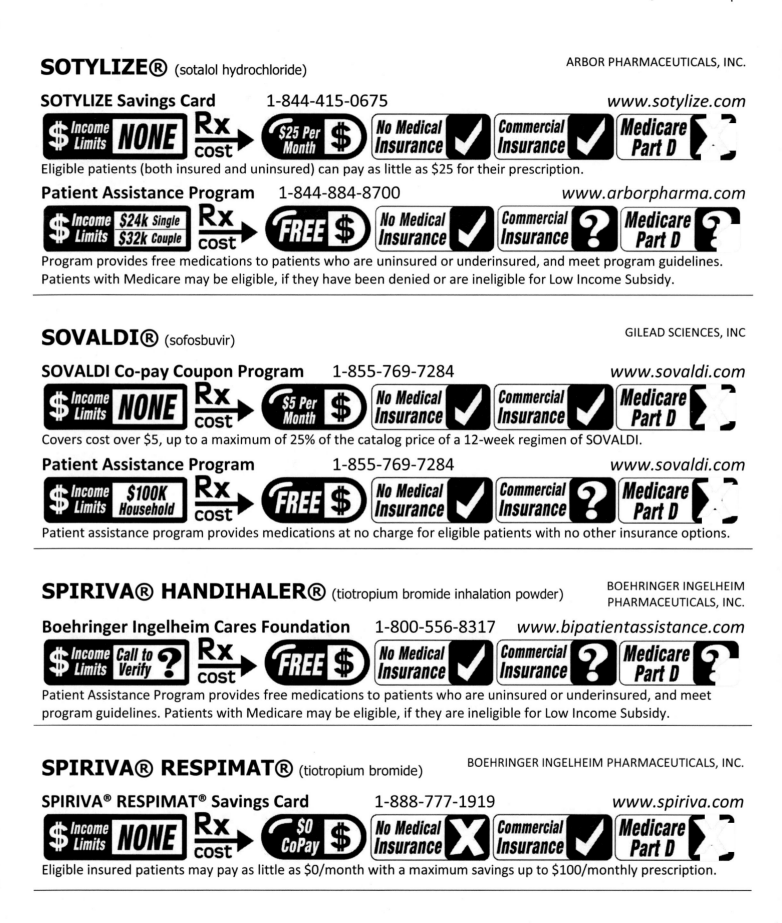

Eligible patients (both insured and uninsured) can pay as little as $25 for their prescription.

Patient Assistance Program　　1-844-884-8700　　www.arborpharma.com

Program provides free medications to patients who are uninsured or underinsured, and meet program guidelines. Patients with Medicare may be eligible, if they have been denied or are ineligible for Low Income Subsidy.

SOVALDI® (sofosbuvir)　　　GILEAD SCIENCES, INC

SOVALDI Co-pay Coupon Program　　1-855-769-7284　　www.sovaldi.com

Covers cost over $5, up to a maximum of 25% of the catalog price of a 12-week regimen of SOVALDI.

Patient Assistance Program　　1-855-769-7284　　www.sovaldi.com

Patient assistance program provides medications at no charge for eligible patients with no other insurance options.

SPIRIVA® HANDIHALER® (tiotropium bromide inhalation powder)　　BOEHRINGER INGELHEIM PHARMACEUTICALS, INC.

Boehringer Ingelheim Cares Foundation　　1-800-556-8317　　www.bipatientassistance.com

Patient Assistance Program provides free medications to patients who are uninsured or underinsured, and meet program guidelines. Patients with Medicare may be eligible, if they are ineligible for Low Income Subsidy.

SPIRIVA® RESPIMAT® (tiotropium bromide)　　BOEHRINGER INGELHEIM PHARMACEUTICALS, INC.

SPIRIVA® RESPIMAT® Savings Card　　1-888-777-1919　　www.spiriva.com

Eligible insured patients may pay as little as $0/month with a maximum savings up to $100/monthly prescription.

SPIRIVA® RESPIMAT® (tiotropium bromide)

BOEHRINGER INGELHEIM PHARMACEUTICALS, INC.

Boehringer Ingelheim Cares Foundation   1-800-556-8317   *www.bipatientassistance.com*

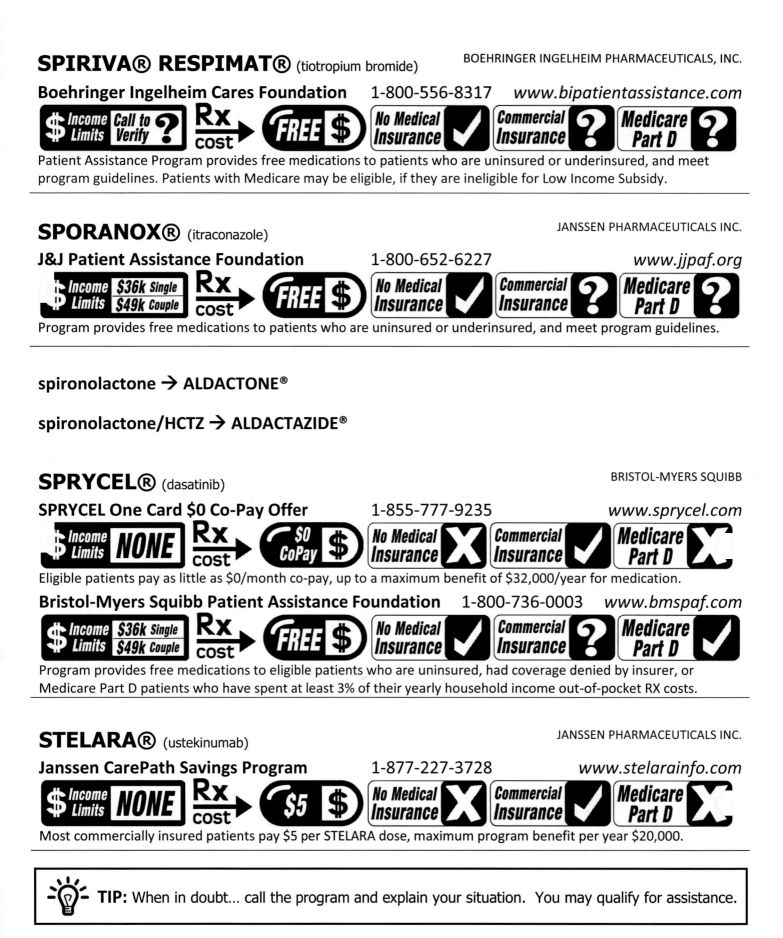

| $ Income Limits | Call to Verify ? | Rx cost → | FREE $ | No Medical Insurance ✓ | Commercial Insurance ? | Medicare Part D ? |

Patient Assistance Program provides free medications to patients who are uninsured or underinsured, and meet program guidelines. Patients with Medicare may be eligible, if they are ineligible for Low Income Subsidy.

SPORANOX® (itraconazole)

JANSSEN PHARMACEUTICALS INC.

J&J Patient Assistance Foundation   1-800-652-6227   *www.jjpaf.org*

| $ Income Limits | $36k Single / $49k Couple | Rx cost → | FREE $ | No Medical Insurance ✓ | Commercial Insurance ? | Medicare Part D ? |

Program provides free medications to patients who are uninsured or underinsured, and meet program guidelines.

---

spironolactone → **ALDACTONE®**

spironolactone/HCTZ → **ALDACTAZIDE®**

SPRYCEL® (dasatinib)

BRISTOL-MYERS SQUIBB

SPRYCEL One Card $0 Co-Pay Offer   1-855-777-9235   *www.sprycel.com*

| $ Income Limits | NONE | Rx cost → | $0 CoPay $ | No Medical Insurance X | Commercial Insurance ✓ | Medicare Part D X |

Eligible patients pay as little as $0/month co-pay, up to a maximum benefit of $32,000/year for medication.

Bristol-Myers Squibb Patient Assistance Foundation   1-800-736-0003   *www.bmspaf.com*

| $ Income Limits | $36k Single / $49k Couple | Rx cost → | FREE $ | No Medical Insurance ✓ | Commercial Insurance ? | Medicare Part D ✓ |

Program provides free medications to eligible patients who are uninsured, had coverage denied by insurer, or Medicare Part D patients who have spent at least 3% of their yearly household income out-of-pocket RX costs.

STELARA® (ustekinumab)

JANSSEN PHARMACEUTICALS INC.

Janssen CarePath Savings Program   1-877-227-3728   *www.stelarainfo.com*

| $ Income Limits | NONE | Rx cost → | $5 $ | No Medical Insurance X | Commercial Insurance ✓ | Medicare Part D X |

Most commercially insured patients pay $5 per STELARA dose, maximum program benefit per year $20,000.

TIP: When in doubt... call the program and explain your situation. You may qualify for assistance.

STELARA® (ustekinumab)

JANSSEN PHARMACEUTICALS INC.

J&J Patient Assistance Foundation   1-800-652-6227   *www.jjpaf.org*

| Income Limits | $36k Single / $49k Couple | Rx cost → FREE $ | No Medical Insurance ✓ | Commercial Insurance ? | Medicare Part D ? |

Program provides free medications to patients who are uninsured or underinsured, and meet program guidelines.

STIMATE® (desmopressin acetate)

CSL BEHRING

CSL Behring Patient Assistance Program   1-844-727-2472   *www.cslbehring.com*

| Income Limits | Call to Verify ? | Rx cost → FREE $ | No Medical Insurance ✓ | Commercial Insurance ? | Medicare Part D ✗ |

Provides meds to qualified patients who are uninsured or underinsured, and cannot afford their prescribed therapy.

STIOLTO® RESPIMAT® (tiotropium bromide and olodaterol)

BOEHRINGER INGELHEIM PHARMACEUTICALS, INC.

STIOLTO® RESPIMAT® Savings Card   1-800-859-2174   *www.stiolto.com*

| Income Limits | NONE | Rx cost → $0 CoPay $ | No Medical Insurance ✗ | Commercial Insurance ✓ | Medicare Part D ✗ |

Eligible insured patients may pay as little as $0/month with a maximum savings up to $380/monthly prescription.

Boehringer Ingelheim Cares Foundation   1-800-556-8317   *www.bipatientassistance.com*

| Income Limits | Call to Verify ? | Rx cost → FREE $ | No Medical Insurance ✓ | Commercial Insurance ? | Medicare Part D ? |

Patient Assistance Program provides free medications to patients who are uninsured or underinsured, and meet program guidelines. Patients with Medicare may be eligible, if they are ineligible for Low Income Subsidy.

STIVARGA® (regorafenib)

BAYER HEALTHCARE PHARMACEUTICALS

Oncology $0 Co-Pay Program   1-866-581-4992   *www.zerocopaysupport.com*

| Income Limits | NONE | Rx cost → $0 CoPay $ | No Medical Insurance ✗ | Commercial Insurance ✓ | Medicare Part D ✗ |

Program covers up to 100% of co-pay/co-insurance amount for those with commercial insurance. Up to a maximum assistance of $25,000/year.

Patient Assistance Program (PAP)   1-866-639-2827   *www.stivarga-us.com*

| Income Limits | Call to Verify ? | Rx cost → FREE $ | No Medical Insurance ✓ | Commercial Insurance ? | Medicare Part D ✗ |

Helps those who are uninsured (no insurance coverage at all) or underinsured (no prescription coverage, a benefits cap, denial of coverage, etc), and cannot afford medications.

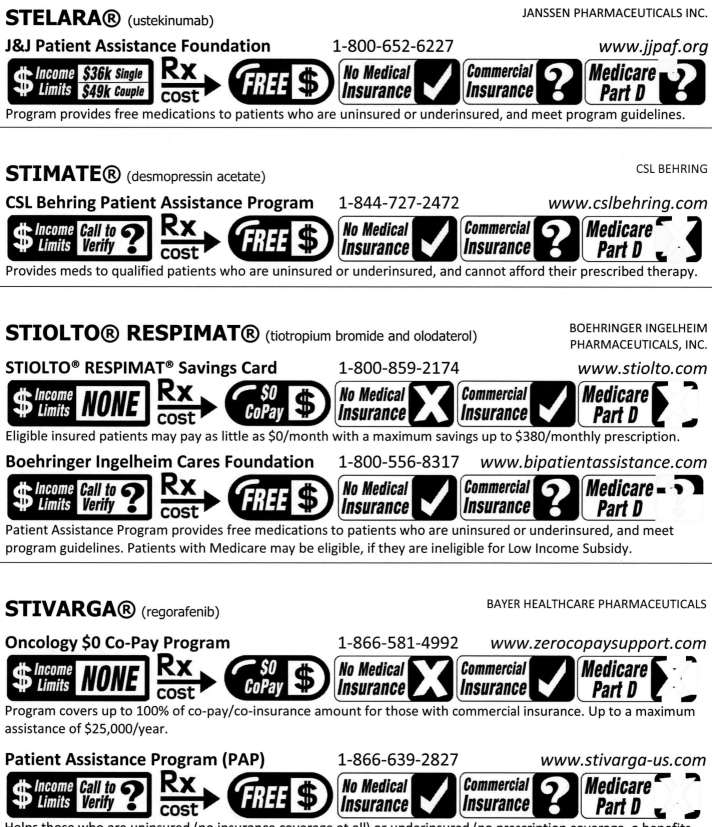

STRATTERA® (atomoxetine)

LILLY USA, LLC

Lilly Cares   1-800-545-6962   www.lillycares.com

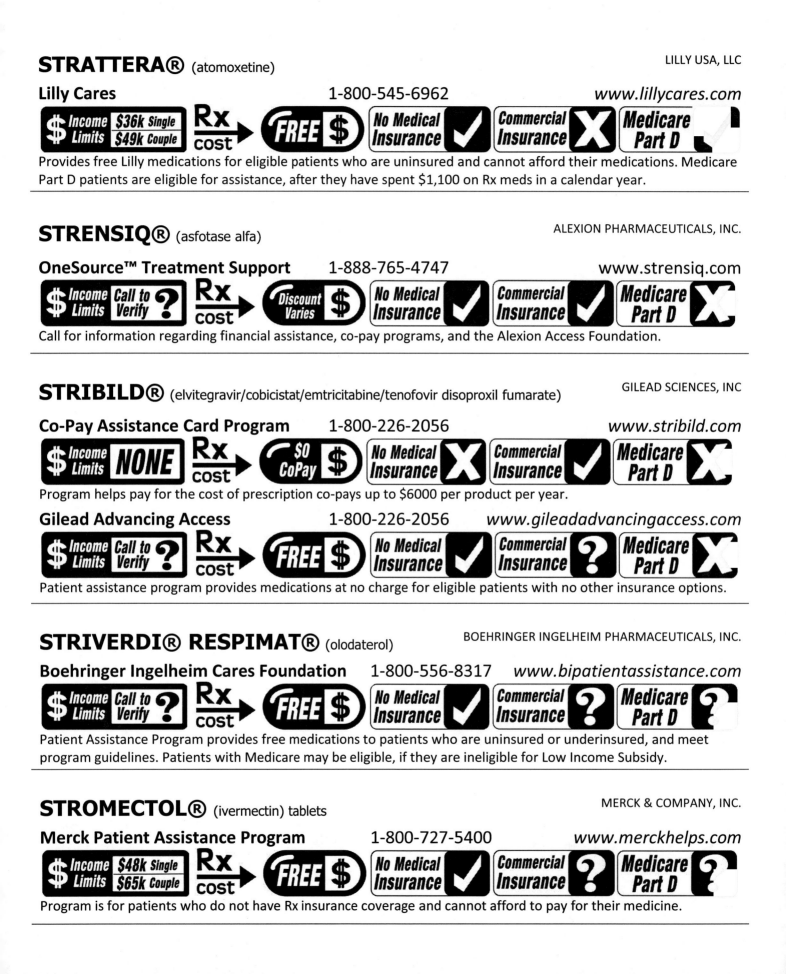

Income Limits $36k Single $49k Couple | **Rx cost** → **FREE $** | **No Medical Insurance** ✓ | **Commercial Insurance** ✗ | **Medicare Part D** ✓

Provides free Lilly medications for eligible patients who are uninsured and cannot afford their medications. Medicare Part D patients are eligible for assistance, after they have spent $1,100 on Rx meds in a calendar year.

STRENSIQ® (asfotase alfa)

ALEXION PHARMACEUTICALS, INC.

OneSource™ Treatment Support   1-888-765-4747   www.strensiq.com

Income Limits Call to Verify ? | **Rx cost** → **Discount Varies $** | **No Medical Insurance** ✓ | **Commercial Insurance** ✓ | **Medicare Part D** ✗

Call for information regarding financial assistance, co-pay programs, and the Alexion Access Foundation.

STRIBILD® (elvitegravir/cobicistat/emtricitabine/tenofovir disoproxil fumarate)

GILEAD SCIENCES, INC

Co-Pay Assistance Card Program   1-800-226-2056   www.stribild.com

Income Limits NONE | **Rx cost** → **$0 CoPay $** | **No Medical Insurance** ✗ | **Commercial Insurance** ✓ | **Medicare Part D** ✗

Program helps pay for the cost of prescription co-pays up to $6000 per product per year.

Gilead Advancing Access   1-800-226-2056   www.gileadadvancingaccess.com

Income Limits Call to Verify ? | **Rx cost** → **FREE $** | **No Medical Insurance** ✓ | **Commercial Insurance** ? | **Medicare Part D** ✗

Patient assistance program provides medications at no charge for eligible patients with no other insurance options.

STRIVERDI® RESPIMAT® (olodaterol)

BOEHRINGER INGELHEIM PHARMACEUTICALS, INC.

Boehringer Ingelheim Cares Foundation   1-800-556-8317   www.bipatientassistance.com

Income Limits Call to Verify ? | **Rx cost** → **FREE $** | **No Medical Insurance** ✓ | **Commercial Insurance** ? | **Medicare Part D** ?

Patient Assistance Program provides free medications to patients who are uninsured or underinsured, and meet program guidelines. Patients with Medicare may be eligible, if they are ineligible for Low Income Subsidy.

STROMECTOL® (ivermectin) tablets

MERCK & COMPANY, INC.

Merck Patient Assistance Program   1-800-727-5400   www.merckhelps.com

Income Limits $48k Single $65k Couple | **Rx cost** → **FREE $** | **No Medical Insurance** ✓ | **Commercial Insurance** ? | **Medicare Part D** ?

Program is for patients who do not have Rx insurance coverage and cannot afford to pay for their medicine.

SUBOXONE® Sublingual Film (buprenorphine/naloxone) INDIVIOR, INC.

SUBOXONE Savings Card 1-877-678-7493 *www.suboxone.com*

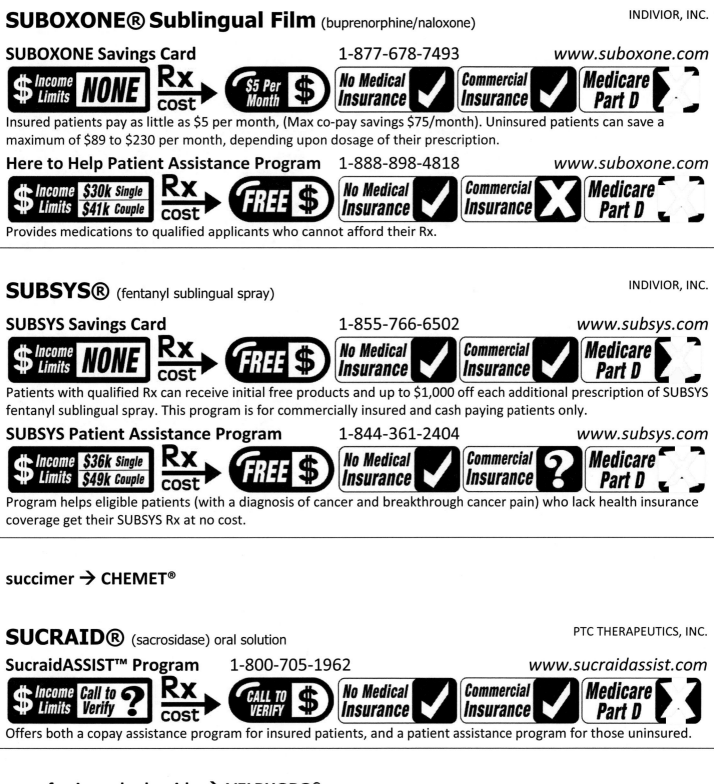

Insured patients pay as little as $5 per month, (Max co-pay savings $75/month). Uninsured patients can save a maximum of $89 to $230 per month, depending upon dosage of their prescription.

Here to Help Patient Assistance Program 1-888-898-4818 *www.suboxone.com*

Provides medications to qualified applicants who cannot afford their Rx.

SUBSYS® (fentanyl sublingual spray) INDIVIOR, INC.

SUBSYS Savings Card 1-855-766-6502 *www.subsys.com*

Patients with qualified Rx can receive initial free products and up to $1,000 off each additional prescription of SUBSYS fentanyl sublingual spray. This program is for commercially insured and cash paying patients only.

SUBSYS Patient Assistance Program 1-844-361-2404 *www.subsys.com*

Program helps eligible patients (with a diagnosis of cancer and breakthrough cancer pain) who lack health insurance coverage get their SUBSYS Rx at no cost.

succimer → CHEMET®

SUCRAID® (sacrosidase) oral solution PTC THERAPEUTICS, INC.

SucraidASSIST™ Program 1-800-705-1962 *www.sucraidassist.com*

Offers both a copay assistance program for insured patients, and a patient assistance program for those uninsured.

sucroferric oxyhydroxide → VELPHORO®

sulfasalazine → AZULFIDINE®

sumatriptan/naproxen sodium → TREXIMET®

sunitinib malate → SUTENT®

SUSTIVA® (efavirenz)

BRISTOL-MYERS SQUIBB

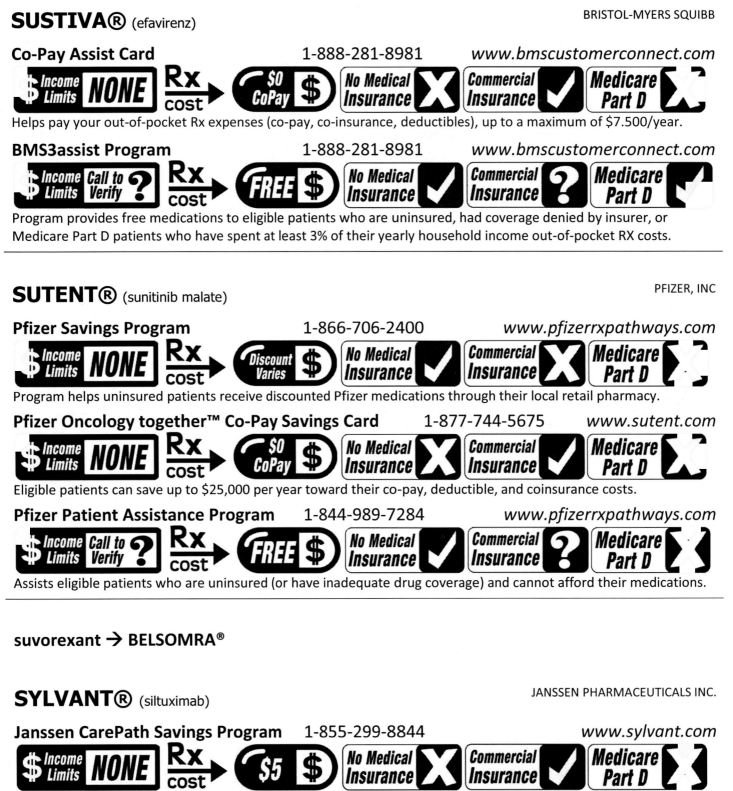

Co-Pay Assist Card   1-888-281-8981   *www.bmscustomerconnect.com*

Income Limits **NONE** | Rx cost → | **$0 CoPay** $ | **No Medical Insurance** ✗ | **Commercial Insurance** ✓ | **Medicare Part D** ✗

Helps pay your out-of-pocket Rx expenses (co-pay, co-insurance, deductibles), up to a maximum of $7.500/year.

BMS3assist Program   1-888-281-8981   *www.bmscustomerconnect.com*

Income Limits **Call to Verify ?** | Rx cost → | **FREE** $ | **No Medical Insurance** ✓ | **Commercial Insurance ?** | **Medicare Part D** ✓

Program provides free medications to eligible patients who are uninsured, had coverage denied by insurer, or Medicare Part D patients who have spent at least 3% of their yearly household income out-of-pocket RX costs.

SUTENT® (sunitinib malate)

PFIZER, INC

Pfizer Savings Program   1-866-706-2400   *www.pfizerrxpathways.com*

Income Limits **NONE** | Rx cost → | **Discount Varies** $ | **No Medical Insurance** ✓ | **Commercial Insurance** ✗ | **Medicare Part D** ✗

Program helps uninsured patients receive discounted Pfizer medications through their local retail pharmacy.

Pfizer Oncology together™ Co-Pay Savings Card   1-877-744-5675   *www.sutent.com*

Income Limits **NONE** | Rx cost → | **$0 CoPay** $ | **No Medical Insurance** ✗ | **Commercial Insurance** ✓ | **Medicare Part D** ✗

Eligible patients can save up to $25,000 per year toward their co-pay, deductible, and coinsurance costs.

Pfizer Patient Assistance Program   1-844-989-7284   *www.pfizerrxpathways.com*

Income Limits **Call to Verify ?** | Rx cost → | **FREE** $ | **No Medical Insurance** ✓ | **Commercial Insurance ?** | **Medicare Part D** ✗

Assists eligible patients who are uninsured (or have inadequate drug coverage) and cannot afford their medications.

suvorexant → BELSOMRA®

SYLVANT® (siltuximab)

JANSSEN PHARMACEUTICALS INC.

Janssen CarePath Savings Program   1-855-299-8844   *www.sylvant.com*

Income Limits **NONE** | Rx cost → | **$5** $ | **No Medical Insurance** ✗ | **Commercial Insurance** ✓ | **Medicare Part D** ✗

Most commercially insured patients pay $5 per infusion, maximum program benefit per year $20,000.

SYLVANT® (siltuximab)

J&J Patient Assistance Foundation   1-800-652-6227   *www.jjpaf.org*

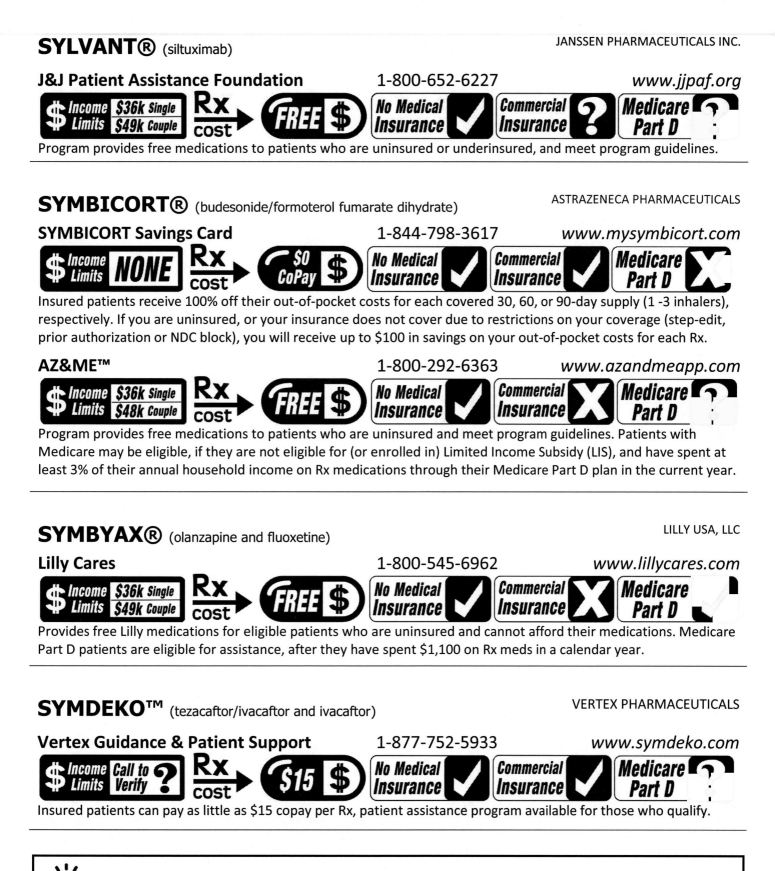

Income Limits $36k Single / $49k Couple | **Rx cost** → **FREE $** | **No Medical Insurance** ✓ | **Commercial Insurance** ? | **Medicare Part D** ?

Program provides free medications to patients who are uninsured or underinsured, and meet program guidelines.

SYMBICORT® (budesonide/formoterol fumarate dihydrate)

SYMBICORT Savings Card   1-844-798-3617   *www.mysymbicort.com*

Income Limits NONE | **Rx cost** → **$0 CoPay $** | **No Medical Insurance** ✓ | **Commercial Insurance** ✓ | **Medicare Part D** X

Insured patients receive 100% off their out-of-pocket costs for each covered 30, 60, or 90-day supply (1-3 inhalers), respectively. If you are uninsured, or your insurance does not cover due to restrictions on your coverage (step-edit, prior authorization or NDC block), you will receive up to $100 in savings on your out-of-pocket costs for each Rx.

AZ&ME™   1-800-292-6363   *www.azandmeapp.com*

Income Limits $36k Single / $48k Couple | **Rx cost** → **FREE $** | **No Medical Insurance** ✓ | **Commercial Insurance** X | **Medicare Part D** ?

Program provides free medications to patients who are uninsured and meet program guidelines. Patients with Medicare may be eligible, if they are not eligible for (or enrolled in) Limited Income Subsidy (LIS), and have spent at least 3% of their annual household income on Rx medications through their Medicare Part D plan in the current year.

SYMBYAX® (olanzapine and fluoxetine)

Lilly Cares   1-800-545-6962   *www.lillycares.com*

Income Limits $36k Single / $49k Couple | **Rx cost** → **FREE $** | **No Medical Insurance** ✓ | **Commercial Insurance** X | **Medicare Part D** ✓

Provides free Lilly medications for eligible patients who are uninsured and cannot afford their medications. Medicare Part D patients are eligible for assistance, after they have spent $1,100 on Rx meds in a calendar year.

SYMDEKO™ (tezacaftor/ivacaftor and ivacaftor)

Vertex Guidance & Patient Support   1-877-752-5933   *www.symdeko.com*

Income Limits Call to Verify ? | **Rx cost** → **$15 $** | **No Medical Insurance** ✓ | **Commercial Insurance** ✓ | **Medicare Part D** ?

Insured patients can pay as little as $15 copay per Rx, patient assistance program available for those who qualify.

TIP: When in doubt... call the program and explain your situation. You may qualify for assistance.

SymlinPen® (pramlintide acetate) injection

ASTRAZENECA PHARMACEUTICALS

MySavingsRx Card   1-855-292-5968   *www.symlin.com*

Income Limits **NONE** | Rx cost → $25 Per Month $ | **No Medical Insurance** ✓ | **Commercial Insurance** ✓ | **Medicare Part D** ⟩

Eligible patients with a valid Rx for SYMLIN who present an activated Savings Card at participating pharmacies may be able to pay no more than $25 per 30-day supply for up to 24 months (maximum savings of $100 per 30-day supply).

AZ&ME™   1-800-292-6363   *www.azandmeapp.com*

Income Limits **$36k Single $48k Couple** | Rx cost → **FREE** $ | **No Medical Insurance** ✓ | **Commercial Insurance** ✗ | **Medicare Part D** ?

Program provides free medications to patients who are uninsured and meet program guidelines. Patients with Medicare may be eligible, if they are not eligible for (or enrolled in) Limited Income Subsidy (LIS), and have spent at least 3% of their annual household income on Rx medications through their Medicare Part D plan in the current year.

SYNAGIS® (palivizumab)

ASTRAZENECA PHARMACEUTICALS

SYNAGIS Patient Savings Program   1-844-275-2360   *www.synagis.com*

Income Limits **NONE** | Rx cost → $30 $ | **No Medical Insurance** ✗ | **Commercial Insurance** ✓ | **Medicare Part D** ⟩

Insured patients pay the first $30 of their SYNAGIS out-of-pocket costs (per dose), and their pharmacy, home care clinic, or prescriber's office will use the Program to cover the balance, up to $2000 per program year.

AZ&ME™   1-800-292-6363   *www.azandmeapp.com*

Income Limits **$36k Single $48k Couple** | Rx cost → **FREE** $ | **No Medical Insurance** ✓ | **Commercial Insurance** ✗ | **Medicare Part D** ?

Program provides free medications to patients who are uninsured and meet program guidelines. Patients with Medicare may be eligible, if they are not eligible for (or enrolled in) Limited Income Subsidy (LIS), and have spent at least 3% of their annual household income on Rx medications through their Medicare Part D plan in the current year.

SYNAREL® (nafarelin acetate)

PFIZER, INC

Pfizer Savings Program   1-866-706-2400   *www.pfizerrxpathways.com*

Income Limits **NONE** | Rx cost → Discount Varies $ | **No Medical Insurance** ✓ | **Commercial Insurance** ✗ | **Medicare Part D** ⟩

Program helps uninsured patients receive discounted Pfizer medications through their local retail pharmacy.

Pfizer Patient Assistance Program   1-844-989-7284   *www.pfizerrxpathways.com*

Income Limits **$48k Single $65k Couple** | Rx cost → **FREE** $ | **No Medical Insurance** ✓ | **Commercial Insurance** ? | **Medicare Part D** ⟩

Assists eligible patients who are uninsured (or have inadequate drug coverage) and cannot afford their medications.

SYNJARDY® (empagliflozin/metformin HCL)
BOEHRINGER INGELHEIM PHARMACEUTICALS, INC.

SYNJARDY® Savings Card
1-866-279-8990 · www.synjardy.com

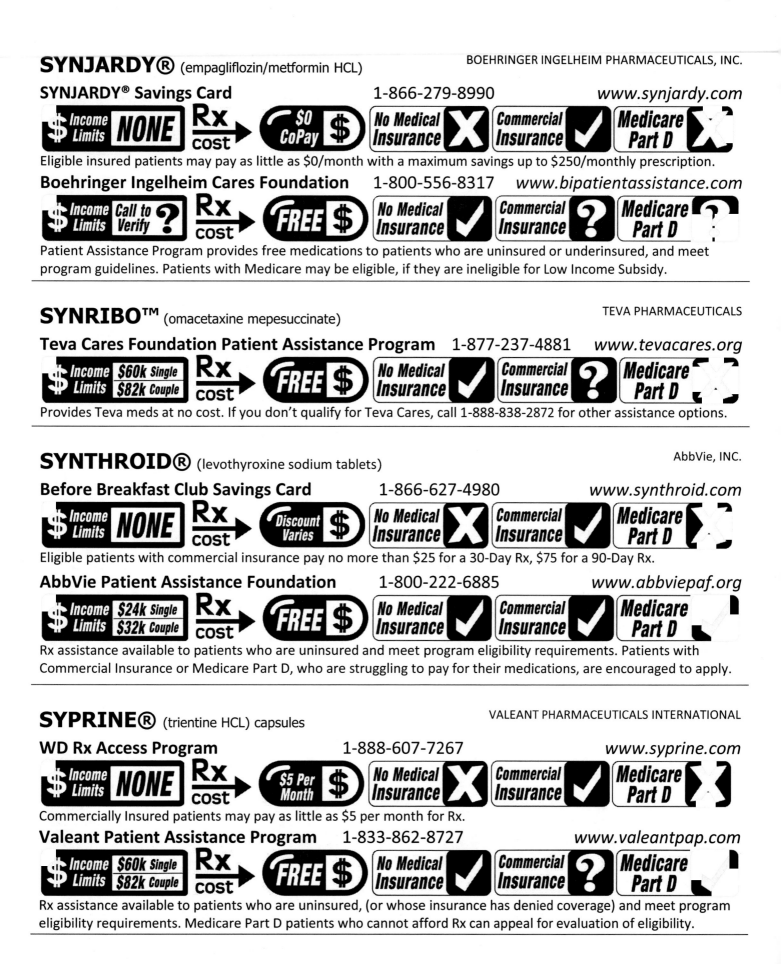

Income Limits: NONE · **Rx cost:** $0 CoPay · **No Medical Insurance:** X · **Commercial Insurance:** ✓ · **Medicare Part D:** X

Eligible insured patients may pay as little as $0/month with a maximum savings up to $250/monthly prescription.

Boehringer Ingelheim Cares Foundation
1-800-556-8317 · www.bipatientassistance.com

Income Limits: Call to Verify ? · **Rx cost:** FREE · **No Medical Insurance:** ✓ · **Commercial Insurance:** ? · **Medicare Part D:** ?

Patient Assistance Program provides free medications to patients who are uninsured or underinsured, and meet program guidelines. Patients with Medicare may be eligible, if they are ineligible for Low Income Subsidy.

SYNRIBO™ (omacetaxine mepesuccinate)
TEVA PHARMACEUTICALS

Teva Cares Foundation Patient Assistance Program
1-877-237-4881 · www.tevacares.org

Income Limits: $60k Single / $82k Couple · **Rx cost:** FREE · **No Medical Insurance:** ✓ · **Commercial Insurance:** ? · **Medicare Part D:** X

Provides Teva meds at no cost. If you don't qualify for Teva Cares, call 1-888-838-2872 for other assistance options.

SYNTHROID® (levothyroxine sodium tablets)
AbbVie, INC.

Before Breakfast Club Savings Card
1-866-627-4980 · www.synthroid.com

Income Limits: NONE · **Rx cost:** Discount Varies · **No Medical Insurance:** X · **Commercial Insurance:** ✓ · **Medicare Part D:** X

Eligible patients with commercial insurance pay no more than $25 for a 30-Day Rx, $75 for a 90-Day Rx.

AbbVie Patient Assistance Foundation
1-800-222-6885 · www.abbviepaf.org

Income Limits: $24k Single / $32k Couple · **Rx cost:** FREE · **No Medical Insurance:** ✓ · **Commercial Insurance:** ✓ · **Medicare Part D:** ✓

Rx assistance available to patients who are uninsured and meet program eligibility requirements. Patients with Commercial Insurance or Medicare Part D, who are struggling to pay for their medications, are encouraged to apply.

SYPRINE® (trientine HCL) capsules
VALEANT PHARMACEUTICALS INTERNATIONAL

WD Rx Access Program
1-888-607-7267 · www.syprine.com

Income Limits: NONE · **Rx cost:** $5 Per Month · **No Medical Insurance:** X · **Commercial Insurance:** ✓ · **Medicare Part D:** X

Commercially Insured patients may pay as little as $5 per month for Rx.

Valeant Patient Assistance Program
1-833-862-8727 · www.valeantpap.com

Income Limits: $60k Single / $82k Couple · **Rx cost:** FREE · **No Medical Insurance:** ✓ · **Commercial Insurance:** ? · **Medicare Part D:** ✓

Rx assistance available to patients who are uninsured, (or whose insurance has denied coverage) and meet program eligibility requirements. Medicare Part D patients who cannot afford Rx can appeal for evaluation of eligibility.

TACLONEX® (calcipotriene/betamethasone/dipropionate)

LEO PHARMA, INC.

LEO Pharma® CONNECT Co-Pay Savings Card   1-855-820-9627   *www.taclonex.com*

| $ Income Limits **NONE** | **Rx** cost → | $20 Per Month $ | No Medical Insurance ✓ | Commercial Insurance ✓ | Medicare Part D ✗ |

Most commercially insured patients pay as little as $20/month. Uninsured patients receive $250 off of cash price.

tacrolimus → ASTAGRAF® XL

tacrolimus → ENVARSUS XR®

tacrolimus → PROGRAF®

tadalafil → ADCIRCA®

tadalafil → CIALIS®

tafluprost ophthalmic solution → ZIOPTAN®

TAFINLAR® (dabrafenib)

NOVARTIS PHARMACEUTICALS

Universal Co-Pay Card   1-877-577-7756   *www.copay.novartisoncology.com*

| $ Income Limits **NONE** | **Rx** cost → | $25 $ | No Medical Insurance ✗ | Commercial Insurance ✓ | Medicare Part D ✗ |

Patients pay the first $25, the program pays the remaining co-pay or coinsurance to max benefit of $15,000/year.

Novartis Patient Assistance Foundation   1-800-277-2254   *www.pap.novartis.com*

| $ Income Limits $75k Single $100k Couple | **Rx** cost → | FREE $ | No Medical Insurance ✓ | Commercial Insurance ? | Medicare Part D ? |

Program assists those without insurance, or with limited/inadequate Rx coverage to receive prescribed medications.

TAGRISSO® Tablets (osimertinib)

ASTRAZENECA PHARMACEUTICALS

AZ&ME™   1-800-292-6363   *www.azandmeapp.com*

| $ Income Limits $36k Single $48k Couple | **Rx** cost → | FREE $ | No Medical Insurance ✓ | Commercial Insurance ✗ | Medicare Part D ? |

Program provides free medications to patients who are uninsured and meet program guidelines. Patients with Medicare may be eligible, if they are not eligible for (or enrolled in) Limited Income Subsidy (LIS), and have spent at least 3% of their annual household income on Rx medications through their Medicare Part D plan in the current year.

talcapone tablets → TASMAR®

taliglucerase alfa → ELELYSO®

talimogene laherparepvec → IMLYGIC®

TALTZ® (ixekizumab)

LILLY USA, LLC

TALTZ Savings Card   1-844-825-8966   *www.taltz.com*

| $ Income Limits | NONE | Rx cost → | $5 Per Month $ | No Medical Insurance ✗ | Commercial Insurance ✓ | Medicare Part D ✗ |

Provides co-pay assistance to eligible insured patients, up to $16,000/year max benefit, pay as little as $5 per month.

Lilly Cares   1-800-545-6962   *www.lillycares.com*

| $ Income Limits | $60k Single $82k Couple | Rx cost → | FREE $ | No Medical Insurance ✓ | Commercial Insurance ? | Medicare Part D |

Provides free Lilly medications for eligible patients who are uninsured and cannot afford their medications, or for those whose insurance has denied coverage. Medicare Part D patients may also be eligible for assistance.

tapentadol → NUCYNTA® / NUCYNTA® ER

TARCEVA® (erlotinib)

GENENTECH, INC.

Co-pay Card Assistance Program   1-855-692-6729   *www.copayassistancenow.com*

| $ Income Limits | NONE | Rx cost → | $5 Per Month $ | No Medical Insurance ✗ | Commercial Insurance ✓ | Medicare Part D ✗ |

Program provides up to $25,000/year in co-pay assistance. Patients pay only $5/month for their prescribed meds.

Genentech Access Solutions   1-866-422-2377   *www.genentech-access.com*

| $ Income Limits | $100K Household | Rx cost → | FREE $ | No Medical Insurance ✓ | Commercial Insurance ? | Medicare Part D ? |

Program provides medications to patients who are uninsured or have been denied coverage by their insurance company. Patients who have insurance, but pay too much out of pocket per year, may also qualify for assistance.

TARGRETIN® (bexarotene) Capsules/Gel 1%

VALEANT PHARMACEUTICALS INTERNATIONAL

Targretin® $0 CoPay Savings Program   1-888-201-1385   *www.targretin.com*

| $ Income Limits | NONE | Rx cost → | $0 CoPay $ | No Medical Insurance ✗ | Commercial Insurance ✓ | Medicare Part D ✗ |

Eligible commercially insured patients may pay as little as $0 for their Targretin Rx.

TARGRETIN® (bexarotene) Capsules/Gel 1%

Valeant Patient Assistance Program   1-833-862-8727   *www.valeantpap.com*

Income Limits $60k Single / $82k Couple — Rx cost → FREE $ — No Medical Insurance ✔ — Commercial Insurance ? — Medicare Part D ✔

Rx assistance available to patients who are uninsured, (or whose insurance has denied coverage) and meet program eligibility requirements. Medicare Part D patients who cannot afford Rx can appeal for evaluation of eligibility.

TASIGNA® (nilotinib)

Universal Co-Pay Card   1-877-577-7756   *www.copay.novartisoncology.com*

Income Limits NONE — Rx cost → $25 $ — No Medical Insurance ✘ — Commercial Insurance ✔ — Medicare Part D ✘

Patients pay the first $25, the program pays the remaining co-pay or coinsurance to max benefit of $15,000/year.

Novartis Patient Assistance Foundation   1-800-277-2254   *www.pap.novartis.com*

Income Limits $75k Single / $100k Couple — Rx cost → FREE $ — No Medical Insurance ✔ — Commercial Insurance ? — Medicare Part D ?

Program assists those without insurance, or with limited/inadequate Rx coverage to receive prescribed medications.

tasimelteon → HETLIOZ®

TASMAR® (talcapone) tablets

Valeant Patient Assistance Program   1-833-862-8727   *www.valeantpap.com*

Income Limits $36k Single / $49k Couple — Rx cost → FREE $ — No Medical Insurance ✔ — Commercial Insurance ? — Medicare Part D ✔

Rx assistance available to patients who are uninsured, (or whose insurance has denied coverage) and meet program eligibility requirements. Medicare Part D patients who cannot afford Rx can appeal for evaluation of eligibility.

TAVALISSE® (fostamatinib disodium hexahydrate)

Tavalisse Co-pay Assistance   1-833-744-3562   *www.tavalissecopay.com*

Income Limits NONE — Rx cost → $15 $ — No Medical Insurance ✘ — Commercial Insurance ✔ — Medicare Part D ✘

Patients pay first $15 of Rx, program assists with remaining out-of-pocket/co-pay costs, max savings $15,000/year.

Regel OneCare   1-833-744-3562   *www.tavalisse.com*

Income Limits Call to Verify ? — Rx cost → FREE $ — No Medical Insurance ✔ — Commercial Insurance ? — Medicare Part D ✘

Provides free meds to eligible patients who are uninsured, or where insurance coverage is delayed.

TAZORAC® Gel/Cream 0.05%/0.1% (tazarotene)

Allergan Patient Assistance Program   1-844-424-6727   *www.allergan.com*

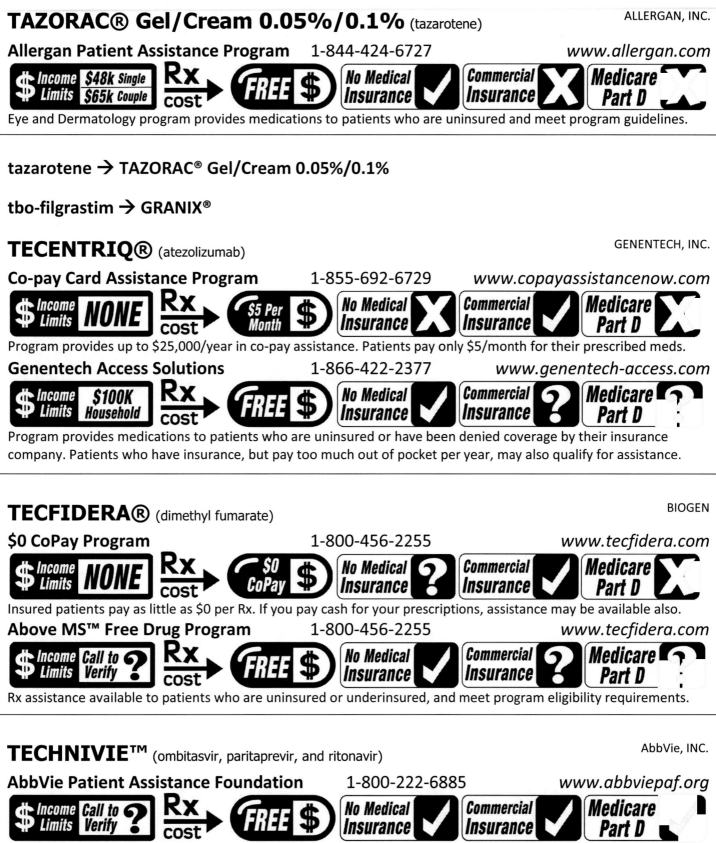

| $ Income Limits $48k Single / $65k Couple | Rx cost → | FREE $ | No Medical Insurance ✓ | Commercial Insurance ✗ | Medicare Part D ✗ |

Eye and Dermatology program provides medications to patients who are uninsured and meet program guidelines.

---

tazarotene → TAZORAC® Gel/Cream 0.05%/0.1%

tbo-filgrastim → GRANIX®

TECENTRIQ® (atezolizumab)

GENENTECH, INC.

Co-pay Card Assistance Program   1-855-692-6729   *www.copayassistancenow.com*

| $ Income Limits NONE | Rx cost → | $5 Per Month $ | No Medical Insurance ✗ | Commercial Insurance ✓ | Medicare Part D ✗ |

Program provides up to $25,000/year in co-pay assistance. Patients pay only $5/month for their prescribed meds.

Genentech Access Solutions   1-866-422-2377   *www.genentech-access.com*

| $ Income Limits $100K Household | Rx cost → | FREE $ | No Medical Insurance ✓ | Commercial Insurance ? | Medicare Part D ? |

Program provides medications to patients who are uninsured or have been denied coverage by their insurance company. Patients who have insurance, but pay too much out of pocket per year, may also qualify for assistance.

TECFIDERA® (dimethyl fumarate)

BIOGEN

$0 CoPay Program   1-800-456-2255   *www.tecfidera.com*

| $ Income Limits NONE | Rx cost → | $0 CoPay $ | No Medical Insurance ? | Commercial Insurance ✓ | Medicare Part D ✗ |

Insured patients pay as little as $0 per Rx. If you pay cash for your prescriptions, assistance may be available also.

Above MS™ Free Drug Program   1-800-456-2255   *www.tecfidera.com*

| $ Income Limits Call to Verify ? | Rx cost → | FREE $ | No Medical Insurance ✓ | Commercial Insurance ? | Medicare Part D ? |

Rx assistance available to patients who are uninsured or underinsured, and meet program eligibility requirements.

TECHNIVIE™ (ombitasvir, paritaprevir, and ritonavir)

AbbVie, INC.

AbbVie Patient Assistance Foundation   1-800-222-6885   *www.abbviepaf.org*

| $ Income Limits Call to Verify ? | Rx cost → | FREE $ | No Medical Insurance ✓ | Commercial Insurance ✓ | Medicare Part D ✓ |

Rx assistance available to patients who are uninsured and meet program eligibility requirements. Patients with Commercial Insurance or Medicare Part D, who are struggling to pay for their medications, are encouraged to apply.

tedizolid phosphate → SIVEXTRO®

teduglutide → GATTEX®

TEFLARO® (ceftaroline fosamil for injection)   ALLERGAN, INC.

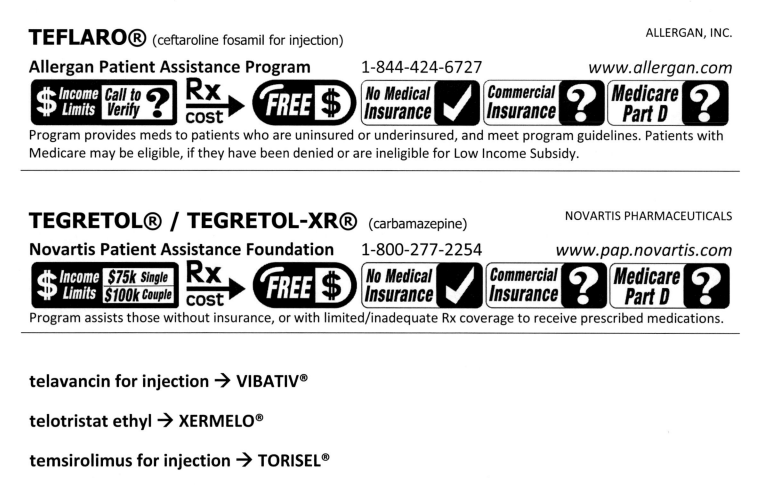

Allergan Patient Assistance Program   1-844-424-6727   *www.allergan.com*

Program provides meds to patients who are uninsured or underinsured, and meet program guidelines. Patients with Medicare may be eligible, if they have been denied or are ineligible for Low Income Subsidy.

TEGRETOL® / TEGRETOL-XR® (carbamazepine)   NOVARTIS PHARMACEUTICALS

Novartis Patient Assistance Foundation   1-800-277-2254   *www.pap.novartis.com*

Program assists those without insurance, or with limited/inadequate Rx coverage to receive prescribed medications.

telavancin for injection → VIBATIV®

telotristat ethyl → XERMELO®

temsirolimus for injection → TORISEL®

tenofovir alafenamide → VEMLIDY®

teriflunomide → AUBAGIO®

teriparatide → FORTEO®

TESSALON® (benzonatate)   PFIZER, INC

Pfizer Savings Program   1-866-706-2400   *www.pfizerrxpathways.com*

Program helps uninsured patients receive discounted Pfizer medications through their local retail pharmacy.

testosterone cypionate → DEPO®-TESTOSTERONE

testosterone gel 1.62%→ ANDROGEL®

testosterone undecanoate injection → AVEED®

tetrabenazine → XENAZINE®

tezacaftor/ivacaftor and ivacaftor → SYMDEKO™

thalidomide → THALOMID®

THALOMID® (thalidomide)   CELGENE CORPORATION

Celgene Co-Pay Assistance Program   1-800-931-8691   *www.celgenepatientsupport.com*

Program can provide up to $10,000/year in Deductible/Co-Pay Assistance, making your Rx cost $25/month or less.

Celgene Patient Assistance Program   1-800-931-8691   *www.celgenepatientsupport.com*

Rx assistance available to patients who are uninsured or underinsured, and meet program eligibility requirements.

THYROGEN® (thyrotropin alfa)   GENZYME CORPORATION

Thyrogen Copay Assistance Program   1-888-497-6436   *www.thyrogen.com*

Commercially insured patients pay as little as $0 copay for their Thyrogen Rx, maximum assistance $1000/year.

Thyrogen Patient Assistance Program   1-888-497-6436   *www.thyrogen.com*

Program provides medications to patients who are uninsured or have inadequate insurance coverage for Thyrogen

thyrotropin alfa → THYROGEN®

tiagabine HCL → GABITRIL®

ticagrelor → BRILINTA®

tigecycline for injection → TYGACIL®

TIKOSYN® (dofetilide)

PFIZER, INC

Pfizer Savings Program   1-866-706-2400   *www.pfizerrxpathways.com*

| $ Income Limits | NONE | Rx cost → | Discount Varies $ | No Medical Insurance ✓ | Commercial Insurance ✗ | Medicare Part D ✗ |

Program helps uninsured patients receive discounted Pfizer medications through their local retail pharmacy.

Tikosyn Co-Pay Savings Card   1-877-845-6769   *www.tikosyn.com*

| $ Income Limits | NONE | Rx cost → | $4 Per Month $ | No Medical Insurance ✓ | Commercial Insurance ✓ | Medicare Part D ✗ |

Eligible patients pay as little as $4 per month for Rx, maximum savings $3000/year..

Pfizer Patient Assistance Program   1-844-989-7284   *www.pfizerrxpathways.com*

| $ Income Limits $48k Single / $65k Couple | Rx cost → | FREE $ | No Medical Insurance ✓ | Commercial Insurance ? | Medicare Part D ✗ |

Assists eligible patients who are uninsured (or have inadequate drug coverage) and cannot afford their medications.

timolol ophthalmic solution → BETIMOL®

timolol maleate → TIMOPTIC® in OCCUDOSE®

TIMOPTIC® in OCCUDOSE® (timolol maleate)

VALEANT PHARMACEUTICALS INTERNATIONAL

Valeant Patient Assistance Program   1-833-862-8727   *www.valeantpap.com*

| $ Income Limits $36k Single / $49k Couple | Rx cost → | FREE $ | No Medical Insurance ✓ | Commercial Insurance ? | Medicare Part D ✓ |

Rx assistance available to patients who are uninsured, (or whose insurance has denied coverage) and meet program eligibility requirements. Medicare Part D patients who cannot afford Rx can appeal for evaluation of eligibility.

tiotropium bromide → SPIRIVA® RESPIMAT®

tiotropium bromide inhalation powder → SPIRIVA® HANDIHALER®

tiotropium bromide and olodaterol → STIOLTO® RESPIMAT®

tipranavir → APTIVUS®

> 💡 **TIP:** Income limits are higher for households with three or more people. Call programs for details.

TIROSINT® (levothyroxine sodium)
AKRIMAX PHARMACEUTICALS

Co-Pay Assistance Card Program
1-866-264-0564   www.tirosint.com

$ Income Limits **NONE** | Rx cost → $35 $ | No Medical Insurance ✔ | Commercial Insurance ✔ | Medicare Part D ✘

Patients pay the first $35, card covers next $35 towards Tirosint Rx costs.

Akrimax Patient Assistance Program
1-855-856-6915   www.akrimaxpap.com

$ Income Limits **$24k Single / $32k Couple** | Rx cost → FREE $ | No Medical Insurance ✔ | Commercial Insurance ✘ | Medicare Part D ✘

Program provides Akrimax brand name medications free of charge, to individuals who meet eligibility requirements.

TIVICAY® (dolutegravir)
ViiV HEALTHCARE

ViiVConnect Savings Card
1-844-588-3288

$ Income Limits **NONE** | Rx cost → $0 CoPay $ | No Medical Insurance ✔ | Commercial Insurance ✔ | Medicare Part D ✘ | www.viivconnect.com

Patients can pay as little as $0 copay, maximum savings $7500/year.

ViiV Healthcare Patient Assistance Program
1-844-588-3288   www.viivconnect.com

$ Income Limits **$60k Single / $82k Couple** | Rx cost → FREE $ | No Medical Insurance ✔ | Commercial Insurance ? | Medicare Part D ✘

Gives meds to patients who are uninsured, lack coverage, or on Medicare and have spent $600 on Rx meds this year.

TOBI® (tobramycin inhalation solution)
NOVARTIS PHARMACEUTICALS

Co-Pay Savings Card
1-844-685-3406   www.copay.novartispharma.com

$ Income Limits **NONE** | Rx cost → $4 $ | No Medical Insurance ✘ | Commercial Insurance ✔ | Medicare Part D ✘

Insured patients pay as little as $4 per Rx, maximum total co-pay benefit of $14,000 per year.

Novartis Patient Assistance Foundation
1-800-277-2254   www.pap.novartis.com

$ Income Limits **$75k Single / $100k Couple** | Rx cost → FREE $ | No Medical Insurance ✔ | Commercial Insurance ? | Medicare Part D ✘

Program assists those without insurance, or with limited/inadequate Rx coverage to receive prescribed medications.

TOBI® Podhaler® (tobramycin inhalation powder)
NOVARTIS PHARMACEUTICALS

Co-Pay Savings Card
1-877-999-8624   www.copay.novartispharma.com

$ Income Limits **NONE** | Rx cost → $0 CoPay $ | No Medical Insurance ✘ | Commercial Insurance ✔ | Medicare Part D ✘

Insured patients pay as little as $0 per Rx, maximum total co-pay benefit of $14,000 per year.

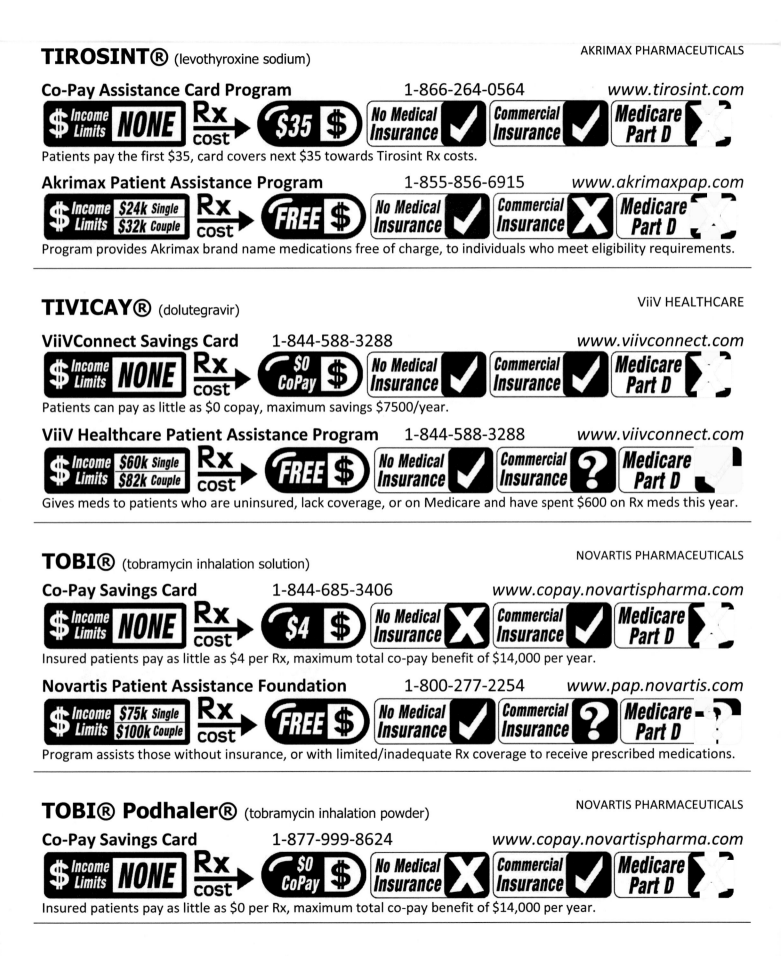

TOBI® Podhaler® (tobramycin inhalation powder)

NOVARTIS PHARMACEUTICALS

Novartis Patient Assistance Foundation   1-800-277-2254   *www.pap.novartis.com*

Program assists those without insurance, or with limited/inadequate Rx coverage to receive prescribed medications.

TOBRADEX®/TOBRADEX® ST (tobramycin/dexamethasone)

NOVARTIS PHARMACEUTICALS

Novartis Patient Assistance Foundation   1-800-277-2254   *www.pap.novartis.com*

Program assists those without insurance, or with limited/inadequate Rx coverage to receive prescribed medications.

tobramycin inhalation powder → TOBI® Podhaler®

tobramycin inhalation solution → BETHKIS®

tobramycin inhalation solution → TOBI®

tobramycin/dexamethasone → TOBRADEX®/TOBRADEX® ST

tocilizumab → ACTEMRA®

tofacitinib → XELJANZ® / XELJANZ XR®

TOFRANIL™ (imipramine pamoate)

MALLINCKRODT PHARMACEUTICALS

Mallinckrodt Patient Assistance Program   1-800-259-7765   *www.mallinckrodt.com*

Program for uninsured patients who may not be able to afford their Mallinckrodt medications, call for application.

topiramate → TROKENDI XR®

tolterodine tartrate → DETROL® /DETROL® LA

topotecan → HYCAMTIN® Capsules

topotecan hydrochloride → HYCAMTIN® for Injection

toremifene citrate → FARESTON®

TORISEL® (temsirolimus for injection)

PFIZER, INC

Pfizer Patient Assistance Program   1-877-744-5675   *www.pfizeroncologytogether.com*

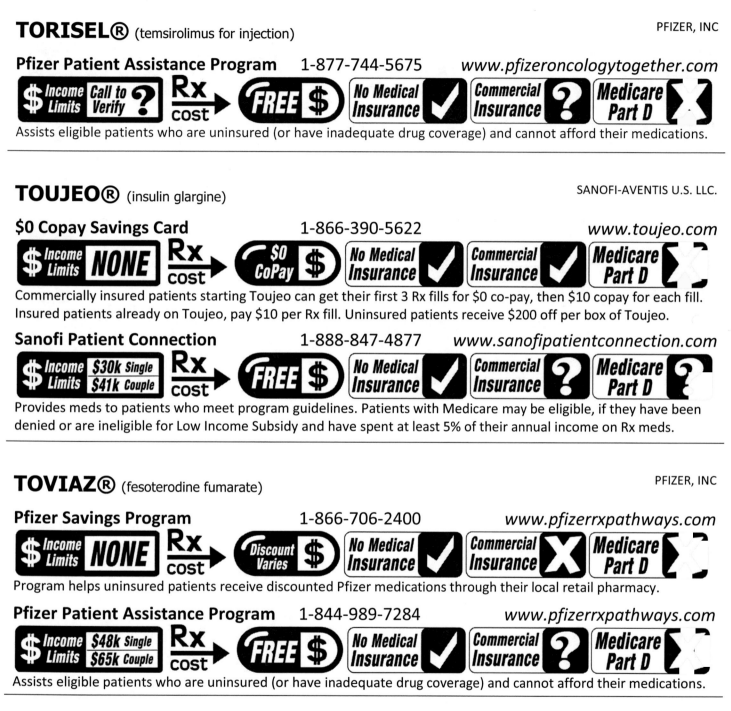

Assists eligible patients who are uninsured (or have inadequate drug coverage) and cannot afford their medications.

TOUJEO® (insulin glargine)

SANOFI-AVENTIS U.S. LLC.

$0 Copay Savings Card   1-866-390-5622   *www.toujeo.com*

Commercially insured patients starting Toujeo can get their first 3 Rx fills for $0 co-pay, then $10 copay for each fill. Insured patients already on Toujeo, pay $10 per Rx fill. Uninsured patients receive $200 off per box of Toujeo.

Sanofi Patient Connection   1-888-847-4877   *www.sanofipatientconnection.com*

Provides meds to patients who meet program guidelines. Patients with Medicare may be eligible, if they have been denied or are ineligible for Low Income Subsidy and have spent at least 5% of their annual income on Rx meds.

TOVIAZ® (fesoterodine fumarate)

PFIZER, INC

Pfizer Savings Program   1-866-706-2400   *www.pfizerrxpathways.com*

Program helps uninsured patients receive discounted Pfizer medications through their local retail pharmacy.

Pfizer Patient Assistance Program   1-844-989-7284   *www.pfizerrxpathways.com*

Assists eligible patients who are uninsured (or have inadequate drug coverage) and cannot afford their medications.

trabectedin → YONDELIS®

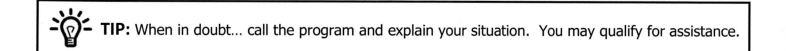

TIP: When in doubt... call the program and explain your situation. You may qualify for assistance.

TRACLEER® (bosentan)

ACTELION PHARMACEUTICALS, INC.

Actelion Oral PAH Therapy

Co-Pay Program   1-866-228-3546   *www.actelionpathways.com*

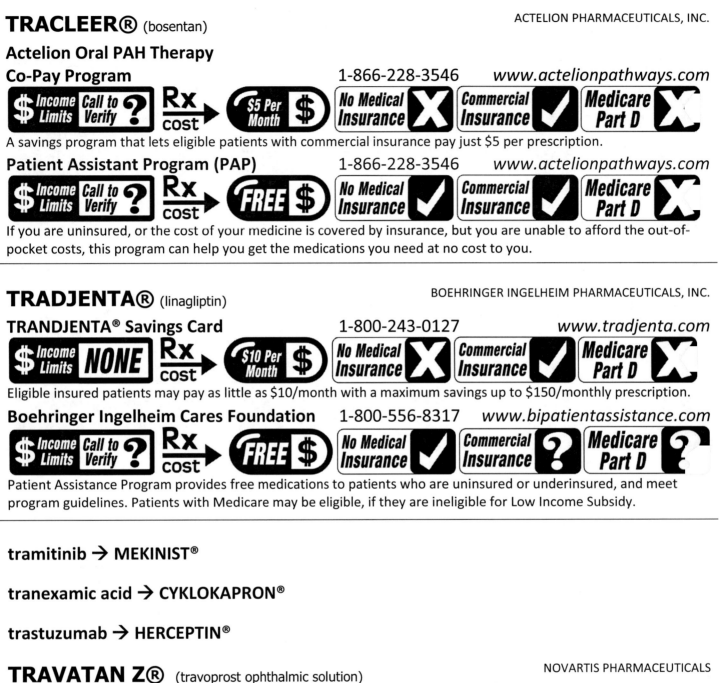

A savings program that lets eligible patients with commercial insurance pay just $5 per prescription.

Patient Assistant Program (PAP)   1-866-228-3546   *www.actelionpathways.com*

If you are uninsured, or the cost of your medicine is covered by insurance, but you are unable to afford the out-of-pocket costs, this program can help you get the medications you need at no cost to you.

TRADJENTA® (linagliptin)

BOEHRINGER INGELHEIM PHARMACEUTICALS, INC.

TRANDJENTA® Savings Card   1-800-243-0127   *www.tradjenta.com*

Eligible insured patients may pay as little as $10/month with a maximum savings up to $150/monthly prescription.

Boehringer Ingelheim Cares Foundation   1-800-556-8317   *www.bipatientassistance.com*

Patient Assistance Program provides free medications to patients who are uninsured or underinsured, and meet program guidelines. Patients with Medicare may be eligible, if they are ineligible for Low Income Subsidy.

tramitinib → MEKINIST®

tranexamic acid → CYKLOKAPRON®

trastuzumab → HERCEPTIN®

TRAVATAN Z® (travoprost ophthalmic solution)

NOVARTIS PHARMACEUTICALS

OPENINGS® Program Savings Card   1-866-972-3008   *www.copay.novartispharma.com*

Insured patients pay as little as $30, the program pays the remaining Rx co-pay with max benefit of $2,000/year.

Novartis Patient Assistance Foundation   1-800-277-2254   *www.pap.novartis.com*

Program assists those without insurance, or with limited/inadequate Rx coverage to receive prescribed medications.

travoprost ophthalmic solution → TRAVATAN Z®

TRAXENE® (clorazepate dipotassium)

RECORDATI RARE DISEASES, INC.

Patient Support Program   1-866-209-7604   *www.recordatiraredieseases.com*

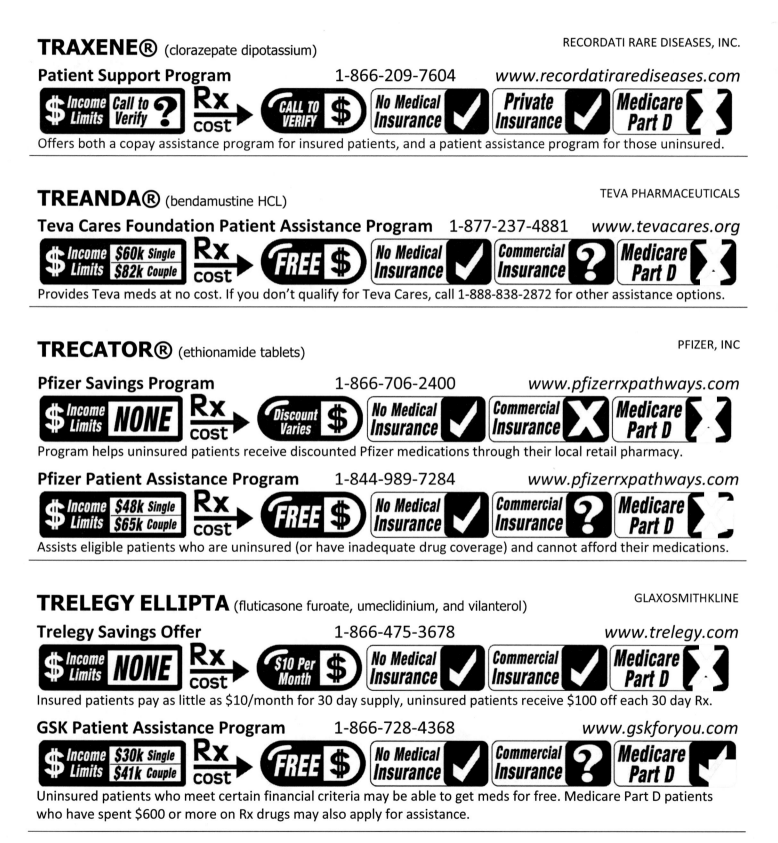

$ Income Limits | Call to Verify **?**   **Rx cost** →   CALL TO VERIFY **$**   **No Medical Insurance** ✓   **Private Insurance** ✓   **Medicare Part D** ✗

Offers both a copay assistance program for insured patients, and a patient assistance program for those uninsured.

TREANDA® (bendamustine HCL)

TEVA PHARMACEUTICALS

Teva Cares Foundation Patient Assistance Program   1-877-237-4881   *www.tevacares.org*

$ Income Limits | $60k Single / $82k Couple   **Rx cost** →   FREE **$**   **No Medical Insurance** ✓   **Commercial Insurance ?**   **Medicare Part D** ✗

Provides Teva meds at no cost. If you don't qualify for Teva Cares, call 1-888-838-2872 for other assistance options.

TRECATOR® (ethionamide tablets)

PFIZER, INC

Pfizer Savings Program   1-866-706-2400   *www.pfizerrxpathways.com*

$ Income Limits | NONE   **Rx cost** →   Discount Varies **$**   **No Medical Insurance** ✓   **Commercial Insurance** ✗   **Medicare Part D** ✗

Program helps uninsured patients receive discounted Pfizer medications through their local retail pharmacy.

Pfizer Patient Assistance Program   1-844-989-7284   *www.pfizerrxpathways.com*

$ Income Limits | $48k Single / $65k Couple   **Rx cost** →   FREE **$**   **No Medical Insurance** ✓   **Commercial Insurance ?**   **Medicare Part D** ✗

Assists eligible patients who are uninsured (or have inadequate drug coverage) and cannot afford their medications.

TRELEGY ELLIPTA (fluticasone furoate, umeclidinium, and vilanterol)

GLAXOSMITHKLINE

Trelegy Savings Offer   1-866-475-3678   *www.trelegy.com*

$ Income Limits | NONE   **Rx cost** → $10 Per Month **$**   **No Medical Insurance** ✓   **Commercial Insurance** ✓   **Medicare Part D** ✗

Insured patients pay as little as $10/month for 30 day supply, uninsured patients receive $100 off each 30 day Rx.

GSK Patient Assistance Program   1-866-728-4368   *www.gskforyou.com*

$ Income Limits | $30k Single / $41k Couple   **Rx cost** →   FREE **$**   **No Medical Insurance** ✓   **Commercial Insurance ?**   **Medicare Part D** ✓

Uninsured patients who meet certain financial criteria may be able to get meds for free. Medicare Part D patients who have spent $600 or more on Rx drugs may also apply for assistance.

TRELSTAR® (triptorelin pamoate injectable suspension)

ALLERGAN, INC.

Allergan Patient Assistance Program   1-844-424-6727   *www.allergan.com*

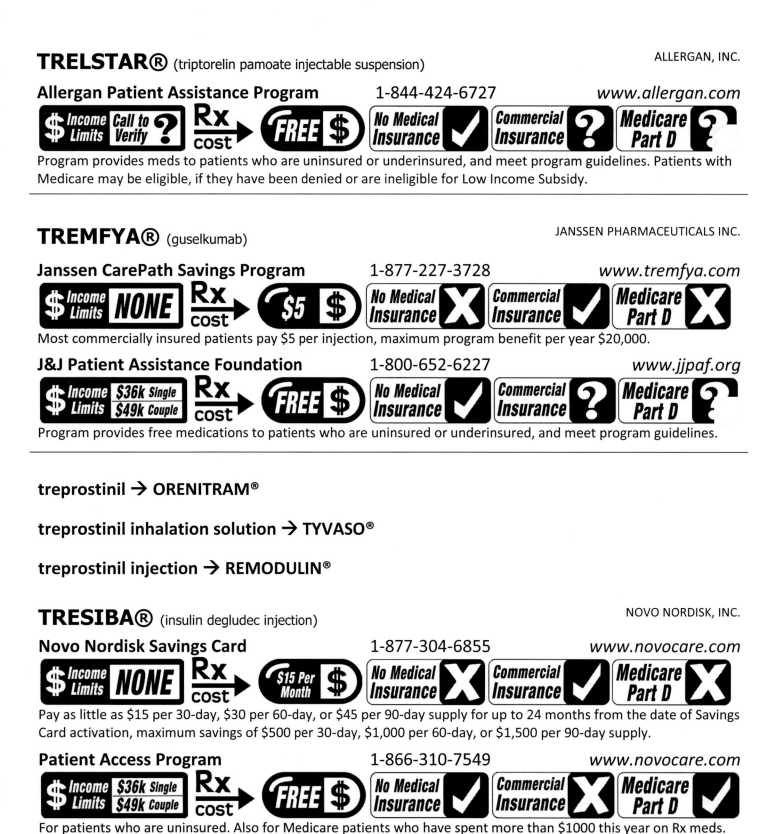

Program provides meds to patients who are uninsured or underinsured, and meet program guidelines. Patients with Medicare may be eligible, if they have been denied or are ineligible for Low Income Subsidy.

TREMFYA® (guselkumab)

JANSSEN PHARMACEUTICALS INC.

Janssen CarePath Savings Program   1-877-227-3728   *www.tremfya.com*

Most commercially insured patients pay $5 per injection, maximum program benefit per year $20,000.

J&J Patient Assistance Foundation   1-800-652-6227   *www.jjpaf.org*

Program provides free medications to patients who are uninsured or underinsured, and meet program guidelines.

treprostinil → ORENITRAM®

treprostinil inhalation solution → TYVASO®

treprostinil injection → REMODULIN®

TRESIBA® (insulin degludec injection)

NOVO NORDISK, INC.

Novo Nordisk Savings Card   1-877-304-6855   *www.novocare.com*

Pay as little as $15 per 30-day, $30 per 60-day, or $45 per 90-day supply for up to 24 months from the date of Savings Card activation, maximum savings of $500 per 30-day, $1,000 per 60-day, or $1,500 per 90-day supply.

Patient Access Program   1-866-310-7549   *www.novocare.com*

For patients who are uninsured. Also for Medicare patients who have spent more than $1000 this year on Rx meds.

TIP: Income limits are higher for households with three or more people. Call programs for details.

tretinoin cream 0.02%→ RENOVA®

tretinoin gel→ RETIN-A MICRO®

TRETTEN® (coagulation factor XIII A-Subunit [rDNA])   NOVO NORDISK, INC.

Co-Pay Assistance Program   1-844-668-6732   *www.tretten.com*

$ Income Limits **NONE** | **Rx** cost → | CALL TO VERIFY $ | No Medical Insurance ✗ | Commercial Insurance ✓ | Medicare Part D ✗

Enrolled patients are eligible for up to $12,000 in co-pay/coinsurance assistance per calendar year for each NNI hemophilia or rare bleeding disorder product. Assistance is retroactive to 60 days.

NovoSecure™ Program   1-844-668-6732   *www.mynovosecure.com*

$ Income Limits $36k Single $49k Couple | **Rx** cost → | FREE $ | No Medical Insurance ✓ | Commercial Insurance ✗ | Medicare Part D ✓

For patients who are uninsured. Also for Medicare patients who have spent more than $1000 this year on Rx meds.

TREXIMET® (sumatriptan/naproxen sodium)   PERNIX THERAPUETICS

Treximet Savings Card   1-855-830-9254   *www.treximet.com*

$ Income Limits **NONE** | **Rx** cost → | $25 $ | No Medical Insurance ✓ | Commercial Insurance ✓ | Medicare Part D ✗

Patients pay as little as $25 when filling Treximet Rx and using savings card.

triamcinolone acetonide injectable suspension → TRIESENCE®

triazolam → HALCION®

TRIBENZOR® (olmesartan medoxomil /amlodipine /hydrocholorothiazide)   DAIICHI SANKYO, INC.

Pre-activated Savings Card   1-877-264-2440   *www.tribenzor.com*

$ Income Limits **NONE** | **Rx** cost → | $5 Per Month $ | No Medical Insurance ✓ | Commercial Insurance ✓ | Medicare Part D ✗

Insured patients pay as low as $5 per 30-day supply ($15 per 90-day supply). Cash patients get $25 off retail Rx cost.

Open Care Program   1-866-268-7327   *www.dsi.com*

$ Income Limits $24k Single $32k Couple | **Rx** cost → | FREE $ | No Medical Insurance ✓ | Commercial Insurance ? | Medicare Part D ✗

Program provides free medications to patients who are uninsured or underinsured, and meet program guidelines.

trientine HCl capsules → SYPRINE®

TRIESENCE® (triamcinolone acetonide injectable suspension)

Novartis Patient Assistance Foundation   1-800-277-2254   *www.pap.novartis.com*

Income Limits $75k Single / $100k Couple | **Rx cost** → **FREE $** | **No Medical Insurance** ✓ | **Commercial Insurance** ? | **Medicare Part D** ?

Program assists those without insurance, or with limited/inadequate Rx coverage to receive prescribed medications.

---

trifluridine and tipiracil → LONSURF®

TRILEPTAL® (oxcarbazepine)

NOVARTIS PHARMACEUTICALS

Novartis Patient Assistance Foundation   1-800-277-2254   *www.pap.novartis.com*

Income Limits $75k Single / $100k Couple | **Rx cost** → **FREE $** | **No Medical Insurance** ✓ | **Commercial Insurance** ? | **Medicare Part D** ?

Program assists those without insurance, or with limited/inadequate Rx coverage to receive prescribed medications.

TRI-LUMA® (fluocinolone acetonide 0.01%/hydroquinone 4%/tretinoin 0.05%)

GALDERMA LABORATORIES

CareConnect Patient Savings Card   1-855-280-0543   *www.triluma.com*

Income Limits NONE | **Rx cost** → **$35 $** | **No Medical Insurance** ✓ | **Commercial Insurance** ✓ | **Medicare Part D** X

Insured patients pay as little a $35 for Rx, uninsured patients pay as little as $125.

---

triptorelin pamoate injectable suspension → TRELSTAR®

TRINTELLIX® (vortioxetine)

TAKEDA PHARMACEUTICALS AMERICA

Instant Savings Card   1-866-279-0287   *www.trintellix.com*

Income Limits NONE | **Rx cost** → **$10 $** | **No Medical Insurance** X | **Commercial Insurance** ✓ | **Medicare Part D** X

Eligible patients pay as little as $35 copay per Rx, maximum benefit of $100 for a 30-day Rx and $300 for 90-day Rx.

Takeda Patient Assistance Program   1-800-830-9159   *www.takedahelpathand.com*

Income Limits $60k Single / $82k Couple | **Rx cost** → **FREE $** | **No Medical Insurance** ✓ | **Commercial Insurance** ? | **Medicare Part D** ?

Provides Trintellix at no cost to eligible patients who do not have insurance or not enough coverage to obtain meds.

💡 **TIP:** When in doubt... call the program and explain your situation. You may qualify for assistance.

TRISENOX® (arsenic trioxide)

TEVA PHARMACEUTICALS

Teva Cares Foundation Patient Assistance Program   1-877-237-4881   *www.tevacares.org*

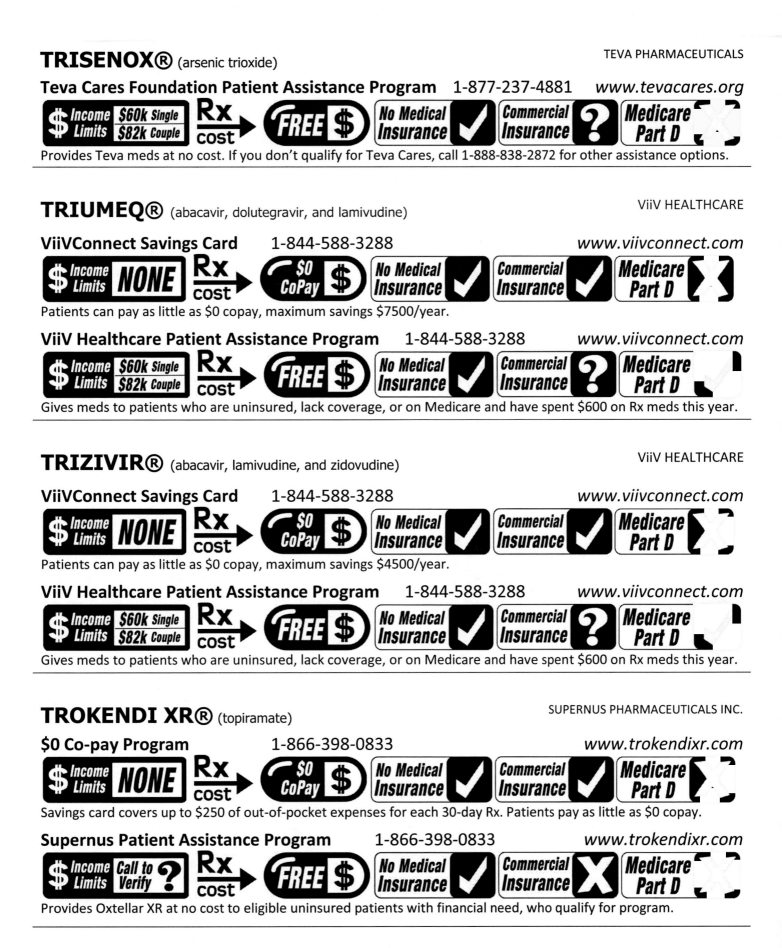

| $ Income Limits $60k Single / $82k Couple | Rx cost → | FREE $ | No Medical Insurance ✓ | Commercial Insurance ? | Medicare Part D ✗ |

Provides Teva meds at no cost. If you don't qualify for Teva Cares, call 1-888-838-2872 for other assistance options.

TRIUMEQ® (abacavir, dolutegravir, and lamivudine)

ViiV HEALTHCARE

ViiVConnect Savings Card   1-844-588-3288   *www.viivconnect.com*

| $ Income Limits NONE | Rx cost → | $0 CoPay $ | No Medical Insurance ✓ | Commercial Insurance ✓ | Medicare Part D ▷ |

Patients can pay as little as $0 copay, maximum savings $7500/year.

ViiV Healthcare Patient Assistance Program   1-844-588-3288   *www.viivconnect.com*

| $ Income Limits $60k Single / $82k Couple | Rx cost → | FREE $ | No Medical Insurance ✓ | Commercial Insurance ? | Medicare Part D ✓ |

Gives meds to patients who are uninsured, lack coverage, or on Medicare and have spent $600 on Rx meds this year.

TRIZIVIR® (abacavir, lamivudine, and zidovudine)

ViiV HEALTHCARE

ViiVConnect Savings Card   1-844-588-3288   *www.viivconnect.com*

| $ Income Limits NONE | Rx cost → | $0 CoPay $ | No Medical Insurance ✓ | Commercial Insurance ✓ | Medicare Part D ▷ |

Patients can pay as little as $0 copay, maximum savings $4500/year.

ViiV Healthcare Patient Assistance Program   1-844-588-3288   *www.viivconnect.com*

| $ Income Limits $60k Single / $82k Couple | Rx cost → | FREE $ | No Medical Insurance ✓ | Commercial Insurance ? | Medicare Part D ▮ |

Gives meds to patients who are uninsured, lack coverage, or on Medicare and have spent $600 on Rx meds this year.

TROKENDI XR® (topiramate)

SUPERNUS PHARMACEUTICALS INC.

$0 Co-pay Program   1-866-398-0833   *www.trokendixr.com*

| $ Income Limits NONE | Rx cost → | $0 CoPay $ | No Medical Insurance ✓ | Commercial Insurance ✓ | Medicare Part D ▷ |

Savings card covers up to $250 of out-of-pocket expenses for each 30-day Rx. Patients pay as little as $0 copay.

Supernus Patient Assistance Program   1-866-398-0833   *www.trokendixr.com*

| $ Income Limits Call to Verify ? | Rx cost → | FREE $ | No Medical Insurance ✓ | Commercial Insurance ✗ | Medicare Part D ✗ |

Provides Oxtellar XR at no cost to eligible uninsured patients with financial need, who qualify for program.

TRULICITY® (dulaglutide)

LILLY USA, LLC

TRULICITY Savings Card   1-844-878-4636   *www.trulicity.com*

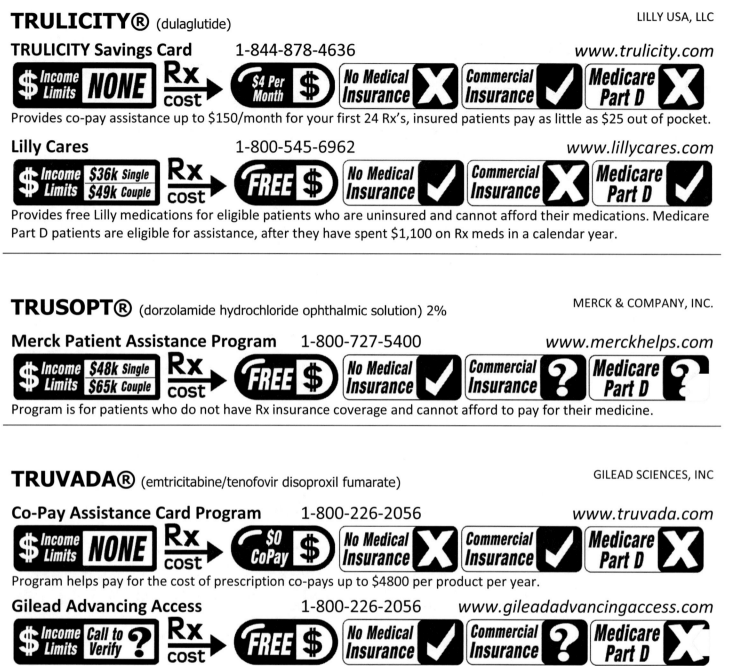

Income Limits NONE | **Rx cost** → **$4 Per Month $** | **No Medical Insurance** ✗ | **Commercial Insurance** ✓ | **Medicare Part D** ✗

Provides co-pay assistance up to $150/month for your first 24 Rx's, insured patients pay as little as $25 out of pocket.

Lilly Cares   1-800-545-6962   *www.lillycares.com*

Income Limits $36k Single $49k Couple | **Rx cost** → **FREE $** | **No Medical Insurance** ✓ | **Commercial Insurance** ✗ | **Medicare Part D** ✓

Provides free Lilly medications for eligible patients who are uninsured and cannot afford their medications. Medicare Part D patients are eligible for assistance, after they have spent $1,100 on Rx meds in a calendar year.

TRUSOPT® (dorzolamide hydrochloride ophthalmic solution) 2%

MERCK & COMPANY, INC.

Merck Patient Assistance Program   1-800-727-5400   *www.merckhelps.com*

Income Limits $48k Single $65k Couple | **Rx cost** → **FREE $** | **No Medical Insurance** ✓ | **Commercial Insurance** ? | **Medicare Part D** ?

Program is for patients who do not have Rx insurance coverage and cannot afford to pay for their medicine.

TRUVADA® (emtricitabine/tenofovir disoproxil fumarate)

GILEAD SCIENCES, INC

Co-Pay Assistance Card Program   1-800-226-2056   *www.truvada.com*

Income Limits NONE | **Rx cost** → **$0 CoPay $** | **No Medical Insurance** ✗ | **Commercial Insurance** ✓ | **Medicare Part D** ✗

Program helps pay for the cost of prescription co-pays up to $4800 per product per year.

Gilead Advancing Access   1-800-226-2056   *www.gileadadvancingaccess.com*

Income Limits Call to Verify ? | **Rx cost** → **FREE $** | **No Medical Insurance** ✓ | **Commercial Insurance** ? | **Medicare Part D** ✗

Patient assistance program provides medications at no charge for eligible patients with no other insurance options.

 TIP: Income limits are higher for households with three or more people. Call programs for details.

TUDORZA® Pressair® (aclidinium bromide inhalation powder)
ASTRAZENECA PHARMACEUTICALS

TUDORZA Pressair Savings Card   1-866-421-2848   *www.tudorza.com*

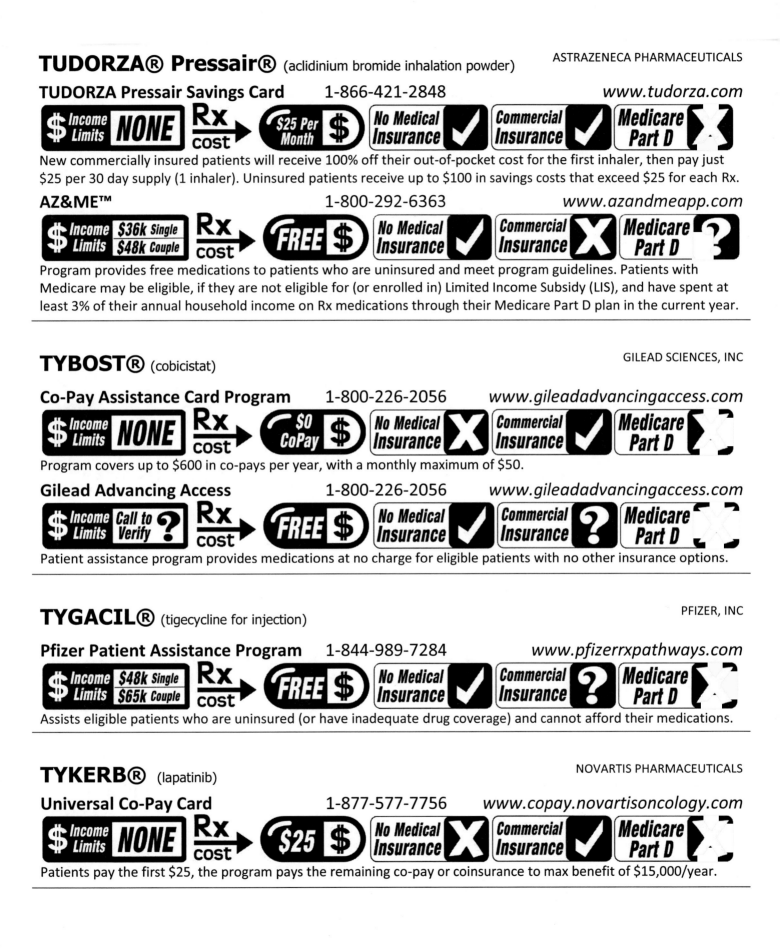

| $ Income Limits **NONE** | **Rx** cost → | **$25 Per Month** $ | **No Medical Insurance** ✔ | **Commercial Insurance** ✔ | **Medicare Part D** ✘ |

New commercially insured patients will receive 100% off their out-of-pocket cost for the first inhaler, then pay just $25 per 30 day supply (1 inhaler). Uninsured patients receive up to $100 in savings costs that exceed $25 for each Rx.

AZ&ME™   1-800-292-6363   *www.azandmeapp.com*

| $ Income Limits **$36k Single $48k Couple** | **Rx** cost → | **FREE** $ | **No Medical Insurance** ✔ | **Commercial Insurance** ✘ | **Medicare Part D** ? |

Program provides free medications to patients who are uninsured and meet program guidelines. Patients with Medicare may be eligible, if they are not eligible for (or enrolled in) Limited Income Subsidy (LIS), and have spent at least 3% of their annual household income on Rx medications through their Medicare Part D plan in the current year.

TYBOST® (cobicistat)
GILEAD SCIENCES, INC

Co-Pay Assistance Card Program   1-800-226-2056   *www.gileadadvancingaccess.com*

| $ Income Limits **NONE** | **Rx** cost → | **$0 CoPay** $ | **No Medical Insurance** ✘ | **Commercial Insurance** ✔ | **Medicare Part D** ✘ |

Program covers up to $600 in co-pays per year, with a monthly maximum of $50.

Gilead Advancing Access   1-800-226-2056   *www.gileadadvancingaccess.com*

| $ Income Limits **Call to Verify** ? | **Rx** cost → | **FREE** $ | **No Medical Insurance** ✔ | **Commercial Insurance** ? | **Medicare Part D** ✘ |

Patient assistance program provides medications at no charge for eligible patients with no other insurance options.

TYGACIL® (tigecycline for injection)
PFIZER, INC

Pfizer Patient Assistance Program   1-844-989-7284   *www.pfizerrxpathways.com*

| $ Income Limits **$48k Single $65k Couple** | **Rx** cost → | **FREE** $ | **No Medical Insurance** ✔ | **Commercial Insurance** ? | **Medicare Part D** ✘ |

Assists eligible patients who are uninsured (or have inadequate drug coverage) and cannot afford their medications.

TYKERB® (lapatinib)
NOVARTIS PHARMACEUTICALS

Universal Co-Pay Card   1-877-577-7756   *www.copay.novartisoncology.com*

| $ Income Limits **NONE** | **Rx** cost → | **$25** $ | **No Medical Insurance** ✘ | **Commercial Insurance** ✔ | **Medicare Part D** ✘ |

Patients pay the first $25, the program pays the remaining co-pay or coinsurance to max benefit of $15,000/year.

TYKERB® (lapatinib)

NOVARTIS PHARMACEUTICALS

Universal Co-Pay Card   1-877-577-7756   *www.copay.novartisoncology.com*

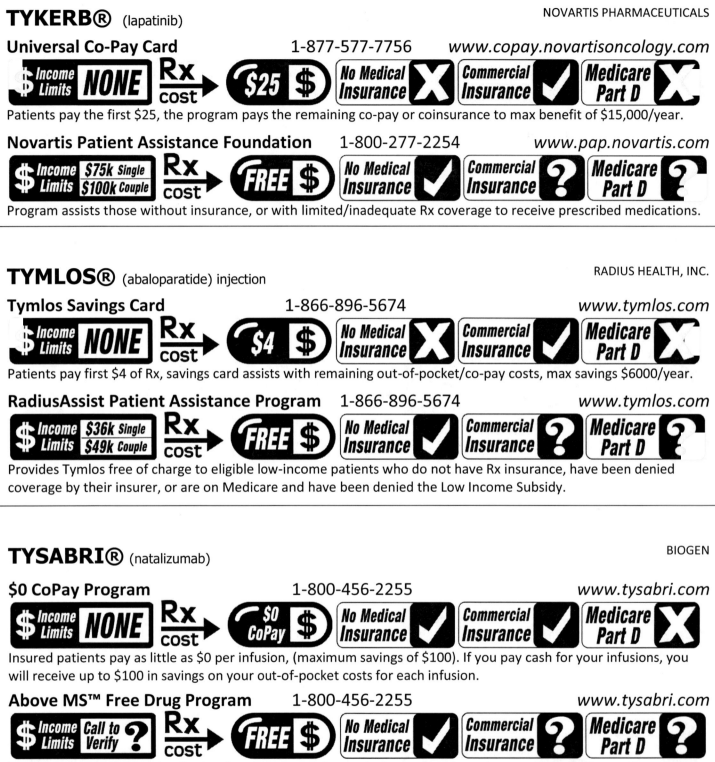

Income Limits **NONE** | Rx cost → $25 $ | No Medical Insurance ✗ | Commercial Insurance ✓ | Medicare Part D ✗

Patients pay the first $25, the program pays the remaining co-pay or coinsurance to max benefit of $15,000/year.

Novartis Patient Assistance Foundation   1-800-277-2254   *www.pap.novartis.com*

Income Limits **$75k Single $100k Couple** | Rx cost → FREE $ | No Medical Insurance ✓ | Commercial Insurance ? | Medicare Part D ?

Program assists those without insurance, or with limited/inadequate Rx coverage to receive prescribed medications.

TYMLOS® (abaloparatide) injection

RADIUS HEALTH, INC.

Tymlos Savings Card   1-866-896-5674   *www.tymlos.com*

Income Limits **NONE** | Rx cost → $4 $ | No Medical Insurance ✗ | Commercial Insurance ✓ | Medicare Part D ✗

Patients pay first $4 of Rx, savings card assists with remaining out-of-pocket/co-pay costs, max savings $6000/year.

RadiusAssist Patient Assistance Program   1-866-896-5674   *www.tymlos.com*

Income Limits **$36k Single $49k Couple** | Rx cost → FREE $ | No Medical Insurance ✓ | Commercial Insurance ? | Medicare Part D ?

Provides Tymlos free of charge to eligible low-income patients who do not have Rx insurance, have been denied coverage by their insurer, or are on Medicare and have been denied the Low Income Subsidy.

TYSABRI® (natalizumab)

BIOGEN

$0 CoPay Program   1-800-456-2255   *www.tysabri.com*

Income Limits **NONE** | Rx cost → $0 CoPay $ | No Medical Insurance ✓ | Commercial Insurance ✓ | Medicare Part D ✗

Insured patients pay as little as $0 per infusion, (maximum savings of $100). If you pay cash for your infusions, you will receive up to $100 in savings on your out-of-pocket costs for each infusion.

Above MS™ Free Drug Program   1-800-456-2255   *www.tysabri.com*

Income Limits **Call to Verify** ? | Rx cost → FREE $ | No Medical Insurance ✓ | Commercial Insurance ? | Medicare Part D ?

Rx assistance available to patients who are uninsured or underinsured, and meet program eligibility requirements.

TIP: Income limits are higher for households with three or more people. Call programs for details.

TYVASO® (treprostinil) inhalation solution

UNITED THERAPEUTICS CORPORATION

Tyvaso Co-Pay Assistance Card   1-877-864-8437   *www.utcopay.com*

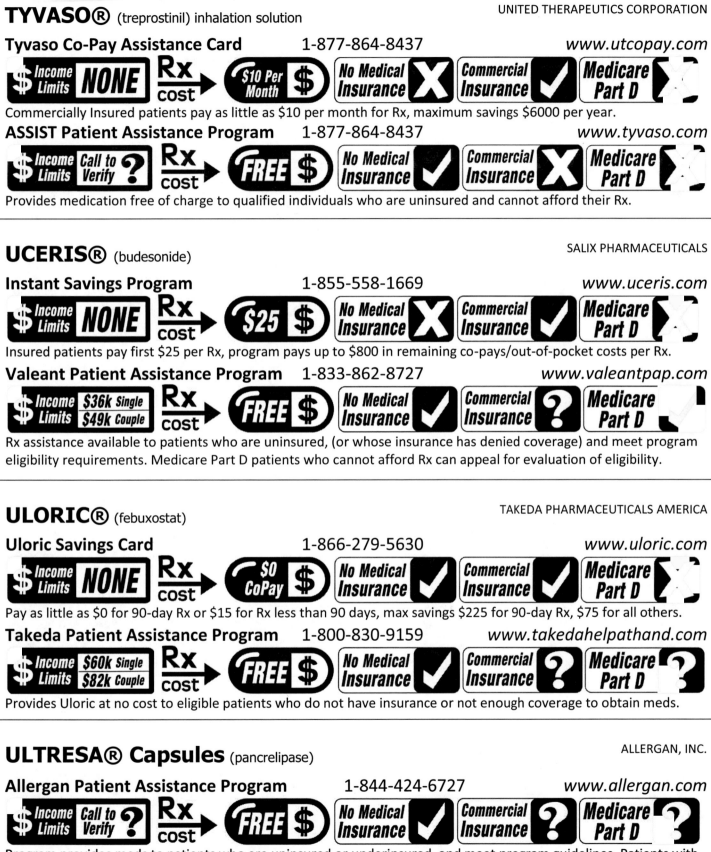

Commercially Insured patients pay as little as $10 per month for Rx, maximum savings $6000 per year.

ASSIST Patient Assistance Program   1-877-864-8437   *www.tyvaso.com*

Provides medication free of charge to qualified individuals who are uninsured and cannot afford their Rx.

UCERIS® (budesonide)

SALIX PHARMACEUTICALS

Instant Savings Program   1-855-558-1669   *www.uceris.com*

Insured patients pay first $25 per Rx, program pays up to $800 in remaining co-pays/out-of-pocket costs per Rx.

Valeant Patient Assistance Program   1-833-862-8727   *www.valeantpap.com*

Rx assistance available to patients who are uninsured, (or whose insurance has denied coverage) and meet program eligibility requirements. Medicare Part D patients who cannot afford Rx can appeal for evaluation of eligibility.

ULORIC® (febuxostat)

TAKEDA PHARMACEUTICALS AMERICA

Uloric Savings Card   1-866-279-5630   *www.uloric.com*

Pay as little as $0 for 90-day Rx or $15 for Rx less than 90 days, max savings $225 for 90-day Rx, $75 for all others.

Takeda Patient Assistance Program   1-800-830-9159   *www.takedahelpathand.com*

Provides Uloric at no cost to eligible patients who do not have insurance or not enough coverage to obtain meds.

ULTRESA® Capsules (pancrelipase)

ALLERGAN, INC.

Allergan Patient Assistance Program   1-844-424-6727   *www.allergan.com*

Program provides meds to patients who are uninsured or underinsured, and meet program guidelines. Patients with Medicare may be eligible, if they have been denied or are ineligible for Low Income Subsidy.

umeclidinium inhalation powder → INCRUSE ELLIPTA

umeclidinium and vilanterol inhalation powder → ANORO® ELLIPTA®

UPTRAVI® (selexipag)

ACTELION PHARMACEUTICALS, INC.

Actelion Oral PAH Therapy

Co-Pay Program   1-866-228-3546   www.actelionpathways.com

A savings program that lets eligible patients with commercial insurance pay just $5 per prescription.

Patient Assistant Program (PAP)   1-866-228-3546   www.actelionpathways.com

If you are uninsured, or the cost of your medicine is covered by insurance, but you are unable to afford the out-of-pocket costs, this program can help you get the medications you need at no cost to you.

ustekinumab → STELARA®

UTIBRON® NEOHALER® (indacaterol/glycopyrrolate)

SUNOVION PHARMACEUTICALS, INC.

UTIBRON NEOHALER Savings Card   1-844-276-8262   www.utibron.com

Insured patients pay as little as $10 for their Rx, max savings $250 per Rx fill for both insured & uninsured patients.

Sunovion Support®   1-877-850-0819   www.sunovionsupport.com

Provides up to 12 prescription fills (equivalent to 12 months of assistance) at no cost to people who qualify.

VAGIFEM® (estradiol vaginal inserts)

NOVO NORDISK, INC.

Instant Savings Card   1-844-449-4712   www.vagifem.com

Save up to $40 on each of your four Vagifem Rx's. Patients pay the first $20 of Rx, savings card covers next $40.

valbenazine → INGREZZA®

valsartan → DIOVAN®

valsartan and hydrochlorothiazide → DIOVAN HCT®

vandetanib → CAPRELSA®

varenicline → CHANTIX®

VARUBI® Tablets/Injectable Emulsion (rolapitant)

TESARO, INC.

Commercial Co-pay Assistance Program   1-844-283-7276   *www.togetherwithtesaro.com*

Eligible commercially insured patients pay as little as $0 per dose, with max savings of $300/tablets, $180/Injection.

Patient Assistance Program   1-844-283-7276   *www.togetherwithtesaro.com*

Provides medications at no cost to eligible patients who do not have insurance or not enough coverage to obtain Rx.

VASCEPA® (icosapent ethyl)

AMARIN PHARMA

Vascepa Savings Card   1-855-497-8462   *www.vascepa.com*

Program can save you up to $70 per month, or $140 for a 90-day Rx. Insured patients pay as little as $9 for 90-day Rx.

VECTIBIX® (panitumumab)

AMGEN, INC.

VECTIBIX FIRST STEP™ Program   1-888-657-8371   *www.amgenfirststep.com*

No out-of-pocket cost for first dose/cycle; $5 out-of-pocket cost for subsequent dose/cycles. Program assists with out-of-pocket costs, maximum benefit of $10,000 per patient per calendar year, via the Amgen FIRST STEP™ card.

AMGEN® Safety Net Foundation   1-888-762-6436   *www.amgensafetynetfoundation.com*

Foundation provides free medications to patients who are uninsured or underinsured, and meet program guidelines. Patients with Medicare may be eligible, if they have been denied or are ineligible for Low Income Subsidy.

vedolizumab → ENTYVIO®

velaglucerase alfa → VPRIV®

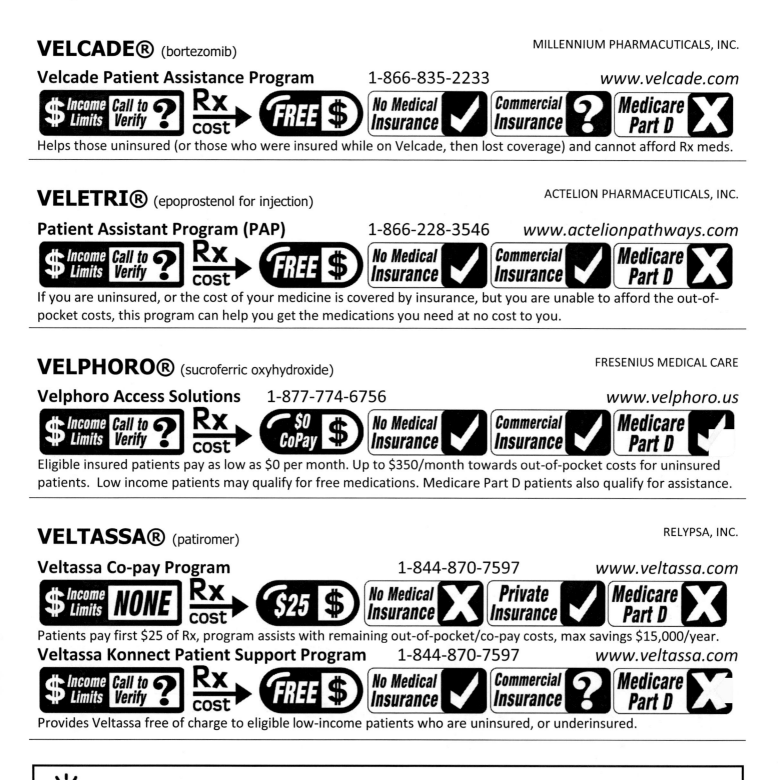

VELCADE® (bortezomib)
MILLENNIUM PHARMACUTICALS, INC.

Velcade Patient Assistance Program   1-866-835-2233   *www.velcade.com*

$ Income Limits | Call to Verify ? | Rx cost → | FREE $ | No Medical Insurance ✔ | Commercial Insurance ? | Medicare Part D ✗

Helps those uninsured (or those who were insured while on Velcade, then lost coverage) and cannot afford Rx meds.

VELETRI® (epoprostenol for injection)
ACTELION PHARMACEUTICALS, INC.

Patient Assistant Program (PAP)   1-866-228-3546   *www.actelionpathways.com*

$ Income Limits | Call to Verify ? | Rx cost → | FREE $ | No Medical Insurance ✔ | Commercial Insurance ✔ | Medicare Part D ✗

If you are uninsured, or the cost of your medicine is covered by insurance, but you are unable to afford the out-of-pocket costs, this program can help you get the medications you need at no cost to you.

VELPHORO® (sucroferric oxyhydroxide)
FRESENIUS MEDICAL CARE

Velphoro Access Solutions   1-877-774-6756   *www.velphoro.us*

$ Income Limits | Call to Verify ? | Rx cost → | $0 CoPay $ | No Medical Insurance ✔ | Commercial Insurance ✔ | Medicare Part D ✔

Eligible insured patients pay as low as $0 per month. Up to $350/month towards out-of-pocket costs for uninsured patients. Low income patients may qualify for free medications. Medicare Part D patients also qualify for assistance.

VELTASSA® (patiromer)
RELYPSA, INC.

Veltassa Co-pay Program   1-844-870-7597   *www.veltassa.com*

$ Income Limits NONE | Rx cost → | $25 $ | No Medical Insurance ✗ | Private Insurance ✔ | Medicare Part D ✗

Patients pay first $25 of Rx, program assists with remaining out-of-pocket/co-pay costs, max savings $15,000/year.

Veltassa Konnect Patient Support Program   1-844-870-7597   *www.veltassa.com*

$ Income Limits | Call to Verify ? | Rx cost → | FREE $ | No Medical Insurance ✔ | Commercial Insurance ? | Medicare Part D ✗

Provides Veltassa free of charge to eligible low-income patients who are uninsured, or underinsured.

TIP: When in doubt... call the program and explain your situation. You may qualify for assistance.

VEMLIDY® (tenofovir alafenamide)

GILEAD SCIENCES, INC

VEMLIDY Co-pay Coupon Program   1-800-226-2056   *www.vemlidy.com*

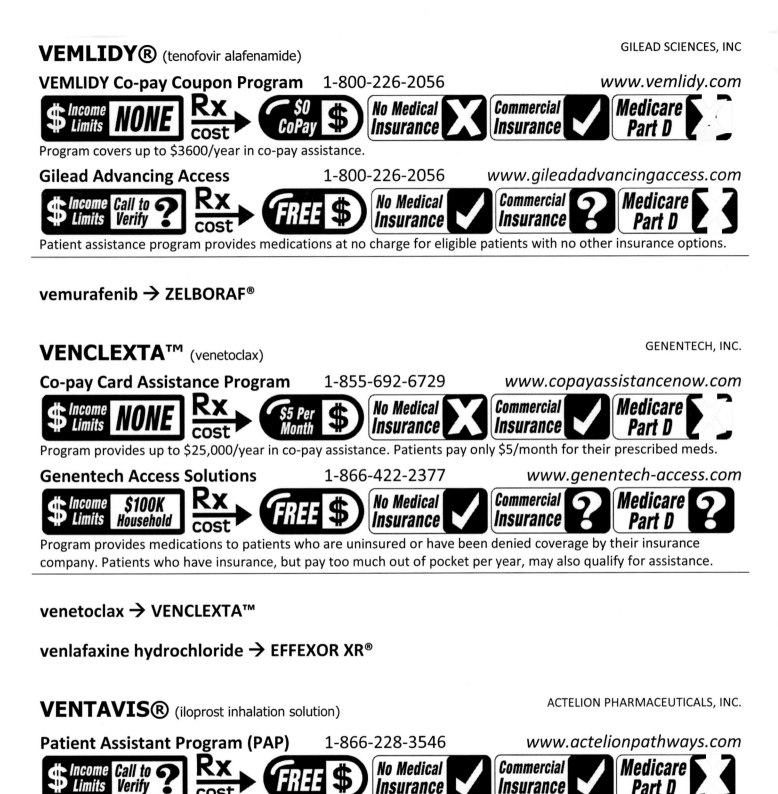

$ Income Limits **NONE** | Rx cost → | $0 CoPay $ | No Medical Insurance ✗ | Commercial Insurance ✓ | Medicare Part D ✗

Program covers up to $3600/year in co-pay assistance.

Gilead Advancing Access   1-800-226-2056   *www.gileadadvancingaccess.com*

$ Income Limits Call to Verify ? | Rx cost → | FREE $ | No Medical Insurance ✓ | Commercial Insurance ? | Medicare Part D ✗

Patient assistance program provides medications at no charge for eligible patients with no other insurance options.

---

vemurafenib → ZELBORAF®

VENCLEXTA™ (venetoclax)

GENENTECH, INC.

Co-pay Card Assistance Program   1-855-692-6729   *www.copayassistancenow.com*

$ Income Limits **NONE** | Rx cost → | $5 Per Month $ | No Medical Insurance ✗ | Commercial Insurance ✓ | Medicare Part D ✗

Program provides up to $25,000/year in co-pay assistance. Patients pay only $5/month for their prescribed meds.

Genentech Access Solutions   1-866-422-2377   *www.genentech-access.com*

$ Income Limits **$100K Household** | Rx cost → | FREE $ | No Medical Insurance ✓ | Commercial Insurance ? | Medicare Part D ?

Program provides medications to patients who are uninsured or have been denied coverage by their insurance company. Patients who have insurance, but pay too much out of pocket per year, may also qualify for assistance.

---

venetoclax → VENCLEXTA™

venlafaxine hydrochloride → EFFEXOR XR®

VENTAVIS® (iloprost inhalation solution)

ACTELION PHARMACEUTICALS, INC.

Patient Assistant Program (PAP)   1-866-228-3546   *www.actelionpathways.com*

$ Income Limits Call to Verify ? | Rx cost → | FREE $ | No Medical Insurance ✓ | Commercial Insurance ✓ | Medicare Part D ✗

If you are uninsured, or the cost of your medicine is covered by insurance, but you are unable to afford the out-of-pocket costs, this program can help you get the medications you need at no cost to you.

TIP: When in doubt... call the program and explain your situation. You may qualify for assistance.

VENTOLIN® HFA (albuterol sulfate)

GLAXOSMITHKLINE

GSK Patient Assistance Program   1-866-728-4368   *www.gskforyou.com*

$ Income Limits | $30k Single / $41k Couple   **Rx cost** → **FREE $**   **No Medical Insurance** ✓   **Commercial Insurance** ?   **Medicare Part D** ✓

Uninsured patients who meet certain financial criteria may be able to get meds for free. Medicare Part D patients who have spent $600 or more on Rx drugs may also apply for assistance.

VERAMUNE XR® (nevirapine)

BOEHRINGER INGELHEIM PHARMACEUTICALS, INC.

Boehringer Ingelheim Cares Foundation   1-800-556-8317   *www.bipatientassistance.com*

$ Income Limits | Call to Verify ?   **Rx cost** → **FREE $**   **No Medical Insurance** ✓   **Commercial Insurance** ?   **Medicare Part D** ?

Patient Assistance Program provides free medications to patients who are uninsured or underinsured, and meet program guidelines. Patients with Medicare may be eligible, if they are ineligible for Low Income Subsidy.

verapamil hydrochloride → CALAN®

verteporfin for injection → VISUDYNE®

VERZENIO® (abemaciclib)

LILLY USA, LLC

Lilly PatientOne   1-844-837-9364   *www.verzenio.com*

$ Income Limits | NONE   **Rx cost** → **$10 Per Month $**   **No Medical Insurance** X   **Commercial Insurance** ✓   **Medicare Part D** X

Eligible patients pay $10 per Rx, program covers remaining co-pay or coinsurance, up to a max of $25,000/year.

Lilly Cares   1-800-545-6962   *www.lillycares.com*

$ Income Limits | $60k Single / $82k Couple   **Rx cost** → **FREE $**   **No Medical Insurance** ✓   **Commercial Insurance** ?   **Medicare Part D** ✓

Provides free Lilly medications for eligible patients who are uninsured and cannot afford their medications, or for those whose insurance has denied coverage. Medicare Part D patients may also be eligible for assistance.

VESIcare® (solifenacin succinate)

ASTELLAS PHARMA, INC.

Momentum Savings Card   1-855-326-1404   *www.astellasaccess.com*

$ Income Limits | NONE   **Rx cost** → **Discount Varies $**   **No Medical Insurance** X   **Commercial Insurance** ✓   **Medicare Part D** X

Saves you up to $50. If your Rx is $70, you pay $20. If your Rx is over $70, you pay $20 plus amount over $70.

VESIcare® (solifenacin succinate)

ASTELLAS PHARMA, INC.

VESIcare Support Solutions   1-800-477-6472   *www.astellasaccess.com*

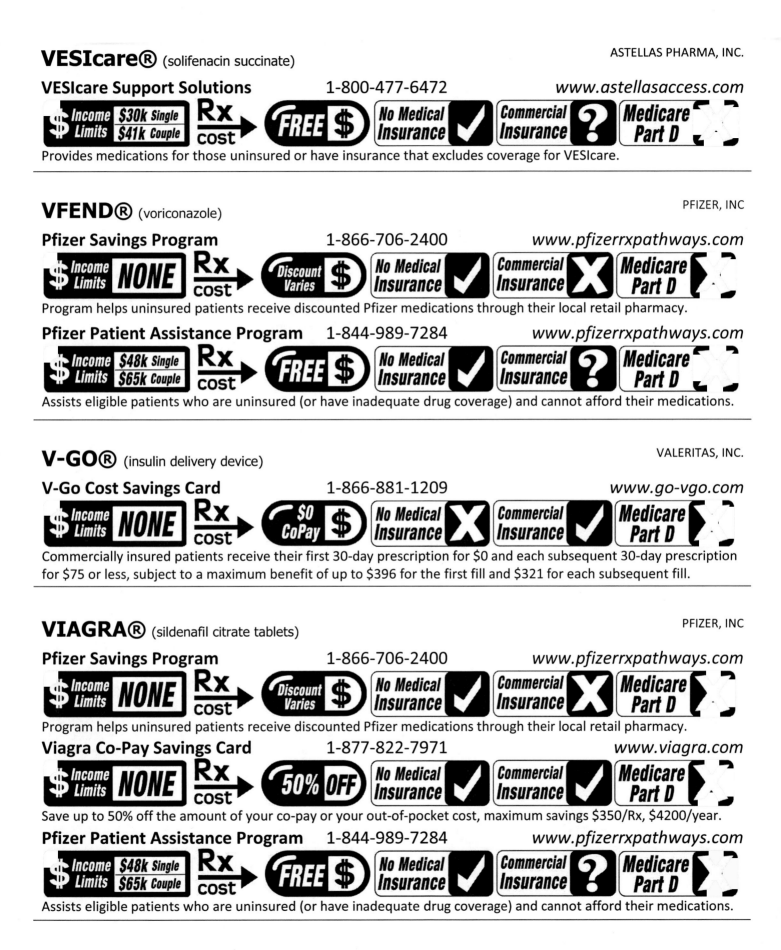

Income Limits $30k Single / $41k Couple | Rx cost → FREE $ | No Medical Insurance ✓ | Commercial Insurance ? | Medicare Part D X

Provides medications for those uninsured or have insurance that excludes coverage for VESIcare.

VFEND® (voriconazole)

PFIZER, INC

Pfizer Savings Program   1-866-706-2400   *www.pfizerrxpathways.com*

Income Limits NONE | Rx cost → Discount Varies $ | No Medical Insurance ✓ | Commercial Insurance X | Medicare Part D X

Program helps uninsured patients receive discounted Pfizer medications through their local retail pharmacy.

Pfizer Patient Assistance Program   1-844-989-7284   *www.pfizerrxpathways.com*

Income Limits $48k Single / $65k Couple | Rx cost → FREE $ | No Medical Insurance ✓ | Commercial Insurance ? | Medicare Part D X

Assists eligible patients who are uninsured (or have inadequate drug coverage) and cannot afford their medications.

V-GO® (insulin delivery device)

VALERITAS, INC.

V-Go Cost Savings Card   1-866-881-1209   *www.go-vgo.com*

Income Limits NONE | Rx cost → $0 CoPay $ | No Medical Insurance X | Commercial Insurance ✓ | Medicare Part D X

Commercially insured patients receive their first 30-day prescription for $0 and each subsequent 30-day prescription for $75 or less, subject to a maximum benefit of up to $396 for the first fill and $321 for each subsequent fill.

VIAGRA® (sildenafil citrate tablets)

PFIZER, INC

Pfizer Savings Program   1-866-706-2400   *www.pfizerrxpathways.com*

Income Limits NONE | Rx cost → Discount Varies $ | No Medical Insurance ✓ | Commercial Insurance X | Medicare Part D X

Program helps uninsured patients receive discounted Pfizer medications through their local retail pharmacy.

Viagra Co-Pay Savings Card   1-877-822-7971   *www.viagra.com*

Income Limits NONE | Rx cost → 50% OFF | No Medical Insurance ✓ | Commercial Insurance ✓ | Medicare Part D X

Save up to 50% off the amount of your co-pay or your out-of-pocket cost, maximum savings $350/Rx, $4200/year.

Pfizer Patient Assistance Program   1-844-989-7284   *www.pfizerrxpathways.com*

Income Limits $48k Single / $65k Couple | Rx cost → FREE $ | No Medical Insurance ✓ | Commercial Insurance ? | Medicare Part D X

Assists eligible patients who are uninsured (or have inadequate drug coverage) and cannot afford their medications.

VIBATIV® (telavancin) for injection
THERAVANCE BIOPHARMA

Theravance Biopharma Patient Assistance Program   1-855-847-9435   *www.vibativ.org*

| $ **Income Limits** $36k Single / $49k Couple | **Rx cost** → | **FREE** $ | **No Medical Insurance** ✔ | **Commercial Insurance** ✗ | **Medicare Part D** ✗ |

Provides assisted for financially diasadvantaged patients w/o public or commercial insurance.

VIBERZI® Tablets (eluxadoline)
ALLERGAN, INC.

Allergan Patient Assistance Program   1-844-424-6727   *www.allergan.com*

| $ **Income Limits** Call to Verify ? | **Rx cost** → | **FREE** $ | **No Medical Insurance** ✔ | **Commercial Insurance** ? | **Medicare Part D** ? |

Program provides meds to patients who are uninsured or underinsured, and meet program guidelines. Patients with Medicare may be eligible, if they have been denied or are ineligible for Low Income Subsidy.

VICTOZA® (liraglutide) injection
NOVO NORDISK, INC.

Novo Nordisk Savings Card   1-877-304-6855   *www.novocare.com*

| $ **Income Limits** NONE | **Rx cost** → | $25 Per Month $ | **No Medical Insurance** ✗ | **Commercial Insurance** ✔ | **Medicare Part D** ✗ |

Pay as little as $25 per 30-day, $50 per 60-day, or $75 per 90-day supply for up to 24 months from the date of Savings Card activation, subject to a max savings of $100 per 30-day, $200 per 60-day, or $300 per 90-day supply.

Patient Access Program   1-866-310-7549   *www.novocare.com*

| $ **Income Limits** $36k Single / $49k Couple | **Rx cost** → | **FREE** $ | **No Medical Insurance** ✔ | **Commercial Insurance** ✗ | **Medicare Part D** |

For patients who are uninsured. Also for Medicare patients who have spent more than $1000 this year on Rx meds.

VIDAZA® (azacitidine for injection)
CELGENE CORPORATION

Celgene Patient Assistance Program   1-800-931-8691   *www.celgenepatientsupport.com*

| $ **Income Limits** Call to Verify ? | **Rx cost** → | **FREE** $ | **No Medical Insurance** ✔ | **Commercial Insurance** ? | **Medicare Part D** ? |

Rx assistance available to patients who are uninsured or underinsured, and meet program eligibility requirements.

VIGAMOX® (moxifloxacin hydrochloride solution)
NOVARTIS PHARMACEUTICALS

Novartis Patient Assistance Foundation   1-800-277-2254   *www.pap.novartis.com*

| $ **Income Limits** $75k Single / $100k Couple | **Rx cost** → | **FREE** $ | **No Medical Insurance** ✔ | **Commercial Insurance** ? | **Medicare Part D** ? |

Program assists those without insurance, or with limited/inadequate Rx coverage to receive prescribed medications.

VIIBRYD® Tablets & Titration Pack (vilazodone HCL)

ALLERGAN, INC.

Allergan Patient Assistance Program   1-844-424-6727   *www.allergan.com*

Program provides meds to patients who are uninsured or underinsured, and meet program guidelines. Patients with Medicare may be eligible, if they have been denied or are ineligible for Low Income Subsidy.

vilazodone HCl → VIIBRYD® Tablets & Titration Pack

VIMOVO® (naproxen/esomeprazole magnesium)

HORIZON PHARMA USA, INC.

VIMOVO Savings Card   1-855-881-3093   *www.vimovo.com*

Helps pay up to $1200 in out-of-pocket expenses for each 30 day Rx. Eligible patients pay as low as $0/month.

Horizon Pharma Patient Assistance Program   1-888-958-5502   *www.vimovo.com*

Helps eligible patients who lack health insurance coverage to get their Rx meds at no cost.

VIMPAT® (lacosamide)

UCB PHARMA, INC.

Vimpat Patient Savings Program   1-888-786-5879   *www.vimpat.com*

Patients pay as little as $20 per month, maximum savings $100 per Rx, $1300 per year.

UCBCares Patient Assistance Program   1-877-785-8906   *www.askucbcares.com*

Provides medication free of charge to those who are uninsured or underinsured, and cannot afford their Rx.

vinCRIStine sulfate LIPOSOME injection → MARQIBO®

TIP: Income limits are higher for households with three or more people. Call programs for details.

VIOKACE® Tablets (pancrelipase)

ALLERGAN, INC.

Allergan Patient Assistance Program   1-844-424-6727   *www.allergan.com*

Program provides meds to patients who are uninsured or underinsured, and meet program guidelines. Patients with Medicare may be eligible, if they have been denied or are ineligible for Low Income Subsidy.

VIRACEPT® (nelfinavir mesylate)

ViiV HEALTHCARE

ViiVConnect Savings Card   1-844-588-3288   *www.viivconnect.com*

Patients can pay as little as $0 copay, maximum savings $4500/year.

ViiV Healthcare Patient Assistance Program   1-844-588-3288   *www.viivconnect.com*

Gives meds to patients who are uninsured, lack coverage, or on Medicare and have spent $600 on Rx meds this year.

vismodegib → ERIVEDGE®

VISTARIL® (hydroxyzine pamoate)

PFIZER, INC

Pfizer Savings Program   1-866-706-2400   *www.pfizerrxpathways.com*

Program helps uninsured patients receive discounted Pfizer medications through their local retail pharmacy.

VISUDYNE® (verteporfin for injection)

VALEANT PHARMACEUTICALS INTERNATIONAL

Valeant Patient Assistance Program   1-833-862-8727   *www.valeantpap.com*

Rx assistance available to patients who are uninsured, (or whose insurance has denied coverage) and meet program eligibility requirements. Medicare Part D patients who cannot afford Rx can appeal for evaluation of eligibility.

VIVITROL® (naltrexone for extended-release injectable suspension)
ALKERMES, INC.

Vivitrol Co-pay Savings Program   1-800-848-4876   *www.vivitrol.com*

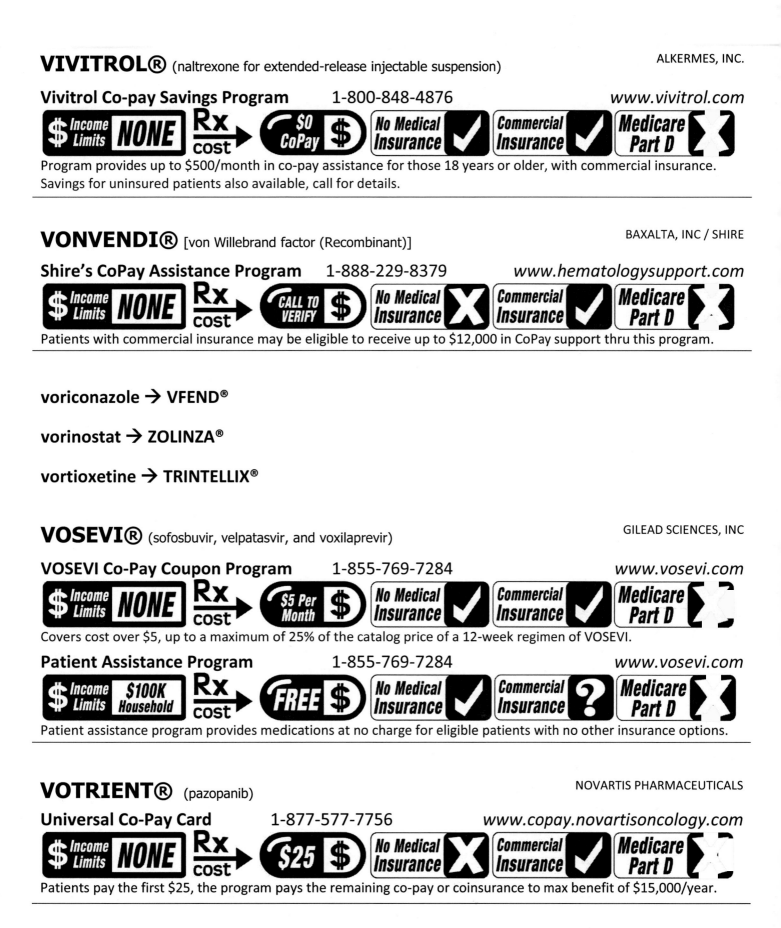

Program provides up to $500/month in co-pay assistance for those 18 years or older, with commercial insurance. Savings for uninsured patients also available, call for details.

VONVENDI® [von Willebrand factor (Recombinant)]
BAXALTA, INC / SHIRE

Shire's CoPay Assistance Program   1-888-229-8379   *www.hematologysupport.com*

Patients with commercial insurance may be eligible to receive up to $12,000 in CoPay support thru this program.

voriconazole → VFEND®

vorinostat → ZOLINZA®

vortioxetine → TRINTELLIX®

VOSEVI® (sofosbuvir, velpatasvir, and voxilaprevir)
GILEAD SCIENCES, INC

VOSEVI Co-Pay Coupon Program   1-855-769-7284   *www.vosevi.com*

Covers cost over $5, up to a maximum of 25% of the catalog price of a 12-week regimen of VOSEVI.

Patient Assistance Program   1-855-769-7284   *www.vosevi.com*

Patient assistance program provides medications at no charge for eligible patients with no other insurance options.

VOTRIENT® (pazopanib)
NOVARTIS PHARMACEUTICALS

Universal Co-Pay Card   1-877-577-7756   *www.copay.novartisoncology.com*

Patients pay the first $25, the program pays the remaining co-pay or coinsurance to max benefit of $15,000/year.

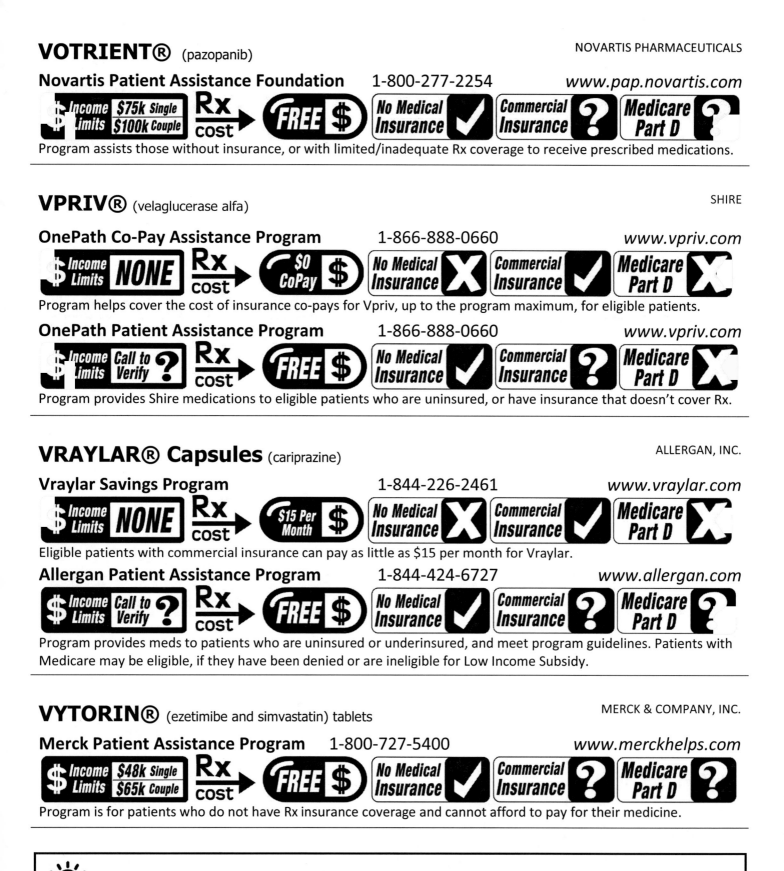

VOTRIENT® (pazopanib)
NOVARTIS PHARMACEUTICALS

Novartis Patient Assistance Foundation 1-800-277-2254 www.pap.novartis.com

Income Limits $75k Single $100k Couple | Rx cost → FREE $ | No Medical Insurance ✓ | Commercial Insurance ? | Medicare Part D ?

Program assists those without insurance, or with limited/inadequate Rx coverage to receive prescribed medications.

VPRIV® (velaglucerase alfa)
SHIRE

OnePath Co-Pay Assistance Program 1-866-888-0660 www.vpriv.com

Income Limits NONE | Rx cost → $0 CoPay $ | No Medical Insurance ✗ | Commercial Insurance ✓ | Medicare Part D ✗

Program helps cover the cost of insurance co-pays for Vpriv, up to the program maximum, for eligible patients.

OnePath Patient Assistance Program 1-866-888-0660 www.vpriv.com

Income Limits Call to Verify ? | Rx cost → FREE $ | No Medical Insurance ✓ | Commercial Insurance ? | Medicare Part D ✗

Program provides Shire medications to eligible patients who are uninsured, or have insurance that doesn't cover Rx.

VRAYLAR® Capsules (cariprazine)
ALLERGAN, INC.

Vraylar Savings Program 1-844-226-2461 www.vraylar.com

Income Limits NONE | Rx cost → $15 Per Month $ | No Medical Insurance ✗ | Commercial Insurance ✓ | Medicare Part D ✗

Eligible patients with commercial insurance can pay as little as $15 per month for Vraylar.

Allergan Patient Assistance Program 1-844-424-6727 www.allergan.com

Income Limits Call to Verify ? | Rx cost → FREE $ | No Medical Insurance ✓ | Commercial Insurance ? | Medicare Part D ?

Program provides meds to patients who are uninsured or underinsured, and meet program guidelines. Patients with Medicare may be eligible, if they have been denied or are ineligible for Low Income Subsidy.

VYTORIN® (ezetimibe and simvastatin) tablets
MERCK & COMPANY, INC.

Merck Patient Assistance Program 1-800-727-5400 www.merckhelps.com

Income Limits $48k Single $65k Couple | Rx cost → FREE $ | No Medical Insurance ✓ | Commercial Insurance ? | Medicare Part D ?

Program is for patients who do not have Rx insurance coverage and cannot afford to pay for their medicine.

TIP: When in doubt... call the program and explain your situation. You may qualify for assistance.

VYVANSE® (lisdexamfetamine dimesylate)
SHIRE

Vyvanse Prescription Savings Offer
1-866-441-3469 · www.vyvanse.com

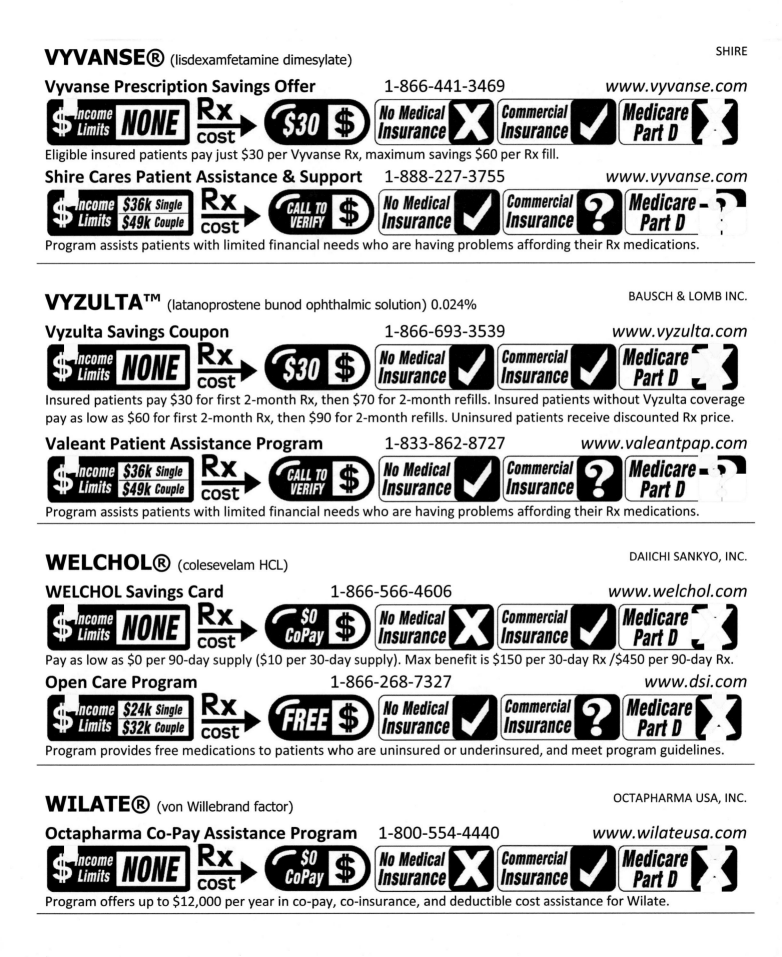

Income Limits **NONE** · Rx cost → **$30 $** · No Medical Insurance **X** · Commercial Insurance **✓** · Medicare Part D **X**

Eligible insured patients pay just $30 per Vyvanse Rx, maximum savings $60 per Rx fill.

Shire Cares Patient Assistance & Support
1-888-227-3755 · www.vyvanse.com

Income Limits **$36k Single / $49k Couple** · Rx cost → **CALL TO VERIFY $** · No Medical Insurance **✓** · Commercial Insurance **?** · Medicare Part D **?**

Program assists patients with limited financial needs who are having problems affording their Rx medications.

VYZULTA™ (latanoprostene bunod ophthalmic solution) 0.024%
BAUSCH & LOMB INC.

Vyzulta Savings Coupon
1-866-693-3539 · www.vyzulta.com

Income Limits **NONE** · Rx cost → **$30 $** · No Medical Insurance **✓** · Commercial Insurance **✓** · Medicare Part D **X**

Insured patients pay $30 for first 2-month Rx, then $70 for 2-month refills. Insured patients without Vyzulta coverage pay as low as $60 for first 2-month Rx, then $90 for 2-month refills. Uninsured patients receive discounted Rx price.

Valeant Patient Assistance Program
1-833-862-8727 · www.valeantpap.com

Income Limits **$36k Single / $49k Couple** · Rx cost → **CALL TO VERIFY $** · No Medical Insurance **✓** · Commercial Insurance **?** · Medicare Part D **?**

Program assists patients with limited financial needs who are having problems affording their Rx medications.

WELCHOL® (colesevelam HCL)
DAIICHI SANKYO, INC.

WELCHOL Savings Card
1-866-566-4606 · www.welchol.com

Income Limits **NONE** · Rx cost → **$0 CoPay $** · No Medical Insurance **X** · Commercial Insurance **✓** · Medicare Part D **X**

Pay as low as $0 per 90-day supply ($10 per 30-day supply). Max benefit is $150 per 30-day Rx /$450 per 90-day Rx.

Open Care Program
1-866-268-7327 · www.dsi.com

Income Limits **$24k Single / $32k Couple** · Rx cost → **FREE $** · No Medical Insurance **✓** · Commercial Insurance **?** · Medicare Part D **X**

Program provides free medications to patients who are uninsured or underinsured, and meet program guidelines.

WILATE® (von Willebrand factor)
OCTAPHARMA USA, INC.

Octapharma Co-Pay Assistance Program
1-800-554-4440 · www.wilateusa.com

Income Limits **NONE** · Rx cost → **$0 CoPay $** · No Medical Insurance **X** · Commercial Insurance **✓** · Medicare Part D **X**

Program offers up to $12,000 per year in co-pay, co-insurance, and deductible cost assistance for Wilate.

XALATAN® (latanoprost)

PFIZER, INC

Pfizer Savings Program 1-866-706-2400 *www.pfizerrxpathways.com*

Income Limits NONE | **Rx cost** → | **Discount Varies** $ | **No Medical Insurance** ✓ | **Commercial Insurance** X | **Medicare Part D** X

Program helps uninsured patients receive discounted Pfizer medications through their local retail pharmacy.

Xalatan Savings Card 1-866-562-6147 *www.xalatan.com*

Income Limits NONE | **Rx cost** → | **$0 CoPay** $ | **No Medical Insurance** ✓ | **Commercial Insurance** ✓ | **Medicare Part D** X

Eligible patients may pay as little as $0 per month for Rx, maximum savings $125 per Rx, $1500 per year.

XALKORI® (crizotinib)

PFIZER, INC

Pfizer Savings Program 1-866-706-2400 *www.pfizerrxpathways.com*

Income Limits NONE | **Rx cost** → | **Discount Varies** $ | **No Medical Insurance** ✓ | **Commercial Insurance** X | **Medicare Part D** X

Program helps uninsured patients receive discounted Pfizer medications through their local retail pharmacy.

Pfizer Oncology together™ Co-Pay Savings Card 1-844-989-7284 *www.xalkori.com*

Income Limits NONE | **Rx cost** → | **$0 CoPay** $ | **No Medical Insurance** X | **Commercial Insurance** ✓ | **Medicare Part D** X

Eligible patients can save up to $25,000 per year toward their co-pay, deductible, and coinsurance costs.

Pfizer Patient Assistance Program 1-844-989-7284 *www.pfizerrxpathways.com*

Income Limits Call to Verify ? | **Rx cost** → | **FREE** $ | **No Medical Insurance** ✓ | **Commercial Insurance** ? | **Medicare Part D** X

Assists eligible patients who are uninsured (or have inadequate drug coverage) and cannot afford their medications.

XANAX® (alprazolam)

PFIZER, INC

Pfizer Savings Program 1-866-706-2400 *www.pfizerrxpathways.com*

Income Limits NONE | **Rx cost** → | **Discount Varies** $ | **No Medical Insurance** ✓ | **Commercial Insurance** X | **Medicare Part D** X

Program helps uninsured patients receive discounted Pfizer medications through their local retail pharmacy.

Xanax Savings Card 1-855-854-4535 *www.xanax.com*

Income Limits NONE | **Rx cost** → | **$4 Per Month** $ | **No Medical Insurance** ✓ | **Commercial Insurance** ✓ | **Medicare Part D** X

Eligible patients may pay as little as $4 per month for Rx, maximum savings $125 per Rx, $1500 per year.

XARELTO® (rivaroxaban)
JANSSEN PHARMACEUTICALS INC.

Janssen CarePath Savings Program   1-888-927-3586   *www.xarelto-us.com*

Income Limits **NONE** — Rx cost → **$10 Per Month** $ — No Medical Insurance ✗ — Commercial Insurance ✓ — Medicare Part D ✗

Commercially insured patients may pay as little as $10 per month for Rx, max program benefit per year $3400.

J&J Patient Assistance Foundation   1-800-652-6227   *www.jjpaf.org*

Income Limits **$36k Single / $49k Couple** — Rx cost → **FREE** $ — No Medical Insurance ✓ — Commercial Insurance **?** — Medicare Part D

Program provides free medications to patients who are uninsured or underinsured, and meet program guidelines.

XELJANZ® / XELJANZ XR® (tofacitinib)
PFIZER, INC.

Co-Pay Savings Card/Hardship Assistance Program   1-844-935-5269   *www.xeljanz.com*

Income Limits **NONE** — Rx cost → **$0 CoPay** $ — No Medical Insurance ✗ — Commercial Insurance ✓ — Medicare Part D ✗

Commercially insured patients can pay as little as $0 co-pay for Rx, maximum benefit $12,000/year. Underinsured patients may receive additional co-pay support up to $10,000/year.

XELSOURCE Patient Assistance Program   1-844-935-5269   *www.xeljanz.com*

Income Limits **Call to Verify ?** — Rx cost → **FREE** $ — No Medical Insurance ✓ — Commercial Insurance ✗ — Medicare Part D ✗

Eligible uninsured/underinsured patients may receive XELJANZ XR or XELJANZ at no charge.

XENAZINE® (tetrabenazine)
LUNDBECK, INC.

Xenazine Copay Assistance Program   1-888-882-6013   *www.xenazineusa.com*

Income Limits **NONE** — Rx cost → **$10 Per Month** $ — No Medical Insurance ✗ — Commercial Insurance ✓ — Medicare Part D

Eligible commercially insured patients pay as little as $10 per 30 day Rx.

XEOMIN® Injection (incobotulinumtoxinA)
MERZ NORTH AMERICA, INC.

Xeomin Patient Savings Program   1-888-493-6646   *www.xeomin.com*

Income Limits **NONE** — Rx cost → **Discount Varies** $ — No Medical Insurance ✗ — Commercial Insurance ✓ — Medicare Part D

Provides support to eligible patients with actual out-of-pocket XEOMIN Rx costs, up to $3,500 per 12 month period.

Xeomin Patient Assistance Program   1-888-493-6646   *www.xeomin.com*

Income Limits **Call to Verify ?** — Rx cost → **FREE** $ — No Medical Insurance ✓ — Commercial Insurance **?** — Medicare Part D

Program is for uninsured or underinsured patients, who cannot afford their medications.

XERMELO® (telotristat ethyl)

LexCares $0 Co-Pay Program   1-844-937-6356   *www.xermelo.com*

$ Income Limits **NONE** | Rx cost → | $0 CoPay $ | No Medical Insurance ✗ | Commercial Insurance ✓ | Medicare Part D ✗

Provides co-pay assistance up to $10,000/year, most patients pay $0 out of pocket for Xermelo.

XERESE® (acyclovir and hydrocortisone) creme

Rx Access Program   1-855-202-3279   *www.orthorxaccess.com*

$ Income Limits **NONE** | Rx cost → | $40 $ | No Medical Insurance ✓ | Commercial Insurance ✓ | Medicare Part D ✗

Most commercially insured patients pay as little as $40 per Rx, once deductible has been met. Those with insurance where drug is not covered pay $75 per Rx, and uninsured patients pay just $100 per Rx.

XGEVA® (denosumab)

XGEVA FIRST STEP™ Program   1-888-657-8371   *www.amgenfirststep.com*

$ Income Limits **NONE** | Rx cost → | $5 $ | No Medical Insurance ✗ | Commercial Insurance ✓ | Medicare Part D ✗

No out-of-pocket cost for first dose/cycle; $5 out-of-pocket cost for subsequent dose/cycles. Program assists with out-of-pocket costs, maximum benefit of $10,000 per patient per calendar year, via the Amgen FIRST STEP™ card.

AMGEN® Safety Net Foundation   1-888-762-6436   *www.amgensafetynetfoundation.com*

$ Income Limits $60k Single / $82k Couple | Rx cost → | FREE $ | No Medical Insurance ✓ | Commercial Insurance ? | Medicare Part D ?

Foundation provides free medications to patients who are uninsured or underinsured, and meet program guidelines. Patients with Medicare may be eligible, if they have been denied or are ineligible for Low Income Subsidy.

XIAFLEX® (collagenase clostridium histolyticum)

XIAFLEX® CoPay Assistance Program   1-800-743-2382   *www.xiaflex.com*

$ Income Limits **NONE** | Rx cost → | $0 CoPay $ | No Medical Insurance ✓ | Commercial Insurance ✓ | Medicare Part D ✗

Most eligible patients with commercial insurance plans pay $0 co-pay. Program can cover up to $1200 of your out-of-pocket costs for each injection of XIAFLEX®. Insured and un-insured patients are eligible for assistance.

TIP: When in doubt... call the program and explain your situation. You may qualify for assistance.

XIFAXAN® (rifaximin)

Instant Savings Card   1-855-250-3759   *www.xifaxan.com*

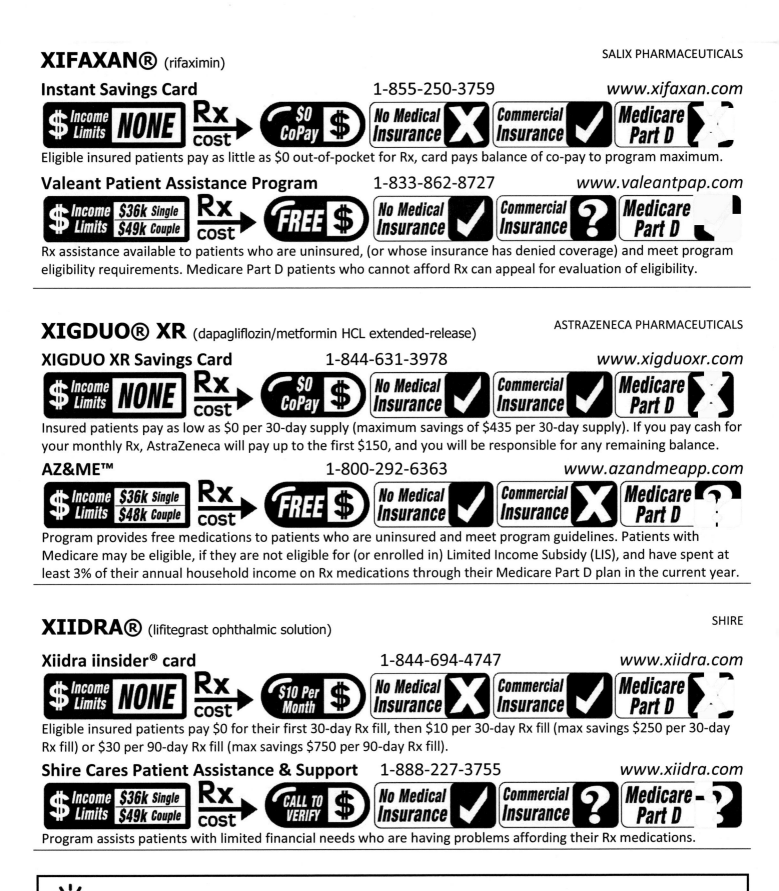

$ Income Limits NONE | **Rx cost** → | **$0 CoPay $** | **No Medical Insurance X** | **Commercial Insurance ✔** | **Medicare Part D X**

Eligible insured patients pay as little as $0 out-of-pocket for Rx, card pays balance of co-pay to program maximum.

Valeant Patient Assistance Program   1-833-862-8727   *www.valeantpap.com*

$ Income Limits $36k Single $49k Couple | **Rx cost** → | **FREE $** | **No Medical Insurance ✔** | **Commercial Insurance ?** | **Medicare Part D**

Rx assistance available to patients who are uninsured, (or whose insurance has denied coverage) and meet program eligibility requirements. Medicare Part D patients who cannot afford Rx can appeal for evaluation of eligibility.

XIGDUO® XR (dapagliflozin/metformin HCL extended-release)

XIGDUO XR Savings Card   1-844-631-3978   *www.xigduoxr.com*

$ Income Limits NONE | **Rx cost** → | **$0 CoPay $** | **No Medical Insurance ✔** | **Commercial Insurance ✔** | **Medicare Part D X**

Insured patients pay as low as $0 per 30-day supply (maximum savings of $435 per 30-day supply). If you pay cash for your monthly Rx, AstraZeneca will pay up to the first $150, and you will be responsible for any remaining balance.

AZ&ME™   1-800-292-6363   *www.azandmeapp.com*

$ Income Limits $36k Single $48k Couple | **Rx cost** → | **FREE $** | **No Medical Insurance ✔** | **Commercial Insurance X** | **Medicare Part D ?**

Program provides free medications to patients who are uninsured and meet program guidelines. Patients with Medicare may be eligible, if they are not eligible for (or enrolled in) Limited Income Subsidy (LIS), and have spent at least 3% of their annual household income on Rx medications through their Medicare Part D plan in the current year.

XIIDRA® (lifitegrast ophthalmic solution)

Xiidra iinsider® card   1-844-694-4747   *www.xiidra.com*

$ Income Limits NONE | **Rx cost** → | **$10 Per Month $** | **No Medical Insurance X** | **Commercial Insurance ✔** | **Medicare Part D X**

Eligible insured patients pay $0 for their first 30-day Rx fill, then $10 per 30-day Rx fill (max savings $250 per 30-day Rx fill) or $30 per 90-day Rx fill (max savings $750 per 90-day Rx fill).

Shire Cares Patient Assistance & Support   1-888-227-3755   *www.xiidra.com*

$ Income Limits $36k Single $49k Couple | **Rx cost** → | **CALL TO VERIFY $** | **No Medical Insurance ✔** | **Commercial Insurance ?** | **Medicare Part D ?**

Program assists patients with limited financial needs who are having problems affording their Rx medications.

TIP: Income limits are higher for households with three or more people. Call programs for details.

XOLAIR® (omalizumab)

XOLAIR® Co-Pay Card Program   1- 855-965-2472   *www.xolaircopay.com*

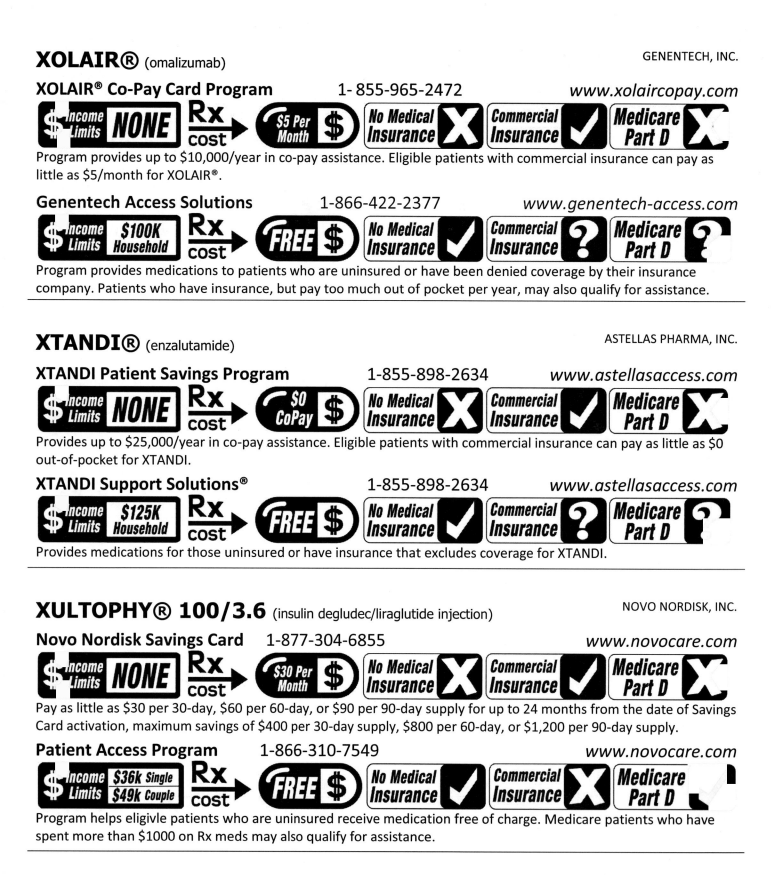

Program provides up to $10,000/year in co-pay assistance. Eligible patients with commercial insurance can pay as little as $5/month for XOLAIR®.

Genentech Access Solutions   1-866-422-2377   *www.genentech-access.com*

Program provides medications to patients who are uninsured or have been denied coverage by their insurance company. Patients who have insurance, but pay too much out of pocket per year, may also qualify for assistance.

XTANDI® (enzalutamide)

ASTELLAS PHARMA, INC.

XTANDI Patient Savings Program   1-855-898-2634   *www.astellasaccess.com*

Provides up to $25,000/year in co-pay assistance. Eligible patients with commercial insurance can pay as little as $0 out-of-pocket for XTANDI.

XTANDI Support Solutions®   1-855-898-2634   *www.astellasaccess.com*

Provides medications for those uninsured or have insurance that excludes coverage for XTANDI.

XULTOPHY® 100/3.6 (insulin degludec/liraglutide injection)

NOVO NORDISK, INC.

Novo Nordisk Savings Card   1-877-304-6855   *www.novocare.com*

Pay as little as $30 per 30-day, $60 per 60-day, or $90 per 90-day supply for up to 24 months from the date of Savings Card activation, maximum savings of $400 per 30-day supply, $800 per 60-day, or $1,200 per 90-day supply.

Patient Access Program   1-866-310-7549   *www.novocare.com*

Program helps eligivle patients who are uninsured receive medication free of charge. Medicare patients who have spent more than $1000 on Rx meds may also qualify for assistance.

XYNTHA® (antihemophilic factor)

Pfizer Factor Savings Program   1-888-240-9040   *www.hemophiliavillage.com*

$ **Income Limits** NONE | **Rx cost** → | **Discount Varies** $ | **No Medical Insurance** ✗ | **Commercial Insurance** ✓ | **Medicare Part D** ✗

Eligible patients can save up to $12,000 per year toward their co-pay, deductible, and coinsurance costs.

Pfizer Patient Assistance Program   1-844-989-7284   *www.pfizerrxpathways.com*

$ **Income Limits** Call to Verify ? | **Rx cost** → | **FREE** $ | **No Medical Insurance** ✓ | **Commercial Insurance** ? | **Medicare Part D** ✗

Assists eligible patients who are uninsured (or have inadequate drug coverage) and cannot afford their medications.

YASMIN® (drospirenone/ethinyl estradiol tablets)
BAYER HEALTHCARE PHARMACEUTICALS

Bayer Savings Card   1-866-203-3503   *www.savingscard.bayer.com*

$ **Income Limits** NONE | **Rx cost** → | **$0 CoPay** $ | **No Medical Insurance** ✓ | **Commercial Insurance** ✓ | **Medicare Part D** ✗

Insured patients pay as little as $0 per month, (maximum savings of $75). If you pay cash for your monthly medications, you will receive up to $75 in savings on your out-of-pocket costs for each prescription.

YAZ® (drospirenone/ethinyl estradiol tablets)
BAYER HEALTHCARE PHARMACEUTICALS

Bayer Savings Card   1-866-203-3503   *www.savingscard.bayer.com*

$ **Income Limits** NONE | **Rx cost** → | **$0 CoPay** $ | **No Medical Insurance** ✓ | **Commercial Insurance** ✓ | **Medicare Part D** ✗

Insured patients pay as little as $0 per month, (maximum savings of $100). If you pay cash for your monthly medications, you will receive up to $100 in savings on your out-of-pocket costs for each prescription.

YERVOY® (ipilimumab)
BRISTOL-MYERS SQUIBB

Oncology Co-Pay Assistance Program   1-800-861-0048   *www.bmsaccesssupport.com*

$ **Income Limits** NONE | **Rx cost** → | **$25** $ | **No Medical Insurance** ✗ | **Commercial Insurance** ✓ | **Medicare Part D** ✗

Patients pay the first $25, program covers remainder of co-pay, up to a maximum of $25,000/year per medication.

Bristol-Myers Squibb Patient Assistance Foundation   1-800-736-0003   *www.bmspaf.com*

$ **Income Limits** $36k Single $49k Couple | **Rx cost** → | **FREE** $ | **No Medical Insurance** ✓ | **Commercial Insurance** ? | **Medicare Part D** ✓

Program provides free medications to eligible patients who are uninsured, had coverage denied by insurer, or Medicare Part D patients who have spent at least 3% of their yearly household income out-of-pocket RX costs.

YONDELIS® (trabectedin)
JANSSEN PHARMACEUTICALS INC.

Janssen CarePath Savings Program   1-844-966-3354   *www.yondelis.com*

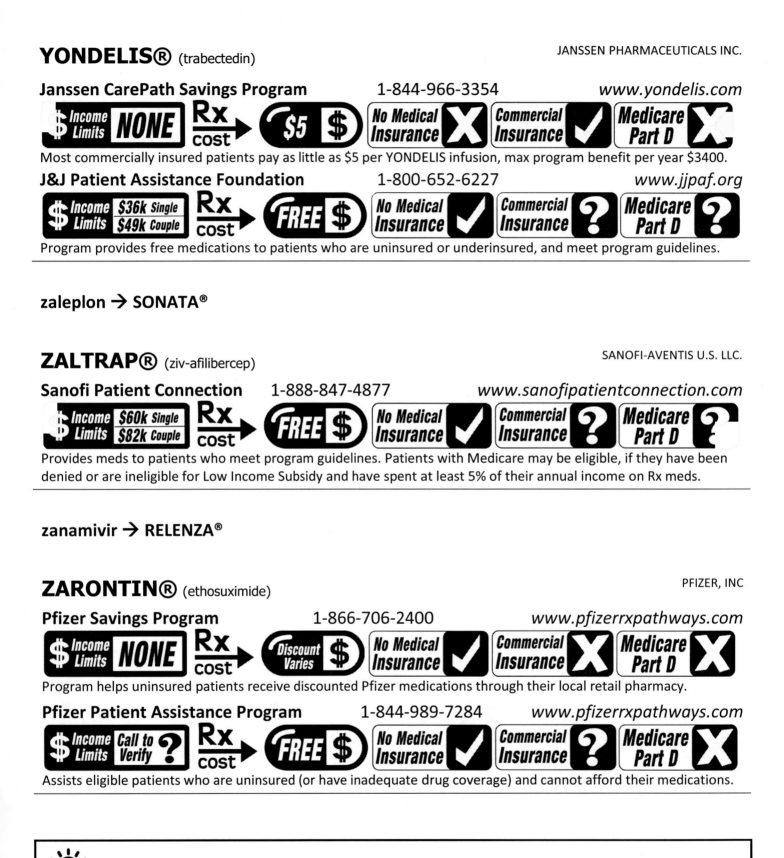

Most commercially insured patients pay as little as $5 per YONDELIS infusion, max program benefit per year $3400.

J&J Patient Assistance Foundation   1-800-652-6227   *www.jjpaf.org*

Program provides free medications to patients who are uninsured or underinsured, and meet program guidelines.

---

zaleplon → SONATA®

ZALTRAP® (ziv-aflibercep)
SANOFI-AVENTIS U.S. LLC.

Sanofi Patient Connection   1-888-847-4877   *www.sanofipatientconnection.com*

Provides meds to patients who meet program guidelines. Patients with Medicare may be eligible, if they have been denied or are ineligible for Low Income Subsidy and have spent at least 5% of their annual income on Rx meds.

---

zanamivir → RELENZA®

ZARONTIN® (ethosuximide)
PFIZER, INC

Pfizer Savings Program   1-866-706-2400   *www.pfizerrxpathways.com*

Program helps uninsured patients receive discounted Pfizer medications through their local retail pharmacy.

Pfizer Patient Assistance Program   1-844-989-7284   *www.pfizerrxpathways.com*

Assists eligible patients who are uninsured (or have inadequate drug coverage) and cannot afford their medications.

TIP: Income limits are higher for households with three or more people. Call programs for details.

ZARXIO® (filgrastim-sndz)
SANDOZ, INC.

Sandoz One Source Co-Pay Program 1-844-726-3691 *www.zarxio.com*

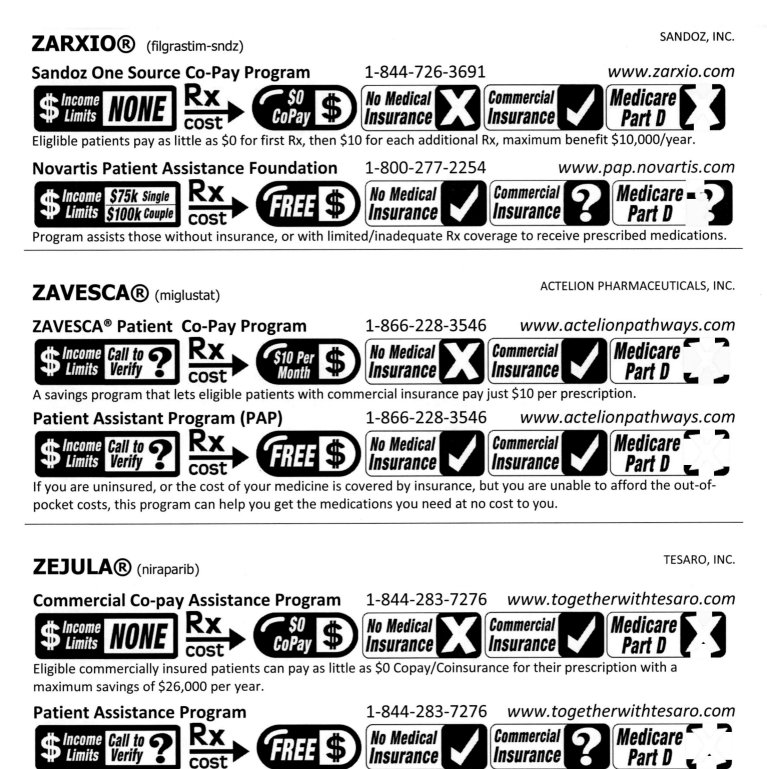

$ Income Limits **NONE** | **Rx** cost → | **$0 CoPay $** | **No Medical Insurance X** | **Commercial Insurance ✔** | **Medicare Part D**

Eligible patients pay as little as $0 for first Rx, then $10 for each additional Rx, maximum benefit $10,000/year.

Novartis Patient Assistance Foundation 1-800-277-2254 *www.pap.novartis.com*

$ Income Limits **$75k Single / $100k Couple** | **Rx** cost → | **FREE $** | **No Medical Insurance ✔** | **Commercial Insurance ?** | **Medicare Part D ?**

Program assists those without insurance, or with limited/inadequate Rx coverage to receive prescribed medications.

ZAVESCA® (miglustat)
ACTELION PHARMACEUTICALS, INC.

ZAVESCA® Patient Co-Pay Program 1-866-228-3546 *www.actelionpathways.com*

$ Income Limits **Call to Verify ?** | **Rx** cost → | **$10 Per Month $** | **No Medical Insurance X** | **Commercial Insurance ✔** | **Medicare Part D**

A savings program that lets eligible patients with commercial insurance pay just $10 per prescription.

Patient Assistant Program (PAP) 1-866-228-3546 *www.actelionpathways.com*

$ Income Limits **Call to Verify ?** | **Rx** cost → | **FREE $** | **No Medical Insurance ✔** | **Commercial Insurance ✔** | **Medicare Part D X**

If you are uninsured, or the cost of your medicine is covered by insurance, but you are unable to afford the out-of-pocket costs, this program can help you get the medications you need at no cost to you.

ZEJULA® (niraparib)
TESARO, INC.

Commercial Co-pay Assistance Program 1-844-283-7276 *www.togetherwithtesaro.com*

$ Income Limits **NONE** | **Rx** cost → | **$0 CoPay $** | **No Medical Insurance X** | **Commercial Insurance ✔** | **Medicare Part D**

Eligible commercially insured patients can pay as little as $0 Copay/Coinsurance for their prescription with a maximum savings of $26,000 per year.

Patient Assistance Program 1-844-283-7276 *www.togetherwithtesaro.com*

$ Income Limits **Call to Verify ?** | **Rx** cost → | **FREE $** | **No Medical Insurance ✔** | **Commercial Insurance ?** | **Medicare Part D**

Provides medications at no cost to eligible patients who do not have insurance or not enough coverage to obtain Rx.

TIP: When in doubt... call the program and explain your situation. You may qualify for assistance.

ZELAPAR® (selegiline HCL)

VALEANT PHARMACEUTICALS INTERNATIONAL

Valeant Patient Assistance Program   1-833-862-8727   *www.valeantpap.com*

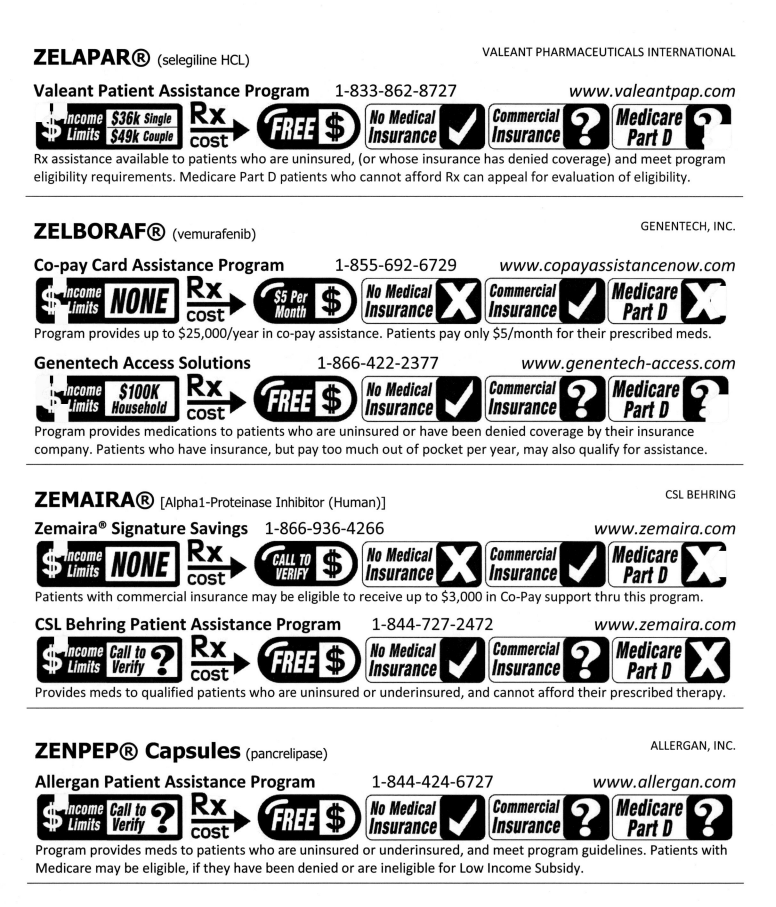

Rx assistance available to patients who are uninsured, (or whose insurance has denied coverage) and meet program eligibility requirements. Medicare Part D patients who cannot afford Rx can appeal for evaluation of eligibility.

ZELBORAF® (vemurafenib)

GENENTECH, INC.

Co-pay Card Assistance Program   1-855-692-6729   *www.copayassistancenow.com*

Program provides up to $25,000/year in co-pay assistance. Patients pay only $5/month for their prescribed meds.

Genentech Access Solutions   1-866-422-2377   *www.genentech-access.com*

Program provides medications to patients who are uninsured or have been denied coverage by their insurance company. Patients who have insurance, but pay too much out of pocket per year, may also qualify for assistance.

ZEMAIRA® [Alpha1-Proteinase Inhibitor (Human)]

CSL BEHRING

Zemaira® Signature Savings   1-866-936-4266   *www.zemaira.com*

Patients with commercial insurance may be eligible to receive up to $3,000 in Co-Pay support thru this program.

CSL Behring Patient Assistance Program   1-844-727-2472   *www.zemaira.com*

Provides meds to qualified patients who are uninsured or underinsured, and cannot afford their prescribed therapy.

ZENPEP® Capsules (pancrelipase)

ALLERGAN, INC.

Allergan Patient Assistance Program   1-844-424-6727   *www.allergan.com*

Program provides meds to patients who are uninsured or underinsured, and meet program guidelines. Patients with Medicare may be eligible, if they have been denied or are ineligible for Low Income Subsidy.

ZENZEDI® (dextroamphetamine sulfate tablets)

Copay Savings Program   1-855-558-1630   www.zenzedi.com

Income Limits NONE | **Rx cost** → Discount Varies $ | **No Medical Insurance** ✓ | **Commercial Insurance** ✓ | **Medicare Part D** ✗

Eligible patients may receive their first prescription for $0. For remaining refills, if your copay exceeds $30 (insured patients) or $75 (noninsured patients), present card to the pharmacist for an instant discount.

ZEPATIER® (elbasvir and grazoprevir) tablets

MERCK & COMPANY, INC.

Merck Patient Assistance Program   1-800-727-5400   www.merckhelps.com

Income Limits $48k Single $65k Couple | **Rx cost** → FREE $ | **No Medical Insurance** ✓ | **Commercial Insurance** ? | **Medicare Part D** ?

Program is for patients who do not have Rx insurance coverage and cannot afford to pay for their medicine.

ZETIA® (ezetimibe) tablets

MERCK & COMPANY, INC.

Merck Patient Assistance Program   1-800-727-5400   www.merckhelps.com

Income Limits $48k Single $65k Couple | **Rx cost** → FREE $ | **No Medical Insurance** ✓ | **Commercial Insurance** ? | **Medicare Part D** ?

Program is for patients who do not have Rx insurance coverage and cannot afford to pay for their medicine.

ZEVALIN® (ibritumomab tiuxetan)

SPECTRUM PHAMACEUTICALS, INC.

Co-Pay Assistance   1-888-537-8277   www.spectrumpatientaccess.com

Income Limits NONE | **Rx cost** → $25 $ | **No Medical Insurance** ✗ | **Commercial Insurance** ✓ | **Medicare Part D** ✗

Eligible patients pay $0 copay for first treatment, $25 for additional treatments with max savings $10,000/year.

Spectrum Therapy Access Resources   1-888-461-2255   www.spectrumpatientaccess.com

Income Limits Call to Verify ? | **Rx cost** → FREE $ | **No Medical Insurance** ✓ | **Commercial Insurance** ? | **Medicare Part D** ✗

Provides free Spectrum meds to patients who meet income, insurance, and citizenship/residency eligibility criteria.

ZIAGEN® (abacavir) Oral Solution

ViiV HEALTHCARE

ViiVConnect Savings Card   1-844-588-3288   www.viivconnect.com

Income Limits NONE | **Rx cost** → $0 CoPay $ | **No Medical Insurance** ✓ | **Commercial Insurance** ✓ | **Medicare Part D** ✗

Patients can pay as little as $0 copay, maximum savings $4500/year.

ZIAGEN® (abacavir) Oral Solution

ViiV HEALTHCARE

ViiV Healthcare Patient Assistance Program   1-844-588-3288   *www.viivconnect.com*

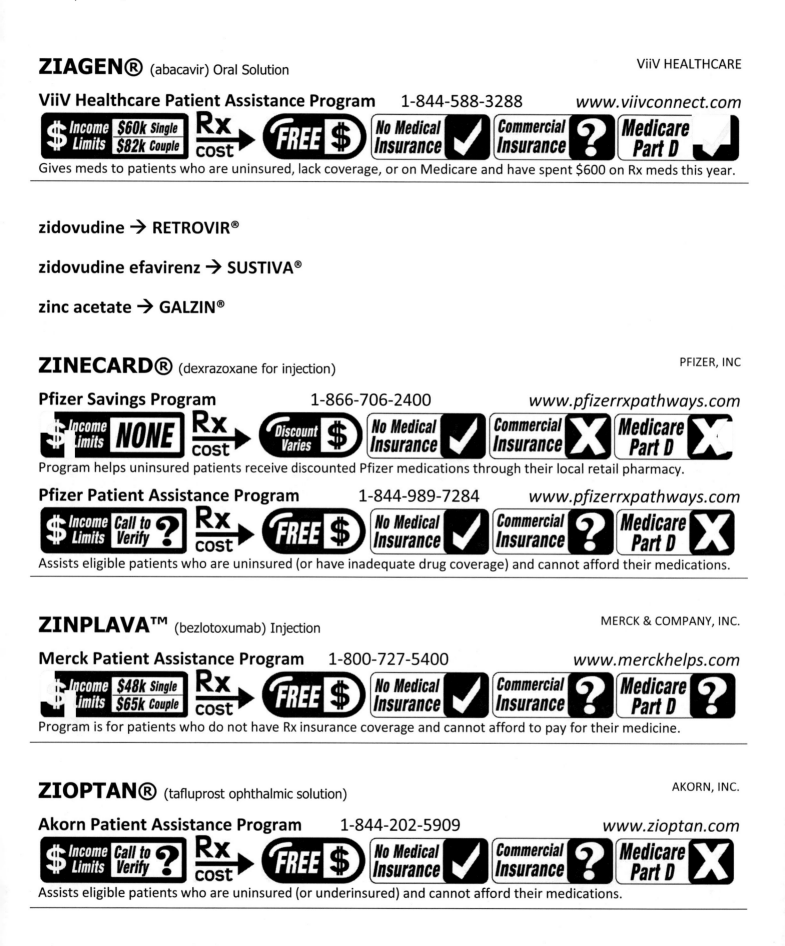

Gives meds to patients who are uninsured, lack coverage, or on Medicare and have spent $600 on Rx meds this year.

zidovudine → RETROVIR®

zidovudine efavirenz → SUSTIVA®

zinc acetate → GALZIN®

ZINECARD® (dexrazoxane for injection)

PFIZER, INC

Pfizer Savings Program   1-866-706-2400   *www.pfizerrxpathways.com*

Program helps uninsured patients receive discounted Pfizer medications through their local retail pharmacy.

Pfizer Patient Assistance Program   1-844-989-7284   *www.pfizerrxpathways.com*

Assists eligible patients who are uninsured (or have inadequate drug coverage) and cannot afford their medications.

ZINPLAVA™ (bezlotoxumab) Injection

MERCK & COMPANY, INC.

Merck Patient Assistance Program   1-800-727-5400   *www.merckhelps.com*

Program is for patients who do not have Rx insurance coverage and cannot afford to pay for their medicine.

ZIOPTAN® (tafluprost ophthalmic solution)

AKORN, INC.

Akorn Patient Assistance Program   1-844-202-5909   *www.zioptan.com*

Assists eligible patients who are uninsured (or underinsured) and cannot afford their medications.

ziprasidone HCL → GEODON®

DEPOMED, INC.

ZIPSOR® (diclofenac potassium)

$0 CoPay Savings Program   1-855-439-2820   *www.zipsor.com*

$ Income Limits **NONE** | **Rx cost** → | **$0 CoPay** $ | **No Medical Insurance** ✓ | **Commercial Insurance** ✓ | **Medicare Part D** ✗

Patients pay as little as $0 for Zipsor. Savings card discount is $70 for Rx of 28 to 59 tablets, $100 for Rx of 60 tablets.

VALEANT PHARMACEUTICALS INTERNATIONAL

ZIRGAN® (ganciclovir ophthalmic gel)

Valeant Patient Assistance Program   1-833-862-8727   *www.valeantpap.com*

$ Income Limits **$36k Single / $49k Couple** | **Rx cost** → | **FREE** $ | **No Medical Insurance** ✓ | **Commercial Insurance** ? | **Medicare Part D** ✓

Rx assistance available to patients who are uninsured, (or whose insurance has denied coverage) and meet program eligibility requirements. Medicare Part D patients who cannot afford Rx can appeal for evaluation of eligibility.

PFIZER, INC

ZITHROMAX® (azithromycin)

Pfizer Savings Program   1-866-706-2400   *www.pfizerrxpathways.com*

$ Income Limits **NONE** | **Rx cost** → | **FREE** $ | **No Medical Insurance** ✓ | **Commercial Insurance** ✗ | **Medicare Part D** ✗

Program helps uninsured patients receive discounted Pfizer medications through their local retail pharmacy.

---

ziv-afilibercep → ZALTRAP®

PFIZER, INC

ZMAX® (azithromycin extended release)

Pfizer Savings Program   1-866-706-2400   *www.pfizerrxpathways.com*

$ Income Limits **NONE** | **Rx cost** → | **Discount Varies** $ | **No Medical Insurance** ✓ | **Commercial Insurance** ✗ | **Medicare Part D** ✗

Program helps uninsured patients receive discounted Pfizer medications through their local retail pharmacy.

---

zoledronic acid → RECLAST®

zoledronic acid → ZOMETA®

TIP: Income limits are higher for households with three or more people. Call programs for details.

ZOHYDRO® ER (hydrocodone bitartrate)

PERNIX THERAPUETICS

Zohydro ER Savings Card   1-844-676-9663   www.zohydroer.com

Commercially insured patients pay $0 for first Rx, then $15 for each refill, max benefit $250 per Rx.

ZOLINZA® (vorinostat) capsules

MERCK & COMPANY, INC.

Merck Patient Assistance Program   1-800-727-5400   www.merckhelps.com

Program is for patients who do not have Rx insurance coverage and cannot afford to pay for their medicine.

ZOLOFT® (sertraline HCL)

PFIZER, INC

Pfizer Savings Program   1-866-706-2400   www.pfizerrxpathways.com

Program helps uninsured patients receive discounted Pfizer medications through their local retail pharmacy.

Zoloft Savings Card   1-855-436-7989   www.zoloft.com

Eligible patients may pay as little as $4 per month for Rx, maximum savings $150 per Rx, $1800 per year.

ZOMETA® (zoledronic acid)

NOVARTIS PHARMACEUTICALS

Novartis Patient Assistance Foundation   1-800-277-2254   www.pap.novartis.com

Program assists those without insurance, or with limited/inadequate Rx coverage to receive prescribed medications.

ZOMIG® (zolmitriptan)

IMPAX LABORATORIES, INC.

ZOMIG Savings Card   1-866-293-5817   www.zomig.com

Patient saves $50 on each Rx for nasal spray, and $25 on each Rx for tablets, using the Zomig savings card.

ZOMIG® (zolmitriptan)

IMPAX LABORATORIES, INC.

Impax Patient Assistance Program   1-877-764-9021   *www.zomig.com*

$ Income Limits — Call to Verify **?** | **Rx cost** → **FREE $** | **No Medical Insurance ✓** | **Commercial Insurance ?** | **Medicare Part D**

Provides free meds for qualified patients that do not have affordable coverage for the Rx. Medicare Part D patients must have spent at least 3% of annual household income out-of-pocket on prescription medicines to qualify.

---

zolmitriptan → ZOMIG®

ZORTRESS® (everolimus)

NOVARTIS PHARMACEUTICALS

$0 Co-Pay Card   1-844-685-3406   *www.copay.novartispharma.com*

$ Income Limits — NONE | **Rx cost** → **$0 CoPay $** | **No Medical Insurance ✗** | **Commercial Insurance ✓** | **Medicare Part D ✗**

Insured patients pay as little as $0 per Rx, maximum total co-pay benefit of $7200 per year.

Novartis Patient Assistance Foundation   1-800-277-2254   *www.pap.novartis.com*

$ Income Limits — $75k Single / $100k Couple | **Rx cost** → **FREE $** | **No Medical Insurance ✓** | **Commercial Insurance ?** | **Medicare Part D ?**

Program assists those without insurance, or with limited/inadequate Rx coverage to receive prescribed medications.

ZOVIRAX® (acyclovir) cream 5%

ORTHO DERMATOLOGICS

Rx Access Program   1-855-202-3279   *www.orthorxaccess.com*

$ Income Limits — NONE | **Rx cost** → **$40 $** | **No Medical Insurance ✓** | **Commercial Insurance ✓** | **Medicare Part D ✗**

Most commercially insured patients pay as little as $40 per Rx, once deductible has been met. Those with insurance where drug is not covered pay $75 per Rx, and uninsured patients pay just $100 per Rx.

ZUBSOLV® (buprenorphine/naloxone)

OREXO US, INC.

Zubsolv Co-Pay Card   1-877-264-2440   *www.zubsolv.com*

$ Income Limits — NONE | **Rx cost** → **$10 $** | **No Medical Insurance ✓** | **Commercial Insurance ✓** | **Medicare Part D ✗**

Insured patients pay as little as $10 for Rx, Max savings for insured/uninsured patients is $225 off each Rx.

Zubsolv Patient Assistance Program   1-888-236-4167   *www.zubsolv.com*

$ Income Limits — $36k Single / $49k Couple | **Rx cost** → **FREE $** | **No Medical Insurance ✓** | **Commercial Insurance ?** | **Medicare Part D ?**

Provides medication to eligible patients who are uninsured, or lack Rx coverage for Zubsolv.

ZURAMPIC® (lesinurad)
IRONWOOD PHARMACEUTICALS, INC.

ZURAMPIC Savings Program
1-855-348-0704   *www.zurampic.com*

$ Income Limits NONE | **Rx cost** → Discount Varies **$** | **No Medical Insurance** ✗ | **Commercial Insurance** ✓ | **Medicare Part D** ✗

Eligible patients may pay as low as $0 for their first prescription of Zurampic (30-day supply) and $15 for the next eleven 30-day supply prescription fills, or receive a total of four 90-day prescription fills for $30 each time.

Ironwood Patient Assistance Program
1-833-557-2413   *www.duzallo.com*

$ Income Limits $36k Single $49k Couple | **Rx cost** → FREE **$** | **No Medical Insurance** ✓ | **Commercial Insurance** ? | **Medicare Part D** ?

Program provides free medications to patients who are uninsured or underinsured, and meet program guidelines. Patients with Medicare may be eligible, if meds are not covered and they are ineligible for Low Income Subsidy.

ZYCLARA® (imiquimod) cream
VALEANT PHARMACEUTICALS INTERNATIONAL

Ortho Dermatologics Rx Access Program
1-855-202-3279   *www.orthorxaccess.com*

$ Income Limits NONE | **Rx cost** → $40 **$** | **No Medical Insurance** ✓ | **Commercial Insurance** ✓ | **Medicare Part D** ✗

Most commercially insured patients pay as little as $40 per Rx, once deductible has been met. Those with insurance where drug is not covered pay $75 per Rx, and uninsured patients pay just $100 per Rx.

Valeant Patient Assistance Program
1-833-862-8727   *www.valeantpap.com*

$ Income Limits $36k Single $49k Couple | **Rx cost** → FREE **$** | **No Medical Insurance** ✓ | **Commercial Insurance** ? | **Medicare Part D** ✓

Rx assistance available to patients who are uninsured, (or whose insurance has denied coverage) and meet program eligibility requirements. Medicare Part D patients who cannot afford Rx can appeal for evaluation of eligibility.

ZYDELIG® (idelalisib)
GILEAD SCIENCES, INC

ZYDELIG Co-pay Coupon Program
1-844-622-2377   *www.zydelig.com*

$ Income Limits NONE | **Rx cost** → $5 Per Month **$** | **No Medical Insurance** ✓ | **Commercial Insurance** ✓ | **Medicare Part D** ✗

Covers cost over $5, up to a maximum of 25% of the catalog price of ZYDELIG.

Patient Assistance Program
1-844-622-2377   *www.zydelig.com*

$ Income Limits $100K Household | **Rx cost** → FREE **$** | **No Medical Insurance** ✓ | **Commercial Insurance** ? | **Medicare Part D** ✗

Patient assistance program provides medications at no charge for eligible patients with no other insurance options.

TIP: When in doubt... call the program and explain your situation. You may qualify for assistance.

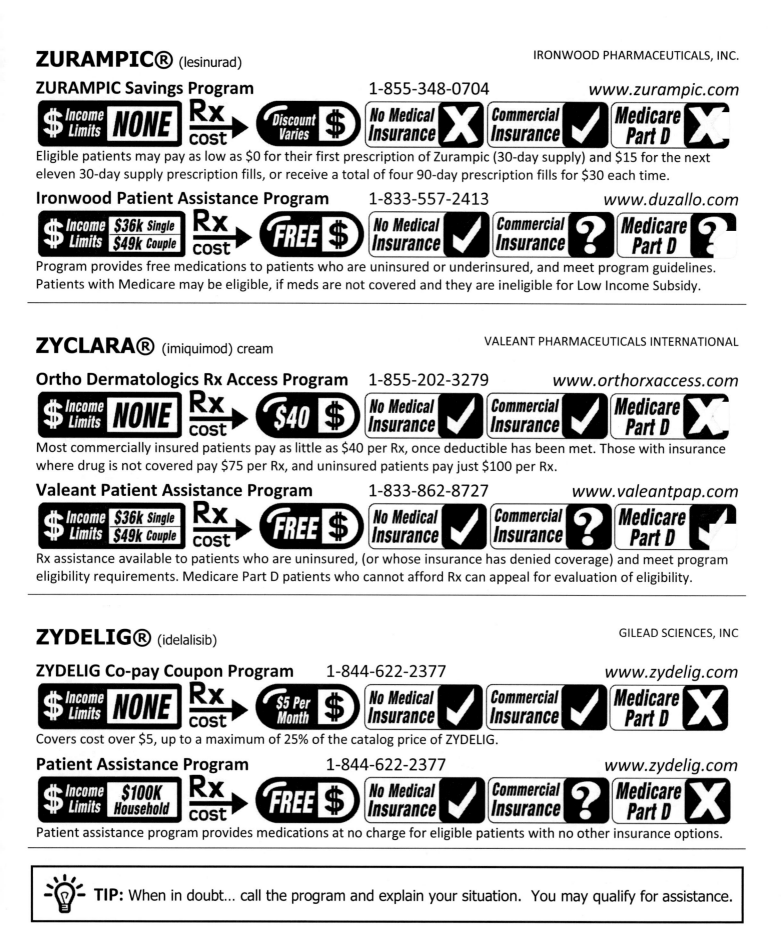

ZYKADIA® (ceritinib)

Universal Co-Pay Card   1-877-577-7756   www.copay.novartisoncology.com

Income Limits **NONE** | Rx cost → **$25** $ | No Medical Insurance **X** | Commercial Insurance **✓** | Medicare Part D **X**

Patients pay the first $25, the program pays the remaining co-pay or coinsurance to max benefit of $15,000/year.

Novartis Patient Assistance Foundation   1-800-277-2254   www.pap.novartis.com

Income Limits **$75k Single / $100k Couple** | Rx cost → **FREE** $ | No Medical Insurance **✓** | Commercial Insurance **?** | Medicare Part D **?**

Program assists those without insurance, or with limited/inadequate Rx coverage to receive prescribed medications.

ZYLET®

(loteprednol etabonate/tobramycin ophthalmic suspension)

Valeant Patient Assistance Program   1-833-862-8727   www.valeantpap.com

Income Limits **$36k Single / $49k Couple** | Rx cost → **FREE** $ | No Medical Insurance **✓** | Commercial Insurance **?** | Medicare Part D ◣

Rx assistance available to patients who are uninsured, (or whose insurance has denied coverage) and meet program eligibility requirements. Medicare Part D patients who cannot afford Rx can appeal for evaluation of eligibility.

ZYPREXA® (olanzapine)

Lilly Cares   1-800-545-6962   www.lillycares.com

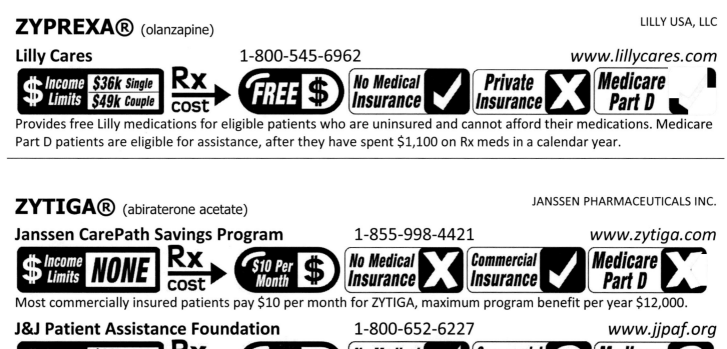

Income Limits **$36k Single / $49k Couple** | Rx cost → **FREE** $ | No Medical Insurance **✓** | Private Insurance **X** | Medicare Part D ◣

Provides free Lilly medications for eligible patients who are uninsured and cannot afford their medications. Medicare Part D patients are eligible for assistance, after they have spent $1,100 on Rx meds in a calendar year.

ZYTIGA® (abiraterone acetate)

Janssen CarePath Savings Program   1-855-998-4421   www.zytiga.com

Income Limits **NONE** | Rx cost → **$10 Per Month** $ | No Medical Insurance **X** | Commercial Insurance **✓** | Medicare Part D **X**

Most commercially insured patients pay $10 per month for ZYTIGA, maximum program benefit per year $12,000.

J&J Patient Assistance Foundation   1-800-652-6227   www.jjpaf.org

Income Limits **$36k Single / $49k Couple** | Rx cost → **FREE** $ | No Medical Insurance **✓** | Commercial Insurance **?** | Medicare Part D **?**

Program provides free medications to patients who are uninsured or underinsured, and meet program guidelines.

ZYVOX® (linezolid)

PFIZER, INC

ZYVOXassist Coupon 1-855-239-9869 *www.zyvoxassist.com*

Eligible patients can pay as little as $1 for Zyvox, depending upon Rx cost. Maximum savings $1000.

Pfizer Patient Assistance Program 1-844-989-7284 *www.pfizerrxpathways.com*

Assists eligible patients who are uninsured (or have inadequate drug coverage) and cannot afford their medications.

Quick Reference Brand Name Index

D

H

I

J

Q

R

T

U

Y

Z